Scenery along the Tippecanoe.
From a photograph.

HISTORIC INDIANA

BEING CHAPTERS IN THE STORY OF THE HOOSIER STATE FROM THE ROMANTIC PERIOD OF FOREIGN EXPLORATION AND DOMINION THROUGH PIONEER DAYS, STIRRING WAR TIMES, AND PERIODS OF PEACEFUL PROGRESS, TO THE PRESENT TIME

BY

JULIA HENDERSON LEVERING

ILLUSTRATED

G. P. PUTNAM'S SONS
NEW YORK AND LONDON
The Knickerbocker Press
1909

COPYRIGHT, 1909
BY
JULIA HENDERSON LEVERING

The Knickerbocker Press, New York

TO THE MEMORY OF

MY FATHER AND MOTHER

WHOSE NOBLE LIVES AND CHARACTERS
WERE A PART OF THE INFLUENCE OF
THE PAST RECALLED IN THIS VOLUME

PREFACE

THE history of Indiana is rich in minor incidents of real interest and of importance; but not in events exclusively its own. The State had its share of the romantic and chivalrous adventures pertaining to the dawn of Western history, its share in the encounter with a savage race, in the self-sacrifice of pioneer days, and the heroic patriotism of the war periods. Following this, it had its decades of social and material development, common to the Middle West. It is a goodly land, most advantageously located, and always ready for its part in the national responsibilities.

The history of Indiana's past is the story of her fast vanishing frontier life and the gradual changes which come in meeting modern conditions. The differences in social life broaden so rapidly in this country, that later generations take a keen pleasure in pages that preserve the scenes and experiences of those earlier days.

Unless it is often retold, the memory of heroic endeavors grows dim. Through history and literature the past accomplishments of a people are perpetuated, and their example has a manifold influence. From the pages of story and verse, the virtues and deeds, the energy and leadership of the best citizens are recalled to the remembrance of another generation.

The intention of this book is to include in a single volume an account of various phases of the development of the Commonwealth, whose history must be learned from many sources, not always accessible. Many who have not time for research, and others who have no taste for reading history, may take an interest in the romance of foreign dominion on the Wabash, and in a plain tale of the early settlers. Some may have aroused within them a just pride in their State, in reading of Indiana's valiant part in war, the development of her vast natural resources, and the advanced position which she has taken among the states in provisions for universal education, and the enactment of beneficent laws.

The author's lifelong familiarity with the scenes, the characters, the movements, and the events mentioned, insures to the reader a sympathetic treatment of the subject. Fireside recitals by aged pioneers, addresses at old settlers' meetings, local historical society papers, reminiscences of early citizens, State records, scholarly monographs and histories have all gone to the making of these pages.

An attempt has been made to accredit, either in the text or in the appended bibliography, the statements and facts, freely gleaned, from every known authority. Acknowledgment and thanks are gratefully rendered to them, and to old settlers for their reminiscences.

If a renewed interest in those authorities is enlisted, and popular attention is attracted to the historic events, which they have all faithfully sought to present, the intention of the present volume will be accomplished.

J. H. L.

La Fayette, Indiana, 1908.

CONTENTS

CHAPTER	PAGE
I.—La Salle and the Exploration	1
II.—French Dominion	15
III.—British Occupation	26
IV.—How Spanish Rule Affected Indiana	32
V.—American Conquest	44
VI.—The Pioneers	60
VII.—Indiana Territory—1763–1816	106
VIII.—The New State—1816	139
IX.—Early Churches in Indiana	166
X.—Crimes of the Border	182
XI.—The Trail—from Birch-Bark Canoe to Electric Trolley	198
XII.—The Social Experiments at New Harmony	240
XIII.—In the Forties and Fifties	271
XIV.—Indiana as Affected by the Civil War	293
XV.—Picturesque Indiana	325
XVI.—An Indiana Type	336
XVII.—Letters and Art in Indiana	350
XVIII.—Education in Indiana	409

Contents

CHAPTER	PAGE
XIX.—The Quality of the People	448
XX.—Agriculture in Indiana	459
XXI.—Natural Resources	479
XXII.—The State Civilization in Indiana as Shown by her Laws	493
Bibliography	525
Index	529

ILLUSTRATIONS

	PAGE
SCENERY ALONG THE TIPPECANOE . . *Frontispiece*	
From a photograph.	
ROBERT CAVELIER DE LA SALLE	4
From an engraving of the original painting.	
"THE MISSIONARIES CAME FROM AFAR" . . .	18
Redrawn from an old print.	
A TYPICAL PIONEER SCENE	62
Redrawn by Marie Goth from an old print.	
THE SPINNING-WHEEL WAS THE STRINGED INSTRUMENT OF THE HOUSEHOLD	64
THE HEROISM OF THE PIONEER WOMEN . . .	68
From an old print.	
A MAP OF INDIANA IN 1817	80
From an old print.	
A VIEW OF THE OHIO RIVER FROM HANOVER COLLEGE	92
The Ohio was the front door into Indiana.	
From a photograph.	
THE SITE OF TIPPECANOE BATTLE GROUND AT THE PRESENT TIME	120

Illustrations

	PAGE
PROPHET'S ROCK	122

    The Prophet stood on the high ground and chanted war songs in a loud voice and assured his followers of victory.

WILLIAM HENRY HARRISON 130

    From an engraving after the painting by Chappel.

THE OLD STATE HOUSE AT CORYDON, INDIANA . . 136

    From a photograph by Mowrer.

"CONSTITUTIONAL ELM" AT CORYDON, INDIANA . 140

    This elm is still standing.
    From a photograph by Mowrer.

AN OLD INDIANA BRIDGE 194

    These picturesque old bridges are fast giving place to modern iron structures.
    From a photograph.

THE INDIAN PERSISTED IN BELIEVING THAT THE THREATENING CREATURE WAS AN OFFENSE TO THE GENTLE RIVER 206

    From an old print.

"JOURNEYING TO THEIR NEW HOMES YOU PASSED PEOPLE SEATED IN THE GREAT CANVAS-TOPPED CONESTOGA WAGONS" 216

    From an old print.

"WE COULD HEAR THE DRIVER WINDING HIS HORN AND IT ALL SEEMED TOO FINE AND GRAND" . . 220

    From an old print.

THE OLD CANAL AND THE DESERTED TOWPATH . 226

OLD MAHOGANY FURNITURE BROUGHT TO THE WABASH BY RIVER AND CANAL . . . 274

    From a photograph.

Illustrations

	PAGE
THE DRESS OF THE FORTIES	276
From a photograph of the period.	
AN ADVERTISEMENT OF THE UNDERGROUND RAILWAY	284
(From *The Western Citizen*, published July, 1844.)	
ONE OF THE OLD COLONIAL HOMES LONG SINCE PASSED INTO OTHER USES	290
SOLDIERS' AND SAILORS' MONUMENT	320
A VIEW ON ONE OF THE BEAUTIFUL RIVER ROADS OF INDIANA	326
THE ENTRANCE TO DONNEHUE'S CAVE IN LAWRENCE COUNTY, SOUTHERN INDIANA	328
From a photograph.	
THE CLIFTY FALLS, NEAR MADISON, INDIANA	330
ONE OF THE GORGES OF MONTGOMERY COUNTY	332
AN OLD MILL	334
One comes upon these old mills unexpectedly at a turn of the road, set amidst the most charming scenery. From a photograph.	
ALBERT HENDERSON	338
THE EARLY POETS ALL SANG OF THE BEAUTIES OF FORESTS AND STREAMS	352
BENJAMIN HARRISON	394
From a photograph by Clark, Indianapolis.	
THE DAUGHTER OF CHIEF MASSAW	400
From a sketch from life by William Winter on the Miami Reservation.	

Illustrations

	PAGE
A MIAMI INDIAN	404

    Sketched from life by William Winter on the Miami Reservation.

YOUNG'S CHAPEL, CONSOLIDATED SCHOOL, UNION TOWNSHIP, MONTGOMERY COUNTY, INDIANA . . 412

    Hacks ready to start home.

A SCENE NEAR HANOVER COLLEGE 424

    From a photograph.

CONSOLIDATED SCHOOL IN UNION TOWNSHIP . . 426

    From a photograph.

FROM THE STATELY ENTRANCE YOU LOOK OUT OVER THE BEAUTIFUL CAMPUS OF "ST. MARY'S OF THE WOODS" 428

STUDENT BUILDING, INDIANA UNIVERSITY, BLOOMINGTON, INDIANA 432

    From a photograph.

INDUSTRIAL TRAINING IN THE PUBLIC SCHOOLS . . 440

    From a photograph by Miner, Fort Wayne, Ind.

CABINET WORK DONE IN THE PUBLIC SCHOOLS OF BLUFFTON 442

MECHANICAL ENGINEERING AT PURDUE UNIVERSITY 446

"OFTEN FROM MORNING UNTIL NIGHT THERE WAS A CONTINUAL RUMBLE OF WHEELS, AND WHEN THE RUSH WAS GREATEST THERE NEVER WAS A MINUTE THAT WAGONS WERE NOT IN SIGHT" . . . 454

    From an old print.

THE ENTRANCE TO SCHOOL GARDEN, DELPHI, INDIANA 460

CHILDREN CRATING THEIR TOMATO CROP IN THE SCHOOL GARDEN AT DELPHI, INDIANA . . . 464

Illustrations

	PAGE
Prize Crop Raised by a Member of the Boys' Corn Club in Laporte County, Indiana	468
The Entrance to Purdue University	472
The Picturesque Sand Dunes Cast up by the Great Lakes	482
Lower Falls Cataract, Styner's Falls	490

Such falls as Styner's Cataract await their development as generators of electric power.

The State Capitol, Indianapolis	500

From a photograph by W. H. Bass Photo Co.

The Indiana Reform School for Boys	512

From a photograph by Deweese, Plainfield, Ind.

ACKNOWLEDGMENTS.

The author gratefully acknowledges the kindness of those who have assisted in the illustration of this volume by permitting the use of photographs belonging to them. Among the friends who have so helped her are: Mrs. Gordon Ball, Mrs. J. H. Styner, Mrs. Julius Hargrave, Mr. William M. Blatchley, Mr. Lawrence McTurnin, Mr. E. L. Hendricks, Mr. Samuel D. Symmes, Mr. Claude Millar, Mr. E. G. Bunnell, Mr. John F. Haines, Mr. W. A. Wirt, the President of Indiana University, the President of Hanover College, and the Sister Superior of St. Mary's-of-the-Woods. Thanks are also offered to Hon. Amos Butler and Superintendent Fassett A. Cotton, who went over certain chapters which were concerned with matters on which they are authorities, and enabled the author to speak with the more confidence regarding them.

"Whatever the worth of the present work may be, I have striven throughout that it should never be a 'drum and trumpet history.' If some of the conventional figures of military and political history occupy in my pages less than the space usually given them, it is because I have had to find a place for figures little heeded in common history—the figures of the missionary, the poet, the painter, the merchant, and the philosopher."

GREEN'S *Short History of the English People.*

HISTORIC INDIANA

CHAPTER I

LA SALLE AND THE EXPLORATION

FLOWING through the most fertile part of the land which stretched from the Alleghanies the Mississippi, was the beautiful river known to the Indians as the Ouabache. It was through the wilderness bordering on that stream that the explorers came who first revealed to Europeans the country south of the Great Lakes.

We are familiar with this domain as a busy section of an established country. We know it as a group of great States, dotted with thriving towns and crossed by thousands of railways; whose trains flash past numberless cultivated farms, and carry their products to the great cities, which have grown up within the territory. But this is only recent history.

Three centuries ago the region north of the Ohio, then covered with a dense wilderness, was a land of adventure, of tragedy and of romance. Here the red man, tracking through his endless forests, encountered a new race, that was to deprive him of his hunting grounds. Other events contributed to the stirring elements of the drama. Scarcely had the canoes of the white race crossed the Lakes, and drifted down the rivers, of what is now known as Indiana, before the history of the Northwest was but the echo of the strife between the Powers of the Old World, and the ominous contest between their colonists with the aborigines. It requires a little imagination to realize that kings and monarchs exercised dominion over Indiana. Nevertheless, from the time that the gallant La Salle opened the way, until the beginning of the nineteenth century, all of the territory of which it is a part was an international shuttlecock. The whole Mississippi Valley was claimed, ceded, and re-ceded by the nations of Europe, as well as by the native chiefs and the American government.

During all of this time, the tragic part of its history was the ever-present menace of the savage tribes, who were being despoiled of their heritage. Such conditions can hardly be called prosaic, and when the true story of explorer, friar, fur-trader, and pioneer are added, it would be a tale hard to match.

It was more than a hundred and seventy-five years after Columbus discovered America, before any European explored the country south of the Lakes, and revealed those magnificent regions to the world. The beginning was the first journey of La Salle. For fifty years the English settlers had been peopling the Atlantic Coast, while Canada had been the objective point of the adventurous French. Following the accessible water-routes, their explorers had reached out along the region north of the Lakes, as far as Lake Superior; and their fur trading-posts and mission-houses had been established at the strategic points.

South of Detroit and the Lakes, the vast territory of fertile soil and more temperate climate lay unexplored. This was from fear of the fierce Iroquois tribes, who intimidated the most courageous traders.

In the year 1669, a new name was enrolled among the intrepid spirits who were willing to dare further dangers of the wilderness for fame and fortune; and the heroic figure of Robert Cavelier, Sieur de La Salle, appears. This brave young man had come out from France three years before, and after studying the explorations already made by others, and addressing himself to the acquisition of seven or eight Indian languages, he considered himself prepared to undertake the realization of his dreams of exploration. Selling all he possessed to defray the cost of the expedition, he threw his whole energies into preparation for the daring venture. His plan was to explore the far country where the "Great River" was said to be, and claim the territory for France. With a little band of fourteen followers, in four frail canoes, he started on the journey from Montreal. The hints grudgingly imparted by the natives, as to the Great River which flowed into the sea, as to fabulous mines in the southwest, and as to a passage to China, he followed eagerly. Except the information regarding the river, the tales were but will-o'-the-wisps.

The "Mississippi" was a name repeated about Canadian camp-fires and in the manors of French chevaliers long before any bold *voyageur* had travelled far enough from his fellows to reach its banks. Four years after La Salle's initial journey toward the west, Joliet and Marquette, going by Lake Michigan and the Illinois River, reached the "Father of Waters"; and published their achievement of that fact to the world, but it is claimed that this *first* voyage of La Salle was probably by another route. The eminent historian Parkman tells us that, by the loss of old records, which have disappeared since 1756, we are deprived of the account of La Salle's movements during the two years following his departure from Canada, on this first mission of adventure. The memorandum that is preserved says that, after leaving Lake Erie, six or seven leagues distant, he finally came to a stream which proved to be a branch of the river we call the Ohio; and that descending it for a long distance he joined that river. Some have maintained that he went beyond the confluence of the Ohio with the Mississippi. As the source of the Wabash is near the west end of Lake Erie, a voyage down that river would naturally lead to the discovery of the Ohio. Doubtless, then, the Wabash country was approached from Lake Erie and the Maumee River, as this route was followed in later journeyings of the French. After crossing the broad Lakes in their slight boats, and paddling up the Maumee to its source, they probably made a short portage of their canoes and camp luggage to the head-waters of the Ouabache, only a few miles overland, and launched their boats for the first voyage through Indiana.

No incident could appeal more to the imagination than this advent of those birch-bark canoes, filled with the denizens of countries overseas, paddling down the newly discovered stream whose rippling waters had flowed for centuries through the vast forest, all undreamed of by white men. The shores they passed were lined with enormous forest trees, festooned with vines and filled with singing birds. Fish abounded in the placid stream, and wild game came unafraid

Robert Cavelier de la Salle.
From an engraving of the original painting.

to the water's brink. Leagues on leagues and miles on miles of unknown lands, sparsely inhabited by savage peoples, stretched away from the narrow river which carried the slight canoes with their handful of men. It is a picture to remain in the mind, this first coming of the old world into the new west. Such slight records of those earlier journeys have been preserved that we must await further research for verification, and for details of the happenings. We know that on later voyages, in the years 1671 and 1672, and again in 1679–1680, La Salle entered the State from Lake Michigan through the St. Joseph River and traversed the northwestern part of what is now Indiana. Following the suggestions of the Indians, he ascended the St. Joseph to about three miles from the present site of South Bend. Here a slight elevation separates the waters that drain into the Gulf of Mexico from those that flow toward the St. Lawrence, and the land flattens out into great stretches of swamp and meadow. Across the grassy plains, covered with game and wild fowl, and strewn with the skulls and bones of buffalo, they carried their boats four or five miles to the origin of the Kankakee. Coming to a little clear thread of water, in the surrounding swamp, it is recorded that they set their canoes on it, and pushed down the sluggish streamlet, looking at a distance like men who sailed on land. Fed by an unceasing tribute of the spongy soil, which extended on either side over sixteen hundred square miles of valley, the stream quickly widened into a winding river, with its two thousand bends. On this stream they floated amidst that voiceless solitude toward the Illinois, and through it to the Mississippi, which was the goal of their wanderings.

From these two journeys through the region that is now called Indiana, La Salle may in truth be called its discoverer. The routes he opened up were followed for many decades by succeeding voyagers. The two parts of the State that he explored were widely different in their physical features. The Wabash Valley was heavily wooded, and the surface of the country high and rolling, while the lands south of Lake Michigan were vast plains dotted with lakes. The explorers wrote to France that they had found the country good and pleasant; that the climate was admirable, and the soil extraordinarily fertile. They found game in abundance, and mentioned particularly the wild turkey.

These first excursions of La Salle into the Indiana wilderness, at the opening of his career, and before jealous enemies tried to thwart his far-reaching plans of dominion, were full of hope and expectation. Later there were stirring tales of his courageous adventures on the Mississippi; the history of his long journeys to France for authority and funds, the counterplotting of Canadian foes, his triumphant recognition by the King, and, last of all, his early death at the age of forty-three, in the Louisiana wilderness. In the preface to *Joutel's Journal*, the following recognition of La Salle's services to France places him among the illustrious heroes sent out by the Grand Monarch. There it is urged:

"Let us transmit their names to posterity in our writings, for the consequences of their labor are most honorable and advantageous to the Nation. . . . La Salle was dignified, bold, undaunted, dextrous, insinuating, not to be discouraged at anything, ready at extricating himself out of any difficulty. No way apprehensive of the greatest

La Salle and the Exploration

fatigues. Wonderful steady in adversity, and, wha[t is] of extraordinary use, well versed in several lang[uages.] Having such extraordinary talents, he was very ac[ceptably] ably employed in these affairs"[1]

and added a domain larger than Central Europe to the possessions of his sovereign.

The quaint language of the faithful Henri de Tonty, friend of La Salle, in his tribute to that leader, picturesquely presents the discoveries as they impressed the explorers themselves.

"Monsieur, the plunderers of your fortune cannot take away that discovery, or blot out the World you then opened. And what is Europe compared to this vast country? At the height of his magnificence, Louis cannot picture to himself the grandeur of this Western Empire. France is but the palm of his hand beside it. It stretches from endless snow to endless heat; its breadth no man may guess. Nearly all the native tribes affiliate readily with the French. We have, to dispute us, only the English, who hold a little strip by the Atlantic, the Dutch with smaller holdings inland, and a few Spaniards along the Gulf. It is an Empire, which Louis might drop France itself, to grasp."

There can be no doubt that La Salle had a clear comprehension of the value, to France, of his explorations, for he not only established trading-posts for gain, but he also endeavored to carry thither people to colonize and preëmpt the territory. The sad ending of his short life came all too soon for the successful carrying-out of his dreams of an Empire, but enough was accomplished by La Salle and Tonty to place

[1] *Joutel's Journal of La Salle's Last Voyage*, Introduction, page 16, Reprint of Caxton Club, 1896.

as the great frontier knights of the middle West
dawn of its history.

or many years after these first voyagers paddled
down the Wabash, the only travellers to the region were the hardy and adventurous *coureurs de bois*. No records were kept of their journeys,—how soon they followed the explorers, or how often they came and went; but long before the French government established military outposts, these wandering traders and trappers, with an occasional zealous priest, were the sole visitors to the wilds of what is now Indiana.

The *coureurs de bois* of Canada ranged over the whole northern and western part of the new continent from Hudson Bay to Louisiana in search of adventure, and to trade with the Indians. They belonged, largely, to the lower classes of adventurers who came out continually from France; but their numbers were constantly augmented by impoverished members of the nobility, or reckless gallants who were reduced in fortune, or fugitives from justice. Inspired by love of adventure, or seeking the oblivion of the forest, these men of gentle blood joined fortunes with the reckless, shiftless *voyageurs*. Hunting, trapping fur-bearing animals, trading with the Indians, and living with the natives in utter abandonment of previous civilization, was the life into which they drifted. As they rowed down the streams, their paddles kept time to the gay strains:

> Tous les printemps, . . .
> Tant de nouvelles . . .
>   Tous les amants . . .
> Changent de maîtresses . . .
>   Jamais le bon vin ne m'endort . . .
> L'amour me réveille . . .

> Tous les amants . . .
>   Changent des maîtresses . . .
>   Qu'ils changent qui voudront . . .
>   Pour moi je garde la mienne . . .
>   Le bon vin n'endort . . .
>   L'amour me réveille . . .

They married the squaws; sold spirits to the braves against all law; ofttimes discarded all clothing; and sometimes conspired against the authorities. They have been known to leave the explorer or missionary alone in the wilderness, to the mercies of the savages. Such were those dauntless adventurers, the *coureurs de bois*, who were peculiar to early Canadian life and history. As most of the territory of which Indiana formed a part was included in that domain in the eighteenth century, these romantic characters were its first white inhabitants. They did not found any homes or towns. They came singing down the rivers in their light canoes, and lodged with the Indians, traded with them, drank with them, and monopolized the forest bargaining. It was through these gay French vagabonds that the savages obtained their bright-colored blankets, their gaudy trinkets, and also the powder, the arms, and the firewater, which made them more dangerous than before. Only such irresponsible, weather-hardened *voyageurs* could have endured the privations of that savage life; and their daring adventurous spirit secured to them the fur-trade of the forest. Not a trace of their existence in Indiana remained at the time of the conquest of 1779, when the French still inhabited the posts. No name, habitation, or landmark was left of those who thus entered and disappeared from the rivers and woods of the Wabash, and whose history reads like a legend.

When the first white explorers came down the Indiana rivers, they found few settled tribes of Indians. This was on account of the recent Iroquois war. But later, numerous Indian tribes, of many different names, roamed the territory, and all belonged to the great Algonquin race, which occupied the whole of the middle West, and the New England coast. These allied families of Algonquins, while often warring among themselves, united their strength in terror of their bitter foes located on either side of them. The cruel Iroquois separated the Eastern forces by occupying the region now known as New York and southward; while the bloodthirsty Siouan tribes held the country west of the Mississippi. The Miami confederacy, whose barbarian villages dotted the central and northern part of Indiana, included the Weas, the Foxes, the Piankeshaws, the Pottawattomies, the Shawnees, the Ouiatanons, and the Kickapoos, with whose barbarous names the early settlers, alas! were to become so familiar, and who were all branches of the Algonquin race.

The regions now called Indiana and Kentucky were reserved as hunting-ground, but they were also perpetual battle-fields. Across this expanse surged these countless allied tribes and their hereditary enemies. Back and forth from east to west, from north to south, from Florida to the Dakotas, they fought in endless warfare against each other and against their foes. To and fro, defeating or defeated, seldom utterly vanquished, unless exterminated, they came and went on the war-path, always planning to return to the fray, if checkmated in their savage raids, when new combinations with more tribes should render them strong enough for a fresh attack.

All of the tribes were passionately fond of the excitement of games of chance, and sat about the fires and gambled until their last possessions were gone; staking clothing, weapons, pipes, ornaments, or wife on the last throw of the dice. It is said that if invited to "come eat" it was unheard of to refuse; the person invited took his dish and spoon and went; grunted "Ho!" upon entering, and to every remark that interested him.

Many of the wigwams or huts of the Indians were fashioned of bark or of skins and were covered on the inside with rude sketches of scenes from the chase and battle, commemorating their deeds of valor. Most of the aborigines painted their faces and bodies with soot, ashes, and the juice of plants. Very often they were cruelly tattooed. They were naturally very fond of ornaments, and were easily beguiled by gifts of finery. One possession all Indians valued above any other, was the belt of wampum. This consisted of beads, white and purple, made from the inner part of certain shells. They were made at the expenditure of great care and labor. The wampum was at once their currency, ornament, pen, ink, and parchment. It is affirmed that no compact, no speech, or clause of a speech, to the representatives of another nation, had any force unless confirmed by the delivery of a string or belt of wampum. It was the task of certain braves, detailed for that duty, to remember and reproduce what each bead recorded. The Indian's idea of music was crude, discordant, and unpleasant sounds, a drum or tom-tom being the most universal instrument of tone. His perceptions of good and evil were shadowy, and belief in a future state of reward and punishment was by no means universal. He thanked the Good Spirit for blessings and prayed to the Evil Spirit, whom he regarded as the agent of disease, death, and mischance.

The Indian had a very material notion of the happy hunting-grounds, and his idea of the fate of the wicked was that he should be doomed to eat ashes in cold dreary regions where there was always snow. All tribes were the dupes of their medicine-men, sorcerers, and witches. As a matter of course, so limited an intelligence believed in magic, in the realities of dreams, and in signs and tokens. Their limited knowledge of the laws of nature kept them in perpetual thraldom to fears of which civilized man knows nothing. Although inhabiting the most desirable area, and living in the most favorable climate on the continent they had attained little intellectual or material advancement and gave no promise of any. Their life was a round of hunting, eating, and fighting. In summer the braves were hunting and fishing when not on the war-path, but with little thought of the future, they stored up meagrely for the needs of the long and cruel winter. The men condescended to build wigwams, fashion the weapons, make their wonderful pipes, and shape their marvellous canoes, but to the women fell all the drudgery. They gathered the fire-wood, dressed the skins, made the cordage and cloth, and prepared the food. In addition they tilled the land for the scanty crops of corn and beans and pumpkins. They planted, hoed, and harvested laboriously with the little stone tools. On the march it was the squaws that bore the burdens and slaughtered the game. In battle they often bore a part. In consequence of their hard life they changed early from comely girls to hideously repulsive hags, many of them more fierce, cruel, and vindictive in war than the men. The children showed no advancement beyond the generation before and were trained in the grim lessons of savage stolidity, superstition, and endurance shown by their ancestors. When food was plenty they all gorged to repletion, and when there was no provender they lived on the roots, bark, and buds of trees.

Indians showed no tenderness or consideration towards the sick or disabled. Each shared with all, in weal or woe. Upbraiding or complaints were unheard.

The Miami tribes of Indians that were living in Indiana were of a degraded type, who practised cannibalism in its most revolting forms, and continued the practice for a hundred years after La Salle's appearance in the West. They had great dread of the evil spirits, whom they tried to propitiate, charm, and cajole. A description of these natives by an explorer characterizes the roving Indians as possessing the sagacity of a hound, the penetrating sight of a lynx, the cunning of a fox, the agility of a bounding roe, and the unconquerable fierceness of a tiger.

There have been many romantic notions of the Indian, and the early settlers were often pressed to the opposite sentiment of vindictive hate. To unprejudiced persons the native was recognized as full of contradictions. The same man who would give way to demoniacal fury, at other times held himself in the most taciturn self-restraint. His pride would sustain him at the stake but did not prevent his begging for whiskey or cast-off food. His skill at hunting and trapping showed him full of perception of nature and his resources in constructing boats, traps, pits, and spears gave evidence of his cunning, but he had little power of reasoning. They had their own form of humor and were fond of telling tales of their prowess by the camp-fire. A practical joke, or the awkwardness of a white man would move them to roars of laughter, and like the white man they were fond of a joke at the expense of the weaker sex. Such were the natives of the Indiana region when the white man came in, and with whom the coming settlers must be brought into close contact. From the mistakes of governments, and the impossibility of the two civilizations mingling peaceably, both races suffered untold misery. No imaginary tale could be more harassing. Their woes appear on each succeeding page of history, insuring them the sympathy of posterity. After the natives acquired from the white man the use of whiskey and firearms, they became what Mr. Roosevelt terms the most formidable savage foes ever encountered by colonists of European stock.

CHAPTER II

FRENCH DOMINION

A CENTURY and a half between La Salle and the beginning of history in the Indiana territory! Truly the new domain waits for its settlement. Silent as the records are of any account of life in the wilderness, we know that the hardy *coureurs de bois* came down the rivers and sojourned among the Indians, trapping and trading for pelts. "For a century and a half fur was king."

A few fugitive *voyageurs* among the more adventurous probably tarried, but the first French colonists, or rather the first inhabitants who made their homes at the posts and brought their families out with them, were the soldiers. The wandering boatmen came and went singly and in pairs without intention of remaining. It was their route for barter, the Indiana rivers being a part of the marvellous continuous waterway from the Lakes to the Mississippi.

"In the opening of the North American Continent," says Mr. Ogg, "the Frenchman had this great advantage over some of his rivals—that he entered the land from the right direction, and at a very strategic point. The St. Lawrence set them on the most inviting path to the vast interior, through the Great Lakes and into the eastern tributaries of the Mississippi, finally down that noble stream to the Gulf. As a consequence of this, and to the further fact that by nature the Frenchmen who came to America were of a more roving disposition than the English, their explorations moved much more rapidly. They had ranged and mapped the country continuously from Labrador to the Gulf of Mexico, before the English yet knew the upper courses of even the James, the Hudson, and the Connecticut."[1]

And yet, if their exploration and trade were more sweeping, their colonization was far less effective and permanent in that far West.

Following La Salle's constant urging of the importance of establishing military posts from Quebec to New Orleans, for the purpose of maintaining the sovereignty of France, against the Spanish and the English, the government of Louis XIV. made some weak establishments on the Lakes and the Mississippi; but they were barely a roof for the wandering missionaries to the savage nations, or a trading station. No posts were established on the Wabash until 1720, and the visitations of the zealous priests to the Indians were the only means of control which France maintained over the wilds of Indiana until that time. During all this period the missionaries were always followed, and sometimes preceded, by a class of traders who gave intoxicating liquors to the Indians in exchange for furs and pelts. "The drink among the Indians is the greatest obstacle to Christianity," wrote the good friars; "they never purchase it, but to plunge into the most furious orgies of riot and bloodshed." For all their despair of the savage character, the Jesuit fathers and the holy friars persisted in their labors, growing old and perishing in their

[1] Ogg, Fredk., *Opening of the Mississippi.*

attempts. Younger ones stepped into their vacant places, and took passage with the *voyageurs* whose little barks penetrated every wilderness.

The gradual movement westward by the British, from the Atlantic Coast, was what prompted the French to establish new posts, and strengthen old ones, along the water-routes from Canada to Louisiana. Several prominent points along the courses were selected and fortified, in the rude frontier fashion of palisades and blockhouses. In these primitive stockades were installed a handful of French soldiers and their families, the priest who guided their very wandering footsteps back to religion, an occasional slave, some half-breed Indians, and a few domestic animals — all of whom were a part of the French system of trade and religion. In a short while each had a plot of garden cultivated by the women, and fruit soon hung on their trees. The posts were not powerful enough for conquest, but they were sufficient to protect the trade with the natives, and to that industry the activities of the lazy little colonies were mainly limited. The post was a convenient rendezvous for the trapper and hunter, and the *voyageurs;* and a point from which the priest reached out to convert the Indians to his faith.

As time went on and trade increased, it came about that, beside the commandants, the most prominent individuals at the trading-posts were the French merchants. The old French merchant, at his post, was the head man of the settlement. Careful, frugal, without much enterprise, judgment, or rigid virtue, he was employed in procuring skins from the Indians or traders, in exchange for manufactured goods. He kept on good terms with the Indians, and frequently fostered a large number of half-breed children. The intermittent traffic on the rivers formed the means of communication between these solitary posts and the outside world. Post Ouiatanon, the first established on the Ouabache, was near the site of the present city of La Fayette, and opposite a group of Indian villages of the Ouiatanon tribes. This post and Fort Miamis, now Fort Wayne, were under the rule of the Canadian Governor and reported to the commandant at Detroit; while the post of Vincennes, established in 1731, belonged to the Louisiana dominion—Terre Haute forming the dividing line between the two districts. Of the Ouiatanon post, so beautifully located, and connected with so many traditions of the past, few traces remain. Its location and career are part of the history of the aboriginal time. The city of La Fayette, which later was founded in that beautiful environment, is located on the hills north of the Indian hamlet. Ouiatanon was the head of navigation on the Wabash for the larger pirogues, on account of the shallow rapids below the present city. All peltries destined for Canada must here be transferred to canoes, and this made the post a natural resting place and point for barter. Twenty thousand skins a year were shipped from Fort Ouiatanon during 1720 and the decade following.

"To watch the English and expel them in case they approach" were the directions to the commandant who established the post at Fort Miamis, now Fort Wayne. The point was an important one as it was near the head of the Maumee River, where the *voyageurs* from over the Lakes re-embarked their canoes for the long river journey. Unlike Ouiatanon, it continued through many vicissitudes and much warlike

"The Missionaries Came from Afar."
Redrawn from an old print.

history, to be the nucleus of a town, and in the present day has grown into one of the important cities of the State.

Post Vincennes also has had a continuous existence from the early part of the eighteenth century; which in Indiana seems like ancient history. The story of Vincennes and vicinity is a large part of the history of the French impression on the State. There were a few scattered families identified with the history of other sections, but all that Indiana knew of a community largely French may be claimed by its oldest town. In 1787, an American soldier writing from Vincennes and giving a description of the mixed population of nine hundred French and four hundred Americans, said: "This town has been settled longer than Philadelphia, and one half of the houses are yet covered with bark like Indian wigwams."

Life at the different posts at that early time was much alike. We are told that each had its large commons for the pasturage of stock, also its common fields, in which each individual's tract was marked off. The houses were grouped about the fort within a stockade as a protection from the savages. After all, the most abiding memory of the influences of the French posts in the early settlements, is that of the brave missionaries, so often spoken of in every record of that remote past. None of the posts contained a large population. The long distances from the coast, either at Quebec or New Orleans, the constant danger of surrounding savages, the rude quarters and great privations, made the interior settlements unattractive to the gregarious French people. Their garden plots were attractive but the agriculture was very shiftless. As the soil was fertile, Indian corn, wheat, tobacco, and all kinds of fruits and melons were easily produced. In time they possessed swine and black cattle, and brought horses from the Spanish settlements in the Southwest. The only vehicle they ever acquired, in their most luxurious days, was the two-wheeled calèche, which was the only serviceable thing in the wilderness without roads. The rivers were the arteries of commerce, and no one could pole a boat like the French Canadian. The priest and chapel held the little isolated communities to something of the old forms and ceremonies of their abandoned civilization, kept them to the prayers and sacraments, taught them to transplant some of the arts of living to the frontier.

They had windmills to grind the wheat into flour, when the earliest English settlers, who lived in a more scattered way, had only corn-meal ground by hand. The women did not spin and weave as the English pioneers did, and the family washing was beaten on the banks of the stream, as was the custom in their home country. French cookery, even in those rude surroundings, was superior to that of other frontier people. Game was plentiful, and their fare included fish, prairie chicken, roast duck, venison pasty, and broiled quail. The costume of these people was picturesque and becoming—it consisted of a buckskin coat, knee breeches, moccasins, and always leggins; a tasselled capote, or in summer a peaked hat of straw, braided by the women, as they gossiped on the little front piazzas. They were fond of wearing a bit of bright color around the throat and at the waist, or bedecked themselves with beads in Indian fashion. In cold weather both men and women wore a long cloak with a hood. The women looked much like the peasants in the old country, with bodice, short full skirt, and little caps.

With true French vivacity and love for social life and amusement, the inhabitants of each little post celebrated feast days, name days, christenings, and weddings with dancing, songs, processions, and feasts; lasting in the case of weddings for two or three days. Fêtes on the river, a row by moonlight, a Christmas morning carol beneath each window, always the New Year's calls by the gentlemen, and the Mardi Gras celebration before the penances of Lent, were the simple round of frontier festivities. We can imagine the scene. Clustered within a palisaded enclosure, surrounded by the interminable forest, were the rude, little whitewashed cabins, bedecked with vines and flowers, and a tiny garden at the side; in the narrow street the small, wiry, dark-skinned French peasants trooping about, babbling in their strange Canadian jargon, the negro slaves, perchance, answering in creole patois; some neighborhood Indians, clad in gay blankets and wonderful eagle-feather head-dresses, looking on in grave curiosity—silent, as the habitants were noisy and chattering. Far from the lands of their ancestry, each nationality lives out its racial traits in the remote wilderness home.

It has always been noted that between wars, there was general friendliness between the French and Indians, in striking contrast to the enmity among the English and the red men. It was the policy of the English to remove the Indians, and of the French to attract them for purposes of trade. Hence, the natives often gathered in settlements around the French posts. They learned a little agriculture and Romanism, but, alas! they also acquired the taste for rum, notwithstanding the selling of guns, ammunition, and "firewater" was against the mandates of the King, and of prudence.

The first slaves in Indiana were owned by these early French settlers. Their holding and treatment were regulated by the French government, in elaborate laws, so that they were not left entirely to the mercy of the owners. The Canadian slaves were generally Indians, called *panis;* and those of the Louisiana district were mostly negroes, brought from the French West Indies. The two races of slaves frequently intermarried, and the government required all to be baptized and instructed in the Roman Catholic faith. The frontier Frenchman was an easy master, lacking thrift and having no pressure of competition.

In trading with the natives for peltries the settlers gave in exchange bright colored cloth, blankets, gunpowder, knives, hatchets, animal traps, kettles, hoes, war paint, ribbons, beads, and rum. By trading and trapping they collected great quantities of furs during the season, which were mostly carried to the Canadian market for European shipments. They raised wheat and ground it into flour at their community windmills. Tobacco was raised and baled. Some pork was cured, then with no undue haste or competition these stores were accumulated, and when a sufficient cargo was secured, a fleet of batteaux would be formed, for mutual protection against the Indians, and the event of the year began; that is the journey thither to Detroit and Montreal, or five hundred leagues down the rivers to New Orleans, which they called "going to town to see their friends." This trip down the river was a long, lazy, delightful journey to those pleasure-loving people. They drifted with the current, telling endless stories of adventure, while they watched the ever-changing views on either shore. Sometimes convoys came from far-off Montreal, to enjoy the winter season. They stayed in New Orleans as long as they could, ofttimes until their money was gambled away. The more enterprising bartered their produce for merchandise, for the return trip, and carried back sugar, rice, cotton, and manufactured articles from France. After much feasting and many formal *congés* among acquaintances they departed for their homes, and then began the long, tedious, toilsome ascent of the river.

From the time when France found it necessary to establish outposts, in 1720, to protect her interests, until the day that Quebec fell into the hands of Great Britain, there were struggles innumerable between the two Powers over their claims to the Western territory. These wars always involved the frontiersmen and the Indians in deadly conflicts, and the blackest pages in American colonial history are the sins of the old world Powers in instigating the natives to massacre the settlers. At length, the English won the great victories at Quebec and along the Lakes. The acquisition of the whole of Canada followed. The Treaty of Peace was concluded in 1763. The English claim included the upper Indiana territory. The inhabitants remained at ease, heeding little of the great change of government and destiny; but the treaties of 1763 closed the brilliant explorations and dreams of American Empire for France. Illustrious explorers, courtly cavaliers, devout priests, reckless *voyageurs*, skilful trappers, and frugal colonists had crossed the Atlantic and traversed the inland lakes and rivers to found a new French dominion and a home in the West. "In the laying of the foundations for an abiding political power they failed. They could have maintained themselves as against the Spaniard or any other possible European competitor, except the very one with whom they had to contend. The contest was essentially a conflict of civilization, the results appear no less inevitable, than necessary to the future of the country."

At the time of the cession to Great Britain there were probably north of the Ohio and east of the Mississippi only about twelve hundred adults, eight hundred children, and nine hundred negroes who were slaves. Many of the French people retired to the western bank of the Mississippi, to the point now called St. Louis, rather than remain British subjects. The French colonies had always been dependencies. Gradually, as the control of the fur trade passed from France to England, the posts languished when they had to depend upon themselves. After a few years, when the Americans in turn took them from the British, the forts were used by the young republic as outposts to protect the settlers against the Indians. Gradually they fell into desuetude, as the native tribes were sent to the farther frontiers. 1791 is given as the date of the final disappearance of Ouiatanon. Towns arose on the site of the other two French posts in Indiana territory, at Fort Wayne and Fort Vincennes. The little French posts of the early half of that century are only a memory. The log chapel where the black-robed priest christened the babe and married the blooming bride, has gone to decay. The vine-covered balcony and its gay peasant family have alike crumbled into dust. There are left no traces of the volatile, pleasure-loving people from overseas, and the silent savage has vanished with his forests. But still a tinge of romance lingers over the palisaded station and its denizens. "Such," says Mr. Dunn in describing those denizens,

"were the French settlers of Indiana—yet not such; for we have scanned too closely what we might esteem their faults, and given little heed to what we must admit to be their virtues. In many respects they were admirable. They were simple, honest, and patriotic. In their social life they were kindly, sympathetic, and generous. The ancient *habitant* rises before us lithe and erect as in his prime. The old capote is there, the beaded moccasins, the little ear-rings, and the black queue. His dark eyes glisten beneath his turban handkerchief as of yore. There stands his old calèche. He mounts upon it and moves away—away—away, until its creaking sounds no longer, and we realize that he is gone forever."[1]

[1] Dunn, J. P., *History of Indiana*, page. 130.

CHAPTER III

BRITISH OCCUPATION

WHEN Great Britain secured Quebec and the control of the St. Lawrence from the French, her grasp of the Western dependencies, along the waterways, followed naturally. The strongholds of French supremacy were in northern and eastern America. The vast tract, inland, was acquired without more fighting, and its fortunes rose and fell with those of Canada. Within a few years of the time that Spain assumed dominion over the Mississippi River, and consequently come vitally into contact with the interests of its tributaries, which we mention elsewhere, England gained possession of the lands through which those rivers flowed. The history of the little settlements on the Maumee and the Wabash under English rule was part of the same period that the struggling settlements were hampered by Spanish interference, at New Orleans.

The British crown owned the territory that is now Indiana less than twenty years. It occupied the scattered military posts scarcely fifteen years before General George Rogers Clark and his little band of American frontiersmen took possession of them in the year 1779. England's title to the wilderness domain made little difference to the scattered French settlements on the Wabash. It being the policy of Great Britain to leave the customs, language, and religion unchanged, the happy-go-lucky class of frontier Frenchmen cared little what government ruled.

When the English troops took possession, in 1765, there were only eighty or ninety French families living at Post Vincennes; and there had been about fourteen families at Fort Ouiatanon during its occupancy, and at the post in the northeastern part of the State there were nine or ten French houses. These three small colonies were, at that time, the only white settlements within the territory which is now the State of Indiana. After the British commandant, with a small detachment of redcoats, had taken possession of the fort, under the Cross of St. George instead of the Lilies of France, and issued a specific proclamation to the settlers, the isolated camps realized little difference by the change of sovereignty. When England took possession of every stronghold from St. Lawrence and the Lakes, south, there were scarcely any American colonists north of the Ohio River and west of the Alleghanies. The savage Iroquois had prevented immigration overland. The American traders who came from the Atlantic colonies, by way of the rivers, were a mere handful and lived among the French at the posts. As soon as Great Britain had extended her control over the West, many English traders and land hunters began to go thither. The home government immediately feared that the section might feel itself so remote, and become so self-reliant, that the settlers would declare an independent government. In consequence of this apprehension, the King of England issued a proclamation forbidding any emigration to the newly acquired section. Six years later, the commander-in-chief wrote to the Colonial Department,

"as to increasing the settlements (northwest of the river, Ohio) to respectable provinces—and to colonization in general terms in the remote countries—I have conceived it altogether inconsistent with sound policy. I do not apprehend the inhabitants could have any commodities to barter for our manufactures, except skins and furs, which will naturally decrease as the country increases in people, and the deserts are cultivated; so that, in the course of a few years, necessity would force them to provide manufactures of some kind themselves, and when all connection upheld by commerce with the mother country shall cease, *it may be expected that an independency in their government will soon follow.*"

Notwithstanding all these prohibitions by the home government, there was an ever-increasing number of hardy pioneers, who ventured down the river from Pennsylvania, or tracked through the forests of Kentucky from Virginia and the Carolinas, to the territory northwest of the Ohio. A few of these came into Indiana. Despite the interdict of Great Britain, and the forbidding attitude of the savages, the population of the English colonists from tidewater kept increasing along the rivers of the West. During all the years of the British occupation, there was a constant menace to the whole border population south and north of the Ohio, from the Indians, who were becoming more and more alarmed at the white man's invasion. It was a time of midnight surprises, swift and sudden attacks and massacres; then an uprising by the whites, and war to the death against the savages. Year in and year out there were always alert anxiety and dread of further disaster, while bitterness of feeling between the races grew ever more deadly. The Indians had no enduring confidence in French, Spanish, or English. They had been used by each in turn, against the other; and were bewildered by the conflicting policies of Europe, which were being fought out in the wilderness.

The situation was most disastrous to both races, and the trouble seemed interminable to the hapless frontiersman.

It was owing to the constant friction with the natives that General George Rogers Clark first came out with a commission from Virginia to help protect the border toward the Ohio River, maintaining that a country which was not worth defending was not worth claiming. It was in defence of Kentucky settlers that he came to the Wabash and the Mississippi. A far more momentous result of that campaign is part of the story of the Revolution. It was to end the dominion of England over the wilds of Indiana. While the puny settlements on Western rivers were struggling with the primeval forces, little affected by the troubles of the American colonists on the Atlantic shore, these colonists had for three years been engaged in a life-and-death struggle for liberty from British rule. The strictures upon emigration to the new lands were part of the cause of revolt. Concentration of population to the narrow strip of country between the Alleghanies and the ocean was resented by the Southern colonies as much as unjust taxation. In fact the war has come to be recognized as a revolt against the attitude of Great Britain in regard to America on many questions. The colonists felt the genius for control of their own affairs.

It required little more than a decade, from the conquest of the French possessions in North America, for the American colonies to throw off the claims of Great Britain. In fact, the military part taken by the colonial troops in that conquest gave them the assurance to begin a protest to the crown.

Professor Hinsdale says:

"The history of French America is far more picturesque and brilliant than the history of British America in that period, but the English were doing work far more solid, valuable, and permanent than their northern neighbors. The French took the lakes, rivers, and forests; they cultivated the Indians; their explorers were intent upon discovery; their traders on furs; their missionaries on souls. The English did not either take to the woods or cultivate the Indians; they loved agriculture and trade, State and Church, and clung to the fields, shops, politics, and churches. As a result, while Canada languished, thirteen English states grew up on the Atlantic Coast, and became populous, rich, and strong. They spread to other colonies. There were 80,000 white inhabitants in New France, and 1,160,000 in the British Colonies at the close of the period." [1]

During the War for Independence, the dramatic movements of General Clark and his Southern soldiers in the Northwestern wilderness were so successful, that the settlements on the Wabash and the Mississippi passed from British control before the contest was over on the Atlantic coast. Indiana territory became an American possession by these brilliant achievements, in February, 1779, four years before England

[1] Hinsdale, Professor, *The Dial*, 1900.

gave up the hope of retaining her colonies. Although the British garrisons lingered, as late as 1796, under one pretext and another, they were but a survival of the past, and scarcely received passing notice from the settlers. The wilderness had become American.

CHAPTER IV

HOW SPANISH RULE AFFECTED INDIANA

SPANISH doubloons paid for the first Indiana homesteads, Spanish silver was the only coin of the realm on the Wabash until 1838. It was barter, or Spanish "pieces of eight," for twenty years after the territory became a State. From whence came this coinage and how did it become the circulating medium of Hoosierdom? Down the Mississippi and its tributaries, was the outlet for the produce of the great valley, and back from the Gulf came pay in Spanish money. The free and uncontrolled navigation of the Mississippi, as the highway to the sea and to Europe, was of the utmost importance to all the adjacent territory, and became the bone of contention for two centuries, among the three great Powers and the colonies. In this way Indiana felt the dominion of Spain, and it became a part of her history, although the territory was never within the possessions of his Most Catholic Majesty.

To appreciate the conditions in the interior along the Wabash, the Ohio, and all the other tributaries of the Mississippi River, a glance at the Spanish claims on this continent is necessary. De Soto had discovered the lower Mississippi River in an overland march from Florida, in search of gold, in 1542. He was buried in its waters—that the Indians might not learn that he was mortal—a hundred and forty years before the Frenchmen, La Salle and Tonty, came down the river from the Great Lakes. In accordance with the custom of nations, De Soto's little band had declared possession in the name of the Spanish monarch, as had been done for all the southern shores. Ever since Columbus's discovery, ships had been sailing away from Spain with their prows turned to the southwest. They had colonized the edges of the shores between Mexico and Argentina before there was a single English settlement on the Atlantic coast. Very naturally the Spanish Government set up priority of claim to the lands along the Gulf. What a vision it must have been to the unaccustomed eyes of the natives of the forest

"when through the gloomy pines there flashed the brilliant arms and trappings of the Spanish cavaliers and their soldiers, whom the Indians took to be gods. They were wearied and tattered with the long and fruitless search for strange cities and gold. Their horses were jaded and their men gaunt, from malaria and lack of food, but when they came upon this mighty river, they compared it to an inland sea and kneeling on the banks, the gallant De Soto declared it to be the possession of the Crown of Spain."[1]

But the aim of De Soto and those who followed him was gold and booty; no colonies were ever founded in the section. A century and a half later, after La Salle had set up the cross of St. Louis, D'Iberville founded the first fort and town on Biloxi Bay, to establish possession. After these two dramatic incidents, the control of New Orleans and the river changed several times between these two nations and

[1] Fiske, John, *Discovery of America*, vol. i., page 68.

for years to come the question was weaving like a shuttle, back and forth, through all the diplomacy of the centuries. The earliest efforts at making settlements in the entrance to the Mississippi were discouraging, but by 1718 France had founded a permanent colony at New Orleans, which proved to be a most loyal and persistently French settlement. We pass over the interesting history of how New Orleans lived through many changes of French rulers, sent out by the kings; under the Treaty of Utrecht, Spain had ceded all of the great territory called Louisiana to France. In 1769 Spain got it all back again and took formal possession of the city, the river, and of the Louisiana territory, by virtue of a secret treaty with France. This compact was made seven years before as a recompense for Spain's loss of Florida to Great Britain, when she was helping France. During this time, in 1763, France, beaten and bankrupt, had finally lost to Great Britain all her dominion of Canada.

Until 1800 the Western settlers in the Indiana territory, with all their trade dependent upon the river transportation, were at the mercy of the Spanish government. The boatmen, with their boats laden with produce and pelts, must await the pleasure of Spanish customs officials. Discommoded as the river voyagers were, under the change of dynasty in 1769 they could not compare with the despondent French citizens of New Orleans. Ten thousand creoles, loyal to their king, resented being used like pawns upon his chessboard, to propitiate a Power whose help he needed in his wars at home. Still the gay creole population of the lower Mississippi submitted without combat to the change, but business was neglected and festivities suspended. The new Spanish Government hung the most prominent French loyalists, ordered the Spanish language to be used, and encouraged immigration from Castile. Then came the sweeping proclamation of dire import to all the *upper country*, that the Mississippi should be closed to all trade outside this province, prohibiting all foreigners from passing through Spanish territory without a passport, and any immigration from the American colonies. These orders could only be overcome by fees and bribes, and all traffic became corrupt and disastrously uncertain. Cargoes decayed on the boats and wharves, at great loss to the settlers along the rivers. In time many of them abandoned tillage and trapping, became more shiftless than ever, and poverty overtook them. Three years later the new Governor, Unzaga, regained the confidence of the French at New Orleans, the colony increased, and agriculture was resumed. Further improvement came under his successor, Galvez, who gradually permitted more heavily laden cargoes to come down the river, and trade revived.

Besides the disasters to the river transportation of Indiana's produce, she encountered Spanish interference in a dash of troops from the little fort at St. Louis, to capture Fort St. Joseph and claim occupation of territory. This was in 1781, during the Revolutionary War. When the claim thus set up reached the distant King of England he had the new American envoys from the colonies to checkmate the design. Great Britain had then lost the war, and Spain's hold on Indiana territory was but as the passing of a shadow.

It was during Galvez's occupancy of the governorship of Louisiana that the struggling American colonies were engaged in the War of Independence.

This contest might have affected far-away Indiana and the other river colonists very slightly, had not Spain engaged in the conflict by declaring war against Great Britain in 1779. This move of the Powers in Europe ruined the commerce on the Gulf of Mexico by checking all shipments to Europe; consequently it again acted disastrously on the sorely tried settlers all the way to the Great Lakes. The cabals at Madrid meant hardships on the frontier. Hopes of permanent relief from all the vexatious hindrances to transportation were revived by the treaty of peace granting American independence, in 1783, wherein, it was fully stipulated that the Mississippi should remain forever free, from its mouth to its source, for navigation by all British subjects and by all citizens of the United States. It would seem that this should have settled the whole matter and there was an immediate response to this measure by increased immigration. Industry and traffic were revived. Alas! Spain was slow to obey the articles of the treaty. Twenty years of delay and continuous vexation followed. They were years of diplomatic dawdling and exasperating fencing, between the commissioners of the American Congress and the ministers of Spain. All this time the patience of the pioneers was tried beyond endurance by their losses in commerce. Property was seized and confiscated from Natchez on down the river.

In 1793 the French Minister, Genet, tried to induce Kentucky and Tennessee to join his standard, in an invasion of Spanish territory, and rid themselves and the French settlers of the foreign yoke. General George Rogers Clark even accepted a command to accomplish this much desired end; but the Federal Government

How Spanish Rule Affected Indiana

demanded the recall of Genet, and that threatened uprising subsided.

At the same time another form of insidious attack by the Spaniards exasperated the founders of the young republic, struggling hard to establish a stable government. This was the constant intrigues, through a long term of years, on the part of the Spanish governors of Louisiana to induce the Southern and Western settlers to secede from the United States, and form an independent government west of the Alleghany Mountains, or join the Spanish territory. The long years of delay in gaining a free outlet to the sea had worn on the disaffected settlers. The Spanish Governor, Miro, incumbent at the time, and his successor Carondelet, sent emissaries through the South and through the Indiana territory, trying to wean the inhabitants from the new American government, and join them to the Spanish territory of Louisiana. They made a secret compact with the American General Wilkinson, who was at the same time engaged in the service and pay of the American Government; making his treachery correspond to his influence. When the leading influential traders came down the river with their fleets, the Spanish Governor granted them extraordinary privileges, and endeavored, in every way, to induce them to join forces with him, and help annex the whole eastern valley of the Mississippi to the western side. From this territory they would create a great internal Spanish domain, reaching from the Alleghanies to the Rocky Mountains. This was during the years 1795 to 1797.

Added to these complications, the new struggling Union had to contend with other foes threatening the continued adherence of the Western settlers. The

British, who had kept control of Canada after the Revolutionary War, endeavored to win the frontiersmen to their standard. The country along the Ohio Valley north and south of that river was infested with emissaries of these insidious and crafty schemers from Canada and the Louisiana territory to win the settler from his loyalty to the United States, but it was all in vain. During all this time the Spanish governors realized the antipathy of the French element among their subjects, from Vincennes to New Orleans. Especially was this so during the French Revolution and the war at that time between France and Spain. In the metropolis on the Gulf, in the little hamlet of Vincennes or Fort Chartres, from the river boatmen poling their batteaux of produce to market down the river, floated the strains of the Marseillaise. In the streets of New Orleans the mobs bawled the Jacobin songs, and drank toasts to liberty and equality. Incendiary letters and documents had to be suppressed and a Spanish alliance with the Indians was made for fear of an uprising of the French against the Spanish rule. In spite of the interdicts on foreigners coming into Spanish territory, in 1795, when Bosa introduced the culture of sugar-cane, which proved so immensely profitable, there was a large immigration from the States.

Spain began to fear a dangerous preponderance of Americans in her meagre settlements. She passed laws restricting immigration, discriminating against Protestants, and denying navigation and the right of deposit of goods. Until the year 1800, these regulations renewed the exasperation of the settlers, to the point of a threatened invasion, when the interdict was removed. Again trade revived, immigrants poured in from the United States, taking up the best lands and startling the Spaniards, until the king ordered that there should be no more grants of land to citizens of the United States, giving as the reason that it would be only a few more years until the tide would rise too high to be resisted. Louisiana would be lost to the king, lost to the Holy Pilgrims, given over to freedom, republicanism, and error. This is a mere outline of the Spanish occupation of that part of America, which so vitally affected the early setlers in Indiana territory. It has left few traces of its connection with the history of the State, but is part of the story of the past. Indiana and Illinois were so dependent in that far-off time, for access to the outside world, upon the Mississippi River, that its century of contest for free navigation was the tragedy of the frontier, second only to the dangers from the Indians. The infant nation on the Atlantic coast hardly dared assert itself against the European Powers who alternately held the fortunes of the West in their hands. As ever, right made slow progress against might. Added to the actual weakness of the American government, some of the seaboard colonies regarded the Mississippi Valley as an undesirable dependency, much as Alaska was afterwards regarded, so that Congress was as slow to act in behalf of the valley as it is slow to act in behalf of suffering Alaska to-day.

During the administration of the Spanish governors, corruption in office was practised in the most unblushing way, indeed both French and Spanish officials, down to the close of foreign domination, were too far from home to pay any heed to an accounting. This, of course, had its effect on the city, and on the river tradesmen; creating very lax morality. To New Orleans came the river boatmen from Indiana and the adjoining territory with their produce. This was where they lingered "to see the world" until their money was squandered.

The more important traders and distinguished men from "up-the-river" also found in New Orleans a social circle that was attractive. The charmingly refined and engaging home life among the upper classes was most delightful after the crude life of the wilderness. We are reminded that throughout the eighty-seven years of foreign control, a steady, if slender, stream of the best blood of France and Spain had trickled into Louisiana. The French Revolution also drove many noble citizens into exile there. From these elements there grew to be a proud and exclusive, if limited, circle of citizens in this wilderness city. Owing to the possession of slaves, and the tropical climate, luxury and ease of life were most alluring to this class. A peculiar phase of society was gradually evolved from these conditions. Social circles possessed little learning perhaps, but the fine manners of the gay polite members could not be surpassed on the continent. French taste, speech, and customs dominated society. After years of control the Spanish had but one school in the city in 1795. Merchants and traders from the Ohio or the Wabash were fascinated with the hospitalities of the exporters with whom they had dealings. They brought home tales of the rose-embowered balconies overhanging the shaded streets, and the low rambling houses with the gay home life within; where light-hearted creole hospitality made New Orleans society famous. As time went on many elegant house furnishings and

European importations of silver, mahogany, silks, laces, and satins found their way in the return loads up the rivers, to the homes of the settlers farther north.

Finally to this Spanish-ruled French city came vague rumors from overseas, that the great Napoleon, who was now ruler in France, had ambitions to regain France's dominion on the Western Continent, and was wringing the Louisiana province from Spain. Such a bargain had really been made, Napoleon ceding Parma in exchange, at Ildefonso, October 1, 1800. But the far-off colonists were left in a state of expectancy, and the Spanish officials were anxious and uncertain, until the treaty was ratified at Madrid in 1801. Even then the French did not come over to take up the government, and all was mystery in the colony. Napoleon had planned to advance to the control of the Louisiana territory from his West India islands, but, being at war with England, that government's fleet ruled the sea and prevented his entering into possession. Political complications on the continent were crowding the French Emperor. He dared not undertake the recovery of the American provinces, but he was determined he would not forfeit Louisiana to Great Britain. Without consulting his own statesmen, he suddenly opened negotiations with the commissioners from the United States, for the cession of that province to the American government. The American commissioners, Mr. Livingston and Mr. Monroe, were in Paris, interceding for free navigation of the Mississippi, and imploring the First Consul to sell their government the island of New Orleans, in order to insure control of the river. In the midst of these modest negotiations, the American gentlemen were astounded when Napoleon proposed to them the sale of the whole province. This was so far beyond their instructions, and even their fondest dreams, that they were dumbfounded. But such a vast acquisition of territory in the heart of the continent being too great a prize to lose by delay, or waiting for power from Congress, they closed the sale forthwith, for sixty million francs, and the fate of the Mississippi navigation was settled forever. Fiske says of this dramatic moment that the payment of a few million dollars, a few strokes of the pen, a discreet silence until the proper moment, and then prompt action, secured what twenty years later could not have been bought with all the treasure of the nation. Jefferson was President at the time, but he had nothing to do with this purchase. In the meantime the colonists in the far-off Mississippi Valley were expecting the French to assume control, not even being asked by your leave in all these transactions, which so vitally affected their interests. In the spring, a French Commandant came over to New Orleans, and was received in state by the Spanish Governor. With great pomp, and surrounded by his soldiers in full uniform, with the whole populace crowded into the streets, the flag of Spain was lowered and the flag of France went up. It was only as a matter of form to mark the transfer of dominion. On the following December 17th (1803), the French Governor Laussat delivered the province, in the name of France, to Governor Claiborne, the representative of the United States; and the foreign rule of Louisiana was over forever.

Spain was furious when she learned that Napoleon had violated his pledge not to cede Louisiana to any other Power and only her weakness prevented her going to war with France, but upon the great territory had finally been bestowed a permanent government with the heritage of freedom and independence. The traffic from the Indiana country could go down the rivers unvexed to the sea, and her settlers be relieved of Spanish interference with trade. For many decades Spain had possessed parts of the territory of the United States along the Gulf and was constantly a power to be reckoned with in any advance in that direction. Our colonial ambassadors had many times "cooled their heels" impatiently in the anterooms of the court at Madrid trying to obtain justice for the frontier, yet after all this history the imprint of that nation was soon effaced. Only along the borders towards Mexico are there any traces of Spanish language and customs. There were few architectural monuments left to bear record of her sway, the remnants of the population were absorbed by the later immigration, and only a few Spanish names are extant in the geography of Indiana or in the families of the State.

CHAPTER V

AMERICAN CONQUEST

BY the time that the colonies had engaged in the War for Independence, Kentucky and the Ohio River had become the front door of the Northwest Territory; of which Indiana formed a part, and all of which was claimed by Virginia. Settlers from the tidewater colonies were going over the mountains to the fertile valleys beyond, and some of these pioneers were looking towards the rich lands of southern Indiana and Illinois. Many of these daring frontiersmen were of the best families in the coast colonies. Among the foremost of these young spirits must be named George Rogers Clark, whose life became so closely identified with Indiana, and whose career is the next phase of her history.

Clark was only nineteen when he crossed the mountains to locate lands for himself, and at the same time act as surveyor for other settlers. Three years later he writes home, "I have engaged as a deputy surveyor under Captain Hancock Lee, for to lay out lands on ye Kentuck, for ye Ohio Company at ye rate of 80£ per year, and ye privilege of taking what land I want." A richer or more beautiful country had never been seen in America, he said. After this surveying journey Clark revisited his Virginia home, and in the spring of 1776 returned to Kentucky, resumed his residence, and soon became a leader. His biographer, Mr. English, describes him as brave, energetic, bold, prepossessing in appearance, of pleasing manner, with all of the qualities, in fact, calculated to win a frontier people. The unorganized and chaotic condition of the country needed such a man, and the man had come. In common with other Virginia emigrants his first object was the desire to secure productive lands, but those lands were of no use unless the inhabitants were safe from the incursions of the savages. George Rogers Clark developed into a political and military leader; it was he who secured the organization of Kentucky into a county of Virginia, and persuaded that State to furnish powder for the defence of this outlying possession. He had served in the Dunmore war, and now he organized and commanded the irregular militia, for the defence of the meagre settlements against the savages, and did most effective work in their protection. At the same time, his alert mind grasped the situation of the whole Northwest. The Revolutionary War was in progress, and the bloodthirsty raids into Kentucky by the Indians were prompted by the British, as well as from their own hatred of the settlers. The order had gone out:

"It is the King's command that you should direct the Lieutenant-Governor Hamilton to assemble as many of the Indians of his district as he conveniently can, and placing a proper person at their head to conduct their parties, and restrain them from committing violence on the *well-affected, inoffensive inhabitants*, employ them in making a diversion and exciting an alarm on the frontier of Virginia and Pennsylvania."[1]

[1] Dunn, J. P., *History of Indiana*, page 131, from Haldimand Coll.

To make them more docile, Hamilton made them an offer of a reward for the greatest number of scalps brought in, from the heads of Americans.[1] The price was one pound, in British money, for the scalp of each woman or child, or for them as prisoners; three pounds for a man's scalp, but no reward for him as a prisoner. They paid five pounds for young women prisoners, and secured by this means some of the comeliest daughters of the frontier as their victims. It was to put an end to this nefarious warfare that Clark and his compatriots enlisted. They were well aware that they had to face the combined forces of the British at the military posts and their savage allies. There is no reason to think that these men did not have visions of securing territory from the British, as well as stopping the Indian forays on their settlements. Certainly Clark moved directly forward along this line. He felt that with a few valiant men he could accomplish much more for the government than to join the army in the East. Nothing but expedition and secrecy could give success to the enterprise. Mr. Clark went to Virginia, took the Governor, Patrick Henry, and Jefferson, Wyeth, and Mason into his confidence, and secured the necessary authority to raise troops, a fund of 1200 pounds in money, and promises of land grants to the troops if successful.

Clark had left Kentucky in October. By the following January, 1778, he had secured his authority and instructions, appointed his officers in Kentucky to enlist men, enrolled a little handful of 150 men in Virginia, and returned down the Ohio before six months had elapsed. In Kentucky the frontier re-

[1] Cockrum, Wm. M., *A Pioneer History of Indiana*, page 26.

cruits joined him. All were volunteers, clad in buckskin, and armed with their own flint-lock rifles and tomahawks. Officers and men were guiltless of uniform or badge. Loyalty to their leader, and hatred of Indians, was the bond which held them together and spurred them forward toward danger. By the last of May the little band of soldiers and followers dropped down the river to the falls of the Ohio, and encamped on Corn Island. Here they left their families and a guard, having only one hundred and seventy-five men to accomplish the great undertaking which they had in hand. Clark moved quickly forward on his desperate enterprise. In his account of this very dramatic journey in his own memoir, he says: "One bright June morning in 1778 our forces embarked in the boats prepared to transport them down the river. We left the little island, ran about a mile up the river in order to gain the main channel; and shot the Falls at the very moment of the sun being under a great eclipse, which caused various apprehensions among the superstitious. As I knew that British spies were kept on the river, below the town of the Illinois, I had resolved to march part of the way by land."[1] Running the boats four days and nights, with relays of oarsmen, they landed three leagues below the mouth of the Tennessee, ran up into a small creek, and rested over-night. Not having enough men to leave a guard, they impressed some hunters, who came along the river from Kaskaskia, into their service as guides, and started across the Illinois country to that post, one hundred and twenty miles, through swamp and wilderness. Clark's warriors had no wagons, pack

[1] Extract from *Memoirs of Gen. Geo. Rogers Clark*, to the Governor of Virginia. Dillon, page 121.

horses, or other means of conveyance for their munitions of war or baggage.

Continuing Clark's own report of the campaign to the Governor of Virginia, we read [1]:

"On the evening of the Fourth of July we got within three miles of the town of Kaskaskia, having a river of the same name to cross before we could reach the town. After making ourselves ready for anything that might happen, we marched after night to a farm that was on the same side of the river, about a mile above the town, took the family prisoners, and found plenty of boats to cross in, and in two hours transported ourselves to the other shore with the greatest silence. I immediately divided my little army into two divisions, ordered one to surround the town, with the other I broke into the fort, secured the governor, Mr. Rochblave, in his bed, in fifteen minutes had every street blocked. Sent runners through the town ordering the people on pain of death to keep to their houses, which they observed, and before daylight had the whole town disarmed. Thus were the British dispossessed forever of this important military post, and of the old historic town of Kaskaskia, about which lingered so much romantic interest."

Bowman, one of the commanders, says that Rocheblave, the British commandant, was made prisoner, with all his instructions received from time to time, from the several governors at Quebec, to set the Indians upon the Americans with great rewards for our scalps.

This is the simple recital of the night surprise and bloodless capture of the post, as told by the commanders. One historian says that Clark had no cannon or means of assaulting the fort, and therefore must

[1] Extract from *Memoirs of Gen. Geo. Rogers Clark*, to the Governor of Virginia. Dillon, page 124.

use stratagem. One of his aids and a small detachment of men entered the fort, and found an American within who conducted them to the very bedchamber of the sleeping governor. The first notice that Rocheblave had that he was a prisoner was Simon Kenton tapping him on the shoulder to awaken him. Later the commandant was sent to Virginia and his goods confiscated. Another pretty story has always been told of this night; that there was a ball being given by the officers of the fort, and that the gay creoles, both men and girls, were surprised at the dance, when Clark and his men looked in on them. He had placed his men on guard, secured the exits, and was calmly leaning against the doorpost, looking at the dancers, when an Indian lying on the floor of the entry, looking up, saw a new pale face and sprang to his feet with the war-whoop. As the dancers rushed towards the door they encountered the commander, but Clark, standing unmoved and with unchanging face, grimly bade them continue their dancing, but to remember that they now danced under the flag of Virginia and not Great Britain. The story is so like the life at the French posts and the cool composure of Colonel Clark, that it is welcome as a reflection of the life and the persons concerned, whether true or not.

The fort, inmates, and stores secured, Clark sent a messenger back to Corn Island to give the good news of a bloodless conquest to those left behind. He then addressed himself to allaying the fears of the inhabitants of the post. The French inhabitants fully expected to be at least exiled from their forest homes, and begged, through their good priest, only not to have their families separated, and to be allowed to take with them some provisions and clothing. To this Colonel Clark says that he replied vigorously:

"Do you mistake us for savages? My countrymen disdain to make war on helpless innocents. It was to prevent the horrors of Indian butchery upon our wives and children that we have taken arms and penetrated this remote stronghold of British and Indian barbarity; and not the despicable prospect of plunder. I further told them that the King of France had united his powerful arms with those of the Americans. . . . That their religion would not be a source of disagreement, as all religions were regarded with equal respect by American laws. And now to prove my sincerity you will inform your fellow-citizens that they are at liberty to conduct themselves as usual without the least apprehension. . . . Your friends who are in confinement shall be immediately released."[1]

He soon made friends and allies of the impressionable French and easily attached them to his standard, as they were never in sympathy with their British rulers. Meantime Colonel Clark's assistant, Captain Bowman, with a detachment of thirty mounted men, was sent immediately up the Mississippi River the very night of Fort Kaskaskia's capture to surprise and take possession of the three other little towns, Prairie de Roche, St. Phillips, and Cahokia. Weary as they were, these determined patriots, without sleep for three more nights, secretly and swiftly marched to, and seized all the hamlets; and within ten days administered the oath of allegiance to three hundred inhabitants of those towns, where Captain Bowman remained to retain possession.

[1] Memoirs from the copy in William H. English's *Conquest of the Northwest*, page 480. Indianapolis, 1896.

Although the British claimed dominion at this time, all the inhabitants of the posts, were still French and their dislike of English rule greatly facilitated Clark's taking peaceful possession. Bowman says that as the towns of white people in the Illinois country east of the Wabash had now been secured Clark was looking with great anxiety to securing Post Vincennes, on the east bank of that river, which he regarded as the most important of all. Father Gibault, the beloved and honored priest of the district, who had labored with his little flock for twenty years, was approached by Colonel Clark with overtures to conduct a peaceable occupation of Vincennes. He knew that the English Governor Abbott had left Vincennes a short time before, leaving the fort and town virtually in the possession of the French settlers. The priest offered to try to secure the feality of the post without a conflict; especially, as he could carry them the news of the new American alliance with France. Ten days after Major Clark's occupancy of Kaskaskia Father Gibault, a French gentleman named Lafont, and a retinue provided by Clark, which included one of his spies to insure fair play to the American forces, made the journey across the prairies of Illinois to the Wabash River, and accomplished the conciliation of the inhabitants of the post at Vincennes. They administered the oath of allegiance in the little log chapel, raised an American flag for the first time on Indiana territory, garrisoned the fort, and returned to Colonel Clark with the joyful news of the peaceful occupation, by the first of August! Every plan had worked out with amazing success. A bold commander with his handful of men, and a peace-loving missionary, had won an area fit for an empire. Captain Helm was placed in command at Vincennes. By securing the sworn allegiance of "Tobacco's son—The Grand Door of the Wabash," a Piankeshaw chief who ruled the tribes along the river, he soon extended the same amicable relations to the Indian towns up the Wabash, as far as the Post Ouiatanon. The whole campaign so far had been a bloodless conquest.

After the British posts were thus secured, and the French habitants so peacefully reconciled to American control, Colonel Clark spent all his energies on making treaties with the surrounding Indians, who had been allied with the British. He showed great tact and sagacity as well as a consummate knowledge of the Indian nature in these negotiations.

When the marvellous news of the peaceful occupation of all the western posts reached Virginia, it created the wildest enthusiasm. The Governor communicated the tidings to the members of the Continental Congress, and planned to accede to Colonel Clark's urgent appeals for help, by sending new troops to the far off wilderness forts.

Two months later the British governor, Hamilton of Detroit, learning that the "American Rebels" had captured the Western outposts, enlisted the services of the Indians in his cause, and with a force of five hundred men of both races, four hundred of whom were savages, came across Lake Erie and down the Wabash, on the six-hundred-mile journey, to recapture the lost posts. As the fort at Vincennes was so miserably weak, and manned by the French habitants, with only two Americans, it was obliged to capitulate on the 15th of December, 1778. But Hamilton did not pursue his advantage and push on to Kaskaskia, as the indomitable Clark would have done with such a force. He contented himself with sending Indian forces to the Ohio River to intercept any troops that might be sent to Clark's relief. By intercepting all messengers, Hamilton prevented Colonel Clark from receiving any word of the recapture of Fort Vincennes by the British until January, when some of the Vincennes men deserted and crossed to Clark's post at Kaskaskia. Later, Colonel Vigo, a Spanish merchant travelling from Vincennes, gave Clark all the details of the strength of the post, and the news that Hamilton had gone back to Detroit to prepare for a spring campaign. He intended to recover the whole country from the Alleghanies to the Mississippi River. Of course, the little bands on the Mississippi were distressed at the recapture by the British of Fort Vincennes, and immediately set about preparations for what proved to be the most spectacular relief expedition in the history of border wars.

Clark's records state that on the first of February men were put to work building a large boat, called a galley or bateau. This boat was to take army supplies and a detachment of troops down the Kaskaskia and Mississippi, and up the Ohio and Wabash to a designated point below Vincennes, probably the mouth of White River, there to await further orders. The vessel was put in condition for use in a few days, and loaded with two four-pound cannon, four swivels, ammunition, provisions, and other army supplies. Nothing equal to this craft had ever been seen at Kaskaskia before, and this added to the already intense military excitement. On the fourth of February, *The Willing*, which was the name given the boat, dropped down the river, amid the cheers of the forty-six men on board, and the applause of four or five companies of soldiers on shore, and most of the men, women, and children of Kaskaskia. After the boat had left on its circuitous water route to Vincennes, the balance of the little force of soldiers, numbering less than two hundred in all, started on foot across the country.

It was one hundred and sixty miles to the point where they were to join those who had gone by boat. The troops going overland had some pack-horses, but no tents, and the whole of this remarkable campaign was made in the worst possible February weather. It rained constantly, and the men were without shelter, or any suitable place to cook or rest. The journals left by the commander and his aide give a most graphic picture of the mid-winter journey. They tell of the constant rain, and the submerged country which only the early settlers, who have seen the Wabash out of its banks, can realize. He says that, after receiving a lecture and absolution from the priest, they crossed the Kaskaskia River with one hundred and seventy men. For a week, they marched over plains covered with water, and encountered incredible difficulties, until they came to the Little Wabash, which was swollen to an expanse of five miles. "I viewed this sheet of water," says Clark, "with distrust, but immediately set to work, without holding any consultation or suffering any suggestions, and ordered a pirogue to be built immediately."[1] In a day it was finished and the baggage and the men ferried over the stream. The horses swam across and were reladened. For seven more days it was their lot to march through water, which in many places was three and four feet deep, or was still deeper where

[1] Extract from Memoirs.

they had to swim. The country was so drowned that no game was obtainable. The men were famished for food and growing weak and miserable. Stopping on a rise in the ground to rest, they made a rude canoe and sent men out in it to steal boats from the shores. The French volunteers wanted to return to Kaskaskia, and the boats were full of the sick and exhausted. Many times the indomitable Clark resorted to solemn or frivolous expedients to hearten his men and urge them on. Once when the water was appallingly deep and swift he set the little Irish drummer on the shoulders of a good-natured six-foot Virginian sergeant, and ordered an advance, with the drummer beating the charge from his lofty perch, while Clark, sword in hand, gave the command to forward march. Elated and amused the men followed and, holding their rifles above their heads, they reached the dry land. A canoe of Indian squaws coming up to town was discovered. The men gave chase, took the canoe, on board of which, it is told, was near half a quarter of buffalo, some corn, tallow, kettles, etc. This was a grand prize. Broth was immediately made and served out to the weakly with care.

Plodding along through further swamps and swollen streams, after eighteen days of this dreary, cold, disheartening, dangerous marching, they finally reached a spot of high ground overlooking the post.

"Our situation was now critical [writes Clark]. No possibility of retreat in case of defeat, and six hundred men in the fort. Our crew on the galley would now have been a re-enforcement of immense magnitude, but it had not come. The idea of being made prisoners was foreign to almost every man, as they expected torture at the hands of savage allies, if they fell into their hands. Nothing but the most daring conduct would insure success."[1]

Colonel Clark now rapidly made his preparations for the assault. He wrote and sent by a Frenchman, whom they had captured out hunting, a friendly proclamation to the French habitants, telling them that he was going to attack with a large force and warning them to stay in their houses on pain of death. Then with flying banners and many evolutions on the edge of the forest he deceived the villagers with the idea of great numbers of troops, and they gave no warning to the soldiers within the post. As dark came on, he divided his little troop and silently advanced. One detachment surrounded the little French town; the other swiftly advanced on the fort, completely surprising the garrison by a deadly rifle attack from behind trees, palings, and huts. So keen and deadly was the marksmanship of the concealed Americans that in a little while no Britisher dared man the cannon in the blockhouses. By morning the tide of battle was in their favor, and they stopped long enough to eat the first breakfast they had had in a week. Clark sent a vigorous and intimidating invitation to the fort to surrender, but it was declined by Hamilton and the fight was resumed. "These frontiersmen were at that time the best marksmen known to the world, and at these distances, from sixty to one hundred yards, a silver dollar was as large a target as they cared for."[2] Whenever a figure appeared at a port-hole, there was one less defender within the fort. Naturally the British became discouraged, and a truce was asked for. After a parley between the officers,

[1] Extract from Memoirs.
[2] Dunn, J. P., *History of Indiana*, page 146.

Clark modified his terms of an unconditional surrender, and required that they surrender as prisoners of war with all stores and supplies.

The fort capitulated; the little army of frontiersmen had conquered with the wounding of only one man. The weary march and unequal task had ended in extinguishing the claim of British dominion on the Wabash. On February 25, 1779, the American flag floated over the post; and two days afterward *The Willing*, ladened with the other troops, arrived. They were too late for the storming of the fort, but in good fighting trim for the very exciting seizure, two days later, of the British re-enforcements coming down the river from Detroit. This picturesque encounter of the British fleet of canoes, filled with red-coated soldiers and their naked savage allies, surprised at a bend of the wilderness stream by the hardy band of Kentucky pioneers, clad in buckskin and armed with their own keen rifles, was a dramatic scene that has never been surpassed on the Wabash. The surprise was complete, and when the British surrendered it meant that they gave up the whole vast interior of the United States. It was Colonel Clark's great desire to push on and capture Detroit, and perhaps secure Canada; but his own handful of troops were worn out, and congressional scrip, wherewith troops were paid, was held at half its face value. No re-enforcements were supplied from the East, and the expedition, greatly to his sorrow, was never resumed. Had he been allowed to gain possession of Canada, the United States could have held it when peace came.

There was great rejoicing in Virginia and all of the Eastern colonies when the news finally travelled over the mountains that the Western outposts were in the hands of the American forces. The results of this campaign were far-reaching in the settlement with Great Britain four years later, when the final treaty of peace was ratified. As a consequence, all the territory between the Ohio River and the Great Lakes became United States possession. In his desolate old age General Clark said, "I have given the United States half of the territory they possess, and they suffer me to remain in poverty."

Colonel Clark returned to the Falls of the Ohio at the close of the victorious summer of 1779, where he afterwards founded the present city of Louisville. Until the close of the war with England he and his volunteers were hard pressed, protecting the frontier from the savages, who were still incited by the British to make raids on the inhabitants. After that war was over, he was for years at the head of the territorial forces who were still called out to contend in bitter warfare against the Indians. Indeed it was a trying time on the frontier. It is known that during the period between the close of the War of the Revolution and the War of 1812, more than two thousand men, women, and children were carried into captivity from Kentucky and the Northwest Territory! To all these heartrending separations, and terrors that dire disasters were surely being visited upon the loved ones thus rudely torn from their families, there was the added sorrow of uncertainty, for only a tithe of the captured ones were ever heard of afterward by their families. Many of those who were carried off were burned at the stake, after being scalped, while the savages gleefully danced around the slow fire. All of the historians concede that there was no more valuable service rendered to the nation, in the War for Independence, than that of these knights of the frontier and their commander. Winsor says that the conquest not only dispossessed England but ruled out the pretensions of Spain and France, who claimed all of the territory from Louisiana to Quebec. "Actual present possession prevailed," says Mr. English, "when the boundaries were finally established. . . . But for General Clark's services, and certainly that of his little band of soldiers, the boundary of the States in the Northwest might have been the crest of the Alleghanies."

Indiana's historian, Mr. Dunn, pays fitting personal tribute to General Clark when he says: "Of all those who preceded or followed him, La Salle is the only one who can be compared to him in the wonderful combinations of genius, activity, and courage that lifted him above his fellows."[1]

Professor Hinsdale gives recognition of the importance of the acquisition of this great territory of which Indiana forms a part: "Next to the planting of English civilization on the Atlantic slope in the first part of the seventeenth century, the planting of American civilization in the Great West in the second part of the eighteenth century is the most impressive event in our history."[2]

[1] Dunn, J. P., *History of Indiana*, page 176.
[2] Hinsdale, Professor, *The Dial*, 1900.

CHAPTER VI

THE PIONEERS

WHEN the very earliest adventurers travelled westward from the Atlantic colonies in the quest for knowledge of the great unknown country, the Indians sent a "speaking bark" from tribe to tribe, passing the word westward, that a new race of pale-faces, neither French nor Spanish, was making its appearance on the western slopes of the Alleghanies.

After General Clark and his company of southern pioneers had wrested the west from the British, many of his little band of soldiers returned to the Territory, and took up lands, which later were granted them by the government for their services. Following them down the Ohio, or on up the Wabash, came others from the South. These men selected homesteads along those rivers, or their tributaries, wherever there was a sightly spot that could be reached by water transportation.

This process was not rapid. In 1787, there were only four hundred Americans within the borders of what is now the State of Indiana. The lands were not ceded by treaty, until 1804. But every little while a quaint flatboat would come floating down from Fort Pitt, or be poled over from the Kentucky shore, and land a family, with its handful of household goods and bare necessities of life, on the banks. Then they would walk, until they found a site that answered their purpose, and another home in the wilderness would be begun. The French settlers had always clustered around the military posts, but each pioneer of English speech built his solitary cabin on his own homestead, in the forest.

Knowing all that they afterwards passed through, it impresses us as a pathetic picture, this, of the primitive craft, drifting down the wilderness rivers, ladened to the water's edge with their nondescript freight and their groups of courageous humanity. They were exposed at any turn in the stream, to the danger of the merciless arrows of savages in ambush, or pursuing canoe. If the newcomers journeyed overland, and most of these walked the entire way, the road was even more perilous. A pioneer said that he knew of few forms of exertion that so thoroughly tested the mettle of men, as journeying across the wilderness. There was nowhere visible the slightest sign that others had ever preceded them, it was all an unbroken virgin forest. The trees were veritable monarchs of the ages. The wind moaned through them; and their dead leaves, of the years before, rustled uncannily under the tread, as they went on and on. Or, warned by native guides, they descended into dark and gloomy ravines, dank with decaying vegetation, to escape the observation of a passing band of savages. It was surely no holiday jaunt. Only the brave started, and only the brave and strong got through. When a newly married couple, or a family, had decided to go to the frontier, their departure meant a long farewell and occasioned many heartaches. As the time really arrived, and the dear ones were to leave, the kinsfolk and neighbors assembled, prayers were said, and hymns sung, such as:

> "When shall we meet again,
> Meet ne'er to sever?"

Then heart-rending good-byes were said, and the wagon creaked off over the trail toward the west. Doctor Ezra Ferris, minister of the Duck Creek Church, has left a graphic account of the journey of his father's family from New England. He says:

"A short time before my father started on his journey to the west, and after he had determined to do so, a sermon was preached at his home on the occasion, from Genesis xii., 1: "Now the Lord said unto Abraham, Get thee out of thy country, and from thy kindred, and from thy father's house, unto a land that I will shew thee." On the twentieth of September, 1789, according to previous arrangement, my father left his native village (Stanwick, Conn.); and separated himself and family from all the associations and endearing ties which had been formed during a life of fifty years, to seek for himself and them a home in the western wilderness. Though I was a boy of only six years of age, I have a very distinct and vivid recollection of the affecting occasion. The enterprise at that time was so novel and daring, it drew together a vast crowd of people to witness the parting scene. Some feared we would fall a sacrifice to savage cruelty; others predicted that we would all be drowned in descending the western rivers. We went down the road on the north side of Long Island Sound to the City of New York. Thence we passed over into New Jersey, travelled through that State and Pennsylvania, over the mountains, down the Youghiogheny, thence down the Monongahela to Pittsburg, thence down the Ohio to Fort Miami, at which our family arrived two months and twenty days after starting on the

A Typical Pioneer Scene.
Redrawn by Marie Goth from an old print.

journey. In approaching the shore we were met by a crowd of smiling faces, to bid us a hearty welcome, and offer us all the assistance circumstances would admit of. An apartment in the fort (of about sixteen feet square) was assigned each family, in which for a time they resided. There were about thirty or more families. Rest was only temporary. Much was to be done to provide for coming wants, and that too in the face of danger. The difficulties were, however, all overcome; who dares to prescribe bounds to what human industry and enterprise may accomplish."[1]

This was a typical journey from the south and east, to the Wabash country. They camped under the stars when night shut down, and often wolves howled about them. Well-to-do families, coming over the mountains from Virginia and Carolina, moved all of their household goods on pack-horses; even bedsteads and bureaus were thus transported. Occasionally a settler would bring out a cow, which must also walk all the way by the wagon side; as at least one maiden did from Carolina, who was too energetic to be content in the slow-moving wain.

Many little bands were surprised by skulking savages, and murdered or scalped by their own camp-fires.

The forest through which they journeyed afforded them plenty of game, and beautiful fish were caught in the streams. In the fall, wild turkey, ducks, and pigeons swarmed in the sky. As the emigrants went, they "blazed" their way by chopping the bark from one side of the trees to guide their return, or mark the way for any one who should come after them. Upon reaching a desirable location, the new

[1] From an old letter.

settlers camped out until they felled trees for a cabin home.

With the help of neighbors, the logs were laid up, notched, and saddled; hand-riven clap-boards were laid on for the roof, and fastened down by weight poles and wooden pegs, never a piece of iron to be had for construction. Nails and hardware were entirely lacking on the frontier. The great fireplaces, five to eight feet wide, and the "cat and clay" chimney were built of stones or sticks, and plastered with clay, and a wide clay hearth was made. The door was rived out of logs, by hand, and battened together with similar boards. This strong barricade was then hung on wooden hinges, and fastened by a heavy wooden latch, which was lifted from the outside by a leather thong made of buffalo or deer hide. This was the latch-string which proverbially hung out, as a token of welcome, and was pulled to the inside only at night, or when Indians were lurking about. At such times the strong door served as a real protection from the invaders.

A puncheon floor was hewed and laid, and the shelter considered complete. Later the chinks between the logs would be filled up before winter set in, and when it was safe from Indians the window openings were cut in the logs and they were "glazed" with greased paper or deer hide. Some of the log taverns and homes were built two stories high, but this was unusual. The rustic logs often put forth leaves, and the outside of the cabin would be covered with green, making a fine screen from the Indians.

John Finley, a pioneer poet, in terms as old-fashioned as his theme, is always quoted as giving in his

The Spinning-wheel was the Stringed Instrument of the Household.

Hoosier Nest the most vivid description of the surroundings of the "squatter" on new lands:

"The emigrant is soon located—
In Hoosier life initiated—
Erects a cabin in the woods,
Wherein he stores his household goods.
Ensconced in this, let those who can
Find out a truly happier man.
The little youngsters rise around him,
So numerous that they quite astound him.
I'm told, in riding somewhere west,
A stranger found a Hoosier's nest,
And fearing he might be benighted
He 'hailed the house,' and then alighted.

The Hoosier met him at the door,
The salutations soon were o'er;
He took the stranger's horse aside
And to a sturdy sapling tied.
Then having stripped the saddle off,
He fed him in a sugar trough.

The stranger stooped to enter in
The entrance, closing with a pin,
And manifested strong desire
To seat him by the log-heap fire.
. . . .

Invited shortly to partake
Of venison, milk, and johnny-cake,
The stranger made a hearty meal,
And glances round the room would steal.
One side was lined with divers garments,
The other spread with skins of varmints;
Dried pumpkins overhead were strung,
Where venison hams in plenty hung;

Two rifles placed above the door,
Three dogs lay stretched upon the floor.
In short, the domicile was rife
With specimens of Hoosier life.

. . . .

Erelong the cabin disappears,
A spacious mansion next he rears;
His fields seem widening by stealth,
An index of increasing wealth;
And when the hives of Hoosiers swarm,
To each is given a noble farm.[1]

In this crude fashion the best of the settlers were obliged to begin life in the wilderness, for the distances were so great, and means of transportation so primitive and slow, that no one brought much with him.

There was, at an early period of the settlements, an inferior kind of land title, which was known as a tomahawk right. This claim was designated by deadening a few trees near the head of a spring, and marking the bark of some of the trees on the boundaries with the initials of the person who thus set up a claim to the tract. Sometimes these rights had to be verified, or paid for, if they were very desirable; but it is certain that they were bought and sold, for a long time. The entry price of regular government land was generally $1.25 per acre.

Some of the early settlers came over the mountains in the spring, and raised a crop of corn, leaving their families at home until a crop was assured. An old pioneer used to tell how his father had brought his wife and children with him when he first came, and the corn-meal gave out six weeks before a new crop

[1] *Indianapolis Journal*, Carriers' Address, 1833.

was ripe. For that length of time they had to live without bread. The grown people told the children to call lean venison and the breast of the wild turkeys bread; the flesh of the bear was called meat. Alas! this artifice, he says, did not deceive the stomach; and for some time they were sickly, being tormented with a sense of hunger. The little ones watched the growth of the potato tops, pumpkins, and corn. They recall to this day the delicious taste of the roasted potatoes; and later the young corn, when they were permitted to pull the new ears. When the corn was hard enough to grate for johnny-cakes, they became healthy, vigorous, and contented. As soon as possible the settlers brought cattle and swine from the older settlements, either driving overland or floating down the river on flatboats. The live stock contributed greatly to their comfort.

There were few household implements, or farm tools, in any cabin home. The shovel plow was the only cultivator. The mortar, in which they pounded the corn into hominy, was made by burning out a hollow in a near-by stump. The corn, for meal bread, was crushed between two flat stones, under a weight. When the corn was still green, they grated and dried the pulp to use for hoe-cake. The trenchers and bowls for kitchen use were hewn from sections of maple logs, and then burned and scraped smooth. Long-handled gourds, of every shape and size, were raised and dried for dippers and drinking cups. Never a cool sparkling spring or cider barrel but had the useful gourd hanging by it. Many of the poorer immigrants, who had walked all of the way from their old homes, had but a single skillet in their cabin. Often they made pots of clay, with their own hands, that served until they could have iron ones. In the more comfortable homes, the cooking was done in iron kettles, hung from a crane, which had been built into the walls of the capacious fireplace. The baking was done in a covered skillet called a "spider." This utensil stood upon feet and was heated on the hearth with hickory coals piled under and over it; no flame was suffered to blaze around the baker.

The apples that were roasted before the fire, and the potatoes and corn which were "roasted in their jackets" in the ashes, had a flavor fit for an epicure. The hoe-cake or johnny-cake was baked on a smooth board, in front of the fire, and there the meat was roasted on a spit or broiled on the coals. When a family became prosperous, they would have a Dutch oven built of bricks, or of clay and boulders. In shape these were long mound-like affairs, and sometimes had great caldrons set in the top, for making apple butter or rendering lard. Fire was built in this oven, and when it was thoroughly heated, the fire was scraped out, the space was swept and garnished, and the rows of bread and pies were put in to bake. There were few cook-stoves, or stoves of any kind, within the State before 1825 to 1830. The furniture of the cabins was all made of riven logs, put together with wooden pins. The bedsteads were made by driving posts in the floor and pegs into the walls; from these, cords or straps of deer hide were drawn, over and across, in place of springs. This network held the pine boughs and afterwards the great feather beds, which were the pride of every housekeeper's heart. Many of the children born on the frontier were rocked in a poplar trough, such as were made for use in sugar camps, and used as a cradle. Lamps were modelled of clay, in the form of cups, fastened on a plate. These were filled with

The Heroism of the Pioneer Women.
From an old print.

bear's-grease, and the wick was made from cotton raised in the door-yard.

A few dishes of pewter-ware brought from home, and some hickory chairs with splint bottoms, were possessed by the more luxurious families, but all had stools and benches, rived out of logs, to sit at table. Every household had its rude loom, and spinning-wheels. Every woman was a weaver, and each householder tanned his own leather, moulded his own bullets, and fashioned his own axe-handles. The dress of the frontier was home-made from centre to circumference. The hunting shirt, breeches, and leggins were made of buckskin, ornamented with fringe of the same. The moccasins were made of the same material, or of the heavier buffalo hide. This foot covering was always made by the people themselves, and was often ornamented with beads in the Indian fashion. In winter the hair of rabbits, squirrels, or deer was placed inside the shoe, for warmth. Buckskin was chosen for clothing, not only because it was available, but because it resisted nettles, briars, the bites of the rattlesnake, and was, as an outside garment, an excellent protection against the cold. Even deerskin had its drawbacks and discomforts, for when it was wet, as must often be the case, the garment would draw up a third of its size, and become stiff and unwieldy. As soon as they could protect a flock of sheep from the wolves, the pioneer had woollen clothing as well. The women made their own soap, moulded their own candles, cured the meats, churned the butter, as soon as they had cows, and wove all of the garments worn by the whole household. They wove linsey-woolsey—the warp of flax and the woof of wool—for winter garments, and tow-linen for summer. The raising of flax was one of the earliest industries in Indiana. Cotton-seed was brought from the South, by the Carolina women, but it would not reach the perfection that it attained in the warmer States. The women spun both wool and cotton yarn for knitting the stockings of the whole household—a task which was eternally in evidence. No one could sit down and hold their hands in that time. 'Coonskin caps and buffalo overcoats formed the outer covering for the men. The women wore shawls, of their own weaving, and the head was covered with a thick quilted hood in winter, and a sun-bonnet in summer. This was universal. When a young girl was married, she put on caps, and henceforth her tresses were covered. All wore mittens made of squirrel or beaver skins, tanned by themselves and stitched by the women of the family.

Horse mills were set up in crudest fashion, as soon as wheat was raised; but as early as possible, in every neighborhood where there was available water-power, one of the settlers would build a dam, and start a mill, either for manufacturing woollens, or grinding grain, or both. The people rode from ten to thirty miles to these mills, and often had to wait three or four days and nights for their grist. The grain was brought in bags on horseback and the boys or men camped about the mill, visiting, playing games, and telling stories until their turn came. The miller took "toll" for his work, generally at the rate of one fourth of the grain ground, and every man had to bolt his own flour from the chaff. From that fact you could always tell when a man had been to mill. In *An Old Settler's Story* Riley gives us a graphic picture of going to mill:

"The Settlement wasn't nothing but a baby in them days, fer I mind 'at old Ezry Sturgiss had jist got his saw and griss-millin' agoin', and Bills had come along and claimed to know all about millin', and got a job with him; and millers in them times was wanted worse 'n congressmen, and reckon got better wages; fer afore Ezry built, ther wasn't a dust o' meal er flour to be had short o' the White Water, better'n sixty mild from here, the way we had to fetch it. And they used to come to Ezry's fer ther grindin' as fer as that; and one feller I knowed come from what used to be the old South Fork, over eighty mild from here, and in the wettest, rainyest weather; and mud! law!" [1]

Every settler tried to have horses, and a horse-thief was punished by beating or death, if caught. The Indians soon learned the luxury of having a beast of burden, other than their squaws, although they had never thought of taming or training the buffalo or any wild animal to work for them; but they were always stealing the horses of the white men. Where there were no roads, wagons were little known. There was only one in the Territory in 1776 and for many years horseback was the general mode of travel. There being no bridges, every stream had to be forded if it was too wide for a tree to span it. In case a tree had been felled across the creek the horses must be trained to "toe the log" across the stream. The few who made themselves wagons, as time passed, made their harness of strips of deer hide and hickory bark, and the horse-collars were braided of corn husks. But horses were very scarce, and two men would often "ride and tie" on their way to town. That is, one would ride a mile or two, then tie the horse and walk on. When the other man came up, he would untie the horse and ride until he overtook his companion. When a man and his wife went on a journey, she rode

[1] Riley, J. W., *Pipes of Pan*, page 101. Indianapolis, 1889.

behind on the same horse; generally both carried a young child in their arms. All of these crude substitutions for our everyday conveniences make us realize what frontier life, of necessity, was.

In those days a new flame must be made by striking fire from two flints, or a flint and a piece of steel. The spark dropping on some inflammable material started the flame. Knots or growths taken from old hickory trees, and called punk, were treasured by every boy for this purpose. Every household had a "tinderbox," which contained pieces of flint from the creek, a bit of steel, a horn of powder, and some punk. This was to rekindle the fire; but when a fire was once lighted on a hearth it was carefully tended, and the embers covered at night, for matches were then unknown.

The food the frontiersman ate was simple as the rest of his living, but his vigorous exercise gave him a prodigous appetite. Housewives varied in the excellence of their cooking then, as now. Corn-pone, hominy, roasting ears, beans, pork, venison, and game were the universal articles of diet. Wheaten bread, tea, and coffee were luxuries seldom seen. Sassafras tea and spicewood tea had to take their place, but the pioneer had the best of syrup and sugar, from the maple trees in the forest. To supply variety for the table, and to take the place of desserts that were no longer obtainable, many new experiments were tried. Sorrel was made into pie, and acorns used for flour. Wild fruit and nuts were eagerly gathered in season and stored for winter. Perhaps no country ever produced a greater variety of wild fruit and berries than the wide, fertile bottom lands of the Wabash and its tributaries. Wild plum trees and crab-apples, gooseberries, strawberries, blackberries, and raspberries, paw-paws (the Indiana banana), persimmons and haws, as well as the many varieties of woods grapes, were gathered by the early settlers, through the years that they were waiting for cultivated orchards. An idea of how plentiful wild game was may be formed from a list of the fur-bearing animals which were hunted for their pelts by the trappers. Bear, deer, buffalo, lynx, wild-cat, opossum, beaver, otter, marten, raccoon, muskrat, and mink were found in great numbers in Indiana. Black, gray, and prairie wolves were so numerous and trespassed so persistently until late times, that the Legislature granted a bounty on wolves' scalps, to encourage their extermination. Buffalo were in such vast herds that the Indians were known to have killed hundreds in a season, to obtain the price of two shillings which they received for the hide! Deer were often shot from the doorstep by the settlers, while wild turkey, pigeons, pheasants, and quail were everywhere. Fire-hunting the deer was a favorite way of killing that animal, which was so much in use for meat and pelt. The hunter would go along the stream in his canoe, with a pine knot or torch flaming from the bow of the boat; when the deer came down to the water's brink to slake his thirst, the light would "shine his eyes," and, startled, he would stand immovably gazing at it while the rifle of the boatman laid him low. The white men learned from the Indians their manner of curing the meat of the deer. It was called jerked venison. An old-timer said that a "hunk of venison" almost invariably hung from the rafters, near the chimney-jamb, in every cabin; and when "a neighbor man" from any number of miles around entered for a visit, he would draw out the universal hunting knife, and slice off a portion of this smoked venison to chew on as the conversation progressed.

Whiskey was invariably offered to a guest in those times. Total abstinence was an innovation of later years, and the farmer who did not supply his field hands with liquor was considered too stingy to work for. There was plenty of this home-made liquid, that was often so cheap that in summer it soured and in winter it froze! "Two fips" a gallon was the price paid for this beverage.

The settlers had great difficulty in securing salt for their food, and to preserve their game. It was the one cash article of commerce, along with powder. Pilgrimages were organized to go to the "licks," in large companies, as a guard against surprises by the Indians. Once arrived at the salt springs, the men camped about until they had evaporated enough salt for a year's supply. One of the perquisites claimed by the Indians, from the government, in settlement of treaties, was their "annuity salt."

The desirable qualifications of a settler were muscular strength and a homely hospitality. One old-timer is glorified in the memory of an early chronicler as a man who had killed more deer, wolves, and rattlesnakes, caught more fish, found more bee-trees, and entertained in a hospitable manner more land-hunters, trappers, and traders than any other private citizen between Vincennes and south of the Solamonie.

After the settler had raised all the provender needed for "man and beast" on his own place, the remainder was bartered down the river, for other necessities. The more enterprising and industrious he was, the more he had to exchange for these luxuries.

The first thing the settler could produce to realize money from was fattening pigs on "oak and beech mast," nuts and acorns, and shipping the pork to New Orleans. Later when a sufficient clearing could be made, and crops raised, he had begun to be a farmer.

At this time a cabinet official of the government referred to the Wabash as marking the uttermost bounds, on the west, of the civilization of the republic.

Neighborhoods grew up, schools were gradually started, and "meetings" were held, when the itinerant preachers came around on their circuit of the isolated settlements. One of the characteristics of the early days was the liberal hospitality connected with the religious meetings. Wherever the associational, synodical, or quarterly meetings were held, each settler of the immediate neighborhood would provide for a score of people that might come from a distance. Long shelves of pies and cakes would be baked, and great quantities of spring chicken, mashed potatoes, corn-pone, succotash and hot biscuits would be provided. As the "meetin' broke," the mother in Israel would go about among the congregation, and gather up a dozen or more of the attendants from the more remote settlements, and take them home to dinner with her.

The social pleasures of the earliest days were largely connected with the helpful neighborhood assistance in the homely, necessary tasks of the frontier. If a new cabin was to be built, the neighbors assembled for the house-raising, for the logs were too heavy to be handled alone. When a clearing was made, the log-rolling followed. All the men for miles around came to help, and the women to help cook and serve the bountiful meals. Then there were corn-huskings, wool-shearings, apple-parings, sugar-boilings, and quilting-bees.

Each of these community tasks was the occasion for a prodigal feast and a visit. Then the isolated households came together for much-needed companionship. After the hard work was over, these rugged laborers were still equal to wrestling matches, shooting for a prize, pitching quoits, tug of war, lap jacket, or any of the tests of strength or skill on which the frontiersman prided himself. Even in the work itself, they "chose sides" and made their labors a contest, to see which could outdo the others. When husking corn they would sit in a circle on the barn floor, so that they could play "brogue it about" (as children play pass the thimble) while they were at work.

Sleigh-riding to the singing-school, or the spelling-match, was the great joy of the winter months, as soon as there were roads made through the forest. For rude, unconventional enjoyment, there have been few pleasures that have atoned for hard labor on the part of the young, equal to the bob-sled with its wagon bed full of country folk, gaily singing as they sped through the clear frosty night. And then the friendly rivalry of the spelling-match at the end of the ride! Ranged in two long lines under their leaders were the contestants, who had been chosen for their knowledge of the columns of the blue-backed spelling-book. The swains and belles of the district spelt each other down, until the best speller was left standing in his or her glory, the object of parental or family pride—for all of their elders were either in the class or ranged around the walls. Of equal social importance was the singing-school, taught by the local "singing master"; tuning fork in hand, and without any accompaniment, he trained the whole neighborhood in reading "buckwheat" notes, and singing the hymns from the *Sacred*

Melodeon, or the *Missouri Harmony*. The little log schoolhouse, or church, would be crowded for these occasions. The classes were divided into the treble, tenor, and bass singers; few of the older books recognizing the alto and baritone parts. The churches reaped the benefit of this practice, in the improvement of their congregational singing. A wedding was also the occasion of all-day hospitality to every one far and wide. While waiting for the ceremony the young fellows used to "run for the bottle"—that is, race their horses for a stake, which was a bottle of whiskey, and then stand treat. Generally the country fiddler came in the evening, and there was a dance on the rude puncheon floor by the light from the fireplace. With swooping flourishes on his violin, his foot patting the accent, and at the same time calling the figures in uncouth buffoonery, the fiddler set merry feet to flying, to the tune of *Old Zip Coon, Jay Bird, Old Dan Tucker*, or *Possum up a Gum Stump*. The dancing was as vigorous as the music. There were "opera reels" and "French fours" and maybe a game of "hunt the squirrel." There was little glide in the movements: high steps and a flourishing swing, with a jig or a "hoe-down" thrown in, was good form in those days. Whitcomb Riley gives the spirit of those parties in his old fiddler's monologue[1]:

"My playin's only middlin'—tunes picked up when a boy,
The kindo'-sorto-fiddlin' that the folks calls "cordaroy."
The Old Fat Gal, and *Rye-Straw*, and *My Sailor's on the Sea*,
Is the old cowtillions I 'saw,' when the ch'ice is left to me."

[1] Riley, James Whitcomb, *Poems*, 1888.

And so I plunk and plonk and plink,
And rosum-up my bow,
And play the tunes that make you think
The devil's in your toe."

The roystering element among the Hoosiers of the backwoods as well as the better families were extremely fond of dancing, and as they were a vigorous, outdoor lot of people their dancing was suited to their natures. The gay ones cut "pigeon wings" or threw in an extra double-shuffle to fill out the measure. Some of the "calls" for the square dances were the product of the wits of the frontier (each neighborhood had its own caller), and for their very crudity are worth preserving. We give one as an example:

"Balance one and balance eight,
  Swing 'em on the corner like you swing 'em on the gate
  Bow to your lady and then promenade,
  First couple out, to the couple on the right,
  Lady round the lady and the gent solo,
  And the lady round the gent and the gent don't go.
  Ladies do-ce-do and the gents, you know,
  Chicken in a bread-pan, pickin' up dough.
  Turn 'em roun an roun, as pretty as you can,
  An' why in the world don't you left alaman.
  Right hand to partner and grand right and left,
  And a big, big swing, an' a little hug too,
  Swing your honey and she'll swing you,
  Promenade eight, when you get all straight.

First couple out to the right—
  Cage the bird, three hands round—
  Birdie hop out and crow hop in,
  Three hands round and go it agin;
  Alaman left, back to partner, an' grand right an' left,

Come to your partner once an' a half,
Yellar canary right, and jay-bird left,
Next to your partner and all chaw hay,
You know where an' I don't care,
Seat your partner in the old arm-chair."

There were some circles where dancing was not approved of, and with these, the chief amusements were forfeit games and marching plays. The frontier youth played with vigorous zest, "We're marching down to old Quebec," "Old Dusty Miller," "I suppose you've heard of late of George Washington the Great," "Come, Philander, let's be a marching," or "Oh! Sister Phœbe, how merry were we, the night we sat under the juniper tree, the juniper tree high ho," with scores of others that were sung to simple airs, while marching with rhythmic motions similar to the quadrille or the Virginia reel. Kissing was less tabooed than the dance. The forfeit games, like "Building the bridge," "Picking cherries," "Drop the handkerchief," "I want no more of your weev'ly wheat," "Chase the squirrel if you please and catch your love so handy," and dozens of others, were the same as are still played by children.

The field sports of the border would be the envy of present-day sportsmen. Besides the daily chance shots at game, for food, there were most exciting neighborhood hunts for wolf, fox, wild hogs, and bear, that required mettle and muscle, and the chase was sometime kept up for days, and much game bagged.

Horses and cattle were most necessary to the pioneers but they were often deprived of their valuable live stock by the bite of poisonous snakes. This occasioned another pursuit; in the early spring days when the warm sunshine began to awaken nature, and great numbers of snakes would crawl out of winter hiding, the frontiersmen would collect themselves into bands and go forth to slay these enemies, often killing hundreds in a day. As to snakes, says an old settler, there was no end to them. Like Pharaoh's frogs of old, they were everywhere, in the forest, yard, house, and among the children. They were met by willing hands and welcomed to hospitable graves.

Young people of the present time can hardly realize that wild beasts were really plentiful within the State, but a couple of true stories, told by Colonel Cockrum, will show that such animals were apt to turn up at almost any place in the woods. In 1817 Joseph Lane—who was afterwards a General, a United States Senator, and a Vice-Presidential candidate—had taken a contract, in partnership with some other young men, to raft several hundred logs down the Ohio to Mr. Audubon's saw-mill, which was over the river, at Henderson, Ky. It was the same Audubon who was, afterwards, the great ornithologist.

"We had landed our fine raft of poplar logs," writes General Lane, "near the mill; and while the raft was being measured, we went to the shanty near by, to eat our dinner. As Mr. Audubon went back to the mill, two large black bears and a small one ran out of the mill, and into a clump of bushes near by. The engineer started up the mill machinery, the saw being an up and down gear. When the men got ready to commence sawing, they discovered that a young bear was under the carriage, with his head fast in a grease pot, which was much smaller at the top than in the middle. The bear had got his head in and could not get it out. When one of the men caught it by the leg, it set up a screaming, strangling noise and the two old bears rushed to its rescue. All of the employees made it convenient to get out of danger. I climbed

A Map of Indiana in 1817.
From an old print.

up a centre post to a crossbeam. The bears had the mill all to themselves. They tried to get the young one away; would roll it and try to make it go, without much success. The engine was running, the saw going up and down. The larger bear was rubbed by the saw; in a minute he threw his paws around the frame it ran in, and such a pounding as that bear got! He kept his hold until he was exhausted, and fell down near the saw blade, which touched his shoulder. He jumped up and made a grab for it. In less than a minute his life was sawed out of him. In the frantic efforts of the old mother bear to release the cub, she pushed it off of the platform on a pile of logs; which broke the pot, released the cub, and he ran off with the rim of the kettle around his neck."[1]

Another tale that Colonel Cockrum tells, is of two young boys who came out west in the early twenties, to visit their uncle, Robert Stockwell.

"A neighbor, who was wise in the lore of wild animals, took the boys out on a longed-for hunting trip. They had gone five or six miles from the village, when they spied a large bear running away from them. Mr. Johnson instructed them to tie their horse to a tree, go to a place he pointed out, and not move from there, on any account, until he returned. On walking around, after waiting a long time, they saw two little animals wrestling much as boys do, rolling and tumbling over each other. They did not have the least idea what they were, but slipped up as close as they could and made a rush to catch them, which they found hard to do, as the little cubs were much more nimble than they looked. They chased them round over chunks and brush. Finally one of them ran into a hollow log and the younger boy crawled in after it. The older boy finally caught the other little bear, when it set up a whining

[1] Cockrum, W. M., *Pioneer Hist. of Ind.*, page 511. Oakland City, Ind., 1907.

noise and at the same time scratched and bit him. In a few minutes he heard the brush crackling, and looking up, saw the old bear coming at him with full force. He let the cub go and climbed up a little tree, fortunately too small for the bear to climb. She would rear up on the tree as though she intended to climb it, and snarl and snort at the boy, who was dreadfully scared. About this time the little boy in the log had squeezed himself through, so that he could reach the other cub, whereupon it set up another cry. The old bear left the treed boy and ran to the log, and over and around it, uncertain where the noise came from. She commenced to tear away the wood, so she could get to her cub, for she was too large to get more than her head in the hole. The boys were thus imprisoned for more than two hours, when a shot was fired not far off. The boy up the tree set up a terrible hallooing, and Mr. Johnson soon came in sight. A second shot soon killed the old bear. The young bear was caught, and tied; and the little boy came out of the log, dragging the other cub, which they also took home for a pet."[1]

In ye olden time, stump speaking during a political campaign was a great social feature and drew the whole countryside together; for the Anglo-Saxon must hear all there is to be said on politics. An old settler writing of these canvasses said that the population was so sparse in the district in which their candidate for Congress was electioneering that it extended from the Ohio River to Lake Michigan, but it contained more Indians, wolves, and wild varmints than voters.

Trading was a feature of every assembling of the people, social, religious, or political. They stood about the church doors before and after "meetin'," or

[1] Cockrum, W. M., *Pioneer Hist. of Ind.*, page 511. Oakland City, Ind., 1907.

around the public square on "court day," to dicker about the articles they needed; for then barter was universal, owing to the dearth of currency. An editor announced that he would take his pay for subscriptions in corn, ginseng, honey, flour, pork, or almost anything but promises. The articles advertised for sale which could be had "for cash only" were powder, shot, whiskey, and salt.

One of the greatest privations of the pioneer's exile was the absence of letters from home. There was no post and everyone was dependent upon chance travellers to "fetch and carry mail." When any one was going on a journey it would be known, and the whole region would bring letters for him to take with him, for postage on a letter cost forty cents. Many of these missives from the frontier were written with a quill pen, dipped in pokeberry juice for ink. It was a great thing, wrote an old lady in later times, when the pioneers began to get mail regularly twice a month. Sounding his horn, the postman approached on horseback, and every one came trooping out of the house hoping to get a letter from "back east." Sometimes he would be several days behind time, on account of high water. It often happened that the postmaster had to spread the mail out in the sun to dry.

The loneliness of their isolated situation made the pioneers very hospitable in their welcome to visitors. One of them writes of the attendance at a land-sale; if men had ever been to the same mill, or voted at the same election precinct, though at different times, it was sufficient for them to scrape an acquaintance upon. Very soon it would come to be known which housewife, on a trail, was the best cook and housekeeper, and that cabin would be singled out as the goal for the day's journey. In this way some of the best families began to "keep tavern." If they did not make a charge, hospitable people were imposed upon by a class of travellers who invariably "sponged their way," as it was termed, for an entire journey. There were men who profited greatly by the "likker sold, and set up reg'lar." To be able to sell liquor, a man must have a tavern license, certifying that he was a freeholder, and that he had two spare beds and two stalls, that were not necessary for his own use! Many wayhouses where the owners would not dispense liquor needed no license and advertised their places as "private entertainment." The usual charges were twenty-five cents for a meal and a "fip" for a "dram." The patrons that the tavern host welcomed came on horseback. Their boots had been well tallowed to resist water, and their legs were swathed in leggins of green baize. They generally dismounted grimy with dust, or bespattered with mud; and were met on the long low porch by a boy with a pair of moccasins or "pomps" in which their feet were shod, while their heavy boots were dried by the great open fire. The merchants and professional men carried a brace of pistols, and across their horse was a pair of saddle-bags. In this receptacle, now obsolete, the gentleman could stow away all of his papers, law books, bottle of bitters, an extra pair of horseshoes, and wearing apparel for the journey. They rode good horses, which often had to be "tethered out" on grass at night for lack of stable room. Other guests of the inn were wagoners, driving oxen or mule teams over the heavy roads to the river towns where they shipped the loads of produce to market. Each tavern had to provide large yards for the wagoners, and for hogs being driven overland.

The accommodations for travellers, in these early taverns, were very primitive, a near-by stream or the pump and a "roller towel" doing duty for a bath, and high feather beds welcoming the weary to rest. Some of these hostelries were noted for the prodigality of plain food and good cheer which was offered to the patrons. Card-playing and toddy, in an upper room, were very general where the landlord was not a temperance man. Then the wee small hours saw lands and chattels change hands, as the game waxed in interest.

Memories of old signboards that used to creak on the corner of these historic buildings come back to old settlers. We are told of one that was fashioned like a gate, and on the pickets was printed,

"This gate hangs high and hinders none,
Refresh and pay, then travel on.
"JOHN FERNLY."

On another notable work of art, which was executed for a tavern on the National Road, there was a portrait of General La Fayette in full uniform. We are told that the board on which it was painted was not long enough for the heroic scale on which the picture was begun, so the legs were cut short and the feet put on where the knees should have been! Red House Inn on the old State Road had for its sign a warhorse rampant and fully caparisoned for battle. The recent War of 1812 with England suggested the sign for another tavern—the painting represented an eagle picking out the eyes of a lion. Like the old "Buck Horn Tavern," which in the palmy days of the National Road is said to have kept over a hundred guests of a summer night, by the aid of the hay-mows and covered wagons of the movers, no hostlery of log cabin days would ever care to acknowledge that there was not room for one more.

Religious meetings in those days were thronged by young and old, wherever a travelling preacher gave out an "appointment" to speak. Some came in ox-carts, others on foot, but mostly the people came on horseback, two and three on behind each other. From eight and ten miles around they flocked to hear the gospel. Marriages were solemnized all along his circuit, and funeral sermons were preached for all the departed who had been buried without any religious rites, in the preceding months since a minister had come that way—even if the remaining bereaved one had been consoled by a subsequent marriage.

Generally these preachers were very practical in their exhortations. The eccentric Lorenzo Dow announced his subject as Repentance.

"We sing, 'while the lamp of life holds out to burn, the vilest sinner may return.' That idea has done much harm and should be received with many grains of allowance. Let me illustrate. Do you suppose that the man among you who went out last fall to kill his deer and bear for winter meat, and instead killed his neighbor's hogs, salted them down, and is now living on the meat, can repent while it is unpaid for? I tell you, nay. Except he restores a just compensation, his attempt at repentance will be the basest hypocrisy. 'Except ye repent, truly ye shall all likewise perish.'"[1]

His sermon lasted thirty minutes. Down he stepped, mounted his pony, and in a few moments was moving through the woods at a rapid gait, to meet another appointment. Restitution before claiming a clear

[1] Smith, O. H., *Early Trials*, page 96. Cincinnati., 1858.

conscience would still be a good doctrine to hold forth. As an example of how primitive the conditions, and unconventional the speakers might be, it is told of one of these circuit riders that he interrupted his discourse, at an outdoor service, by exclaiming, as he gazed upward into a tree, "I want to say right here, that yonder is one of the best forks for a pack-saddle I ever saw in the woods, and when the services are over, we will get it."

Besides the preachers, there were colporteurs, now long obsolete and forgotten, who went about distributing Bibles and tracts from the publication societies. They were far more welcome to those isolated inhabitants than we can imagine, in these sophisticated days.

Next to the ministers, the most accepted nomadic characters were the tinkers, who travelled through wide regions, repairing the clocks. In later times the spinster tailors, and the local cobblers, who came semi-annually, to mend and make clothes and shoes for the entire family, were a regular institution. If one could not get to the shop the shop must come to the customer. These welcome tradesmen had their rounds, and their coming was counted on; not only for the very necessary services they rendered, but for the gossip they brought, from far-off neighborhoods.

A frontier personage who has passed into oblivion with the water-diviner, is the bee-hunter. Sweets were a great rarity. Maple sugar and wild honey were the confections of the wilderness. The wild bees made their honey in the hollows of the trees and the bee-man was a wonderfully acute naturalist, who, by long observation of the habits of the bees, could tell in which tree the honey could be found. On his decision, great trees were felled, even on a stranger's land, to secure the coveted honey. One long, lank bee-hunter, who looked like a ferret, declared that "on a clear day I can see a bee a mile." In those times peddlers, with packs on their backs, journeyed through the country with "notions and small ware" for exchange or sale.

The frontiersman's most valued possession was a dog; this animal was not only a prized friend and hunting companion, but was invaluable to give warning of approaching Indians.

In these troublesome times, the militia were always being called out for actual warfare against the savages, and there was regular "muster day" and an attempt at regular drill. Muster day was the great gala occasion of the border. People gathered from far and near to visit together. Oliver Smith gives us a hint of the crude equipment with which the men appeared for duty, by the commands given on the parade ground which he rehearses: "Officers to your places. Marshal your men into companies, separating the barefooted from those who have shoes or moccasins; placing the guns, sticks, and cornstalks in separate platoons. Form the line ready to receive the Major."[1] They were not a very gallant looking troop perhaps, but they were brave, and wise in the cunning of the savage forms of warfare.

The schooling of this pioneer period in Indiana was of the crudest form. The schoolhouses were like the homes, log cabins with puncheon floors and great open fireplaces into which the big boys must roll in logs for the fire. Those who sat near roasted, and the pupils farther away froze their toes. The seats were logs or benches, without either backs or desks. The

[1] Smith, O. H., *Early Trials*, page 167. Cincinnati, 1858.

theory of instruction was "no lickin' " no larnin'."
There was a long writing-bench placed against the wall.
It was made of a riven board or a puncheon, smoothed
off and supported by great wooden pegs. At this
the pupils took turns in copy-book work, writing with
a pen made from a goose-quill, and using pokeberry
juice for ink. A spelling match on Friday afternoon
was an inalienable right of every district school,—an
older custom even than speaking pieces, that universal
practice which occasioned so much tremor and glory
among the pupils. Boys and girls often attended
school in the fall long after the hard frosts came, and
even after the ice had begun to form, with their feet en-
cased in old socks or stockings. Sanford Cox, in his
Wabash Valley, draws a graphic picture of juveniles
skating upon the ice, some with skates, some with
shoes, and some barefooted. The author of the
History of Monroe County says that it was then the
custom to go to school, winter and summer, barefooted. That seems unreasonable, but it was done.
The barefooted child, to begin with, had gone thus
so long that his feet were hardened and calloused to
resist the cold by several extra layers of epidermis.
He would take a small piece of board, say a foot wide
and two feet long, which had been seasoned and
partially scorched by the fire, and after heating it until
it was on the point of burning, he would start on the
run toward the schoolhouse, with the hot board in his
hand, and when his feet became too cold to bear any
longer, he would place the board upon the ground and
stand upon it until the numbness and cold had been
partly overcome, when he would again take his " stove."
in his hand and make another dash for the schoolhouse.
Sometimes a flat, light piece of rock was substituted

for the board and was much better, as it retained heat longer. Often boys would rouse up a cow and stand in the place she had warmed, to prevent their feet from freezing. To save their shoes, it was very general for people to walk barefooted along the dusty roads, until they approached the " meeting house," and then sit down by the roadside and put on their stockings and shoes.

New homes were sometimes started with very little capital in hand. Many stories are told of these primitive weddings. It is recorded that one morning, a certain Esquire Jones saw a young man ride up with a young lady behind him. They dismounted; he hitched his horse and they went toward the house and were invited to be seated. After waiting a few minutes the young man asked if he was a 'squire. He informed him that he was. He then asked the " 'squire " what he charged for tying the knot. "You mean for marrying you?"—"Yes, sir." "One dollar," says the 'squire— "Will you take it in trade?"—"What kind of trade?" "Beeswax."—"Bring it in." The young man went to where the horse was tied and brought in the beeswax, but it lacked forty cents of being enough to pay the bill. After sitting pensive for some minutes, the young man went to the door and said: "Well, Sal, let's be going." Sal followed slowly to the door, when, turning to the justice, with an entreating look, she said: "Well, 'Squire, can't you tie the knot as far as the beeswax goes anyhow," and so he did, and they were married.

One of the customs in the very first settlement of the territory was that those arrested for crimes and misdemeanors were chained to a tree or pinioned under some logs until trial could be held, if not more summarily disposed of by the Regulators! Afterwards there were jails built of logs, as also were the courthouses, and the prisoner worked out his sentence by grubbing stumps to clear the streets of the town.

Sickness was one of the ever-present dreads of the frontier. The very fertility of the soil in Indiana made it miasmatic. Ponds and streams bred mosquitoes to spread malaria to the—all unknowing—settlers. Exposure in all kinds of weather, and the opening up of the forests, the turning up of the new earth, all contributed to slow fevers, and the shaking ague then so universal. Many years in the autumn season there were more people sick than were well. Sometimes there were scarcely enough in health to care for those who were ill. Quinine bark, calomel, and boneset were the principal articles of commerce at those times.

One of the worst ills with which those people had to contend was what was known as milk sickness. Even scientific men, with all their investigation, have not been able to discover what plant caused this pestilence. They only know that with increased cultivation of the fields it disappeared, but in the early part of the Western settlement whole families were prostrated in a week, from using the milk of one cow. Sometimes they would drag around like living skeletons, and finally succumb. It destroyed the value of the lands, as people moved from neighborhoods where it was known cows had got access to it. Sometimes the settlers would move away, on the theory that it was the water.

Whiskey was a remedy in almost universal use against malaria. It did not require a physician's prescription, but the effects were often worse than the malady.

In Mrs. Blake's *Heart's Haven*[1] there is a pen picture of a typical cabin home on the lower Wabash, and the effect of the deadly malaria and whiskey used as an antidote:

"They were rich in youth, health, and courage, and the young wife's bright spirit turned the difficulties and privations into a romantic experience. She helped to clear the land, build the cabin, and plant the fields. She learned to shoot bears, defend herself from Indians, and kill snakes; to weave, to brew, and to nurse sick neighbors. Every year she brought a child into the world of want and hardship, until now there were two little graves in the woods for those who could not stay, and six little creatures in the comfortless cabin, that was no larger and no better, for all of their work and self-denial. The wife was changed, gaunt, sallow, shaken by ague, consumed by fevers, worn by toil, hardened and embittered by life's broken promises. The change maddened the husband. He saw that hardship was destroying her,—hardship that he was powerless to help. He could not conquer circumstances, he could only suffer in them, but he could drug his feelings in whiskey,—whiskey which made it possible to counteract the miasma of the middle West; which was the panacea for ague, snake bites, and poisons. It also fortified men for explorations, Indian raids, struggles with wild beasts, and Herculean toil, and it could also make them forget their hard conditions. Alas! it could also instigate foolishness and cruelty."

Many tales are told of the doctors, to whose practices the early settlers were subjected. In Mr. Duncan's very interesting reminiscences, he humorously remarks, that they generally provided themselves with a goodly supply of the largest lancets and unmeasured quantities of English calomel. A flaring sign painted on a clap-

[1] Blake, Mrs., *Heart's Haven*, Indianapolis, 1905.

A View of the Ohio River from Hanover College.
The Ohio was the front door into Indiana. From a photograph.

board was hung out, and as opportunity offered they went forth; first to take from the unfortunate patient all the blood that could be extracted from his veins without killing on the spot; then he was dosed with calomel enough to kill a gorilla, confined in a close room, and was to neither eat nor drink. The treatment killed quickly but cured slowly. Many of these early practitioners were dubbed "Death on a pale horse." Doubtless the openness of the log cabins, admitting plenty of air, saved many a poor soul racked with fever. Some of these men were educated, but others entered on their careers with the barest preparation possible, and those who brought the profession into contempt often had no knowledge of medicine at all. There were root doctors and mesmerists and all sorts of frauds who hung out their sign and made themselves dangerous to the community. To one ignorant pretender, who had gone into the practice without any preparation, an acquaintance said: "Well, Doctor, how goes the practice?"—"Only tolerable; I lost nine fine patients last week, one of them being an old lady that I wanted to cure very bad, but she died in spite of all I could do. I tried every root I could find, but she steadily grew worse." And still he got patients.

An old pioneer told, in the following quaint fashion, his experience with the early practitioners. About his seventeenth year he was taken ill. The neighbors said he had a kind of bilious fever. The only doctor was living over on Middle Fork, several miles away; he came on horseback with his saddle-bags of medicine, comprising tartar-emetic, calomel, jalap, castor oil, salts, and a thumb and spring lancet. After counting the beats of the patient's throbbing pulse, he proceeded to give him an emetic, then had him take calomel and jalap. Returning two days later he administered more emetics and bled him with his spring lancet until the boy fainted. The doctor said he was taking him through a course of medicine to prostrate his system, to break the fever. After continuing his visits for about two weeks, he said he always succeeded in curing by salivating his patients. The boy on the bed was now reduced to a mere skeleton. To be sure the fever was broken, for there was little left to create a fever. "The old doctor believed that the salivation was the salvation of me, but with all due respect," said he in after years, "I believe nature got the upper hand and cured me in spite of his strong medicine, bleeding, and tinkering; but he damaged my tenement irreparably."

Unfortunately, from these old stories, some still associate these early ailments with Indiana at its present state, when in fact it is one of the healthiest sections of the Union. Cultivation of the soil and drainage have eliminated the danger which beset the health of the early settlers.

In later years, when the prairies attracted emigration, another terror of the frontier was experienced by the settlements of the northern part of Indiana. This was the prairie fires. From fall to spring, the season when the grass was dry and Indians or campers' fires might spread disaster, the settlers would sleep with one eye open, to be ready to fight the destruction of their homes and improvements. It was an unequal combat at best. Often the lurid light of the oncoming flame would light the whole visible world. Sometimes the wall of fire would reach from ten to fifty feet in height. A horse could not outtravel it. Snakes, wolves, and deer would run before the advancing heat, and frightened birds would fly screaming before the flames. After the fire had passed, the smoke was suffocating, and for months afterwards the charred and blackened waste marked the path of the fire. Often the only shelter of the poor settlers was left in ruins.

Earlier than we should now think possible, when we consider how entirely the Western pioneers were cut off from communication with the older settlements, those hopeful toilers added to their homes more and more of the comforts of life. Many of the large log cabins were covered with weather-boarding, and stood for years as substantial colonial homes. The example of the thrifty helped the more shiftless to improve. Fruits and vines were planted. Houses were added to, and furniture and china were brought up the river. Neighborhood cabinet-makers fashioned cupboards, beds, and bureaus of the wild-cherry lumber, and owing to the honest workmanship they last until this day. All the conditions of living constantly improved. Innovations were a source of wonderment to the real backwoods element, and amusing instances happened. In one section where the Rev. Samuel R. Johnson had brought a piano out with him, when he moved his family from New York, it happened that a parishioner from the Wild-Cat Prairie called to see the Rector. In the parlor of the parsonage she saw, for the first time in her life, a piano, and had no idea what it was. Pianos were square in those days and this one was closed, with the round stool placed in front of it. After looking a long time at the great polished piece of furniture she exclaimed: "Well, that is the biggest work-box and the mightiest pincushion I ever saw." The first stoves that were brought into any section drew curious visitors from miles around, to see the new invention for making life easy!

"We are having innovations betokening too much fashion," says an old letter; "one of our dandies appears daily wearing silver spurs and embroidered gloves!" In those days patterns and styles came ambling at a deliberate pace, to the remote West, one year or the next making little difference.

There was little money in circulation then, and it took very little to sustain life on the frontier. At twenty years of age, a man, afterwards famous, started in as a lawyer in Indiana, with the noble ambition of securing a practice worth four hundred dollars a year.

In the life of privation and toil on the border, there were many homes where the traditions of gentleness and culture were maintained, and every effort to improve their growing children was made.

In writing his very interesting history of the Lake counties, and their early settlement, Mr. Ball says of that section, what was true of the whole frontier: that home life being an important part of true life, and as we have looked into these early homes, we have seen that warmth and light, and industry and thrift were there. In these homes you would find the mother and sisters knitting or spinning, the father and boys, fashioning a new axe handle or braiding a whiplash, and another roasting the apples and mulling the cider on the hearth, while an older sister or the boarding "school-ma'am" reads aloud from Robbie Burns or Bunyan or Shakespeare. We realize that isolation in the forest, sometimes, meant time for culture, as well as toil. If they were shut in to themselves, there was an uninterrupted existence which our rapid transportation, with its flittings south in the winter, to the sea-shore or mountains in summer, and maybe Europe in between times, may have destroyed; and some of the pleasures of continuous family life may have been lost.

In a country so free and where all had equal opportunity, men were ambitious. Only the most ignorant and benighted were ever content, unless they were increasing their possessions. Work was so honorable that these pioneers ostracized a man who was considered "a little slack in the twist" about avoiding labor. In marked contrast to the dull hopelessness of the Old World from which the foreign settlers had emigrated, was the determined purpose of the people of the West. As has been truly said, through the whole household there shone the light of a fine vigor and bright expectancy. The women were as courageous, as capable, and as zealous as the men. They became inured to toil, privations, and dangers. A story is told of one woman on the prairies when the wind was blowing a perfect hurricane, to the great terror of a transient guest: the hostess gently admitted, that the wind "*was noticeable.*" Many a woman, when notified that the Indians threatened a raid, refused to leave her cabin to their desolating firebrands, and they defended their homes by firing through the chinks between the logs, until help came from the settlements. When widowed, they kept their children together, and with the help of their boys they ran the farm in the lonely clearing.

"There are many diseases now, unheard of then," said Mrs. Rebecca Julian who was one of these very pioneers, "such as dyspepsia, neuralgia, etc. It was not fashionable at that time to be weakly. We could take up our spinning-wheel and walk two miles to a spinning frolic, do our day's work after a first-rate supper, join in some amusement for the evening. We never thought of having hands just to look at."[1] A managing mother would take a probable suitor for her daughter's heart around the cabin and show the bundles of yarn the young girl had spun, and the coverlids she had woven. The frontier mother's hands were never idle. From flax to linen from wool to cloth, from spinning the yarn to finished stocking, she was the manufacturer for her household. Nor was it possible to accomplish all of these duties by daylight. Back and forth by the firelight of the great open fire which enabled the father and son to shape the scythe handles and cobble their own shoes, the graceful girl passed to the hum of the whirring wheel. Her swift expertness as she deftly turned the thread in her fingers, made a picture of industry and skill, very captivating to the country swain. The spinning-wheel, wrote Judge Ristine, was a stringed instrument which furnished the principal music of every household, high or lowly. These home manufacturers dyed their yarns with the ooze from the bark of different trees, and vied with each other in the skill of coloring.

A traveller in 1830, writing of the excellent dames of Brookville, including the wife of the United States Senator, said they, in the exercise of "woman's rights," milked their own cows, churned their own butter, and made their own brooms.

A few extracts from the private journal of a newcomer among these pioneer mothers will give an idea of their lives upon the frontier.

"November 10th—To-day was cider-making day and all were up at sunrise.

[1] *Personal Reminiscences.*

"December 1st—We killed a beef to-day, the neighbors helping.

"December 4th—I was very much engaged in trying out my tallow. To-day I dipped candles and finished the *Vicar of Wakefield.*

"December 8th—To-day I commenced to read the *Life of Washington,* and I borrowed a singing book. Have been trying to make a bonnet. The cotton we raised serves a very good purpose for candle-wicking, when spun."

It seems incredible that the own granddaughters of these toiling women now find themselves on the very same spot, living in a factory age where every article they use or eat may be bought ready-made. Truly, as Jane Addams has pointed out, the present generation of women should feel and show every consideration for the factory hand, who performs the labors by machinery which formerly must all be done in the homes. Factory labor has lifted the burden of actual manufacture of every article used in the home from the women of the third generation.

Many a frontier mother, in addition to all her toil, taught her children their lessons, before there were any schools available. Had there been less labor, and no terror of the savages, wild beasts, and snakes, nor anxiety over wasting fevers, still the isolation and homesickness in the wilderness would have been enough to make the stoutest hearts quail before the undertaking.

But the dark side of the picture of early emigration seems to have had an overweaning bright side, which drew the people like a magnet to the West.

In an old-settlers' meeting a pioneer of Milton was called on for his experience. He gave an account of his removal to the region, and the gratification he felt in exchanging the red soil, full of flint stones, of his native Carolina, for the black and fertile lands of Indiana. In the vigor of his youth, he regarded not the Herculean labors and hardships which then rose before him, for, to use his own words, he felt that he had a fortune in his own bones. Those from well-to-do Southern families immediately took an interest in politics and gained preferment in office-holding, as well as lucrative law practice. Land speculation was in the minds of those who had some money. It was not only the rich soil, the broad acres, the greater opportunity for the young beginner, which lured them hither. With many, it was a vision of the greater freedom in the wilderness, the sense of space on the prairies. It is often a matter of wonder to older civilizations, why these pioneers came to the forbidding frontier. Often they left good homes, friends, families, comforts, safety, and advantages of culture and social intercourse. As Julian Hawthorne has said, pioneering was in their blood, and in their traditions. They had listened in childhood to tales of adventure told by the fireside, half true and half apocryphal. They were familiar with the log cabin, the rifle, and the saddle. They went forth to win an independent footing in the world. It was seldom the hegira of an organized community; each individual or family set forth on an independent basis.

Besides these families of sterling character who came West and made the "bone and sinew" of the nation, we have seen that there were many individuals known as "poor whites," of no occupation, who migrated two or three times in one lifetime. Starting from "Ole Caroline," they came up through "Kentuck," sojourned a year or two in Indiana and moved on westward, until their bones finally rested in Pike County, across the Missouri. The story of one of these migratory families, who formed an entirely different class from the real pioneer settlers, is told by a centenarian daughter of one of these men.

"When I was a woman grown and married, with children of my own, my man and daddy took a notion they'd try Injianny. So we all came, with just one wagon to carry our things and the children, while the rest of us walked, me toting my baby. We didn't seem to do as well here, and by 'n' by daddy wanted to go back and we went with him. Then we seemed to do worse than ever there, and daddy said he'd try Injianny again, and we come. Injianny didn't 'pear to be much better than Tennessee, and daddy took a notion again. I was getting despert tired of travel, but daddy coaxed me and mammy coaxed me, and this time they promised they would stay, and seeing they were bent on it I agreed. So five times, I walked back and forth between Tennessee and Injianny, kase I would have followed my daddy and mammy to the ends of the earth."[1]

But it was not alone the shiftless ones who changed their abiding-places. "I must be moving on" quoth Daniel Boone, who had come out from the New Carolinas to the wilds of Kentucky. "Why, a man has taken up a farm right over there, not twenty-five miles from my door." He could only breathe freely in vast solitude. These hardy adventurers were not the only emigrants. Some of the best English families, well-to-do where they were, moved forward in each generation. The Lincolns, through which the President's genealogy is traced, were for six generations, with a single exception, pioneers in the settlement of the new

[1] *Indiana Magazine of History*, vol. i., page 107.

countries. John Richmond left an ancient manor in south England, to establish a sea-coast colony in Massachusetts; his descendants moved to the Berkshire Hills, in the western part of that State; and their son settled in eastern New York. After John, of the next generation, had seen Fulton take the first steamboat up the Hudson River, he moved to the West, and was an old settler when he witnessed the first railroad train come into Indianapolis. To take up lands unhampered by the towns, his son Corydon Richmond moved his medical practice to the wilderness of Howard County, then still in the possession of the Indians.

Miss Anna Jenners tells of a pioneer woman who it must be admitted, had endured the extreme experiences of this spirit of Westward Ho! She used to recount how her father and mother had been one of the earlier couples to migrate from the East to Ohio, where they settled themselves in the wilds of the forest, and hewed out for themselves a home. In time, they acquired the comforts of home life, including all of the necessary buildings, gardens, and orchards of the most prosperous settlers. Here it would be supposed they would have lived to an old age; but the new lands opened to settlement in Indiana attracted the father; and after selling his beautiful homestead, he carried his family to the more fertile banks of the Wabash. In a rude cabin in the woods, where at night they often heard bears scratching on the low roof, they began the task anew. Always prosperous, the father cultivated his virgin acres successfully, until broad fields were added, and a large house was planned. For the new residence he sent all the way back to Ohio and had bricks hauled out, and interior finish and cabinet work made, which it

was not possible to have manufactured on the frontier.
When the comforts and luxuries had become attainable,
the daughter married; and soon the broad prairies of
Kansas lured her *husband* toward that new territory;
and again she passed through the discomforts and experiences
of border life. In her old age, though possessed
of a good home and vast acres, she was dragged to the
new Dakotas by her *son*, who perpetuated the pioneer's
longing for the frontier.

When Marion County was still a wilderness, one of
its young men, feeling crowded by incomers, slung
his rifle over his shoulder and disappeared farther
west beyond the Mississippi, and was never heard of
again by his family, until the Civil War broke out.
Then he reappeared as a bugler in an Oregon regiment,
old and gray, but still ready for adventure and unafraid
of hardships, as long as it was life in the open.

These sketches of family histories are outlined because
they are widely typical of many of Anglo-Saxon
lineage, who had the love of the soil in their blood.

The same impulse which prompted the Teutonic
race to make their incursions on Britain, and led
their descendants across the Atlantic, seemed to have
possessed each succeeding generation until the Pacific
was reached and the western coast was settled. The
Middle West was but the Atlantic colonies transferred
to a freer life and ideals one more remove from Old-
World standards. The opening up of new fields to
the race proved a wonderful stimulus to the national
life, and the growth of the United States as a world
power. When these people settled the western
borders they took with them their intelligence, virility,
love of country, passion for liberty, and desire for
knowledge. Hence, orderly governments, schools,

courts of justice, and charitable institutions sprang up from their efforts. The wilderness, to such natures, meant opportunity and freedom. As one said, "You do not need to keep on the path for there is no path. Each may mark out a future for himself, nor did we miss the satisfaction that comes from the constant victory over odds."

In addition to this love of space and freedom, many frontiersmen had a perception of the picturesque and the poetic. Their letters were full of the beauties of river, woodland, and flowers. The verse of the day was largely descriptive of the ocean-like prairies, the brook that runs murmuring by, the arching sky and flowering earth, and "The Bonnie Brown Bird in the Mulberry Tree."

On the frontier, equality of circumstances, common dangers, hopes, privations, and mutual interests created a homely tie of brotherhood and true democracy, dear to the Anglo-Saxon nature. As time passed in their forest isolation, intermarriages of the families strengthened the bonds of union.

Of the character of these first pioneers, no better portrayal could be made, than in the eloquent tribute of Reverend Jenkin Lloyd Jones to the father of Abraham Lincoln.

"Only he who knows what it means to hew a home out of the forest; of what is involved in the task of replacing mighty trees with corn; only he who has watched the log house rising in the clearing and has witnessed the devotedness that gathers around the old log school house and the pathos of a grave in the wilderness can understand how sobriety, decency, aye, devoutness, beauty, and power belong to the story of those who began the mighty task of changing the wild west into the heart of a teeming continent. In pleading for a more just estimate of Thomas Lincoln, I do but plead for a higher appreciation of that stalwart race who pre-empted the Mississippi Valley to civilization, who planted the seed that has since grown school houses and churches innumerable. They were men not only of great hearts, but of great heads, aye, women, too, with laughing eyes, willing hands, and humble spirits."[1]

[1] Address at Lincoln Centre, 1906.

CHAPTER VII

INDIANA TERRITORY

1763–1816

"I SHALL stand 'til morning in the path you are walking," said the Chief Pontiac to Major Rogers, who, with his English forces, was sent out from Montreal to take possession of the western posts, after the French had surrendered Canada. To a council of Indians the same Chief said: "The Great Spirit has appeared and spoken,—why do you suffer these dogs in red clothing to enter your country and take the land I gave you."[1]

Such was the first effect of English victories and the withdrawal of the French authority.

From the earliest landing of the first Europeans in America, there had been innumerable and continuous conflicts between the races. Although not appearing in this conflict so early as the Atlantic colonies, the Northwest Territory, of which Indiana formed a part, suffered in consequence of the war of races, from the time La Salle first explored her forests to within the memory of persons now living. And the history of Indiana's Territorial period is the story of that encounter.

After Pontiac's War in the autumn of 1764, when

[1] Dillon, J. B., *History of Indiana*, page 68. Indianapolis, 1859.

peace with the Indians was declared, the British again assumed control of all the western posts and held them, until, as we have recorded, fourteen years later, when General George Rogers Clark captured the forts for the American colonies. One of the pioneers has left an interesting account of the mode of savage warfare which prevailed through all the years of settlement. He says that the Indians in attacking a place are seldom seen in force upon any quarter, but dispersed, and acting individually or in small parties; they always conceal themselves in the bushes or weeds, or behind trees or stumps, or waylay the path or field where the settlers are obliged to work, and when one or more can be taken down, they fire the gun or let fly the arrow. If they dare they advance upon this killed or crippled victim and take his scalp or make him prisoner. They cut off the garrison by killing the cattle and watch the watering-places and pick off the inhabitants in detail. They crawl towards a fort until within gunshot and wait, and whoever appears gets the first shot. They often make feints to draw out the garrison on one side of the fort, while some of their numbers surprise another entrance. In combat they were brave, in defeat they were dextrous, in victory they were cruel. Neither sex nor age nor the prisoners were exempt from their tomahawk or scalping-knife. When the Indians went off for game or into camp, the white man would plough his corn, or gather his crop, or hunt deer, or get up his cattle for his own food. Often the women would keep watch with rifle in hand while the father or husband drove the plough.

An old settler tells us of the manner in which he used to work in those perilous times:

"On all occasions I carried my rifle, tomahawk, and hunting-knife, with a loaded pistol in my belt. When I went to plough, I laid my gun on the ploughed ground and stuck a stick by it for a mark, so that I could get it quickly in case it was needed. I had two good dogs. At night I took one into the house, leaving the other out. The one outside was expected to give the alarm, which would cause the one inside to bark, by which I would be awakened, having my fire-arms always loaded. During the two years I never went from home with any certainty of returning."[1]

Neither was there any certainty of finding his family unmolested upon his return. Many times children were sent for wood or water and were captured or scalped within sight of the home, and boys were murdered at the wood-pile. So harassed were the settlers that in one of the records of those times we find that in 1794 a reward of one hundred and thirty-six dollars was offered on the Kentucky shore for every Indian scalp having the right ear appended. An old army officer of the time has left a graphic description of one of the many councils when General Clark was trying to negotiate a treaty with the tribes in 1785.

"Three hundred of their finest warriors set off in all their paint and feathers, filed into the council houses; their number and demeanor was altogether unexpected and suspicious. The United States stockade mustered only seventy men as against their three hundred. In the centre of the hall at a little table sat the commissioners, and General Clark, the indefatigable scourge of those very marauders. On the part of the Indians an old council sachem and a war chief took the lead; the latter a tall, raw-boned fellow with a bold, villainous look, made a

[1] *Conversational Reminiscences.*

boisterous speech, which operated effectually on the passions of the Indians, who set up a prodigious whoop at every pause. He concluded by presenting a black and white wampum, to signify that they were prepared for either event, peace or war. General Clark exhibited the same unalterable and careless countenance he had shown during the whole scene, his head leaning on his left hand and his elbow resting on the table, with very little ceremony. Every Indian immediately started from his seat with one of those sudden, simultaneous, and peculiar savage sounds, which startle and disconcert the stoutest heart, and can neither be described nor forgotten. At this juncture Clark rose and the scrutinizing eyes cowed at his glance. He stamped his foot on the prostrate and insulted symbol of wampum and ordered them to leave the hall. They did so involuntarily. They were heard all that night debating in the bushes near the fort. The chief was for war, the old sachems for peace; the latter prevailed, and the next morning they came back and sued for peace."[1]

When General Clark made the conquest of the Northwest, it was the fourth white man's government the natives had encountered claiming rule over that region. With their limited knowledge of the Old World and their confused ideas of what Europe really was, what wonder that their minds were befogged and perplexed over the changes from French King to Spanish and from English Monarch to American Congress. First one "Big Knife," would solicit them as an ally to kill off the other nation, and then the next power to gain authority would announce that their chief was the "Great Father," and they in turn would use the savages against the settlers.

In recalling the intercourse between the natives and

[1] Vincennes, *Western Sun*, Oct. 21, 1820.

the white man, it is interesting to look over the articles for which the Indians bartered with the Europeans, and the following is the price received in 1775 in exchange for a great tract of land on the Ouabache River, well and truly delivered for the use of the several tribes: " Four hundred blankets, twenty-two pieces of stroud, two hundred and fifty shirts, twelve gross of star gartering, one hundred and fifty pieces of ribbon, twenty-four pounds of vermilion, eighteen pairs of velvet-laced housings, one piece of malton, fifty-two fusils, thirty-five dozen large buck-horn handle knives, forty dozen couteau knives, five hundred pounds of brass kettles, ten thousand gun flints, six hundred pounds of gunpowder, two thousand pounds of lead, five hundred pounds of tobacco, forty bushels of salt, three thousand pounds of flour, three horses; also the following quantities of silverware, viz.: Eleven very large arm bands, forty wristbands, six whole moons, six half moons, nine ear-wheels, forty-six large crosses, twenty-nine hairpins, sixty pair of ear bobs, twenty dozen small crosses, twenty dozen nose-crosses, and one hundred and ten dozen brooches; wherefore we have granted, bargained, sold, altered, released, enfeoffed, ratified, and fully confirmed unto the said gentlemen, etc."

Many stories are told of children who were stolen by the Indians in Territorial days and carried off, sometimes never heard of again. None of these tales has a more romantic interest than the well-known one of Frances Slocum, who lived as the wife of a Miami chief on the Mississinewa River near Peru, Indiana, until 1847. In the far-off country near Wilkesbarre, in the month of July and the year 1778, a tribe of Delaware Indians, incited by the British troops, swooped down on the Wyoming Valley, made a sudden attack upon the little settlement, killed the boys that were out of doors, and every one rushed for protection. In the stampede, little five-year-old Frances was forgotten, and knowing there was danger she crawled under the stairway to hide from the savages who were ransacking the house. Unfortunately they spied her little feet sticking out and pulling her out one of them swung her over his shoulders and they carried her and a neighbor boy away. Although pursued by soldiers sent out to the rescue, the Indians circumvented the troops, and the child disappeared from their ken. Within a month her father was murdered by the savages. She was taken to New York State near the falls of Niagara and was adopted by the chief; dressed out in blanket and gay wampum she grew up among the savages, and the Indians were good to her. In time there was only a hazy memory of her origin. She was called the White Rose and had been married to a Delaware Indian who proved unworthy of her and later she was wed by her adopted father to a Miami chief, She-buck-o-nah, who was deaf. After the death of her adopted father she and her husband left New York State and went to the home of his tribe in Indiana. She had three daughters. Frances's Indian name was Ma-con-a-quah. In the year 1839, Mr. George Winters, an Indiana artist, went to Deaf Man's Village, on the Mississinewa River, near Peru, and painted a portrait from life, of Frances Slocum; and he describes her as she appeared in her old age, arrayed as she wished to be painted. She was dressed in a red calico "pes-mokin" or skirt, figured with large yellow and green figures. Her nether limbs were clothed with red leggings winged with green ribbon, her feet were bare and moccasinless. Her forehead was singularly interlaced with angular lines, and the muscles of her cheeks were ridgy and corded. There were no indications of unwonted cares upon her countenance, beyond time's influence. Her hair, originally brown, was now frosted. The ornamentation of her person was very limited. In her ears she wore small silver ear bobs.

Colonel Ewing, a successful trader, who knew the Indian language, and had known Frances Slocum by her Indian name for many years, was called in one day when she was so ill that they thought death was near. The nameless longing, of which she had never spoken, came over her, and she revealed her life's story to Colonel Ewing. She told him she had been carried away, and had never heard of her people again; that it was far back "before the last two wars." She remembered her family name of Slocum, but had forgotten her own given name. After recovery from this illness, she relapsed into her Indian reserve, and told no one of her history.

Colonel Ewing wrote an account of the revelation made to him by this aged white woman, who was known as an Indian; and in 1837 it was published in a Lancaster, Pennsylvania, newspaper, with an appeal for news of the family. The story became widely circulated throughout the State, and finally reached the ears of her two brothers and a sister. The mother had died thirty years before, grieving to the last for the loss of her baby girl. She had spent thousands of dollars in searching and advertising for the child. A purse of five hundred guineas had been offered for her restoration. Eleven years after Frances was kidnapped an exchange of prisoners was arranged

on the frontier, and Mrs. Slocum journeyed thither
to see if her child was among the little ones, but she
had to return home saddened by disappointment.
She was not among the white prisoners. For thirty
years more the sorrowing mother waited and watched
for some tidings of the lost daughter and died without
the sight. Her brothers and sister grew to be prosperous citizens and were past middle life before this
published account of the confession of the aged white
woman, out among the Miamis, was brought to their
notice. With impatient speed they arranged to journey
westward for an interview. It was in the month of
September, 1837, fifty-nine years after the abduction,
that the sister and brothers reached the Indian village
on the Mississinewa. They had to communicate with
her through an interpreter, for she had entirely lost
her mother tongue. Her older brother identified her
beyond doubt by the nail being gone from her left
front finger, as it had been when she was lost, and
she recalled her name of Frances when it was spoken
to her. They learned that she had always been kindly
treated by the Indians, and universally respected by
the savages and white settlers. They begged her to
return with them, if only for a sight of old home surroundings, but she resisted their pleadings. She said,
"I am an old tree and cannot be transplanted." By
long habit she had become an Indian with precisely
their manners and customs. It is interesting to learn
that her changed environment at such an early age
caused her to grow so exactly like the savage people
with whom she was thrown. We are told by all that
she looked entirely like an Indian, talked like one,
slept, ate, and reasoned like them, and was as stoical
and reserved. The only difference seemed to be in

the purity of her life and behavior, and the fact that she acquired property, and provided for the future, in a way unknown among the aborigines. On the day after the surprise of the visit of her family, according to her promise to them, she rode into town to return their visit arrayed in her best barbaric attire and accompanied by her daughter and son-in-law and carrying a quarter of a deer for a present. She seemed to feel that their relations were established and enjoyed her visit, but again would not listen to their plans to have her return with them, seeming to feel no longings for home or kindred or race. With tearful adieus on their part and stoical reserve on hers, attended by her Indian offspring she mounted her pony and rode back to her forest home. Frances Slocum's history is but one of many tales of Indian kidnapping and reprisals which, if they could be given a place, would be more thrilling than any in fiction.

The story is told of a family near Pendleton, who had one son of the house who was proverbially slow. He was sent by his mother for an armful of fire-wood with the admonition, "Now don't be gone seven years." An Indian lurking in the woods near by seized the boy and carried him off. It was seven years before the lad found an opportunity to steal away from the tribe and return to his home; as he neared the house, the memory of his taking-away came back to him vividly and he gathered up an arm-load of wood and carried it in to his mother, who had long mourned him as dead. A young girl in Ohio County named McClure saw all of her kindred tomahawked before her eyes and then the Indians carried her off and sold her to the British with whom she remained in captivity until recaptured at the battle of the Thames.

In the earliest settlement of the Whitewater country, one of the Holman families suffered the kidnapping of their son by the Indians, who kept the youth for seven years. Among the thrilling experiences of his captivity was one time when he is said to have refused to carry a heavy burden which he had been ordered to shoulder. A council of savages was held to determine what they should do with him. The usual punishment was decided upon, of running the gauntlet between two files of men and squaws who were to buffet him as he passed or discharge their arrows at him. He was too useful to them to be killed and he finally escaped from the savages and lived to a good old age in southeastern Indiana.

John Conner, the founder of Connersville, was taken by the Shawnee Indians when a mere youth and was brought up and trained in Indian life, language, and manners. He knew their nature so well that in after life he was saved from their treachery while travelling in the northern part of the State, by a feeling that they were ill-intentioned and keeping himself awake. His apprehension was justified, for about midnight a friendly Indian came to his tent and warned him not to be there or his life would be forfeited. When dressed in their costume and painted it was difficult to distinguish Conner from a real savage. On one occasion in later years he came to Andersontown, then the lodge of a large band of Indians under Chief Anderson. He was dressed and painted as a Shawnee and his granddaughter says, when he heard Tecumseh was absent, he pretended to be that warrior. As is usual with the Indians, he took his seat on a log in sight of the Indian encampment, quietly smoked his pipe, waiting the action of Anderson and his under chiefs. After an hour he saw approaching him the old chief, himself, in full ceremonial dress, smoking his pipe.

"As the old chief walked up to me I rose from my seat, looked him in the eyes, we exchanged pipes, and walked down to the lodge without exchanging a word. I was pointed to a bearskin—took my seat with my back to the chiefs. A few minutes later I noticed an Indian, who knew me well, eying me closely. I tried to evade his glance, when he bawled out in the Indian language, at the top of his voice,—interpreted, 'You great Shawnee Indian, you big John Conner.' The next moment the camp was in a perfect roar of laughter, all yelling over the great joke. Chief Anderson ran up to me, jumping, throwing off his dignity, 'You great representative of Tecumseh,' and burst out in a loud laugh."[1]

His granddaughter, Mrs. Christian, says that the Indians seemed to retain an affection for her grandfather, but hated his second wife who was a white woman.

The Indians were always fond of making grave declarations in the councils, and many of the set speeches were incorporated in and could be unearthed from the commissioner's reports to the government, when treaties were being arranged. None of these orations are more familiar, to those who declaimed it when school children fifty years ago, than the stirring address of Logan, the Shawnee chief, which was translated by General Gibson.

"I appeal to any white man to say, if he ever entered Logan's cabin hungry, and he gave him not meat; if he ever came cold and naked, and he clothed him not. During

[1] "Reminiscences of Sarah C. Christian" in *Indiana Magazine of History*, vol. iii., No. 2, page 87.

the course of the last long bloody war, Logan remained idle in his cabin, an advocate for peace. Such was my love for the whites that my countrymen pointed as they passed, and said, 'Logan is the friend of the white men.' I had even thought to have lived with you, but for the injuries of one man. Colonel Cresap, the last spring, in cold blood and unprovoked, murdered all the relations of Logan, not even sparing my women and children. There runs not a drop of my blood in the veins of any living creature. This called on me for revenge. I have sought it; I have killed many; I have fully glutted my vengeance; for my country, I rejoice at the beams of peace. But do not harbor a thought that mine is the joy of fear. Logan never felt fear. He will not turn on his heel to save his life. Who is there to mourn for Logan? Not one."[1]

Tecumseh, who came to be the best known chief in the Northwest Territory, was not only a leader of shrewdness and intelligence but his powers of oratory were so great that he fascinated even groups of savages that listened to his eloquent speeches, and other chiefs were wont to shield their tribes from his influence.

The effect on the natives of contact with the white race was flattering to neither. The historians of the early periods of American history have all testified to the disastrous results from the sale of firearms and liquor, and drink is still the worst enemy of the remaining tribes on the reservations. Of the aborigines in Indiana Territory, its historian, Mr. Dunn, says: "It does not appear that the French civilization had any material effect on the manners and customs of the Indians in general. Some of them were converted to Catholicism, a few undertook something like an agricultural life; as a rule these advances were merely

[1] Dillon, J. B., *Hist. of Indiana*, page 97. Indianapolis, 1859.

grafted on the savagery which still remained."[1] The Reverend Isaac McCoy, a Baptist missionary, who, with his faithful wife, labored with the Pottawattomies, the Miamis, and Kickapoos for years and taught them agriculture and instructed their children, in his last days sighed over their inability to grasp the truths—"How few of the Pottawattomie tribes have reached the abode of the blessed." In one respect, at least, they were infinitely worse off than they were before the white man came. They acquired the appetite for rum, to satisfy which they were ready and willing to sacrifice anything they possessed. No tribe escaped this curse. The Indians themselves, in their sober moments, lamented their weakness, but there was no cessation of debauchery. In 1805, when Governor Harrison was urging the Territorial Legislature to adopt some measure to prevent this drunkenness, he said:

"You are witnesses to the abuses; you have seen our towns crowded with furious and drunken savages; our streets flowing with their blood; their arms and clothing bartered for the liquor that destroys them; and their miserable women and children enduring all of the extremities of cold and hunger. So destructive has the progress of intemperance been among them, that whole villages have been swept away. A miserable remnant is all that remains to mark the names and situation of many numerous and warlike tribes. In the energetic language of one of their orators, it is a dreadful conflagration, which spreads misery and desolation through the country and threatens the annihilation of the whole race."[2]

Contemplate this picture drawn by Governor Denonville in 1690:

[1] Dunn, J. P., *Hist. of Indiana*, page 122. Boston, 1888.
[2] Burr, S. J., *Life and Times of Wm. H. Harrison*, page 86. N. Y. and Phil., 1840.

"I have witnessed the evils caused by liquor among the Indians. It is the horror of horrors. There is no crime nor infamy that they do not perpetrate in their excesses. A mother throws her child into the fire; noses are bitten off. It is another hell among them during their orgies, which must be seen to be credited. There is no artifice that they will not have recourse to, to obtain the means of intoxication." [1]

Notwithstanding all the terrors and sorrows it brought to the settlers, the people who trafficked in liquor still sold it to the natives just as they do to our own people in the present day. Many Indians would get drunk to incite themselves to fresh atrocities on those they hated. They would sell anything they possessed to obtain "fire-water." Said a Shawnee chief in 1732: "The Delaware Indians wanted to drink the land away"; whereupon we told them, "Since some of you are gone to Ohio, we will go there also, we hope you will not drink that away too." But they did drink much of Ohio away and many other lands. Besides their passion for liquor the Indians of Territorial Indiana were very fond of games of chance and there were many forms of gambling in vogue among the various tribes. The game of "Moccasin and Bullet" as played by those inveterate gamblers, the Delawares, the Miamis, and the Pottawattomies, is thus described by Mr. Robert Duncan in his memoirs. He well recollected frequently seeing them playing the game, which was played in this wise: The professional gambler would spread upon a smooth level grass plot a large, well-dressed deerskin, upon which he would place in a semicircular form, within convenient

[1] "N. Y. Col. Doc.," vol. ix., quoted on page 123, Dunn's *Indiana*. Boston, 1888.

reach of the player, a half-dozen newly made moccasins. The game consisted in the use of a large-sized bullet held in his hands, and shown to those looking on and desiring to take part in the game, and then in a hurried and very dextrous manner, placing his hand under each moccasin, leaving the bullet under one of them. Betting was then made as to which one of the moccasins the bullet was under. As the manner of shuffling the hands under each moccasin was done so rapidly and skilfully that it was impossible for the bystanders to see under which the bullet was left, it will be seen that the chances were largely in favor of the gambler.

The names of some of the Indians of this time we learn from their signatures on old land sales. Twenty Canoes, Full Moon, Dogs 'Round the Fire, Dancing Feather, Corn Planter, Loaded Man, and Thrown in the Water, were among those on record, as ceding their titles to the invading settlers.

A detailed history of the Indian wars in Indiana Territory would be wearisome. It was an interminable maze of attacks by the natives, counter-attacks by the whites, in a few months, fresh reprisals, and then revenge taken on some other settlement. Often there were raids made on some innocent neighborhood for an injustice done to Indians miles away. Then the militia would be ordered out and the whole border "checkered" by the troops, in search of marauders. When it is remembered that over forty different treaties, in regard to the lands alone, not to mention peace pipes that were smoked pledging temporary peace, were made with the different tribes between 1796 and 1840, it is easy to imagine the constant conflict during that whole period. If Canada had been secured when the Independence of the United

The Site of Tippecanoe Battle Ground at the Present Time.

States was declared, the situation would have been greatly bettered. For many of the savage raids in the Northwest were incited by the British who kept the Indians constantly stirred up against the colonists. As an example, the tribes knew there was to be fighting between the two nations, long before the war was declared in 1812. British commanders had summoned the chiefs to Canada, and British agents went all over the West, distributing presents to the tribes and stirring up the bloodthirsty natives against the Americans. Tecumseh, the Shawnee chief, died in the British service, and his brother, "The Prophet," received a pension from the British Government until his death in 1834. Nor were the French guiltless for they had always incited the savages against the English settlers.

There was continued fighting in scattered localities throughout the Territory during the whole of the disturbance from 1808 to 1815, occasioning much misery and suffering, but wearisome to recall in detail. The battle of Tippecanoe was one of the best remembered of those Indiana conflicts. It was fought by General Harrison and his troops against the Prophet Elkswatawa (Loud Voice) who was a brother of the Shawnee chief Tecumseh and Kanskaka, triplets born at one birth. Tecumseh was a man of vast influence with all of the Miami Confederation. Tecumseh, who was an Indian of talent, skill, and bravery, and became one of the most celebrated aborigines on the continent, came down the Wabash attended by a large retinue of four hundred braves, fully armed, and appearing before Governor William Henry Harrison in August, 1810, made a long speech against allotting particular tracts of land to each tribe, and against the late purchase of lands by the white people.

"I am a warrior," said he, "I am the head of them all, and all the warriors will meet together in two or three moons from this, then will I call for those chiefs who sold you the land and shall know what to do with them. I will take no presents from you. By taking goods from you, you will hereafter say that with them you purchased another piece of land."[1]

Tecumseh had no claim or title to any of the lands which had been sold by the six tribes and their own chiefs. For ten days the haughty Shawnee chief and Governor Harrison held daily councils,—the Governor trying to reason and explain the new conditions to the aboriginal mind. Events that followed showed that the lengthy pow-wow, and all subsequent warnings, accomplished nothing. At the close of the visit Harrison told Tecumseh that his claims and pretensions would not be acknowledged by the President of the United States. "Well," said the astute Indian, by his interpreter, "as the Great Chief is to determine the matter, I hope the Great Spirit will put sense enough in his head to induce him to direct you to give up this land. It is true, he is far off and will not be injured by this war; he may sit still and drink his wine while you and I fight it out."[2] After this, the chief and twenty followers, who probably had intended to make an attack on Vincennes at this time, but were overawed by the presence of the United States troops, passed on down the river to the South to enlist more tribes in a great revolt they had planned embracing the whole territory from the Lakes to the Gulf. While he was gone on this mission, his brother, the Prophet, stirred up the natives and continued the

[1] Dillon, John B., *Hist. of Ind.*, page 444. Indianapolis, 1859.
[2] *Ibid.*

Prophet's Rock.

The Prophet stood on the high ground and chanted war songs in a loud voice and assured his followers of victory.

agitation in the Territory. Two months afterward the Governor, in his message to the Territorial Legislature warned them of the ominous clouds hovering over the Wabash; told them of the failure to induce the natives to take up agriculture, as game disappeared, and settle down on lands of their own.

"As long as a deer is to be found in these forests they will continue to hunt. Are then these extinguishments of native titles which are at once so beneficial to the Indian, the territory, and the United States to be suspended on account of the intrigues of these few individual leaders? Is one of the fairest portions of the Globe to remain in a state of nature, the haunt of wretched savages, when it seems destined by the Creator to give support to a large population?"[1]

Until the present moment these are the arguments of the opposing civilizations. Four hundred years of contact since the discovery have not changed the point of view of either race. Governor Harrison, ever wise in his dealings with the natives, endeavored to break up the confederacy of the Indians at the Prophet's town. He sent them the following letter addressed to the Prophet and his brother:

"Brothers, listen to me. This is the third year that all the white people in this country have been alarmed at your proceedings. You invite all the tribes of the North and West of you to join against us. You shall not surprise us as you expect to do. As a friend, I advise you to consider well of it. Brothers, do you really think that the handful of men you have about you are able to contend with the seventeen fires (U. S.) or even that the whole of the tribes united could contend against the

[1] Burr, S. J., *Life of Wm. Henry Harrison*, page 127. N. Y. and Phil., 1840.

Kentucky fire alone? Brothers, I am myself of the Long Knife fire; as soon as they hear my voice, you will see them pouring forth their swarms of hunting-shirt men, as numerous as the mosquitoes on the shores of the Wabash. Brothers, take care of their stings. It is not our wish to hurt you. With regard to the lands, it is in the hands of the President; if you wish to go and see him, I will supply you with the means."[1]

For months these negotiations were kept up, the Indians denying the threatened uprising and promising that they would send messengers among the tribes to prevent depredations. At the same time the Prophet was drawing the natives to his standard. In the autumn the signs grew ominous and Governor Harrison having lost hopes of a peaceful solution of difficulties determined upon an aggressive policy. He, with a force of troops, marched northward from Vincennes toward the Prophet's town to settle the question before winter set in, and ere Tecumseh should return from the South. The malign influence of the Prophet had reached all the tribes. In a speech to his followers, the Prophet had declared that his tomahawk was up against the whites, that nothing would induce him to take it down, unless the wrongs of the Indians about their lands were redressed. When Governor Harrison and his troops drew near the Indian forces the Prophet sent out a chief to call them to halt. Governor Harrison explained that he had no intention of attacking him, until he discovered that they would not comply with his demands. "At present my object is to find a good piece of ground to encamp on, where we can get wood and

[1] Burr, S. J., *Life of Wm. Henry Harrison*, page 127. N. Y. and Phil., 1840.

water."[1] The chief pointed out an oak grove which has since become so famous. It was on a table-land of the lower ground, which the troops settled on, and mutual promises were made for a suspension of hostilities until there was an interview on the following day, when General Harrison hoped to make peace settlements. Nevertheless, the army encamped in battle array and slept on their arms, for Governor Harrison was an old Indian fighter and knew their ways. He was none too wary. Before sunrise the Indians attacked so suddenly that they were in the camp before many of the soldiers could get out of their tents, and the battle of November 7, 1811, was on. The Prophet stood on high ground and chanted war songs in a loud voice and assured his followers of victory. When they were vanquished and the day was lost, they lost faith in the Prophet, deserted his standard, and he slipped away from the vengeance of the whites and joined the Wyandots.

It was on the return march from this battle of Tippecanoe that the soldiers from Kentucky gathered the seed of the blue grass which they found growing in Indiana, and carried it home with them thinking it was a superior variety, because it satisfied the hunger of their horses so that they would not eat their corn. It flourished so well on the limestone soil of central Kentucky that it made that State famous. Among the immediate results of the battle of Tippecanoe were the signal destruction of the Prophet's influence over the tribes, their dispersion from their settlements on that river, the complete defeat of chief Tecumseh's designs for a general uprising of all the allied tribes,

[1] Burr, S. J., *Life of Wm. Henry Harrison*, page 142. N. Y. and Phil., 1840.

and a little relief to the frontier from the incursions of the savages.

An appreciation of William Henry Harrison's official services to Indiana Territory belongs in its history. He understood how to deal with the Indians and by his victories in the border forays at Tippecanoe, at Fort Meigs, and jointly with Lieutenant Perry in making peace, he made it possible for the settlements throughout the whole Ohio Valley to enjoy a measure of safety. It is vastly to his honor that in the hotly contested campaign of 1840, when he was the Presidential candidate, it was never intimated that any taint of misapplied funds, or dishonest dealings could be attached to his administration, either as a commissioner, a military officer, or as an Executive. His zeal in the service and fidelity to the Territory made for General Harrison a most honorable record.

It is always to be remembered, in the annals of these Territorial days in Indiana, that the relief accomplished by any battle was temporary, that there would often be an outbreak in some other section in a short time. For example, a distressing massacre occurred in the following year, within the present limits of Scott County. In 1812, there was a place that was called the Pigeon Roost settlement. It consisted of a few families, isolated from other settlements, by a distance of four or five miles. During the afternoon of the third of September two of the men, who were out hunting for "bee trees" in the forest, about two miles from home, were surprised and killed by a party of Indians, consisting of ten or twelve warriors, mostly Shawnees, who afterwards attacked the settlement and in an hour, about sunset, killed one man, five women, and sixteen children, after a determined defence on the part of the few settlers. As soon as it grew dark two men, one woman, and five children eluded the savages, struck out through the woods, and by daylight reached the home of a neighbor six miles distant. The militia went to the scene of the disaster only to find the houses a smoking ruin and the victims of the savage warfare burned in their cabins. They buried the murdered persons in one grave on the spot where they died, and which they had suffered so much to attain.

The same month of the disaster of the "Pigeon Roost" settlement, Fort Wayne, which was more than a hundred miles away, was surrounded and held until the troops from far-off Ohio and Kentucky relieved it by dispersing the savages. Again, two months later, troops had to be sent to the Mississinewa River, to destroy the Miami villages and disperse those warlike bands. Only a few of the many conflicts between the natives and the white settlers can be recounted here. Indeed the alarms were so frequent that in 1812 the Territorial Legislature did not convene in regular session because so many of the members of that body were on military duty. Mr. Dillon says that twenty battle-fields and the ashes of fifty Indian towns are among the memorials of that triumph of civilized man in this region. The deaths and desolate homes of the white people have never been fully enumerated. Their graves are unmarked. Near their forest homes many times the ashes of both were found together and told the tale. The whole situation was deplorable, and continued so for years, but enough has been recounted for later generations to appreciate the conditions of living in Indiana when it was a Territory. Many interesting details of the encounters with the Indians in this particular State may be found in Colonel Cockrum's *Pioneer History of Indiana*. Throughout the continent the white man was a usurper from the Indian's standpoint, whether the lands were purchased or appropriated. It was their hunting ground they wanted preserved. It has been said that the English race of settlers extinguished the Indian title by the simple expedient of extinguishing the Indian. All of the European races who came in must ever stand accused of many violations of faith with the natives, and of horrible retaliations for all the savage atrocities committed by the red man.

Unless the whole continent was to be retained as a vast hunting ground, and forever closed to the overcrowded population of the rest of the world, border war was inevitable. The tribes had always battled among themselves for the same reason, and constantly depleted their own race in appalling conflicts for their "game preserves." If the white race finally conquered, it was not an easy victory, as we have seen.

In Indiana Territory the Indians resisted the advance inch by inch. Pleadings, protestations, strategy, cunning, cruelty, and massacre were tried to maintain their sway in the land. It is needless now to deplore or recriminate for the part our nation played in the Indian question. Like negro slavery, it was instituted by the different European nations who started the settlement of this continent before there was any American government. English, Spanish, French, and Dutch trafficked in slaves, and pushed the Indians back long before the Republic existed. We may regret it, deplore it, and be thankful that slavery finally was abolished; but the inception of both Indian and negro injustice was European, and the American nation inherited the two problems with the domain. We must shoulder our own share of the responsibility for mistakes in trying to adjust the difficult relations between the different civilizations, but Europe must share with us the beginning of sorrows. Neither of the two dark races has been able to develop sufficiently to "catch step" with the descendants of the Europeans. An ironical form of the Indian's retaliation for the loss of domain might be recognized in the money loss to the world by his introduction of the use of tobacco. Possibly the living descendants of the departed braves could spend the rest of their days in computing the cost, to the nations, of the wealth "gone up in smoke" from the use of the weed made known to the white man on the banks of the James. It might be a grim satisfaction to Big Chief, fretting on Western "farms in severalty," to reflect that, at an ever-increasing ratio, his mild poison is absorbing the revenues of the European races; that the value of his lost lands will be a mere bagatelle, compared with the cost of the tobacco which is being consumed at the rate of four hundred million dollars a year, within that same domain.

Notwithstanding the continued Indian troubles, the Northwest Territory increased in population and in material wealth. After the Revolutionary War, in 1785 the disbanded soldiers began drifting westward in large numbers. After Virginia and the other Atlantic colonies had ceded their individual claims to the Federal Government, Congress completed the organization of the lands north of the Ohio and east of the Alleghanies into the tract known officially as the Northwest Territory, and adopted the famous

"Ordinance of 1787" for its government. In the year 1800, with a population of 4700 white people, an independent territory, extending to the Mississippi River, and called Indiana, was organized with William Henry Harrison as Governor. Four years later it was granted a Representative in Congress. In 1808, when the population had increased to 17,000, the part east of the Wabash River was divided from Illinois. In 1816, Indiana was admitted into the Union. "She has come in free," was the glad word carried from hamlet to village. This meant that slavery existed on this soil, in the early history of Indiana. Slaves were brought with the settlers from the South, others were sold "up the river" by the Spanish; and Louis of France, by a royal ordinance in 1721, had authorized the importation of negro slaves into his territory, and slaves were still held by Americans who had come from the South. When the United States secured control of the territory the struggle began between those who wished slavery continued within its borders, and those who strenuously opposed it. Mr. J. P. Dunn, in his interesting and exhaustive history of Indiana as a Territory, and its redemption from slavery, covers every phase of the discussion the reader may wish to investigate. He gives due weight to the historical fact that the local slavery question was the paramount political influence in Indiana up to the time of the organization of the State government; and he brings clearly to light the causes which produced the pro-slavery feeling, and the difficulties which the anti-slavery sentiment was obliged to overcome. Here it will suffice to recall that, as the French settlers already had slaves under the crown, which they brought up the river upon their return from the trading trips

William Henry Harrison.
From an engraving after the painting by Chappel.

to New Orleans, it was natural that the early pioneers from the South who had slaves should retain them, it still being in accordance with the law. At the same time there had come into the Territory many Quakers, who always discountenanced slavery; and large numbers of the citizens from the South, who had left slave States at great sacrifice, on account of their disapproval of slavery, many of whom were of Huguenot descent, had been joined by people from New England. These elements made a strong minority, who persisted in a conscientious and continued fight against perpetuating the practice in the new Territory. It is a fact that, when the constitution for the new State was adopted by the commission appointed for that purpose, freedom won by only two votes! A traveller through Indiana at this time wrote home: "These people are forming a State government. The question in all its magnitude, whether it should be a slave-holding State or not, is just now agitating. Many fierce spirits talked about resistance with blood, but the preponderance of more sober views and habits of order and quietness prevailed." Indiana came in as a free State.

One of the perplexing and vexatious things in frontier life was the frauds practised in entering claims to the public lands. The times were so threatening in 1804 that the Commissioners, appointed to adjust the land titles for the Federal Government, in closing their report, said: "We close this melancholy picture of human depravity by rendering our devout acknowledgment that it has pleased Divine Providence to preserve us both from legal murder and private assassination."[1] The rapacity of land

[1] Dillon, J. B., *History of Indiana*, p. 434. Indianapolis, 1859.

speculators, the dishonesty of land agents, and the grasping covetousness of some settlers kept up a constant source of hardship and discontent. Soldiers and the earlier inhabitants sometimes sold their lands to cunning speculators as low as thirty cents an acre, and then were paid in bogus scrip. The very first settlers came into the Territory before there were any surveys, and had to prove up after the government was ready to grant a title. Actual settlers tried to adjust their selections without dissensions or bidding against each other, sometimes casting lots to decide who should secure a certain tract. We read in an old journal that "the settlers tell foreign capitalists to hold off till they enter the tract they have already settled upon, and that then they may pitch in; that there will be land enough for all. If a speculator makes a bid or shows a disposition to take a settler's claim from him, he soon sees the whites of a score of eyes. A few days of public sale sufficed to relieve hundreds of their cash, but they secured their land, which will serve as a basis for their future wealth and prosperity, sure as time's gentle progress makes a calf an ox." Some speculators swept whole townships at a purchase. The fortunes of many who were afterwards the rich men of Indiana were made by securing cheap government lands, and not "signing deeds." The story is told by Sanford Cox of a clever ruse played upon land speculators that were constantly scouring the country.

"A man who owned a claim on Tippecanoe River, near Pretty Prairie, fearing that some one of the numerous land hunters might enter the land he had settled upon before he could raise the money to buy it, seeing one day a cavalcade of land hunters riding in the direction of his claim, mounted his horse and started off at full speed to meet them, swinging his hat and shouting at the top of his voice: ' Indians! Indians! The woods are full of them, murdering and scalping all before them!' They paused a moment, but he cried: 'Help! Longlois,—Cicots, help!' They turned and fled, giving the alarm to the settlements, and never came back. As soon as the alarmer could gather up money enough, he slipped down to the land-office town, and entered his land, chuckling in his sleeve over outwitting the land hunters."[1]

At one time "land spies" and "land sharks" were circumvented by a whole neighborhood of settlers dressing up like Indians and making a noisy attempt to surround the speculators, who hastily left and spread the alarm of savages coming.

In December, 1811, the month after the battle of Tippecanoe, Territorial Indiana and the whole Mississippi Valley experienced the terrors of an earthquake. It was the first disturbance of that character since the country had been explored, and no seismic phenomena have ever been so violent in the Middle West since. The first shock occurred the fifteenth of December, and they were repeated at intervals for two or three months. A resident of the valley at that time wrote that the shocks of these earthquakes must have equalled, in their terrible upheavings of the earth, anything of the kind that has been recorded. We are accustomed to measure this by the buildings overturned and the mortality that resulted, but here the country was thinly settled. The houses, fortunately, were of logs, the most difficult to overturn that could be constructed. Yet, as it was, whole tracts of land were plunged into the river. This was the "Great

[1] Cox, Sanford C., *Old Settlers*, p. 53. La Fayette, 1860.

Shake" of 1811, as it was felt in the centre of the district affected. Up and down the tributary rivers the terror was only less felt, as the settlements were distant from that centre. Indiana Territory had so few towns, of any size, at that time that the experience came mostly to cabin settlements and solitary homesteaders in their isolated clearings.

An interesting fact in connection with the Mississippi River intrigues was that in the year 1806 the Territory of Indiana had many valuable accessions, in the deluded followers of Aaron Burr. These learned on their way down the Ohio that Burr's followers were regarded as traitors by the government; that if they proceeded farther toward the Mississippi they would be seized by soldiers, who had been detailed to watch the river and make arrests of the adherents of Burr. These deluded people saw the dreams of empire, with which that conspirator had enticed them away from their homes, to join with him in his scheme of establishing a great inland, independent government, vanish into an illegal myth. To protect themselves, they left the rivers and retired into the fastnesses of southern Indiana, where they began anew, under great hardships, to make homes for themselves. They became valuable settlers, but cherished no regard for that arch schemer, who lured so many from their old habitations.

We have already recounted, in the chapter on Spanish dominion, how in 1803, shortly after Indiana attained the rank of separate Territorial government, the long-drawn question of the free navigation of the Mississippi River, whereby the commerce of the Wabash and the Ohio might have an outlet, was finally settled by Napoleon selling the whole of Louisiana Territory to the American Government. During these troublesome times on the frontier, the settlers upbraided the New Englanders for their indifference to the troubles of the West. They wrote to them that

"three times the quantity of tobacco and corn can be raised on an acre here than can be within the settlements on the east side of the mountains, and with less cultivation. Do you think to prevent the emigration from a barren country, loaded with taxes, to the most luxurious and fertile soil in the world? We are determined that the Spaniards shall not trade up the river, if they will not let us trade down it. In case we are not succored by the United States, our allegiance will be thrown off and some other power applied to. Great Britain stands ready with open arms to receive and support our claims. When once re-united to them, 'Farewell, a long farewell' to all your boasted greatness. You are as ignorant of this country as Great Britain was of America."[1]

This whole question, which had annoyed the settlers for two decades, we dispose of in a few paragraphs, but their vexations had been most disheartening, and they hailed the opening of the river with rejoicing.

Seemingly this would have ended forever the battles of the river, but nine years afterwards, in the War of 1812 between the United States and Great Britain, the Western border was again disturbed and Indiana's commerce congested by the blockade of New Orleans, whereby it was intended to make a permanent conquest of the lower Mississippi, and to secure for Great Britain in perpetuity the western bank of the river. Says Fiske: "In order to effect all this, it seemed necessary to inflict upon the Americans one crushing and humiliating defeat. That this could be done few

[1] *Ind. Magazine of History*, 1906, vol. ii.

Englishmen doubted, and so confident was the expectation of victory that Governors and Commandants for the towns along the Mississippi River were actually appointed and sent out in the fleet."[1] Thus we see the great significance to the Indiana settlers, clustered along the Ohio and Wabash with all their tributary streams, of the great victory gained by Andrew Jackson at New Orleans, with his army of scarcely six thousand sturdy frontiersmen from the valley territory, when he met a force of twelve thousand British regulars on that December day in 1814.

"The faultless frontier marksmen, who thought nothing of bringing down a squirrel from the top of the tallest tree, wasted very few shots indeed. In just twenty-five minutes the British were in full retreat, leaving 2600 of their number killed and wounded. The American loss was only eight killed and thirteen wounded, for the enemy were mowed down too quickly to return an effective fire. This victory, like the three last naval victories of the war, occurred after peace had been made by our Commissioners at Ghent. Nevertheless, no American can regret that the battle was fought. Not only the insolence and rapacity of Great Britain had richly deserved castigation, but Jackson's victory decided that henceforth the Mississippi Valley belonged indisputably to the people of the United States."[2]

And it was the last struggle with a foreign power for its possession.

The state of advancement in Indiana at this time may be understood from some passages in the Gov-

[1] Fiske, John, *Essays, Historical* and *Literary*, vol. i., "Andrew Jackson," p. 248. New York, 1902.
[2] *Ibid.*, page 251.

The Old State House at Corydon, Indiana.
From a photograph by Mowrer.

ernor's message to the Territorial Legislature when it met in 1813. Governor Posey rehearsed the causes of the war then going on with England, and then urged the Assembly to pass laws for raising revenues for roads and schools and the reorganization of the militia for better protection against the Indians! In the formal response of the Legislature, that august body of pioneers, clad in deerskin, replied in imperious language, calling attention to the fact that the American nation had been forced into the war by the indignities practised on her by Great Britain, and added: "With you, Sir, we abhor that cringing and detestable policy which would submit to British aggression, and cherish a hostile colony—a scourge on our borders. We are astonished at the mistaken and obstinate policy of the New England States, in opposing the junction of the Canadas to the Union."[1]

After living under the Territorial form of government for seven years, Congress granted Indiana the right to call a convention for the purpose of framing a constitution preparatory to admission into the Union of States. This convention assembled in the little town of Corydon, which had just been made the capital. It was in the month of June. In southern Indiana, when the corn is growing finely, the temperature can be like the torrid zone. The honorable body which had assembled for the work found such weather prevailing, and held most of the sessions under a great spreading elm-tree, which still stands. The limbs of this tree cover nearly one hundred and twenty-five feet in diameter, and its shade was gratefully cool to the ardent law-makers who were assembled to close the Territorial stage of her history.

[1] Dillon, J. B., *History of Indiana*, page 529. Cincinnati, 1858.

With the opening of the nineteenth century, Indiana was to come into the galaxy of States, nearly a century and a half after La Salle revealed her fertile lands and streams to the people of the other continent, and under conditions daily growing more favorable to peaceful occupancy.

CHAPTER VIII

THE NEW STATE—1816

INDIANA Territory, as well as the others west of the intervening Alleghany Mountains, was a long distance from the immediate watch-care of the Central Government, and in common with Territories at the present day felt the delays and the indifference to its necessities and peculiar conditions. In 1815, Congress received a petition from the settlers of Indiana, reciting that they now had 60,000 white inhabitants within their borders, and asking that honorable body to order an election for representatives to form a State government; and very significantly expressing at the same time the hope that if a State was organized, it would be permitted to be a free and not a slave State. "Let us be on our guard when our convention men are chosen," wrote good old Dennis Pennington, in 1815, "that they may be men opposed to slavery."

The following April, a bill favorable to the organization of a new State was passed in Congress, and a month later the election occurred. The commission sat in June to frame the constitution. Of those hardy frontiersmen who were to assume the responsibilities of forecasting the future commonwealth, Mr. Dillon says:

"The convention that formed the first constitution of the State of Indiana was composed mainly of clear-headed, unpretending men of common-sense, whose patriotism was unquestionable and whose morals were fair. Their familiarity with the theories of the Declaration of Independence—their Territorial experience under the provision of the Ordinance of 1787—and their knowledge of the principles of the Constitution of the United States were sufficient, when combined, to lighten materially their labors in the great work of forming a constitution for a new State."[1]

This is really a modest estimate of the commission, when we compare the instrument which they prepared with State measures originated by others, even in this day! The new constitution was comprehensive, dignified, and so liberal in its provisions for the future that it was a half century in advance of the times. It declared for reform and not vengeance, as the object of State punishment for crimes; it imposed on future Legislatures the requirement of providing asylums for the unfortunate; it prohibited the establishment of banks for the purpose of issuing bills of credit, or bills payable to order or bearer, except the regular State bank and its branches; and it is claimed that, previous to Indiana, no State had in its constitution declared for a graduated system of schools, extending from the district schools to the university, equally open to all, on the basis of gratuitous instruction. The legislation of the next thirty-five years did not accomplish the ideal of these early framers of the first constitution in regard to education, and it was over three quarters of a century before the penal code of the State contained as enlightened provisions as they had outlined.

[1] Dillon, J. B., *History of Indiana*, page 559. Cincinnati, 1858.

"Constitutional Elm" at Corydon, Indiana.
This elm is still standing. From a photograph by Mowrer.

As an illustration of the primitive conditions which prevailed at that date, it is recalled that the commission held its sessions under a great elm in the yard, and the chairman of the Constitutional Commission, who was also the builder that was erecting the new State-house, was often called from hammer and trowel, to decide upon questions of State.

The duties of Statehood were assumed by thirteen sparsely settled counties lying along the Ohio and the southern part of the Wabash River. Less than one-fourth of the territory had been ceded to the white race. Two-thirds of the domain was still the hunting-ground of the Indians.

The men who had controlled political affairs during the Territorial time led in the organization of the State and portioned the offices and honors among themselves, very much after the present fashion in politics. Jonathan Jennings became Governor. James Noble and Walter Taylor were elected to the United States Senate, and Williams Hendricks went to Congress. The first Assembly after the State was admitted into the Union convened in the new capital at Corydon on November 4, 1816. Governor Jennings's message to the first General Assembly was full of appreciation of the dignity and importance of the occasion, and the responsibilities of the Legislature in striking a high plane for their deliberations and enactments. An idea of the issues of the day may be gleaned from the points brought out in his address, some of which still have a familiar ring, and others passed with the passing of the pioneer conditions. He pointed out the necessity of providing for general education; urged the necessity for better roads; that certainty of punishment must be established, as the surest way of preventing crime.

He urged better protection from the Indians, and that there was need of laws prohibiting any attempts to seize and carry into bondage persons of color legally entitled to their freedom, and at the same time laws to prevent slaves, from elsewhere, seeking refuge within the limits of the State.

The tax rates for the year of admission into the Union are also interesting as an index of the times. For each one hundred acres of best land, the tax was one dollar. For each bond-servant over twelve years of age, three dollars; thirty-seven cents for each horse or mule. For each ferry across streams, from five to twenty dollars. Town lots were assessed fifty cents; and each "pleasure carriage" with two wheels, one dollar; four wheels, one dollar and a quarter; each silver watch, twenty-five cents; gold watch, fifty cents; for every billiard table, fifty dollars. We wonder of how many the crude wilderness towns could boast?

At this time there was not a mile of turnpike, plank road, or canal in the State! The Indian trails, which could only be travelled by a rider on horseback, were the only roads outside of the towns. It took the members elected to the National Congress twenty-eight days to travel on horseback to reach the sessions of that body.

The description of the diminutive county towns, in William Dudley Foulke's very interesting biography of Governor Oliver P. Morton, gives the reader a graphic picture of the county seat in that early time. He says that

"thither flocked the men of the county upon all great occasions, to the trials and to the musters. They brought with them their own food in their wagons or saddle-bags, and sought the shelter of the Court-house or of the great

The New State—1816

trees near by. The men were clad in deerskin trousers, moccasins, and blue homespun hunting-shirts, with a belt to which hung a tobacco pouch made of polecat skin. The women wore gowns of homespun cotton, with calico or gingham sun-bonnet. The country folks came to town on horseback, the women sitting behind the men on the same horse."[1]

At the same time the people in the towns were surrounding themselves with better homes and more of the conveniences of life. The impetus given to the development of the State, by having its own government and increased security from Indian raids, may be realized when it is recalled that the population increased eighty-seven thousand in the next four years. By 1820, there were 147,178 people in the State. New settlements were founded, homes rebuilt or enlarged, schoolhouses and churches built, orchards planted, and roads hewn through the forest.

There were few newspapers anywhere in that day, and on the border candidates for office were wont to issue flaming handbills, and broadsides, setting forth their own virtues, and the drawbacks from the election of their opponents. There were no caucuses or conventions then. Every candidate brought himself out and ran on his own merits. Modesty generally was its own reward! Then, the best men succeeded in capturing office by sounding their own praises from the stump. It really was stump-speaking in those primitive times. The political candidate would round up a few voters at a battalion muster on training-day and harangue them; or, appoint a meeting, where there were a few logs in a clearing for the benches, on which the choppers gathered to listen, and a broad stump

[1] Foulke, Wm. D., *Life of Oliver P. Morton.* Indianapolis, 1900.

for the speaker, and you had a "log convention," such as downed slavery in the new Territory. Many amusing stories are told of these frontier campaigns. When Jonathan Jennings, who afterwards was the first Governor of the State, was running for Congress against Mr. Randolph, they both went about among the different neighborhoods 'lectioneering. Mr. Dunn tells the story of Mr. Randolph coming to a log-rolling on horseback, being received by Farmer Ruse with the salutation, "'Light you down"; he dismounted, and after chatting a few minutes was asked into the house. Randolph accepted the invitation, and, after visiting with the women folks a short time, rode away. On the next day Jennings came, who had a similar reception, but to the invitation to repair to the house, he replied, "Send a boy up with my horse and I'll help roll," and help he did until the work was finished, and then he threw the maul and pitched quoits with the men, taking care to let them outdo him, although he was very strong and well skilled in the sports and work of frontier farmers. So he went from house to house. People used to treasure up their anecdotes of his doings in his campaign, and how he would take a scythe and keep ahead of half a dozen mowers.

Captain Lemake, with his keen sense of humor, has told in his *Reminiscences of an Indianian* a very amusing story of a canvass for votes which he made in his youth. It was in a contest for sheriff of Vanderburg County to which he had been nominated, against his vigorous protest.

"I found this race a bitterly contested fight and no comfortably padded job. Through the out townships, over rough and muddy roads, in buggy and on horseback, day and night I beat the bush. And all the time there rang in my ears the professional office-seeker's chant:

> He greets the women with courtly grace,
> And kisses the babies' dirty face;
> He calls to the fence the farmer at work,
> And bores the merchant, and bores the clerk;
> The blacksmith while his anvil rings,
> He greets. And this is the song he sings:
>
> 'Howdy, howdy, howdy do?
> How is your wife, and how are you?
> Ah! it fits my fist as no other can,
> The horny hand of the working-man.'

"One day when riding along a country road looking for voters, I spied a dilapidated old Reuben plowing a field. No sooner had I tied my horse than the intelligent agriculturist left his plow and came over to the fence. After shaking his gnarly claw in the hearty manner that candidates have, I began my spiel. He listened patiently until I got through, and then with hems and haws said: 'Well, Cap, I'd like to vote for you firstrate, but the other fellow is sort o' kin to me and I don't like to vote agin him.' Rather taken back, I queried what relationship he claimed with my opponent; when he, with subdued pride, drawled out, 'Well I got an idee that he's the father of my oldest boy.'"[1]

Politicians were often the butt of the proverbial Hoosier humor, and on account of it sometimes lost their election. Of one politician it was said that there was no tangible objection to him, but it was rumored that he could see a short rich man over the head of a tall poor man. The same humor sometimes came out in plea for office, as when a candidate for justice of peace boasted that he "had been sued on every

[1] Lemcke, J. A., *Reminiscences of an Indianian*, page 66. Indianapolis, 1905.

section of the statutes, and ought to know all about the law."

Political influence and office went in the olden time, as much as now, to the lawyers; commercial life had a narrower horizon in those days than at present, and the young men of wit, who were selecting a career, turned very often to the profession of law. In the reminiscences of one of these men, who figured largely in the early bar of Indiana, he says that the lawyers were the most important personages in the country. They were universally called " 'squires " by old and young. Queues were much the fashion, and nothing was more common than to see one of these 'squires with a queue three feet long, tied from head to tip in an eel skin, walking in evident superiority, in his own estimation, among the people in the court-yard, sounding the public mind as to his prospects as a candidate for the Legislature. The crowds of that day thought the holding of court a great affair. The people came hundreds of miles to see the judges and hear the lawyers plead, as they called it. When court adjourned, the people returned to their homes and told their children of the eloquence of the attorney.

The dress of the prominent men of this time was of blue cloth with brass buttons, buff small-clothes, a white vest, and fine linen ruffled shirts, the hair in a queue, and the hat of beaver. A list of prices charged for tailor's work in 1816 mentions three dollars as the charge for making a gentleman's cloak, five-fifty for a surtout, two-seventy-five for hussars, three dollars for shirrivallies, two-fifty for short breeches, and five dollars for making a dragoon's coat. If mother did the sewing, as in most families at that time she did, the tailor would cut a man's coat for a dollar, and

The New State—1816

the waistcoat and pantaloons for thirty-seven and a half cents each.

The court-houses in those days were built of logs, and the sheriffs seem to have been selected as officials, on account of their fine voices to call the jurors and witnesses from the woods to the door of the court building, and their ability to run down and catch offenders. The condition under which justice was dispensed is reflected in the memory of a prosecuting attorney in the Third District. He says:

"We rode the circuit on horseback. There were no bridges over the streams, but we rode good swimming horses, and never faltered for high water, but plunged in and always found the opposite side somehow. The great variety of trials and incidents in the circuit gave to the life of a travelling attorney an interest that we all relished exceedingly. There was no dyspepsia, no gout, no ennui, no neuralgia. All was good humor, fine jokes well received, good appetites and sound sleeping, cheerful landlords and good-natured landladies at the head of the tables in the taverns. We rode first-class horses, costing from fifty to ninety dollars, the highest price. They were trained to travel on cross-pole and to swim the creeks."

The story of the change of capitals is a reflection of the development of the Territory from the French trading era through American settlement to a realization of future conditions, when the whole State should be inhabited. Vincennes was one of the oldest towns in the western part of the continent. We know it first as the French trading-post. The antiquity is not so great as the lack of written history. Judge Law claimed 1710 as the year of the building of the fort, and that Father Mermat was the first missionary, and was sent to the post in 1712. Mr. Myers has made most interesting researches into the subject, and Mr. Dunn, after a careful survey of all of the evidence obtainable, places the first foundation of a town in Indiana at the military post at Vincennes, about the year 1731. From the first it was included by the French Government in the Province of Louisiana; it was located on the east bank of the Wabash amidst broad prairies. As time went on, English-speaking people were added to the original French inhabitants, and when the American Congress granted Territorial government Vincennes was designated as the little capital, and the Legislature sat there until 1814. Governor William Henry Harrison had occupied this town as his official residence, while ruler of the Northwest Territory. The Vincennes University was granted a charter in 1807, and with it authority to raise by lottery twenty thousand dollars for its establishment and maintenance. In that time lotteries constituted a very prevalent way of raising funds with which to build churches and schools, to pave the streets, to construct turnpikes, and to buy fire-engines. When the Territorial Legislature was in session, in 1813, it passed a bill, much against the wishes of the old French town, removing the seat of Territorial government from Vincennes to the town of Corydon, in Harrison County, where the Assembly met the following December. One argument that was used for the necessity of this removal was the peril from hostile Indians on the border of the State, and the danger in which the archives might be found in case of an incursion! Madison, Salem, and other towns aspired to become the seat of government; the latter village threatened to take up the capital, and bear it off bodily! Madison offered one thousand

The New State—1816

dollars bonus to secure it! In the year 1820, after much heated discussion, and many objections from the southern section of the State, the General Assembly of Indiana appointed ten commissioners, from as many different counties, to select a site for the permanent seat of the State government. It was recognized that in time the capital must occupy a central location. This would make the proposed site come within what was then the wilderness, called the "New Purchase," a tract ceded by the Indians ten years before. It would also rule out any favoritism toward sections already occupied. The commission met at the house of William Conner, on the west fork of the White River, in May of the same year. That well-known citizen, General John Tipton, one of the commissioners, has left a journal, which is a circumstantial account, of great interest, describing the journey taken in the work of determining the exact location for the future permanent capital of Indiana. General Tipton had been a soldier in the battle of Tippecanoe, nine years before, and knew the territory that was to be traversed. It was he who purchased the land on which that battle was fought, where the soldiers, who fell in that conflict, were buried, and presented the historic field to the State. He was afterwards United States Senator. A few extracts from General Tipton's diary will give an idea of the frontier conditions which prevailed at that time where the new capital was to be founded. We reproduce it without corrections. He says:

"On Wednesday the 17 of May 1820 I set out from Corydon in Company with Gov'r Jennings. I had been appointed by the last legislature one of the commissioners to select & locate a site for the permanent seat of govern-

ment of the state of Ind'a (we took with us Bill a Black
Bouy) Haveing laid in plenty of Baker [bacon?] coffy &c
and provided a tent we stopt at B. Bells two hours then
set out and at 7 came to Mr. Winemans [?] on Blue River.
stopt for the K't [night] "thursday the 18th. "some
frost; set out early Stopt at Salem had breckfast paid
$1.00 B &c and Bo't some powder paper &c paid 2.12 ½
Set out at 11 crost Muscakituck paid 25 cts and stopt at
Col Durhams in Vallonia who was also a Commissioner
here we found Gen'l Bartholomew one of the commissioners
I cleaned out my gun after dinner we went to shooting"

"Sunday 21 set out at ½ p 4; at 5 passed a corner of
S 36 T 11 N of R 4 E passed a plaice where Bartholomew
and my self had encamped in June 1813 missed our way
traveled east then turned Back; at 8 stopt on a mudy
Branch Boiled our coffy set out at 9 or ½ p 9. I killed
a deer the first I have killed since 1814 at 10 came on the
traice at creek, found tree where I had wrote my name
and dated the 19th June 1813 we traveled fast and at 7
encamped on a small creek having traveled about 45
miles (horseback of course)

Monday, 22d

"a fine clier morning we set out at sunrise at ½ p 6 crost
fall creek at a ripple stopt to B [bathe?] shave put on
clean clothes &c this creek runs between 30 & forty miles
perrelled with White river and about 6 or 8 miles from
it in this creek we saw plenty of fine fish; set out at 9
and passed a corner of S 32 & 33 in T 17 N of R 4 E at 15
p 11 came to the lower Delaware Town crost the river
went up to the n w side and at once came to the house
of William Conner the place appointed for the meeting of
the commissioners he lives on a Prairie of about 250
acres of the White R bottom a number of Indian Huts
near his house: on our arrival we found G Hunt of Wayne
County John Conner of Fayette Stephen Ludlow of Dearborn John Gilliland of Switzerland & Thos Emmison
(Emerson) of Knox waiting us Wm Prince and F Rapp

not being up, we waited until late in the evening We then met and were sworn according to law and adjourned until tomorrow evening"

"Wednesday the 24th a dark morning. at 9 Gov'r Jennings with the other comr. came on us set out for the mouth of fall creek Last Kt I staid in an Indian town saw some drunk Indians this morning sat at the Table of a Frenchman who has long lived with the Indians and lives with them he furnished his table for us with eggs: altered times since 1813 when I was last there hunting the Indians with whom we now eat drink and sleep they have now sold their land for a trifle and prepareing to leave the country, where they have laid their fathers and relatives, in which we are now hunting a site for the seat of Govrt of our State."

After selecting a site near Fall Creek and having it surveyed, they started homeward, concluding the journal with this entry:

"Sunday the 11. Stopt at Major Arganbrites [?], had dinner, etc. At dark got safe home, having been absent 27 days, the compensation allowed us commisioners by the law being $2 for every 25 miles traveled to and from the place where we met, and $2 for each day's service while engaged in the discharge of our duty, my pay for the trip being $58—not half what I could have made in my office. A very poor compensation."[1]

The site selected was a heavily wooded miasmatic wilderness, sixty miles from nearest civilization, and at that time most inconveniently inland, so far as real navigation was to be had; and this remained the handicap of Indianapolis for a decade. Indian trails were the only paths to the place, and there

[1] Tipton, John, "Journal," published in vol. i., No. 2, p. 74, *Ind. Mag. of Hist.*, 1905.

were no accommodations upon arrival. There were few people in the village, and settlers were so slow to choose it as a place to live, that at the end of the time named, when the Legislature should actually sit in the new capital, it had only one thousand population. The jealousy felt by the other sections against the new seat of government was shown in many ways. In 1820, Brookville had been made headquarters for the entries of lands, for all the State northward of the Wabash. All purchasers must visit that village. For five years, the little town had enjoyed the prosperity and distinction of being the political and social centre of that part of the State. When the land office was moved to the new capital, the change was most bitterly opposed. In a pompous speech by one of the local celebrities, he referred to the little insignificant capital in the woods, as a place buried in miasmatic solitude and surrounded by a boundless contiguity of shade. There was much discussion about what the embryo capital should be called. Indian names seemed to be in the minds of all. "Tecumseh" was rejected, as too closely connected with past horrors, and "Suwarrow" was also dropped. Finally Indiana–polis was agreed upon, as combining a notion of the aborigines and a future metropolis.

The county was organized, and in 1821 Alexander Ralston and his assistants laid out the capital on the present beautiful lines. Ralston was a Scotchman of ability, and fortunately had seen Old World cities and had assisted in the work of surveying the city of Washington, which gave him the advantage of a broader view of the future requirements of a capital city than would have been supplied by a frontiersman. To this training, and the sense of space which the wilderness must have impressed on one, the city is indebted for its broad streets and liberal plan.

The lots were offered for sale to secure funds to build the State buildings, but few buyers came forward. The important business lots of the present day, on the corner of Washington and Delaware Streets, sold for $560.00, and others likewise. After ten years the authorities put the price at $10.00 for the lowest lot, and in 1842, they had closed the city out for $125,000.00! With this fund they built the State-house, Court-house, Governor's residence, Clerks' Office, and Treasurer's Office, which would not allow much margin for "graft," even in the crude architecture adopted for these State buildings. In November, 1824, Mr. Samuel Merrill, the Treasurer, brought the State papers and books from Corydon to the new capital in one wagon, with his family in another. The roads were so execrable at that season of the year that twelve miles and a half a day was all the distance they could cover. In January, 1825, the first Legislature met in Indianapolis, and the permanent capital was established. For several decades many other towns in the State, especially those on the rivers, were of more commercial importance, and more attractive socially, than Indianapolis. The meeting of the Legislature was the only event of interest; and it was twenty-two years before the first railroad made the town accessible.

In 1825, when General de La Fayette made a tour of America, he could not journey to the capital of the new State and Indiana's Governor went to Jeffersonville, on the Ohio River, to welcome the hero to Indiana soil. In the forest adjoining that village a feast was spread, to which the General was conducted by the State militia and children strewed flowers in his path. At the head of the long two-hundred-and-fifty-foot table, was an arch with the inscription, "Indiana welcomes La Fayette, the champion of liberty in both hemispheres."

After Indianapolis actually became the seat of government, the authorities being anxious to have the streets opened up, gave the magnificent timber, in what is now Washington Street, to the contractor for removing it. After the trees were felled, there were no mills to cut them up, and no demand for lumber, so the logs were rolled up in piles and burned, to the loss of the contractor and the regret of later generations. Great sugar groves occupied the ground where the Soldiers' Monument now stands, and where the State-house is situated. The first mail route was established in 1822 by popular subscription, and in the same year a newspaper appeared, as the forerunner of that brilliant series of journals which have since characterized the city. In the following year, a Union Sunday-School was started and the first of several Presbyterian Churches was organized a few months later. Said Henry Ward Beecher when pastor of one of them: "We have given Indianapolis a deep-blue Presbyterian tinge, which should last for several generations to keep her straight."

The first violators of the law in the village had to be sent sixty miles overland to Fayette County, to the nearest jail; and the earliest couples that were married went to the same county-seat to get a license. As there was no outlet to markets, corn sold for ten cents a bushel, butter from three to eight cents a pound, eggs for five cents a dozen, and chickens for sixty cents a dozen. Dr. W. H. Wishard said in an address on the medical men and the practice in the early day in that city:

The New State—1816

"Indianapolis was laid out in a dense forest with a heavy undergrowth of spice wood, prickly ash, weeds, and grapevines, that made it impossible, in many places, for a man to go through the forest on horseback. There was but one road open that might be called a highway. That was from Brookville. There was an Indian trail from Strawtown and Conner's Prairie to Vincennes. In 1821, there was not one well person in ten. Dr. Coe was the only physician able for duty. He could be seen at all hours of the day and night wending his way from cabin to cabin, through the most impenetrable forest; the owls hooting and the wolves serenading him in his lonely walk, and the rattlesnakes shaking their tails every few rods to notify him that they were on the warpath. This picture is not overdrawn. The sickness and fatality of that year brought Indianapolis into such disrepute that it discouraged emigration. As the doctors had to ride into the country ten or fifteen miles, it was no unusual thing for a doctor to get lost and have to spend the night in the saddle or up a sapling. Such nights were not the most pleasant. The music was varied between the panthers, wolves, owls, and raccoon fights."[1]

In this fashion the practice of medicine was followed in Indianapolis when the capital was moved to the town in 1824. In those times, the regular practitioners had the competition of certain old crones, who gathered herbs and simples in the right time of the moon, and administered this tea with weird and mysterious incantations, which the ignorant believed was working wonderful cures. There were no grist mills, and all the flour and meal must be carted a distance of sixty miles. The "cassimeres, bombazettes, dress shawls, cap-stuff, nankeen, and cambrick," that

[1] Wishard, Dr. W. H., *Address*, printed by State Medical Society of Indiana.

were advertised for my lady's Sunday apparel, were brought from Cincinnati in pack-saddles, when the roads were too bad for the professional teamsters to pass over the trail. Teaming was a calling in those days for the stout-hearted. They decorated their horses with bows over the hames, which were hung with bells to make music wherever they floundered. Twelve days from Cincinnati, and ten from Lawrenceburg, was the length of time required when the roads were at their best. Two dollars a hundredweight was the minimum charge, and it took four horses to pull the load even when the weather was fine.

But in time, fertile lands and official importance offset the lack of river transportation, and gradually an excellent class of settlers was attracted to central Indiana. Mr. Fletcher wrote back to a Virginia friend:

"I am much pleased with the inhabitants of this new purchase. We have none here but independent freeholders, and a much more enlightened set of people than any others I have seen in a western country. We have emancipators from Kentucky, who are a sober class, and we have the thrift of Ohio. Our laws and constitution are truly republican. All fines on military delinquents and for misdemeanors are appropriated to the use of the county seminaries in the State."[1]

Judge Banta told of one bully, who used to boast that he maintained one corner of Johnson County Seminary, by his fines for disturbing the peace. Through two decades, Indianapolis sought by the construction of turnpikes, the National road, and canals, to overcome the disadvantages of its inland location until railroads were introduced. After the Civil War, Indianapolis

[1] *Indiana Magazine of History*, vol. ii., 1906.

became the metropolis as well as the beautiful capital. In the last quarter of a century, she attained her present reputation for commercial, intellectual, and social leadership, as well as being the official centre of the State.

The new State was now steadily growing in population and wealth, in fact the population doubled between 1830 and 1841, but in 1832 there was a border war that startled the settlers and brought out the State militia and a large number of volunteers from Indiana. Black Hawk, the chief of the Sac Indians, with headquarters on Rock River in Illinois, had refused to submit peacefully to the banishment of the tribes west of the Mississippi. He was a cunning and skilful leader and rallied the Fox and Sac tribes into armed resistance. The northwestern part of Indiana was but sparsely settled at that time. The lonely homes that dotted the prairies, west and north of the Wabash River, were still exposed to attack from any band of Indians that might steal upon them from northern Illinois. The Pottawatomie and Miami tribes were still on their reservations, on the Mississinewa River. In May, 1832, the Governor of Illinois had called his troops to arms; and the news came that several persons had been murdered on Hickory Creek, and that the hostile Indians were infesting the country around Chicago. The counties along the Wabash hastily assembled bands of volunteers, and rode forth to defend the outlying borders. Scouts ranged over the country in every direction, hunting for detached bands of savages. The settlers on the border, from Vincennes to La Porte, flocked into the villages and camped around the towns for protection. The scattered people in the outlying counties gathered into the fort and blockhouses, in terror of the scalping invaders. Many false reports further terrified the poor squatters: at one time it would be that the Miamis were rising; at another that the Indians, a thousand strong, were crossing Nine-Mile Prairie killing as they went; again word would come in from Sugar River that the whoop of the invaders was ringing through the forest there. Meanwhile the Illinois troops fought several fierce engagements and were driving the savages from their State towards Wisconsin. On the second of August Black Hawk was overtaken, his troops defeated, and he foiled in his desperate plans. The chief was made a prisoner; which terminated the horrors of that short but savage war. Indiana was not invaded; the troops she raised were not needed, but there was every reason for the terrors of the settlers and the prompt response of the volunteers. The people throughout that region were familiar with danger from experience not long past. The bloody tragedies enacted in the earlier settlements were fresh in their memories. There were but few families then residing in the State who had not lost some of their number by the hostile Indians.

Col. Cockrum tells a droll story of this war, illustrative of the courage of pioneer women. The head of a family, living west of Lafayette, in great affright, gathered up his children in a cart, and, driving up to the door, was amazed to find that his wife had no intention of running from the savages on hearsay of danger. She told him that if he wished to go he might, but that when he recovered from his scare he would find her and the baby at the same old cabin. Bidding her a final, affectionate farewell, he still insisted on her going with him. "No," she said; "take the children and go. If I never see you again, I shall die with the satisfaction of knowing that I had a husband who thought too much of his scalp to permit any Indian to have his black glossy locks as an ornament to his helmet." The husband and children remained away a few days, and no Indians materializing, he returned and found Bowser and Tige barking a welcome. Upon going into the cabin, they were welcomed by the courageous wife, who had one foot on the rocker and the other on the treadle of the spinning-wheel, while both hands were busy with the distaff. Looking around the house, the brave man espied a fine wild gobbler ready for dinner and a fresh coon-skin hanging on the wall. With beautiful consistency he exclaimed: "Mandy, why in thunderation have you been so free in using my powder?" She composedly replied: "Never mind, Ebenezer, there is plenty left. If you hear of an Indian crossing the Mississippi River, you wont need it, for you'll be on the go to Lafayette again."

In the beginning of Indiana's history as a separate commonwealth there was no State currency in circulation. Barter was universal. The only specie ever seen was the British and Spanish silver coinage. There were no gold coins in circulation in this section of the country until after the discovery of gold mines in California. For small change, Spanish dollars were cut into quarters, eighths, and sixteenths. These were called "bits," "two-bits," and "fo-pence" pieces. A fip was equal to five cents, you often heard an article priced at a "fip-and-a-bit.' The government demanded cash payments for lands, but aside from this purchase only salt, hardware, and a few such imported commodities brought actual money; all else was trade in the West.

The first constitution of Indiana had tried to safeguard the currency of the future; but financial troubles began before the organization of the State, with the volume of Ohio bank-notes, which were disbursed by the General Government during the War of 1812-14. The Territorial bank which had been chartered at Vincennes was made a State institution in 1817, with branches at Corydon, Brookfield, Vevay, and Madison. This little chain of banks began well, and would have been a great financial blessing to the new country had they not drifted into reckless ways. Soon they contracted debts to an amount double that of their deposits, embezzled large sums from those deposits, and, issuing currency beyond all possible means in their power of redemption, brought ruin upon themselves and thousands of people. This heedless pace caused them to forfeit their charter in 1821. The one at Madison was more honestly managed, and eventually redeemed its notes. So serious was the condition of affairs that it became necessary for the Federal Government to reduce the price of entry lands from two dollars to a dollar and a quarter per acre, to cancel its claims to interest, and permit a re-arrangement of smaller holdings, clear of debt, for the larger tracts then in the possession of settlers. At this time the demand for the produce of the West had fallen off, three years of devastating sickness prevailed in the section, and the new State passed through a period of the deepest gloom, followed by fairer sailing and better times. A determination to overcome the lack of transportation facilities originated the system of internal improvements, which was inaugurated in 1832, and prosecuted during the years immediately following. Again there was a season of prosperity. As the public works progressed, and the amount of money in circulation increased from the dispersion of United States Bank funds, the population of the State and nation plunged into an orgy of land speculation on credit. They based the prospect of immediate increase of values on the usefulness of the coming canals and roads. The contractors brought disaster by paying the laborers, very largely, in the fiat money just then being issued by Michigan, which would not pass current in the seaboard centres of trade, where the merchant must meet his obligations. In 1832, President Jackson had abolished the United States Bank and the people of Indiana had begun to agitate the pressing need of some provision by the State for a safe currency. After conservatively adjusting their differences of opinion, the charter of 1834 was granted for the State Bank of Indiana. This bank with its centre at the capital and thirteen branches in the larger towns, was established on sound principles, and throughout its history was so well conducted on conservative lines, that it remained a model for other States, and was a safe institution during the life of its charter, which expired in 1857. It was this institution that was required to hold every branch thereof mutually responsible for all of the debts and engagements of each other. In case of failure the debts of an insolvent branch must be paid by the others, in proportion. As each branch was represented on the general board it insured unremitting vigilance, and a close watch being kept on the departments by all of the others. The board of control had unlimited authority over all of the branches. It was devised by the founders that the accumulated profits were to be turned over to the school fund, at the termination of the charter, which resulted in netting three million dollars to the permanent endowment of the public school system. There were many far-sighted provisions in the law founding this bank, which insured to the people a safe place of deposit and the advantage of a sound currency for twenty years. The conservative management and high moral standard of the men in control of the institution assured the great success which it enjoyed, and distinguished it from other State banks of that time. It outrode the panic of 1837, and the financial difficulties which stranded the treasury of the State on the shoals of no more credit for public improvements.

National and foreign credit was at this time exhausted, as well as that of the Western States. To assist the treasury of Indiana, the Legislature of 1839 authorized the issue of State scrip to the amount of a million and a half dollars; and private individuals, also disdaining the lessons of history, proceeded to try for themselves the experiment of manufacturing money by the printing-press, regardless of any specie basis. Not only were the State treasury notes floated as currency, but shop-keepers, packers, and traders issued bills in payment for debts. When all of their fictitious values were depreciated, the State money came to be known as "Red Dog," from the paper on which it was printed; and the plank-road scrip was called in derision "Blue Pup." It seems strange that so few saw that ruin was inevitable. This currency was soon worthless, business was prostrated, and values destroyed.

The successful State Bank was a monopoly. As the years passed, others grew envious of its prosperity and wanted like opportunities. The discontented element secured a clause in the new constitution of 1851 empowering the Legislature to grant new charters. A free banking law was the result. This statute opened the door for another season of disaster. Banks of issue sprang up everywhere on hilltops, on a stump, anywhere that a man chose to issue currency. These firms made no pretension to be banks of deposit, their only business being to issue and float notes. "A few men would get together, purchase a few thousand dollars worth of the depreciated bonds of some far-away municipality, deposit them with the auditor of State, and receive authority to enter upon the manufacture of paper money." They would issue bills, to an amount two or three times greater than the value of the securities deposited, put them in circulation, and then the bank, the officers, and the directors would disappear and the notes be worthless. Forty-eight hours was too long a time to pass, without a decision whether the money you had received was worth fifty cents or a dollar. Many of these free banks started on their career with no more actual capital than was expended on the engraving of their currency notes, and desk room in an office. Mr. McCulloch says, "Their life was pleasant and short; their demise ruinous and shameful. As soon as their notes began to be presented for payment they died without a struggle."[1] The panic of 1857 put an end to the inglorious existence of the fraudulent concerns. The exploit of basing a currency on nothing and floating it in the air was never more wildly attempted than at this time in Indiana. No doubt it was the experience of this debased money that made the State spurn the free silver doctrine a half century later.

As the time approached for the expiration of the

[1] McCulloch, Hugh, *Men and Measures of Half a Century*, page 126. New York, 1888.

charter of the reliable State Bank, and the citizens realized the necessity of a safe currency, a group of influential men united in a quiet movement to secure a charter from the Legislature of 1855 for the Bank of Indiana. After obtaining this valuable franchise they sold to the old organizations the permit for the districts where they were so honorably established and new ones were organized for other sections. This institution was guided into a safe and honorable career by its first president, the Hon. Hugh McCulloch. It weathered the financial storm of '59 in great credit. At a time when old established banks in New York and everywhere were obliged to suspend, and private institutions went to the wall by the score, the Bank of Indiana redeemed its obligations in specie without interruption. This institution went into liquidation when the tax was increased on other notes than those of national banks, and most of the branches reorganized under the Federal statute. No safer banking laws could be found anywhere than the statutes of this State thereafter, the savings banks being modelled for the benefit of depositors, and to induce frugality. The securities allowed are based on real estate, the improvements are not included in the valuations.

The new constitution was adopted by Indiana in the fifties to replace the one formulated for primitive times, when it was not so queer to have the Legislature regulate local and even personal affairs. Under the old law, the granting of divorces, electing part of the State officers, abolishing county offices, and creating new ones, and the granting of charters for the incorporating of railroads and business concerns, whereby abuses crept in and legislators were corrupted, were all in the hands of the legislative body! In the new constitution this was corrected. A reminder of the old contention in Indiana, regarding negroes, was incorporated in the later organic law, when it was provided that no negro or mulatto should have the right of suffrage, and furthermore that they should not come into, or settle in the State. Even after the Civil War was over, when the fifteenth amendment to the Federal Constitution was submitted to the Legislature, the Democratic members all resigned, rather than ratify it; and upon the newly elected ones also tendering their resignations, the amendment was declared passed by a Republican speaker ruling that a quorum was present, by counting the Democrats as present and not voting. In the next session, when the Democrats attempted to rescind the action of the preceding assembly, the Republican members prevented its repeal by resigning.

After the adoption of the new constitution, Indiana may be said to have passed from the pioneer period of her history. By the progressive measures adopted then and by the school legislation which followed, by the improved means of transportation, which gradually ensued upon the introduction of railroads, her future was assured. The increase of population has been uninterrupted, and the accessions have been a desirable class. Fifteen counties have had no emigrants from foreign countries in late years. The manufacturing centres and the mining regions have had many, but they are industrious. The foreigners, who came into the State two or three decades ago, have become assimilated with the general population, and have contributed to the sum of good citizenship within the State. The future status of Indiana must depend upon the quality of the representatives that she sends to the State Legislature.

CHAPTER IX

EARLY CHURCHES IN INDIANA

IN fancy we may picture the long procession of churchgoers, during the different decades of history in Indiana, as they are reflected in the mirror of the past.

In the very beginning, we see the zealous French priest, arrayed in his long black robes, holding a crucifix aloft, as he stands in the little log chapel, attached to the military post, and blesses his wildwoods parishioners. It is a saint's day. The Jesuit father has come hundreds of miles in his canoe to instruct and absolve the sins of the little isolated flock. Filing into his presence, we see the motley throng that lives within the stockade. First comes the haughty commandant in the full uniform of Louis of France, attended by a detachment of soldiers in their blue coats with white facings, and short clothes. Following them come the peasants wearing the long, coarse blue surtout, red sash, and cap, of their native land, and the deerskin moccasins which they have adopted from the Indian. With them come the women in short skirts and bodice, wearing the peasant's cap, and the ribbons, ornaments, and beads, brought by some admiring boatman, upon his return from far-off Canada. The reckless *coureurs de bois*, dressed in fringed buckskin and embroideries, with a knife in the belt, lounge in with the half-breeds. Following these are the taciturn savages, from the forests round about. With great satisfaction in the forgiveness of all their misdeeds, the assembly kneels on the floor of the rude chapel, counts its beads, and gains absolution. After the benediction, and making the sign of the cross from the font, they pass out into the sunshine; and the happiness of a volatile pleasure-loving people is theirs, as they spend the rest of the day, gaily dancing upon the green.

Before these scenes have passed away, the Anglo-Saxon race has straggled into the wilderness. In one of their own cabin homes, or in summer, in the groves, which were God's first temples on the frontier, the scattered settlers gather for worship. It might be said to hear preaching, for the service is wholly unlike the Canadian Frenchman's at the post. In buckskin and homespun these settlers came together during two whole generations. The backwoods preacher who travelled far and wide on horseback, and ministered unto the scattered settlements, was as the faithful "voice of one crying in the wilderness, prepare ye the way of the Lord." During long weeks between their visitations, there was no observance of the Sabbath, except where a godly father or mother took down the old Bible, and read aloud to the family. In a wide country, with large districts, sparsely populated, there were comparatively few stationary ministers; but there were many, embracing all denominations, who traversed the whole country. They formed an itinerant corps, who visited in rotation, within their respective bounds every settlement, town, and village. Living remote from each other as the people then did, and spending much of their time, in domestic solitude in vast forests, or widespreading prairies, the "Appointment" for preaching was often looked upon as a gala day.

In organization, Charleston, on Silver Creek, claims that the first Protestant Church was organized there, in November, 1798. It was a Baptist Church, and had a struggle for existence. The first Methodist Church organized, is dated in 1803, and the Presbyterian in 1806. Whether Methodists or Baptists were the first to enter on evangelistic work in Indiana, matters not. People belonging to both denominations came early, and their travelling preachers came with them. These hardy, zealous, earnest men built their own cabins and then began their spiritual ministrations throughout the thinly scattered population.

The Baptists were much hampered in their progress, at first, because of the large number, of what was then known, as "Hard-shell Baptists." This sect was a nonprogressive people who were against all missionary efforts, because of their belief that all who were predestined to be saved, would be saved, without any missionaries. The Missionary Baptists were a live progressive body, and were independents in organization. They were a revolt from tradition and church authority back to the Bible—the Bible only. Their pioneer preachers were noted for their simple eloquence and the democratic methods of their teaching. The Methodist preachers of that early time were unconventional, candid, brusque, emotional speakers, and were picturesque and rugged characters. It is said that Rev. Asbury, during a long ministry, rode a distance that would have taken him twelve times around the world. No doubt Peter Cartwright and several other faithful exhorters on the Wabash could score as many leagues in their ministrations.

Alexander Campbell made a great impression on the people of many sections of Indiana. The sect he founded, especially at the capital, is still large and has an educational institution of prominence, originated by its membership.

Owing to their disapproval of slavery, many of the early settlers from the Carolinas, who came into the free State of Indiana, were Quakers. Wherever this peace-loving people formed a settlement, they immediately established a "meeting", and at the same time, a school for the instruction of their youth. The southeastern part of the State, particularly, felt the high moral influence of the Society of Friends, in the development of social conditions. Their churches and schools were a controlling, repressing, quieting, elevating influence, over the boisterous element of the frontier. The numberless teachers supplied by this sect extended this influence, and made known the tenets of freedom, sobriety, education, and a simple living, held with such tenacity by that congregation. The Presbyterians instituted, from the first, a centralized system of organization, and held to a rigorous theology. They maintained an educated ministry, and located their little churches in the towns, instead of in the country. This gave them a prestige, from the very first. There were many educated persons in their membership and little sensationalism in their service, or preaching, to attract the multitude. The schools this denomination established were among the most enduring influences of the new State.

Of the faithful men who ministered unto the border people, too much cannot be said in praise. A writer of forty years ago quaintly said that a decidedly religious stamp was given to Indiana character by the preachers of an early day. They were often men of intellect, as well as of zeal. They found their way to the backwoods, and preached Christ from a cabin door, or from the shade of a spreading tree, to the sunburned men and women gathered from the region round about. It was thanks to these fervid laborers, that the little church was erected, as soon as the log cabin afforded the shelter of a home. The contemptuous application of "North C'lina church" was applied to men of notoriously worldly or otherwise wicked character.

The trials and privations of the earlier preachers, if told to-day, would be beyond belief. Isaac McCoy and his wife, who spent their lives as missionaries to the Indians, labored the whole time in direst poverty, utter isolation, constant danger, failing health, and great privation, before rest came in death. He wrote that he did not know what to do about taking his fourteen-year-old daughter into the wilderness, away from all educational advantages; but that the Lord solved the problem by suddenly taking her to himself. The women in these families were left alone in their solitary cabins, when the minister went off on his long itinerary. Sickness, raids of savages, wild beasts were the dangers they had to face, while the minister travelled the circuit. Most of the ministers cleared, and cultivated their own homesteads and supported their families by other labor, at the same time ministering unto the people, on the Sabbath day. Indeed in the very earliest days, a man was held in scorn who did not labor with his hands.

There have always been men, in every locality, who were independent in their thinking, and identified with no church. One of the earliest settlers of Indiana, born in 1781, left the following record of his religious views, written in his seventy-third year.

"As to religion: 'Happy is he, the only man, who, from *choice*, does all the good he can.' The world is my country, and my religion is to do right. I am a firm believer in the Christian religion, though not as lived up to by most of its professors of the present day. In the language of Jefferson, I look upon the 'Christian Philosophy, as the most sublime and benevolent, but most perverted system that ever shone on man.' I have no use for the priesthood, nor can I abide the shackles of sectarian dogmas. I see no necessity for confession of faith, creeds, forms, and ceremony. In the most comprehensive sense of the word, I am opposed to all wars, and to slavery; and trust the time is not far distant when they will be numbered among the things that were, and viewed as we now look back upon some of the doings of what we are pleased to style the dark ages." [1]

To an Orthodox woman who thought a soul lost that did not belong to a church, an old pioneer—in fact the first Lieutenant-Governor of Indiana—answered, "God is love. Love never lost anything. It is infinitely tender, and infinitely forgiving."

In Indiana, as elsewhere in America, the freedom of thought and independence of character, fostered by frontier life and an absence of ecclesiastical control, occasioned the rise of many religious sects. Some of these have entirely disappeared from the theological horizon. Their very names would have no significance now. There was a great variety of opinions on minor subjects, even in the earliest times and this occasioned

---

[1] Anonymous, *Reminiscences*.

the scores of denominations. In an address by a citizen of Indianapolis, delivered in the fifties, it was proudly claimed that there were twenty thousand inhabitants, and behold the spires of her twenty-seven churches, of the different denominations of Christians, shooting upward toward the clouds! Rev. Nathaniel Richmond wrote from a little hamlet in central Indiana in 1843: "There are two kinds of Methodists, two of Quakers, and two kinds of Presbyterian Churches here. And all of the talk is of 'means and anti-means.' The Baptists are mostly anti-mission. Dr. Dollinger exclaimed, 'How can I live in a country where they found a new church every day!'"

The sermons in those days were one, two, or three hours long. Reading sermons was not tolerated on the frontier. The minister must speak extemporaneously, and with fire and zeal. The preaching, as well as the discussions of laymen, was largely doctrinal and controversial as was the custom of the times, elsewhere.

Series of debates between noted preachers were held, and people went miles to the "meeting"—doubtless as much to hear the discussion as for worship. They debated on such points as free-will *versus* predestination, falling from grace *versus* the final perseverance of the saints, good works *versus* justification by faith, immersion *versus* sprinkling, and election *versus* free grace. Good men believed these subjects vital, and the certain terrors of hell were imminent, for those who did not settle the question. It was the vividness of this impending danger, which wrought up the otherwise grave and unexcitable people, to such strong, emotional excitement. The differences of opinion were dwelt upon and this held the people apart.

It was said in jest, that the only difference between the new school and old school of one denomination was that one stood up, and the other sat down when they prayed in church. Sects sprang up, named for their founders who started the agitation. Alexander Campbell won thousands of followers, and then another branch had New Light. An estimate given by an old timer, of the preachers to whom he listened, in his youth, gives an excellent idea of the type of men who were then acceptable to the ministry. Of one he says:

"He was the Napoleon of the Methodist preachers of eastern Indiana, I knew him well. He seemed to be made for the very work in which he was engaged. He had a good person, a strong physical formation, expanded lungs, a clear and powerful voice, reaching to the verge of the camp-ground, the eye of the eagle; and his talents as a preacher were of a very high order. I never heard but one man that was like him in his meridian days. He could feed his babes with the 'milk of the Word' and hurl the terrors of the law at old sinners." [1]

The itinerant preacher riding up to the cabin, and "hallooing the house" to see if any one was at home and unloading his saddle-bags to stop for the night, was a welcome occurrence on the frontier. In the isolation of the wilderness the settlers longed for companionship, and as the minister was the most considerable personage of the community, he was always sure of a warm welcome and a good chicken-dinner. These men were representative of the muscular Christianity required on the frontier and were a part of what Mr. Nicholson has termed, that vigorous Protestant evangelization of Indiana, which triumphed

[1] Smith, Oliver H. *Early Trials*, page 264. Cin., 1858.

over mud and malaria, and carried the gospel far beyond the sound of church bells. There were many union churches formed on the frontier, when there were few of each denomination in a neighborhood. Differences of opinion were tenaciously held in those days, and the various sects in the congregation would soon arrange to hold services of their own on alternating Sundays. "Once a month" preaching, or four churches to each minister, was the rule, in all the struggling communities. Congregational singing was universal in the early churches. Often there was a choir to lead, but there were no organs. Indeed, the innovation of an organ or fiddle being introduced has repeatedly been the occasion of churches dividing. There were few hymn-books; the minister "lined off" the hymns, the leader gave the pitch from his tuning fork, and all joined in with enthusiasm and fervor, seldom heard in these days of paid choirs. Hearts were uplifted in singing the old hymns, and their spiritual effect was as great as that of the sermon. In those days, there was a holy awe of the terrors and punishments awaiting the unconverted. The consequent spiritual exaltation, and fervor of those who hoped they had escaped these terrors by the grace of God, was as extremely emotional. From the scarcity of buildings, there grew up the custom of holding camp-meetings in the beautiful forests. An old annalist gave the following quaint account of the first of these meetings held during the years 1799 and 1801. A vast concourse of people assembled under the foliage of the trees, and continued their religious exercise day and night. This novel way of worship excited great attention. In the night, the grove was illuminated with lighted candles, lamps, or torches. This, together with the stillness of the night, the solemnity which rested on every countenance, the pointed and earnest manner with which the preachers exhorted the people to repentance, prayer, and faith, produced the most awful sensations in the minds of all present. At these gatherings, the people fell under the power of the Word "like corn before a storm of wind"; many thus affected arising from the dust with divine glory beaming upon their countenances gave utterance to strains of ecstatic gratitude.

Few escaped without being affected. Such as tried to run away from it were frequently struck on the way, or impelled by some alarming signal to return. Great numbers fell unconscious, and remained so for hours. To prevent their being trodden under foot by the multitude, they were collected together and laid out in order, where they remained in charge of friends, until they should pass through the strange phenomena of their conversion. In consequence of such vast assemblages of people, it was impossible for one person to address them, hence they were divided into groups. At times the whole grove resounded with the praise of God, and at other times was pierced with the cries of distressed penitents. The number that "fell" at some of these meetings in trance or ecstasy of excitement reached the number of three thousand! This form of religious meeting was found in every Western State.

About 1843 there arose a religious frenzy over the immediate second advent of Christ, which swept over the country, and made a distinct impression on certain temperaments in Indiana. The belief in the speedy return of Christ for a glorious reign on earth has always elicited enthusiasm, and in the early part of the nineteenth century, in New England, William Miller became the founder of a sect holding peculiar views on the subject of the millennium. His followers increased until there were over 50,000 people in America and England who had embraced his hopes. The Millerites believed that their leader had found out the meaning of Daniel's incomprehensible prophecies; that he had worked out like a sum in arithmetic, the exact day when the end of the world was to come, and that was in August, 1843. They became fanatically responsive to the exhortation to be ready for the immediate Judgment Day, and thought the clergy inconsistent, who professed to believe in prophecy and yet discarded this revelation. These teachings had spread over the East, and made their way as far as the Western frontier.

The fierce polemical discussions and the conclusive sectarianism of that day had taught the people anything but the "modesty of true science," and we are told by the people who were living at that time, that the unsolvable problems of the centuries were taken out of the hands of puzzled scholars, and settled summarily and positively by the imaginative laymen.

Many persons in various parts of the country had become such fanatics that they had sold or given away their lands and possessions, in awestruck anticipation of the immediate end of all things; also as a testimony to their belief. Shrewd sharpers played upon credulity and bought up for a small pittance the property of the deluded. This happened in various localities east and west. Later, when the catastrophe did not take place, there were many lawsuits and lifelong feuds over property so disposed of. We are told by old citizens who remember this wave of fanaticism, that trade took up the craze. One enterprising manufacturer had table covers of oil-cloth, printed, on which was a design of a wheel displaying all these figures of Daniel's prophecies. They were eagerly bought by the deluded followers, and were used long after the failure of the millennium to appear; and the ascension robes did duty as frocks for festival occasions. After months of preaching and exhortation to be ready for the end, the religious excitement reached its culmination as the tenth and eleventh of August came on. Some made ascension robes. Work was suspended everywhere. The people who did not believe in the new cult, felt sorry for the frenzy of the deluded ones and wished the time were passed.

A witness of the scene said that the sun on the eleventh of August rose gloriously. People pointed to it with trembling and said it would rise no more. Men said: "Behold the beginning of the fervent heat that shall melt the elements." Night grew on, and every "shooting star" was a new sign of the end. In their different neighborhoods the people assembled out of doors to await the coming. They sang hymns, exhorted each other, shouted with excitement, some fainted from sheer terror, and some nervous temperaments lost their reason during the strain of the last hours. In many districts the torrid summer heat was broken by violent thunder-storms, which added to the agitation and terror of the excited multitudes. The lightning flashed, and the rain poured down in torrents on the kneeling congregations.

When the tragical night had passed, without the day of judgment being ushered in, and the clear fresh morning dawned, cool and refreshed by the rains, it found the credulous people dazed and exhausted.

The reaction, was, in many ways, disastrous to belief and morals.

Early settlers from the Atlantic States, had never known of Sunday-schools, and brought no plans with them for such services. Indeed many church members in Eastern cities at that time would not permit their children to attend the "new fangled" Sabbath-schools. The little children sat, or slept, through three-hour sermons, and that was the limit of their Sabbath-day diversions. In Indiana, as elsewhere, when Sunday-schools were inaugurated they were used to instruct children and adults, how to read; and many an ignorant pioneer youth has learned his letters from Watts's *Hymns* or the Bible. One of the verses committed to memory by the children of those days will give an idea of the cheerful character of the theology taught:

> "Why should I love my sports so well,
>   So constant at my play,
> And lose the thoughts of heaven and hell;
>   And then forget to pray?"

From *Historical Sketches of Sunday-school Work* by Wm. H. Levering, who spent his life in the work, and sixty years of that time laboring in the Indiana field, we learn the following facts regarding Sabbath-schools in Indiana:

"While much has been done and written about the early churches yet almost no mention was made of Sunday-schools. This was owing to the fact that there were but a few or none; for be it known that prior to a half a century ago, Sunday-schools were in disfavor with a large number of the churches. The writer well remembers that in his earliest experiences the churches gave a cold shoulder to Sunday-Schools, faithful women persisted in maintaining them, and in time, when their great value as a 'nursery of the church' was forced upon the attention of the ruling members the church opened its heart and its doors."[1]

In the year 1828, a young Christian missionary came from Connecticut to Washington in Daviess County, Indiana, the Reverend Ransom Hawley, and much of his earliest efforts and time were devoted to organizing and building up Sunday-schools in Washington, and its vicinity. The houses of worship were cold, and many of these country schools could not be kept open in the winter months. Mr. Hawley has recorded that

"some who commenced with the alphabet can now read. Those who religiously instruct their offspring have found Sabbath-schools not interfering with their rights, but an auxiliary in bringing up their children in the nurture and admonition of the Lord."

This old memorandum reminds us of two facts regarding the changes since the Sabbath-school movement began. Now spelling lessons are no longer necessary, and to-day, perhaps, the Bible training is largely from the Sunday-school, instead of at the mother's knee. Committing verses of Scripture to memory was a marked feature of the teaching in those days. Whole books of the Bible were recited each Sabbath. Great familiarity with the text of Holy Writ was acquired and remained in the memory.

[1] Levering, Wm. H., Pamphlet, *Historical Sketches.* La Fayette, 1906.

Reverend Hawley adds:

"At first our books were the New Testament and Watts's *Psalms and Hymns*. On August 7, 1829, we sent $40.37½ to New Albany for books. These were library books published by the American Sunday-school Union, and spelling books published by the same society. All of these schools were conducted on Union principles—that is all denominations participating. I do not know of any other kind of schools until after 1840. My journeying in preaching was done mostly on horseback, and I have ridden thus more than 90,000 miles. One, Reverend Isaac Reed, Presbyterian missionary, arrived in New Albany in 1818 and there organized the first Sunday-school in Indiana."

After two previous short-lived attempts, a permanent organization of the State Sabbath-school forces was accomplished in 1865 and is still flourishing under the name of the Indiana State Sunday-school Union. The last statistics that he records gives the number of Sabbath-schools in the State as 5617; officers and teachers, 45,600; scholars, 515,568. Mr. Levering was nine times elected president of this State union. As in other States the Sabbath-schools of Indiana now may truly be called the Church at work.

In the temperance work, the early churches took little part; but their good membership formed various organizations for the control of the liquor traffic and the persuasion of the intemperate. The first temperance paper published in the West is credited to an Indiana man. John W. Osborne, a worthy citizen of Greencastle began issuing the *Temperance Advocate*, in 1834; and for many years he sent out this sheet at his own expense. There have been many temperance organizations of Christian people since then and the sentiment against general drinking is very different from pioneer times.

The student of the early history of the Western States will find in the reminiscences of old settlers no more interesting chapters than their recollections of the pioneer churches and their ministers. Into the fruits of their ardent labors, the present generations have entered; their memories are a heritage. Here, the subject may only be brought in as one of the influences in the development of the State. Indiana's obligation to these influences cannot be calculated. The present and future generations can scarcely measure their indebtedness to those devoted Christian forefathers. A record of their labors in their various neighborhoods would be an invaluable addition to the archives of the Commonwealth. It is scarcely possible that an acquaintance with the greatly good, an intimate knowledge of their unpretending heroism, a sympathy with their unselfish sorrows and their lofty joys will not refine and elevate our lives.

CHAPTER X

CRIMES OF THE BORDER

IN common with all other frontiers, Indiana had grave tales of outlawry and crime in the early days. The reprisals on the Spanish traders of the river towns and the confiscation of their goods were among the earliest depredations that occurred after the Americans were responsible for the Territory. In their anger over the closing of navigation on the Mississippi River, the settlers would become completely exasperated over the embargo and confiscation of their goods. In this temper, they would form bands of raiders and seize every boatload of commerce, on the small rivers, belonging to Spanish boatmen. They would also appropriate every vestige of merchandise owned by Spanish merchants in the towns on the shore. These forays would be followed by appeals to the Spanish Governor at New Orleans, and the whole matter of reprisals and open navigation would be carried on up to Madrid. These international squabbles on the frontier made stirring times in Indiana Territory. The Indian warfare is recounted in the story of the Territorial period. We come now, upon the consequences of that warfare. The very license and necessity of carrying deadly weapons for defence against the savages made the people familiar with arms and bloodshed. Every pioneer carried a rifle, a knife, and a tomahawk or axe, when he was laboring. The members of the organized militia were required by law to attend church in full fighting trim, to be ready for any surprise by the Indians. From these customs, it came about that, in any sudden heat of passion or enmity, assault was pretty sure to follow an encounter. It is also necessary to remember that some of the frontier people had come from the rougher border element of the Southern mountains. While having their own code of honor, which governed their fights, they were essentially a rude, boisterous, drinking, fighting class of people. They were always a source of displeasure and offence to the much larger class of law-abiding citizens. When they gathered, as was their custom, on Saturday afternoon or on muster day, and whiskey had circulated freely, the causes for which they might take umbrage increased hourly. During the homeward ride, on horseback, the road was one wild "halloo" of racing and banter, often ending in a free-for-all fight. They had an unwritten code which required that "all fights must be fit fairly"; and when the "under dog cried 'nuff'" the striking, gouging, kicking, and hair-pulling contest must be acknowledged settled, at least for that time. Much of this fighting was pure banter, without any quarrel to start the fray. Mr. Parker recalls the fact that differences of opinion were not even necessary. Neat clothing, correct speech, and gentlemanly bearing were often a sufficient provocation; or a bully might choose to "Renown it" by drawing a circle about himself, and defying any one to enter the space, claiming that he could "whup". the whole town.

Political strife in hotly contested campaigns sometimes called into use the handy weapons that were worn for defence. And so through all the experiences of the border there crept in lawless deeds among the hardy frontiersmen. It is not only of these encounters, but of organized bands of freebooters, horse-thieves, counterfeiters, kidnappers, and the excesses of the bands of Regulators, that sensational stories were told by old settlers.

Shortly after the War of 1812, before steamboats were in use on the rivers of Indiana, there was a class of bargemen who used to loaf about the landings. They were a hardy, roistering, fearless set of fellows, and none of them more muscular or more daring than one Mike Fink. With his drinking, laborious, sturdy crew, he spent much of his time, when the river was low, in the towns along the Ohio. Mike and a friend named Carpenter used to practise rifle-shooting, by filling a tin-cup with whiskey, placing it, in turn, on each other's head, and shooting at it at the distance of seventy yards. It was always pierced, without injury to the one on whose head it was placed. After showing their confidence in each other in this way for a number of years, they quarrelled over an Indian squaw, and henceforth there was smothered hate. Later they pretended to "make up and call it off with a drink." To show that peace was declared they were to shoot for the cup, as of yore. Bequeathing his trusty rifle, shot-pouch, powder-horn, and wages to a friend, Carpenter took his position with the cup of whiskey on his head. Mike loaded, picked the flint, drew a bead, and called out: "Hold your noddle steady; don't spill the whiskey—I shall want some presently." Cocking his rifle again he took aim, and his foe fell, shot in the centre of the forehead. The law was too uncertain, and Fink was "removed" by a friend of the murdered man. He also went unpunished. Mike Fink was once convicted for shooting off a negro's heel as he was standing on the wharf. He gave as his justification, that the darky's heel projected too far behind, preventing him from wearing a genteel boot, and he wished to correct the defect. Such marksmen as these used to pride themselves on "barking a squirrel"—that is shooting so close to it, without scratching it, that the animal was killed by concussion. They were fond of snuffing a candle, at fifty yards, for the drinks.

As horses were the most necessary possession of the new settler, the loss of an animal meant great hardship and was desperately resented. Until the middle of the last century, farmers in the outlying districts suffered from the depredations of horse-thieves. They were the boldest of all the marauders of the border. They often went in gangs, rode away with the best horses in the neighborhood, and divided the plunder among them. Stringent laws were passed for their punishment. The code was, that a man who was guilty of stealing a horse should be whipped fifty to one hundred lashes; for a second offence, hanging was the penalty. Receiving stolen horses was a crime punishable by death. Very often the thief was whipped, and then drummed out of the country.

In the earliest time, when courts were few and distant, the people often took the law into their own hands, and were regularly organized into "Regulators." These bands hunted down marauders. They also often held court, very informally, for flagrant misdemeanors, and Judge Lynch executed sentence. The lash was considered very efficacious in 1816, and was the punishment imposed by law universally. Twenty strokes were given and a fine of five dollars was added for altering bounds. For manslaughter, a man was branded in the hand with the letters M. S.

Prompt measures often checked further disturbance to the settlers. A story is told of a frontier judge whose common-sense rulings stopped the incursions of one gang. Indiana was still a Territory. The country was a wilderness, except a few posts and settlements. Governor William Henry Harrison had moved to Vincennes, as the Executive of the Territory. The country was filled with Indians, friendly and hostile, when a gang of desperate horse-thieves from Kentucky, Ohio, Pennsylvania, and Virginia began to cross the river and steal and drive away the horses of the white men and Indians, indiscriminately. The settlers were for lynch law and hanging, or at least whipping; but the opinion of the Governor, that the laws should be enforced upon the offenders, prevailed, and many thieves were taken and confined, ready for the sitting of the court. At the next term, trial after trial, with convictions, was held, but the United States Attorney was a young green lawyer, and every conviction was followed by successful motions in arrest of judgment, for some defect in the indictments. The clamor against the court reached the ears of the judge and he resigned, when General Marston G. Clark, a cousin of General George Rogers Clark, was, by consent, appointed judge to fill the vacancy. The General was no lawyer—was brought up in the woods of Kentucky, could scarcely read a chapter in the Bible, and wrote his name as large as John Hancock's in the Declaration of Independence. He was about six feet in his stockings, very muscular—wore a hunting-shirt, leather pants, moccasins, and a foxskin cap, with a long queue down his back. Court came on, Judge Clark on the bench. The jail was full of horse-thieves. The penalty was not less than thirty-nine lashes on the bare back. The grand jury turned into court indictments against each of the prisoners. Here is an account of the proceedings:

"Judge Clark—'We will try John Long first, as he seems to be a leader in this business. Bring him into court.' Sheriff—'There he sits, I brought him with me. John Long, stand up.'—'You are indicted for stealing an Indian pony; guilty or not guilty?' Counsel—'May it please the Court, we plead in abatement that his name is John H. Long.'—'That makes no difference; I know the man, and that is sufficient.'—'We then move to quash the indictment before he pleads in chief.'—'State your objections.'—'First. There is no value of the horse laid. Second. It is charged in the indictment to be a horse, when he is a gelding.'—'I know an Indian pony is worth ten dollars; and I shall consider that a gelding is a horse; motion overruled.' Plea of not guilty; jury impanelled; evidence heard; proof positive; verdict, guilty; thirty-nine lashes on his bare back. Counsel—'We move in arrest of judgment, on the ground that it is not charged in the indictment that the horse was stolen in the Territory of Indiana.'—'That I consider a more serious objection than any you have made yet. I will consider on it till morning. Sheriff, adjourn the court, and keep the prisoner safe till court meets.' The judge kept his seat till the sheriff returned from the jail.—'Sheriff, at twelve o'clock to-night you and your deputy take Long into the woods, clear out of hearing, and give him thirty-nine lashes on his bare back, well laid on; put him in jail again; *say nothing*, but bring him into court in the morning.' The order was obeyed to the very letter, and the next morning

Long was in the box when court opened, his counsel ignorant of what had taken place. Judge Clark—'I have been thinking of the motion in arrest, in the case of Long; I have some doubts that the evidence proved that he did steal the horse in this Territory, and I think I ought not to sustain a motion that, I understand, will discharge the prisoner after he has been found guilty by the jury, but I feel bound to grant a new trial.'—Long, springing to his feet, cried out: 'Oh, no, for heaven's sake! I am whipped almost to death already. I discharge my attorneys and withdraw their motion.' Judge Clark—'Clerk, enter the judgment on the verdict, and mark it satisfied.' The other prisoners were brought up in succession, and convicted. No motion to quash, or in arrest, was afterward made. The prisoners were whipped and discharged, carrying with them the news to all of their comrades. Not a horse was stolen in the Territory for years afterward."[1]

Sometimes the self-constituted "Regulators" were the ones who were in the wrong. One of the most substantial men of the whole countryside in central Indiana was for many years pointed out as the man who had been hung and yet was alive. His history was that in the early times, before the days of railroads and mail communication, he had gone overland to the Territory of Illinois. He had journeyed with another man who drove his own team of horses, hitched to his spring wagon. They investigated the prairie lands and the stranger decided to settle there; but the man from Indiana preferred to return to his own section. He purchased the horses and wagon, from the man, and drove back to his former neighborhood. From the intimations of some evil-disposed persons,

[1] Smith, Oliver H., *Early Trials*, page 160. Cincinnati, 1858.

who wished to do the young man a harm, the report gained credence that he had murdered the stranger out on the lonely plains and taken the vehicle and horses. Of course he stoutly denied the slanderous story, but it grew with the telling of it, until the word went around that the whole tale was known to be true. The Regulators took it up, and seized the young man for murder and horse-stealing. Because he admitted that he had no witnesses to prove his innocence of the terrible charges, the border ruffians put a rope around his neck, passed it over the limb of a tree, and hanged him. After a few awful seconds, they eased up on the rope and let him down on to the ground. Some of the less cruel ones in the crowd tried to resuscitate the victim. Their efforts were rewarded with signs of life, and when the man could speak again, he promised them that, if they would give him a chance to have a court trial, he would take them to the spot where he had buried the man! This was news indeed. The next day a posse of men went with the accused, and after a long journey across country he led them about from one settler's cabin to another, until he found and produced the man, alive and well, whom they had accused him of killing! He explained to them that he had only promised them that he would point out the burial-place just to gain time and an opportunity to convince them of his innocence by showing them the man. He told them that he recognized the fact that in their unreasonable frame of mind it was the only way to secure a reprieve long enough to clear himself for all time.

In early days, counterfeiting seemed to be a most fascinating way of making money easily. Driving through the lonely districts of the State, in after years, a mysterious cave or a deserted cabin would be pointed out to the traveller as the place where some noted counterfeiter's band had been taken "red-handed." Desperate characters, who would dare to pass off spurious currency, would ally themselves with a more or less skilled engraver with a moral bias; and while he plied his expert trade in seclusion, the "gang" would roam to other parts, and buy guns, ammunition, horses, or lands with the false coin or scrip. The price he paid the men was generally "sixteen to one," but in counterfeit dollars. In Mr. Howe's tales of *The Great West*, he gives an account of one of the most successful of these counterfeiters, named Studevant, who lived in several States—as the exigencies of his business demanded,—but whose imitation currency was circulated all over Indiana. Mr. Howe says that he was a man of talent and address, possessed mechanical genius, was an expert artist, skilled in some of the sciences, and excelled as an engraver. For several years he resided in secluded spots, where all of his immediate neighbors were his confederates, or persons whose friendship he had conciliated. At any time, by the blowing of a horn, he could summon from fifty to a hundred armed men to his defence. He was a grave, quiet, inoffensive-looking man, who commanded the obedience of his comrades and the respect of his neighbors. He had a very excellent farm; his house was one of the best in the country.

"Yet this man was the most notorious counterfeiter that ever infested the country, and he carried on his nefarious art to an extent which no other person ever attempted. His confederates were scattered over the whole Western country, receiving, through regular channels of intercourse, their regular supplies of counterfeit bank-notes, for which they paid him a stipulated price—sixteen dollars in cash for one hundred in counterfeit bills. His security arose partly from his caution in not allowing his subordinates to pass a counterfeit bill or do any other unlawful act in the State in which he lived—measures which effectually protected him from the civil authority."[1]

But he became a great nuisance from the immense quantity of spurious paper which he threw into circulation; and Studevant, though he escaped the arm of the law, was at last, with all his unprincipled confederates driven from the country by the enraged people. As late as 1840, a man who had been passing counterfeit money, in payment for labor, supplies, and implements, made a narrow escape from the officers of the law. They had traced the offence to some passenger on the boat which had landed at the last town and they boarded the canal boat. Immediately the guilty one recognized the officers, and before they could identify him he slipped into the hold of the boat, and secreted himself in the part where the mules were kept. As soon as it was dark, so that he could not be seen by the passengers on deck, he slipped into the water, unfastened the belt from around his waist, in which the false coin was secreted, and dropped it silently into the waves. This done, and no traces of his guilt remaining, the man swam to shore and disappeared in the shadows of the forest. The officers of the law were baffled; the guilty man reappeared later, and pursued his career of amassing wealth.

Travellers in those early days travelled overland on horseback, or later by driving. They almost always carried their funds with them, in the form of coin

[1] Howe, H., *The Great West*.

or currency, as there were few banks to honor checks or drafts. This fact was well known, and often prompted highway robbery. The well-known stage driver, Winslow, once had a large sum in coin to carry overland. When stopping at the tavern for dinner, he took off his overshoes and slipped a sack of gold into each shoe. He carried the shoes in his hand into the dining-room, placed them under his feet at table, where he could feel the money safely resting, and no one was the wiser of his treasure. The bandits generally plied their trade in twos and threes. They would often stop at the same tavern, with the man of business, learn the direction he was going, and ride on ahead, or join him socially as he was leaving. When well out of hearing of any settlement, or in some lonely spot, the thief would be joined by a confederate, and after a struggle they would secure the booty. Sometimes mine host of the inn was in partnership with the outlaws, and many a citizen has lodged where he would not allow himself to fall asleep for fear of an attack. Travellers in those days always provided for such alarms by wearing a brace of pistols and a bowie-knife; the money was carried in a belt about the waist, or in the saddle-bags. Hardy frontiersmen were often as good shots as the freebooters, and declined in vigorous fashion to surrender their possessions, and there would be one less robber on the highway after such an encounter. Prairie bandits infested Newton and Jasper counties, within the memory of some of the citizens now living in those sections. Many of the streams in Indiana were spanned by heavy wooden bridges which were covered, both on the sides and roof, to preserve the timbers. These long tunnel-like structures are now fast disappearing before the modern iron bridges, but they were almost universal in an earlier day. They proved a refuge in time of storm, and a source of terror to many a faint heart who had heard tales of highway robbery committed in their dark interiors.

One of these stories is so typical that it must be recounted. A well-to-do citizen, had sold his cattle in the great market at Cincinnati, and was feeling so good over his returns for the year that he bought some "store goods" for the goodwife at home, had a round game of poker at the tavern, and started homeward. It was later than he would have had the hardihood to attempt had he not imbibed a drop too much over the friendly game. Owing to these circumstances the farmer did not reach the inn, where he was accustomed to "put up for the night" on his regular trips. The darkness fell when he was emerging from the hills, and where the lands were so poor that no one was very prosperous. Consequently, the landlord of the log tavern was not above suspicion. But convivial indulgence had limited the hours of day and determined the stopping-place for the night. Our traveller entered the hostelry with suspicion, which turned into foreboding after supper was over, and he surveyed the groups about the bar-room. A lame peddler asleep on his pack was the most innocent guest about the fire, and he looked like a cutthroat. The keeper of the road-house was playing a desperate game of cards with some men who turned out to be confederates of his in waylaying travellers. The man of means slept with his pistols ready and arose weary in the dawn to resume his journey. Against his wishes, two of the men who were at the card-table the night before rode out of the stables, as he was leaving, and hallooed him as a fellow traveller. They rode along but a few miles when they said they must turn off at the crossroads, and, much to his relief, bade him adieu. Five miles down the road, where the way narrowed into one of those long bridges, a bear ran across from a thicket, pursued by three hunters. Our traveller's horse shied at the animal, ran into the bridge, and threw his rider heavily against the timbers, just as the highwaymen thought he would. But the man was not so unconscious from the fall as they had hoped. When they were absorbed in rifling his saddle-bags, he raised on one arm, and drawing his big horse-pistol shot two of the thieves, and was wounded by the third. With this one he then entered into a life-and-death struggle. Both men were so furiously engaged that they did not hear the approach of a settler who had heard the shots, and, knowing the presence in the woods of the gang of outlaws, had crept up to the entrance of the bridge to see what was going on. Realizing the desperate straits of the traveller, he clipped off the brigand with his rifle and ended the life of the last one of the thieves that had infested the neighborhood for months. The bear was part of their plot to take travellers at a disadvantage, for he was a pet and had often been used. One of those who lay dead was the landlord of the tavern. The two others were his guests of the night before, all disguised as half-breed Indians.

Along the Wabash there were many rough-and-tumble fights among the belligerent Irish who were brought in to dig the canal. These immigrants were in no sense highwaymen, their "ructions" were generally *en masse*, a free-for-all fight without warning,

An Old Indiana Bridge.

These picturesque old bridges are fast giving place to modern iron structures. From a photograph.

and generally without any provocation—unless it was cheap whiskey. A misunderstanding was enough to set them all at loggerheads, and soon the whole gang would be using their shillalahs. An old citizen of the Wabash tells the following incident, which is so very characteristic of these laborers from Erin that it may be accepted as typical of scores of other occurrences. In 1834 there had been a freshet sufficient to float a steamboat as far up the river as Peru and Chief Godfrey's village. The steamboat was just leaving the little town of Peru for the return trip. He tells the tale in this wise:

"I made haste to get on board, and just as I was stepping on board the plank that led on to the boat, a fight commenced between a party that came up from Logansport and some Peruvians, which blocked up the gangway so that I could not get on the boat. The excitement ran high throughout the crowd. The Logansport party was about to prove too hard for their antagonists, who began to sing out for help. There were several hundred Irishmen near at hand, working on the Wabash and Erie canal, who, observing the foray, and considering it a free fight, could no longer resist the temptation to pitch in; and gathering their picks and spades, they rushed in platoons upon the belligerents, and soon vanquished the party that had proved strongest in the mêlée, compelling them to betake themselves to the boat, in double-quick time, shouting, 'The Greek, the Greek.' On looking up and down the line of the canal for a mile and a half in either direction, Irish recruits were seen pressing for the scene of action, with picks in their hands and wrath on their faces. 'We will sink your d——d dugout, be jabers' rung like a knell upon the ears of the astonished boat crew, who at the Captain's command pulled in the plank and pushed off into the river, to keep the enraged Hibernians from demolishing his vessel. At first the boat dropped slowly along with the current, and the Captain motioned for those who had failed to get on board to follow along the shore where he would land and take them on."[1]

From the time that Indiana came into the Union a free State, there were crimes committed continually in the kidnapping of free negroes within the State, and selling them into Southern slavery. Sometimes the ignorant blacks were persuaded to go aboard river boats to work, in some instances they were carried forcibly by outlaws across the river, in all cases, when once over the line, they were taken in bands to the Cotton States and heard of no more. This lucrative iniquity, as Captain Lemcke termed it, was very profitable, and the guilty bands of desperadoes would cross from one State to another, eluding pursuit. It is said that they were regularly organized, having rendezvous and passwords, leaders, and methods of distributing the spoils of their trade in human suffering. As late as 1833, an attempt was made to steal two black boys from a field as far north as the Wea plains. After the Fugitive Slave Law of 1850 was passed, there were great numbers of slave-hunters raiding the border States under the authority of that obnoxious statute. It continued to be a disastrous time for negroes, who were enticed from their own masters, then claimed as runaway slaves and sold by their persecutors into slavery; some negroes were resold three and four times at a thousand dollars apiece. Fortunately the abolition of slavery ended these crimes.

[1] Cox, Sanford C., *Recollections of the Wabash Valley*, page 145. La Fayette, 1861.

Immigration was so continuous and the population increased so rapidly that Indiana very early passed from the condition of a border State, and excepting the outrages by isolated bands of white-cappers in the hill counties, the crimes peculiar to a frontier country ceased.

CHAPTER XI

THE TRAIL—FROM BIRCH-BARK CANOE TO ELECTRIC TROLLEY

THE pirogue of the French *coureurs des bois* gliding athwart the Indians' birch-bark canoe, on the gently flowing Ouabache, is the earliest picture of the first modes of travel in Indiana. It was only on foot or by boat that there was any way of penetrating the wilderness, for many decades following its exploration. The American aborigines had no horses at the time of the discovery, and when they first saw the Spanish soldier on horseback, the natives thought horse and rider were one, and imagined they were gods. When the Indian learned the usefulness of the horse in covering distances without the fatigue of long marches, it became his most valued possession, and appealed to his cupidity to secure by any means in his power, be it theft or murder. The deftness and skill shown by the Indians in fashioning their birch-bark canoes and dugouts indicated the experience of ages of savage ancestry. Into the Indiana region, birch canoes must be brought from the north and east, but the natives there made canoes of hickory or elm bark turned inside out; and their dugouts were fashioned from the trunks of large trees, hollowed out by burning and scraping, and the ends pointed with their stone axes. These pirogues were long and strong, and as claimed by a traveller, "required us and everything in them to be exactly in the bottom and then to look straight forward and speak from the middle of our mouth, or they were other side up in an instant." The rivers could tell many tales of adventure, of battle, and of romance, but they are all silent about the long procession of French fur-traders, Spanish merchants, British soldiers, and American settlers, whose primitive barques have glided down the Indiana waters into oblivion. There are many old settlers still living, who recount lively tales of the commerce by boat when the homes were being pre-empted along the streams. When the American colonists opened up the forests for farming, they brought beasts of burden to their aid. There was only a "blazed traice" through the trees for many years, and the universal means of transportation across the country to the river landing was by horseback. The Indian understood so thoroughly the topography of the country, that the white man could rarely improve on the routes which his stealthy footsteps had traced through the forests for ages. Along those narrow defiles, on horseback, until the boat was reached, the commerce of the West was carried for more than a century and a half. The early American settlers in Indiana followed the same natural outlets to the sea that the French had before them. They brought rowboats with them, and the shaping of canoes was learned from the Indians; but the settlers soon astonished the savages by a new craft. These were the flatboats, which were shaped like scows, sometimes having a shed over the centre of the craft. Of these useful boats, so well adapted to the shallow streams, it was quaintly said that they drew about as much water as a sap trough. There was a long steering oar at the stern of the boat, and a sufficient number of side oars to propel it, with the help of a pole, which was handled by a man who stood in the stern, to push over sand-bars and obstructions. Wags used to say that these boats, in going down-stream, managed to keep up with the current. Coming up-stream, the boats were cordelled, as the French boatmen had named the process of towing by hand. There was scarcely a man of large undertakings but shipped his fleet of flatboats, rafts, and scows down the Mississippi to market. There he sold his produce, bartered for supplies for his neighborhood, and came back by rowboat, or mayhap walked the entire distance home, as did Abraham Lincoln. Mr. Henry T. Sample, a veteran pork packer, told the writer that he had walked from New Orleans to the Wabash country sixteen times.

Before a merchant left on one of these tours, weeks and months were consumed in bartering for his cargo of grain, pelts, venison, bear's grease, lard, flour, and pork; also in gathering the great rafts of logs, to be taken down and sold for their lumber. Pork-packing for export to the seaboard was, during the winter season, the most lucrative industry of river towns, and it laid the foundation of many early fortunes. Three hundred barrels of pork was the usual load for the average flatboat, and that product was one tenth of the export trade, and another tenth was lard. Corn was the great crop of Indiana, then as now, and from five to ten thousand bushels of corn could be carried on one of these boats. Cattle, horses, oats, venison hams, hickory nuts, and walnuts made up the balance of the annual $1,000,000 trade by flatboat.

Many boats were collected to make up these fleets. It took nearly a month to pole this type of craft to New Orleans, and the merchant capitalist generally accompanied his cargo and crew. The flatboats were generally sold or abandoned at the end of the journey. A return cargo of sugar, tobacco, rice, furniture, and dry goods was brought up the river on the return trip, in rowboats, or keel boats poled and pulled by oars or sweeps, at a snail-like pace. These boats made a long hard journey up-stream, and the labor was excessive. By avoiding the swift current and keeping close to the shore, and employing oars, poles, and a cordelle or tow line, a distance of six miles was all that could be made in a day! "I shall long remember," writes Captain Lemcke, "the low-lying islands, tedious bends, long reaches, treacherous cut-offs, and bristling snags; the confusing fogs, and the sombre density of the unbroken forests."[1]

The first line of "Packet Boats" on the Ohio River, in which Indiana people were carried to their new homes, was advertised in 1793. These were flatboats for hire, to accommodate passengers. They were to leave Cincinnati every Saturday for Pittsburgh, and one month was the required time for a round trip! In the advertisement of the new line of transports, we have a picture of the border life. The management stated that no danger could be apprehended from the enemy, as every person on board would be under cover, made proof against rifle or musket balls, and

[1] Lemcke, J. A., *Reminiscences of an Indianian*, page 142. Indianapolis, 1905.

that there were portholes for firing out! They were also amply supplied with ammunition and strongly manned with choice hands to fight the Indians! A separate cabin was to be portioned off for the accommodation of the ladies. This enterprising line of up-to-date boats did not always go on schedule time, as there is a record extant that the packet which was to leave November 30th did not get away until December 10th, and the passengers had to await its departure!

From twelve to fifteen hundred flatboats a year went from the White River, and the Wabash country, to New Orleans. The *Emigrants' Guide*, published in 1832, said that at least one thousand flatboats entered the Ohio from the Wabash in one month in the previous spring. When a fleet would be ready, all the village would assemble on the bank of the river to see it depart on its long journey, and be there again to welcome the weary boatmen upon their return.

We can imagine the lively interest taken in the contents of the return load, with its barrels of syrup, sacks of coffee, quaint Chinese boxes of tea, its sugar loaves, and all its suggestions of the outside world, so remote from their wilderness home. China and silks from France, mahogany and silver from England, found their way, as time went on, into the river hamlets of this far West.

During these days, the travel across country being on horseback, the invariable outfit of the traveller was a pair of saddle-bags which could be thrown across the horse, to carry the rider's wardrobe and papers. His limbs were always wrapped in leggins of heavy green baize cloth, now no longer sold; these were to protect his clothing from the mud. If it were wintry weather he wore a buffalo overcoat and coonskin cap. The early preachers and lawyers, whose calling made it necessary for them to "ride the circuit," came to know the best trail through the woods, just how their horses would ford the streams, and where the most hospitable cabins were located, from whose occupants they could ask a night's lodging.

A new epoch dawned in transportation for the inhabitants along the Ohio River when they hailed, with eager curiosity and delight, the first steamboat, which was run from Pittsburgh to New Orleans, in the year 1811. It was built by a relative of the President, Nicholas J. Roosevelt, and made the trip in the wonderful time of fourteen days. For several years there were other small steamboats plying on the river, but flatboats and barges continued to be the principal means of transportation, as the small rivers were always too shallow to make it profitable to use steam for propelling their craft. Mr. Dunn says that no steamboat ascended the Wabash until the summer of 1823. When it came the villagers gathered on the river banks to welcome the new-fashioned transport,—the wonderful new craft which could go up-stream as well as down! How was the flatboat to stand against such a competitor? Now prosperity would bless the frontier!

Mr. Condit tells us in a graphic way the effect upon the savages:

"The barge or keel-boat, and the skiffs, though they had surprised the Indians, yet they neither alarmed nor offended them, but upon the first appearance of the steamboat, breathing out its white steam, black smoke, and belching forth its red fiery sparks, the poor affrighted

Indian fled as from a huge unearthly monster. Even after explanations and assurances were given, and he had become somewhat acquainted with its working, he was still superstitious and fearful, and persisted in believing that this ugly, threatening creature was an offence to the gentle river."[1]

To the white man, it was a wonderfully advanced method of reaching the outside world, and brought a great increase in population and prosperity; and soon regular packet boats had their appointed days of arrival and departure. When Nathaniel Bolton's mother came west in 1820, she refused to travel on the steamboat, thinking it a dangerous-looking craft, and her husband secured transportation on a timber boat. Upon this, her daughter records, the family floated down the river quite comfortably. The rude craft had fireplaces at each end, in front of which they did their cooking. In a few years it came to be a regular event for a fleet of steamers to be seen wending its way up the Wabash, laden with passengers and merchandise. When the boats from New Orleans would pull up at the wharf at La Fayette—which was the head of navigation for the larger steamers—the whole landing was the scene of liveliest interest. Barrels of sugar, coffee, molasses, and tobacco would be unloaded, and rolled up along the side of Main Street, for blocks away. The odor of teas and savory spices pervaded the air. Mysterious bales and boxes, suggestive of new fashions and fabrics, lined the approaches to the wharf. The names of some of these old steamers are still remembered; as, the *Paul Pry*,

[1] Condit, Blackford, D. D., *History of Early Terre Haute*, page 26. New York, 1900.

the *Daniel Boone*, the *William Tell*, the *Facility*, and many whose names suggested the frontier, and whose whistles could be recognized a mile away by all of the small boys along the shore. The youth of the river towns aspired to the career of being steamboat captains. As Captain Lemcke recalls, from an early day, it was the ardent wish and nightly dream of every barefooted boy on the banks of the rivers to be or become the commander of one of these fiery dragons with glittering interior.

In the towns located on the rivers were great warehouses, generally owned by the leading capitalist of the town. They were built as places of storage for every kind of river merchandise, and costly freight and furniture that had voyaged, said William Tarkington, from New England down the long coast, across the Mexican Gulf, through the flat delta. They had made the winding journey up the great river a thousand miles; and almost a thousand miles more up the great and lesser tributaries. There was in this cargo cloth brought from Connecticut; and Tennessee cotton, on its way to Massachusetts and Rhode Island spindles. These imports lay there beside huge mounds of raw wool, from near-by flocks, ready for the local mills. Dates and nuts from the Caribbean Sea, lemons from the tropics, cigars from the Antilles, tobacco from Virginia and Kentucky were on the wharf; and most precious of all, the farmers' wheat from the home fields. This was the commerce of the Indiana rivers, as carried on in the packets and steamboats, before the days of railroads. The first steamboats were little, ill-smelling, craft, with a single dining-cabin, around which was a row of berths, hidden by faded curtains. Early in the forties, however, there were announced the splendid three-decked monarchs of the rivers, surpassing in luxury any sea-going vessel. The most picturesque life was then on the river. Taking trips by boat was a novelty. Society often went afloat, and the provender was fine. There was always music on the big boats, and an almost permanent feature was the singing of the crew as the steamer landed or resumed her course in the channel. One of the favorite songs of the deck hands was:

"The Captain's in a hurry, and I know what he means;
He wants to beat the other boat down to New Orleans.
Then, roll out and heave that cotton,
Roll out and heave that cotton,
For we ain't got time to stay."

When the first steamboat went down the Ohio River, it made the seven hundred miles from Pittsburgh to Louisville in seventy hours, down-stream. A citizen of the place, at that time, has left an account of the impression that the wonderful new craft made on the frontier people. He says that the novel appearance of the vessel, and the fearful rapidity with which it made its passage over the broad reaches of the river, excited a mixture of terror and surprise among the people gathered on the banks, whom the rumor of such an invention had never reached. On the unexpected arrival of the vessel before Louisville, near midnight on a still moonlight night, the extraordinary sound which filled the air as the pent-up steam was suffered to escape from the valves on rounding to produced a general alarm, and multitudes rose from their beds to ascertain the cause. It is said the general impression was, that the comet had fallen

"The Indian persisted in believing that the threatening creature was an offense to the gentle river."
From an old print.

into the Ohio. The comet had been the sensation of the year.

As the steamboats became factors in the life along the tributaries of the Mississippi River the frontier settlements rejoiced in their touch with the outside world. A writer in the *Western Monthly Review*, in 1827, said:

"An Atlantic cit, who talks of us under the name of backwoodsmen, would not believe, that such fairy structures of oriental gorgeousness and splendor as the *Washington*, the *Walk in the Water*, the *Lady of the Lake*, etc., etc., had ever existed in the imagination, much less that they were in actual existence, rushing down the river, as on the wings of the wind, or plowing up between the forests, bearing speculators, merchants, dandies, fine ladies, everything in the form of humanity, with pianos, stocks of novels, and cards, and dice, and flirting, and lovemaking, and champagne drinking, and on deck perhaps three hundred fellows who have seen alligators, and neither fear whiskey, nor gunpowder. A steamboat coming from New Orleans brings to the remotest villages of our streams, and the very doors of our cabins, a little of Paris, a section of Broadway, or a slice of Philadelphia, to ferment in the minds of our young people the innate propensity for fashions and finery."[1]

Steamboats reduced the freight rates along the rivers to one third the former price. The great impetus to agriculture created a surplus which developed the interior of the country, and attracted so many settlers that by 1835 the exports had accomplished the economic independence of the United States.

As may be imagined, all this traffic did not go on

[1] *Western Monthly Review*, May, 1827, i., 25.

without frights and delays and accidents. There were whole months when the rivers were so low that snags and sandbars endangered craft of the lightest draft. In fact the old joke about the boats being obliged to run on a heavy dew originated along these Western streams, where there were such extremes of low water and great freshets. One accident on the Ohio River, near where Evansville stands, was of national interest. It was in the year 1825, when the illustrious General La Fayette was touring the country, as the guest of the grateful nation. The General and a distinguished party of civilians and military men were on board the steamboat *Mechanic*, coming up the river. It was in the month of May and all the passengers had retired for the night; suddenly the boat struck a snag in the very middle of the stream, and immediately began to settle. The night was dark, most of the travellers and crew were asleep, and the call of danger caused great confusion. General La Fayette was hurried on deck, and helped over the side of the steamboat, where a small boat had been launched to take him ashore. In the haste and excitement, he fell overboard, and was nearly drowned before assistance reached him. The General lost all of his effects, and eight thousand dollars in money, as did the captain, who also suffered the loss of his steamer.

Travel on the steamboats was more picturesque than on the modern railway. The voyage was long, and people took time to draw leisurely breaths of enjoyment. There was usually a pleasure party on board. Sometimes they were bound for the Mardi-Gras. They danced, they flirted, and they always gambled. An old traveller recalls that every boat had its corps of courteous, low-voiced, well-dressed gentlemen, who lived by "running the river." The traveller who knew them excused himself from playing with them; if he did not know them, he paid the penalty. The "river blackleg" was the typical sinner of that day. He was recognized as an emissary of Hell, and pointed the moral of many a sermon.

No one has pictured the traffic by steamboat so graphically as Mark Twain. He makes one live over again those deliberate times when the commerce was spasmodic, and the sleepy towns drowsed between arrivals of the transport. We see how presently a film of dark smoke appears above a remote point, some lusty wagoner on the lookout for trade yells, "S-t-e-a-m-b-o-a-t a-comin'," and the scene changes. The town drunkards stir; the clerks wake up; a furious clatter of drays follows. Every house and store pours out its human contribution, and all in a twinkling the dead town is alive and moving. Drays, carts, men, boys all go hurrying from all quarters to a common centre, the wharf. After the cargo is unloaded, and new freight and passengers taken on, the boat steams away over the placid waters, and the town resumes its normal state.

Mr. Cottman has given an interesting account of river navigation in Indiana, and the vital importance which that form of transportation assumed in early days. Among other things, he tells of the strenuous insistence on considering, as navigable, streams that were hopelessly useless for such purpose, ofttimes approaching the ludicrous. As an example, Indianapolis, for nearly two decades after its founding, *would have* White River a highway of commerce, in spite of nature and the inability of craft to get over ripples, sandbars, and drifts. As early as 1820, it was officially declared navigable. In 1825, Alexander Ralston, the surveyor, was appointed to make a thorough inspection of the river and to report in detail at the next session of the legislature. The sanguine hopes that were nourished at the young capital are shown by existing records.

"For three years past efforts had been made by Noah Noble to induce steamboats to ascend the river, and . . . very liberal offers had been made by that gentleman to the first steamboat captain who would ascend the river as far as this place. . . . As early as February, 1827, he offered the Kanawha Salt Company $150 as an inducement to send a load of salt, agreeing to sell the salt without charge.

"In 1830, Noble offered a Capt. Stephen Butler $200 to come to Indianapolis, and $100 in addition if Noblesville and Anderson were reached, though what efforts were made to earn these bonuses is not known. From time to time the newspapers made mention of boats which, according to rumor, got 'almost' to the capital and eventually one made for itself a historic reputation by performing the much-desired feat. This one was the *General Hanna*, a craft which Robert Hanna, a well-known character in early politics, had purchased for the purpose of bringing stones up the river for the old National road bridge. The *Hanna*, which in addition to its own loading, towed up a heavily-laden keel-boat, arrived April 11, 1831, and, according to a contemporary chronicle, every man, woman, and child who could possibly leave home availed themselves of this opportunity of gratifying a laudable curosity to see a steamboat. On Monday evening and during the most of the succeeding day, the river bank was filled with delighted spectators. Captain Blythe and the artillery company marched down and fired salutes. The leading citizens and the boats' crew peppered each other with elegant, formal compliments, and the former, in approved parliamentary style, 'Resolved, That the arrival at Indianapolis of the Steamboat *General Hanna*, from Cincinnati, should be viewed by the citizens of the White River country and of our State at large, as a proud triumph and as a fair and unanswerable demonstration of the fact that our beautiful river is susceptible of safe navigation.'

"A public banquet in honor of the occasion was arranged, and the visiting navigators invited to attend, but they were in haste to get out of the woods while the water might permit, and so declined with regrets. Legend has it that the boat ran aground on an island a short distance down the river, and there lay ignominiously for six weeks, and that was the last of the 'proud triumph' and White River 'navigation.'

"But despite these and many similar absurdities, the Indiana streams were a factor, and an important one, in our earlier commerce. The number of rivers and creeks that have been declared 'public highways' by our legislators is a matter for surprise. An examination of the statutes through the twenties and thirties discloses from thirty to forty. According to Timothy Flint, who wrote in 1833, the navigable waters of the State had been rated at 2500 miles, and this estimate he thought moderate. These streams ranged in size from the Wabash to insignificant hill drains that run down the short water-shed into the Ohio, some of which, at the present day at least, would scarce float a plank. Such streams were, however, supposed to have sufficient volume during high water to float flatboats and the purpose of the legislation was to interdict impeding of the waterway by dams or otherwise, and the clearing of the channel was under State law. To this end many of these streams were divided into districts, as were the roads, and worked."[1]

[1] *Magazine of History*, 1907, Geo. S. Cottman, Editor.

That is, the streams were cleared of drifts, and other obstructions, by the male residents living adjacent to either shore.

During all this time of steamboat commerce, the wagon roads were being slowly opened up through the forests to the river towns. The lands were so rich and mellow, through which the roads passed, that these highways were a vexation to the soul of the settlers for many years, until the days when they were made into turnpikes. In that early time the cattle and hogs were driven overland to the packing centres, the drivers walking the weary way back and forth. Hog driving was a separate occupation, and teaming was a regular business. An idea of the toil and weariness encountered on these overland trips may be gleaned from Mr. Smith's story of John Hager. He says:

"As I was travelling one rainy day on horseback through the woods, between Indianapolis and Connersville, near where Greenfield now stands, I heard a loud voice before me, some half a mile off. My horse was wading through the mud and water, up to the saddle-skirts. I moved slowly on, until I met John Hager driving a team of four oxen, hauling a heavy load of merchandise, or store goods, as he called it, from Cincinnati to Indianapolis, then in the woods. He had been fifteen days on the road, and it would take him three days more to get through, but said he must move on, as they would be anxiously looking for him at Indianapolis, as they were nearly out of powder and lead when he left, and they could get none until he got there, as his was the only wagon that could get through the mud between Cincinnati and Indianapolis, and it was just as much as he could do. He hallooed to the oxen, plied the lash of his long whip, and the team moved on at the rate of a mile an hour—the wheels up to the hub in mud, carrying the whole commerce between the Queen city and the Railroad city of the West, in that early day."[1]

When the Rev. Thomas Goodwin, the pioneer Methodist preacher, was journeying to Asbury College in 1837, he passed over the roads when the fifty miles toward Indianapolis were one great quagmire. He tells the old story of the passengers having to get rails from the near-by fence, to help pry the stage-coach from the mudholes. When the wagon broke down beyond repair, the driver took young Goodwin's trunk on the horse before him, and the mail agent, with his mail-bag in front of him, and the student up behind, rode the other horse into the capital. When he reached his destination, he had travelled four days and two nights, to cover 124 miles.

It would look very strange to the moderns, accustomed as we are to rapid transit means of locomotion, to see slow plodding oxen used, but in that day they were worked on all of the Western roads. Heavy loads over rough highways could be hauled by these strong beasts of burden even better than by horses. Until after the Civil War, the making of neck-yokes was a regular trade in every community, and the patient ox was a common sight on the roads.

The fertility of the soil, which produced such spreading forests, shading the lands and preventing the equally deep soil on the roads from drying out, was what attracted immigration, and also what made it necessary to build roads, before the country could properly develop. Four years after the organization

---

[1] Smith, O. H., *Early Trials*, page 583. Cincinnati, 1858.

of the State, and when it had been determined to place the capital inland, a real system of wagon roads was projected. Twenty-six turnpikes were planned in 1820; five were to centre at Indianapolis, the others were to connect the older towns of the State; and the revenues for their establishment and maintenance were designated from the sale of public lands, and a road tax, and labor per capita, to be rendered. As in other public works, the enactment of laws did not make good roads immediately. Travelling by land was still travelling by mud and water, as the depressed Professor Hall termed it, at that time. Legislation was but a beginning. The work went slowly on through corduroy and toll roads, until the belated discovery that they had excellent gravel beds within the borders of the State made it improvident to have further delays. Even the National road limped lamely across Indiana; the only real work being the clearing of the trail, and plowing drains by the side of the roadway. East of the Alleghanies and across Ohio, it gave emigrants and commerce a famous highway toward the West. When Ohio and Indiana were admitted into the Union, Ohio fourteen years previous, there was a provision made by Congress reserving two per cent. from the sale of public lands within their limits, to be held and applied to the construction of a public highway, leading from the coast to a point to be designated within their borders. In 1806, Congress authorized President Jefferson to appoint a commission to lay out the best route; and the trail from Cumberland, Maryland, across a part of Pennsylvania and Virginia, on into Ohio was chosen. It was eventually carried forward, in a much less thorough manner, and very imperfectly constructed, through

Indiana to Vandalia, Illinois. For a half-century, the legislation regarding this highway had dragged its way through political campaigns, the sessions of Congress, and the various legislatures. It was never satisfactorily constructed at full length, and was very shiftlessly maintained; but it served a great purpose. It developed a vast territory, and served as a bond of communication and union between the tide-water States and the prairies. It also connected a network of State roads, which gave access to the whole interior of the Ohio Valley. It reduced freight rates one half. In 1820 three thousand wagons ran from Philadelphia to Pittsburgh for this trade, reaching a value of eighteen millions annually.

Travel was not then the matter-of-course affair of a few hours to the coast that it is in these days. The coaches driven over that old Cumberland road went across the mountains at the rate of five miles an hour, changing horses three or four times a day, and stopping for rest over night at the famous old wayside taverns. The merchant who went east in those days, and the belle who had spent a season in Philadelphia or Boston, were envied personages, who really had seen the world, had actually known life! If a citizen and his wife contemplated a journey to their old home, on the coast, it was an event to be planned months in advance. A new dozen of shirts, all of finest linen, must be hand-stitched for the journey. His best blue broadcloth clothes, and flowered waistcoat, must be brushed, his gold fob polished, and the beaver hat remodelled and ironed. Mother would content herself with a made-over outfit, so that she might purchase "brand new" peau de soie and French merino at the centres of fashion. Their clothes were packed in the old hair trunk, studded with brass nails; and the things for the journey were placed in the huge carpet-bag of gay flowered brussels. In it, were letters from all of the neighborhood, to friends in the East; for postage was ruinously high then, and it was a matter of etiquette for every traveller to carry mail for his friends. Funds for the journey were carried very secretly in a belt about the waist, with a brace of pistols for defence against possible highwaymen. Family and friends gathered at the gate to say good-bye to the travellers when the gay stage-coach, with its six spirited horses, drew up at the door with many a dash and flourish. The fellow-passengers, who were held in close companionship for this long journey, had plenty of time to exhaust topics of conversation. The talk ranged from predestination, high tariff, federalism, border wars, and early planting, to the latest news from the State and National capitals. And then there was always politics to be discussed, and new stories to be told. If there were lady passengers, no man would presume to light a cigar, for in those days such a lack of deference was unknown in America. Hospitable inns, with great blazing fires and a lavish table of homely fare, were established at intervals on the route. There is said to have been a score of these old taverns in Wayne County alone, which shows how much travel there was by the old National road. Recalling these journeys, an old timer mused: What stories they told, too, around that fire after supper! Men took time to tell stories in that day. Each had his half-dozen narratives, carefully elaborated, and given with dramatic effect. It was something to be a raconteur on the road. The best drivers, too, of these coaches on the pike

"Journeying to their new homes you passed people seated in the great canvas-topped Conestoga wagons."
From an old print.

reached a position of national distinction. Sometimes in lonely stretches of interminable forest, your only vis-à-vis might be a villainous-looking cutthroat, whose side glances would make one feel to see if his holsters were in place. Journeying to their new homes, you passed people seated in the great canvas-topped Conestoga wagons, going towards the setting sun.

"Old America seems to be breaking up and moving westward," wrote Morris Birkbeck in 1817. On the National road he said that "we are seldom out of sight of family groups, behind and before us. No possessions but two horses and sometimes a cow or two; excepting a little hard-earned money, for the land office of the district, where they may obtain a title for as many acres as they have half dollars, being one fourth of the purchase price. The family are seen before, behind, or within the vehicle, according to the road, the weather, or perhaps the spirit of the party. Sometimes a horse and a pack saddle afford the means of transfer."[1]

A traveller would pass in one journey four to five thousand hogs being driven to the Eastern market. In Benjamin Parker's reminiscences, we gain a vivid impression of the vast commerce and travel, which passed toward the West; and also have a quaint picture of the little Indiana boy, who was afterwards to be noted as one of her writers, as he sat by the roadside of the great national way, and observed the travel from that mysterious East toward the setting sun. He wrote:

"From morning till night there was a continual rumble of wheels, and, when the rush was greatest, there was

[1] Birkbeck, Morris, *Notes on a Journey from Virginia*, pages 25, 26.

never a minute that wagons were not in sight. Many families occupied two or more of the big red wagons then in use, with household goods and their implements, while extra horses, colts, cattle, sheep, and sometimes hogs were led or driven behind. Thus, when five or ten families were moving in company, the procession of wagons, men, women, and children and stock was quite lengthy and imposing. Now and then there would be an old-fashioned carriage, set upon high wheels to go safely over stumps and through streams. The older women and little children occupied these, and went bobbing up and down on the great leather springs, which were the fashion sixty years ago. But everybody did not travel in that way. Single families, occupying a single one or two horse wagon or cart, frequently passed along, seeming as confident and hopeful as the others. With the tinkling of bells, the rumbling of wheels, and the chatter of the people as they went forever forward, the little boy who had gone to the road from his lonesome home in the woods was captivated, and carried away into the great active world. But the greatest wonder and delight of all was the stage-coach, radiant in new paint, and drawn by its four matched horses in their showy harness, and filled inside and on top with well-dressed people. We could hear the driver playing his bugle as he approached the little town, and it all seemed too fine and grand to be other than a dream." [1]

In the early thirties, a new mode of reaching the centres of trade was advocated. Steam, applied to the running of boats, had worked wonders for those sections lying adjacent to the navigable streams. Alas! the fertile districts along shallow streams, and those remote from the waterways, including the inland capital of Indiana, were greatly retarded in their

[1] Parker, Benjamin, " Pioneer Days," in vol. iv., Ind. *Mag. Hist.*, 1908.

development by lack of adequate transportation.
Railroads had only appeared on the horizon, and the
agitation for the building of *canals* began. To-day
we should hardly regard a slow-going canal-boat,
travelling at the rate of eight miles an hour, as a great
socializing influence; but in that earlier time, when
the canals were first opened up, a traveller wrote
back home from Ohio, that it was well worth while
to make a trip to Cincinnati or Toledo, just to enjoy
the luxury of the passage.

The development of the State under this new mode
of transportation is a very definite and interesting
phase of Indiana's history. As Mr. Dillon has said:

"the State system of internal improvement, which was
adopted by Indiana in 1836, was not a new measure, nor
did the adoption of the system at that time grow out of
a new and hasty expression of popular sentiment. For a
period of more than ten years, the expediency of providing
by law for the commencement of a State system of public works had been discussed before the people of the
State by governors, legislators, and distinguished private
citizens."[1]

They instanced the Erie Canal, which was begun by
New York State in 1817, and within a decade after
its completion the tolls repaid the cost of construction.
In 1823, two years before steam was applied to the
locomotive, the subject of connecting the Maumee and
Wabash rivers by a canal over the old Indian trail,
thus opening up navigation to the Lakes, had attracted the attention of the legislative authorities of
Illinois and Indiana. The agitation entered politics,

[1] Dillion, J. B., *Hist. of Ind.*, page 569. Indianapolis, 1859.

divided families, and sundered friendships. In 1816, the year that the State was admitted, there was an act passed by the legislature reserving five per cent. of the proceeds of sales of all public lands within its territory as a fund for the construction of roads and canals and three-fifths of this fund was to be expended by act of legislature. In 1821, this famous "three per cent. fund" was first drawn upon. In 1826, the State obtained from the general government a grant of land two miles and a half wide on each side of the proposed canal and projected State road, making 3200 acres per mile, and the whole grant was valued at a million and a quarter of dollars. The sale of the government lands was to aid in the construction of the proposed improvements. Great inland districts were to be connected with shipping privileges. The rivers had long been hampered by the obstructions in their channels, and canals were to be substituted, as a better means of transportation, with lateral canals and turnpikes, opening up other districts. These ambitious and far-reaching plans for internal improvements included the Wabash and Erie Canal, covering 459⅝ miles, and extending from Lake Erie down the Wabash where it was to be connected with the Ohio River, which Mr. Benton, in his very interesting monograph on the canal, calls the Indiana Appian Way; the Central Canal which was to connect the inland city, Indianapolis, with the Wabash and Erie, via Muncietown and the White River Valley, and another branch to place the capital in connection with Evansville; there was also to be built the Whitewater Canal, which was to be a cross-cut canal from the Ohio River and was completed to Brookville; the Erie and Michigan Canal, from Fort Wayne to

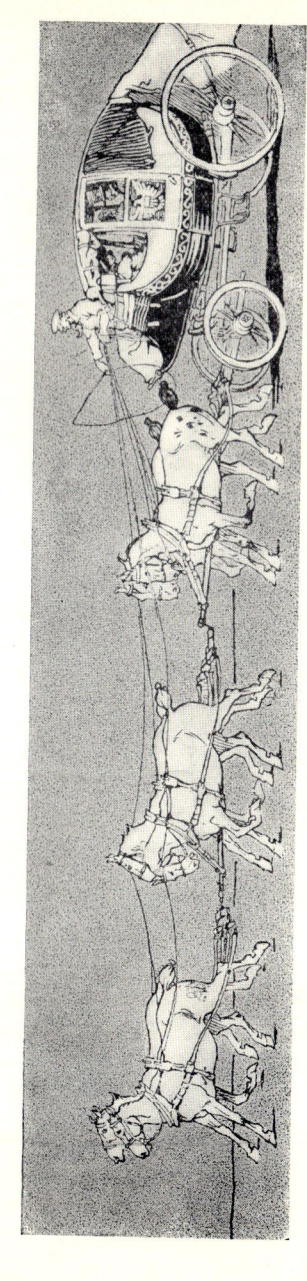

"We could hear the driver winding his horn and it all seemed too fine and grand."
From an old print.

Lake Michigan, and the National road. The last was the turnpike continuing that road from the Ohio State line, and extending thence to Indianapolis, and from there west to Illinois, and by a State road toward the north to Lake Michigan. There were also to be constructed turnpikes from the capital to La Fayette, and to Jeffersonville. The Wabash River channel from Vincennes to the Ohio was to have the obstructions removed. Before these grand schemes for transportation in Indiana were entirely outlined, steam had been applied to railroads in England, and such a road was added to the project and planned to run from Madison to Indianapolis. Other railroads were also suggested. Even a casual glance at this bare outline of roads and canals, mapped out by the State Commissioner, will reveal the deeply felt demand for means of reaching the markets.

When we follow the itinerary of a load of merchandise from New York to Indiana, we can realize through what a tortuous journey it passed and what length of time it took to transport merchandise. From New York, goods by freight were taken by boat up the Hudson River, to Albany, then fifteen miles over the turnpike to Schenectady, up the Mohawk by man power, through the canal and eight locks, around the Falls, and on from Utica to Lake Oneida by a canal and creek, through that lake to Onondaga and Oswego River—into Lake Ontario; thence to Lewiston, then overland along the Niagara, by boat on Lake Erie; thence by land to Fort Bœuf, again by water to Pittsburgh and down the Ohio and up the Wabash River. One hundred thousand bushels of salt, annually, passed this way from Central New York to Indiana.

The passage of the bill authorizing the internal

improvements was vastly popular. The news was carried from village to village and celebrated with the ringing of bells, firing of cannon, and processions marching through the streets. The people rejoiced over the prospect of an outlet to the seaboard for the products of the country, of which they could raise so much more than they could use. Work was begun on the Wabash Canal in 1832, on the White-water in 1836, and on the Central Canal in 1837. It was undertaken in sections, and in different parts of the State at the same time, by different contractors. Immediately, labor was in demand, and immigrants from Ireland and Germany were brought into the State to work on the canals. These families remained as permanent residents, and many of them became prosperous. In time, they were thoroughly absorbed into the body politic, as loyal citizens. For the next four years, the work went on throughout the projected system of public improvements. Along the lines of the canals, Paddy, just over from Ireland, and Hans from Germany, were making the dirt fly; and laborers, already resident, were employed on the turnpikes, or in building warehouses and wharves, for the opening of commerce. The only grumbling heard came from the counties through which none of the projected highways were to pass. There were citizens who, for economic reasons, had opposed the whole scheme of internal improvements being undertaken by the State; but the majority had won. As soon as the bill had passed, the wildest speculation in lands ensued; farmers added to their farms and investors flocked into the State. If all had been paid for, distress need not have followed, but many of the ventures were undertaken on credit, and ruin of fortunes came.

People had visions of the revenues from the canals and roads paying all taxes, and the dawn of a new era was prophesied. While manual labor on the various public works was progressing in many sections, a cloud appeared on the commercial horizon, to disquiet careful citizens. Grave errors in financing the system of highways were made, which brought financial disaster to the State, long before anything had approached completion. The total of the canals, turnpikes, and railroads surveyed and included in the estimates, under the Act of 1836, was about twelve hundred and eighty-nine miles; which, it was estimated then, would incur an expenditure of $19,914,-244.00. A permanent Commission was created to represent the State, in organizing the department of construction, and negotiating for funding the debt to be assumed. To meet the amounts necessary, so large for a frontier commonwealth, required wisdom and exceedingly provident management. This, the momentous question certainly failed to receive. Many mistakes were made. One of the fundamental errors was the result of pressure from each section, that their improvements should be executed at once; and the Board tried to satisfy public clamor, by endeavoring to construct all of the projects simultaneously. Then when the bonds were issued to raise the funds to build the canals and roads, they were sold on credit. As a consequence, there was, very soon, no money to meet the demands of contractors for supplies and construction. The wages of laborers went far in arrears and, of course, this immediately affected the small shopkeepers and general trade. Construction would be suspended for months, until funds might be forthcoming, causing great unrest and distress. To add to the misfortunes of the people, the great panic of 1837 swept over the nation, and financial disaster was general to the whole country.

An additional short-sighted financial measure at the very beginning was, that even the money to pay the very interest on the debt was borrowed; which compounded the indebtedness to the further embarrassment of the Treasury. In 1839, a large portion of the contemplated improvements were abandoned. The construction of the railroads was left to private enterprise. The Wabash Canal, which had been started before the General Improvements Bill had passed, was now in use over part of the route and yielding a revenue. This was not abandoned, as it had the land grants from the general government still unsold, from which it could yet realize funds. In 1842, when of the twelve hundred miles of improvements contemplated, 281 miles had been completed, the State found itself in debt, for all causes, $207,894,613. Thus, Indiana, like several other States at that period, faced bankruptcy. It was often heard said, Indiana cannot pay the interest on her public debt. Her resources were very much crippled on account of her remoteness from markets, which limited production. As in some other States, it was openly claimed that the indebtedness would have to go by default, but this was abhorrent to honest citizens and was very widely opposed. Sensational speeches were made in the State Assembly about "preserving the honor of the State, sir," one member asserting that he would chop wood to pay his proportion of the State debt before he would listen to repudiation. Mr. Butler and others representing the foreign bondholders spent season after season in the State, trying to avoid total loss, and have the work go on until revenues might be realized. Finally most of the works were permanently abandoned, and the Wabash and Erie Canal, with its lands and tolls, was taken in part payment of the claims, the bondholders promising to complete the canal. This they did by 1851. This waterway extended from Evansville, on the Ohio, to Toledo, 379 miles of it lying within the State of Indiana. After the introduction of railroads had made the canal unprofitable, the legality of the compromise was questioned, and the bondholders wanted the State to pay half of the debt for which the canal had been taken, as they claimed they had been defrauded of tolls, on account of the franchise granted to the railroads. They never realized more than $9\frac{1}{2}\%$ of their principal, making the investment disastrous individually. The whole project had been so to the State exchequer; but the canal was a wonderful impetus to the development of the West.

It has always been conceded that the economic and social influence of the public works was far reaching. Every mile of improved transportation by turnpike facilitated the mail service and overland immigration, and made it possible for the inland settlers to reach the waterways with their produce. The canal increased the production of the country in a wonderful way. Before its completion, trade was stagnant. There was little incentive for industry among the people, for there was no market for more produce than could be consumed within their own territory, and lands lay idle. At one time, when Mr. Henry T. Sample was going overland, collecting pelts for a cargo, his business led him across the fertile Wea plains, fit to be called the Garden of the Gods. He soliloquized thus to himself and his gray pony: "This stretch of country is beautiful beyond compare, but I would not give this bale of pelts for the whole of it, as I could not sell what it would produce." He lived to see the plains then stretched before him, worth millions of dollars.

Before the canal was built, wheat sold for 37 to 45 cents a bushel and corn from 10 to 20 cents a bushel, while at the same time for their imports they paid $10.00 a barrel for salt, and sugar brought from 25 to 35 cents per pound. A Putnam County settler says that prior to the completion of the canal he hauled a load of wheat (25 bushels) to Hamilton County, Ohio, a distance of 150 miles, for which he received 38 cents a bushel.

In less than two years after the canal reached a district, wheat advanced to 90 cents a bushel and salt could be bought for less than $4.00 a barrel. Mr. Benton says that

"before the opening of the canal in 1844, the zone of the Maumee and upper Wabash valleys had sent towards Toledo only 5622 bushels of corn, five years later the exports from the same region, sent to that port, reached 2,755,149 bushels.

"For home consumption, the large number of laborers added to the population increased the demand for produce, and much more money than ever before came into circulation.

"When the canal was begun, the upper Wabash Valley was a wilderness. There were only 12,000 scattered population in all that district, but people began to flock in by wagon-loads so that the number had increased to two hundred and seventy thousand by 1840. In 1846, over thirty families every day settled in the State. Five

The Old Canal and Deserted Towpath.

new counties were organized in three years following the opening of the first section of the canal from Fort Wayne to Huntington. Thirty per cent. of the emigrants entering the port of New York passed into the group of States where the Erie Canal and its connections were being constructed. The boats that took grain up the canal brought back emigrants and homesteaders from the East. Thirty-eight counties in Indiana and nine in southeastern Illinois were directly affected by the new waterway. Long wagon trains of produce wended their way to the towns on the shores of the canal. In the year 1844, four hundred wagons in a day were waiting to unload at points like La Fayette and Wabash."[1]

Towns rose and grew as a result of the canal commerce, and the larger ones, which grew into cities, owed their first impetus to the same cause, and the railroad which succeeded it made their existence secure. We are told that in 1836 alone the land sales in Indiana amounted to three million acres. In addition to the enormous impetus given to agricultural exportation, the canal also supplied water-power for manufacturing. In one year nine flour mills were built along the new line, and eight saw-mills, and paper, woolen, and oil mills came into existence, doing a flourishing business. The population of the counties bordering along the canal increased 397% from 1840 to 1850, while counties containing better lands, but more remote from the waterway, only increased 190% in the same decade. The incoming population was of the most desirable quality, the majority being from Eastern and Northern States, and it was this interstate migration of American-born people which caused

[1] Benton, Elbert Jay, *The Wabash Trade Route in the Development of the Old Northwest*, Indiana Hist. Soc. Publications.

an entire political change in the State. The element which came in from the North helped to counterbalance the early settlement of Southern pro-slavery people along the Ohio and lower Wabash rivers. The canal, also, largely reversed the tide of trade from New Orleans to New York, and changed the centre of population. In 1830, five-sixths of the people within the State lived in the southern tier of counties bordering on the navigable streams. Ten years later, says Mr. Benton,

"the line had pushed up and by 1850 there was an equal distribution, about as many living in the canal zone as the river counties. In 1860, the population on the Wabash was from forty-nine to ninety to the square mile, while along the Ohio River it varied from eighteen to forty-five persons to the square mile."[1]

The Virginia, Carolina, and Kentucky settlements formerly had outnumbered the combined totals of New England and Middle State emigration. The finest flower of the Western States was from the intermarriage of these families from the East joined with the South. Of the valuable acquisition of foreign laborers, it should be remembered that the Germans who came in were tired of monarchical traditions, and, attracted by the name and the opposition to slavery, they very largely attached themselves to the Republican party. Owing to the Know-Nothing agitation, just at this time the Irish became to a great extent affiliated with the Democrats, all of which helped to maintain the balance of numbers between the two parties in Indiana, and made it, proverbially, a battle-ground in politics.

[1] Benton, E. J., *The Wabash Trade Route*, Publications of Ind. Hist. Soc.

The period from 1841 to 1843 saw the opening of through traffic on the Wabash and Erie Canal from the Lake to La Fayette. Ten years later, after passing through deep financial hindrances, as we have seen, it was completed—the 459 miles to Evansville. The years from 1847 to 1856, says Mr. Benton, may be considered the heyday of the canal. Within that period the tolls and income reached the highest mark, amounting in 1852 to $193,400.18. The passenger "packets" ran regularly, proceeding in a most leisurely way, stopping at every wharf for produce and passengers. The little towns on the way could be reconnoitred during the delay of taking on and putting off freight, and one could call upon a friend, or conclude a business transaction, before the next stage of the journey was begun! Weary with the monotony of the journey, travellers often strolled along the towpath ahead of the boat, while it was going through the locks, and they would gather berries or wild flowers along the banks. If it chanced to be in the autumn, they sometimes went nutting in the near-by forests. Games at cards were a great relief to the tedium of the voyage, and often the play ran high, and bunco men followed the line, as they did on the river steamers. There was time for reading and reflection on such a journey. Lifelong friendships were formed during the leisurely passage, and children played about as if at home. In pleasant weather the passengers always sat about on the top deck of the boat, arrayed in holiday attire, now unknown in travelling, and gliding smoothly along past field and forest, they found it a delightful way of seeing the country.

Sometimes we read tales of hot summer nights in stuffy staterooms and cabins, and marvellous stories of swarms of mosquitoes, which were probably the cause of malarial fevers often contracted en route. One young girl has left a bitter complaint, in print, of her various experiences along the way, and added that all the mosquitoes ever hatched in the mud puddles of Indiana were condensed into one humming, ravenous swarm about their heads.

Notwithstanding the beneficial effects on commerce, from the introduction of steamboat and canal transportation, as compared with old flatboats and wagon trains, their doom in turn was approaching. Steam had been applied to rail locomotion; even before Indiana's dearly bought system of internal improvement had been fairly inaugurated, the very masses of immigrants brought in by the waterways made more rapid transit of merchandise imperative. Says Mr. Benton:

"While the canals were immensely stimulating the business of the State and encouraging immigration, the very enlargement of the volume of traffic, in turn, called for a more general system of transportation. As a direct result, there grew up a railroad system which ruined the canals."[1]

In the thirties, the friends of internal improvement were sharply divided concerning the relative merits of canals and railroads. It was admitted that for novelty and speed, a railroad might be preferable to stage-coaches and canal boats, but it was contended that for a long journey, or for a man travelling with a family, a canal was better! It was pointed out that on a canal boat passengers could eat their meals, could walk about, write a letter, or play a game of

[1] Benton, E. J., *Wabash Trade Route*, Indiana Hist. Soc. Pub.

poker, whereas in a railway carriage these things were impossible! In a canal boat, too, the passengers were as safe as at home, whereas in a railway car nobody could tell what might happen! The incoming of the railways was necessarily gradual and river traffic died as gradually. For example, it took eight years to complete the first railway in the State, and it stretched only from the Ohio River to the capital of the State. Vast sums had been expended in the canal ventures, and the bondholders tried to maintain the business. Steadily, the whole system refused to become profitable, and repairs were too expensive to be undertaken in the face of the new steam power. After dragging along for years in a dying condition, the Whitewater Canal was sold, for railroad right of way, in 1862 and 1865. The last section of the Wabash Canal was abandoned in 1874. Only the towns that chanced to lie along the route that was touched by the railroads survived. The immense old warehouses were abandoned to humbler uses, and to this day may be seen, where there is no longer any sign of the old canal save a depression in the surface of the land, grown up with reeds and rushes. Shadowy advertisements of the imports of teas, coffees, and spices may be deciphered, we are told, on the beams and walls; but the channel, which carried that merchandise, has gone like a tale that is told. Only a right of way for some other mode of transportation can be resurrected from its past.

The old National road, already referred to, proved to be an open sesame to the West, a great impetus to immigration and commerce. For years it was the highway from the Southeast.

During the years that the Internal Improvement

Act was being carried out by the building of turnpikes and canals to give other outlets to market, the traffic southward by steamboats on the rivers had continued to prosper. There were always passengers travelling on the steamers, as well as the freight they carried, all of which was often interrupted by obstructions in the rivers. The streams continued difficult of navigation, and the building of railroads was urged to further commerce. The same innovation which caused the canals to be unprofitable and finally abandoned, also made the river traffic languish and die.

When the national tragedy of the Civil War was ended, the steamboat owners awoke to the fact that their calling was gone forever. That enemy of the river boats, the railroad, whose growth even the war could not check, had rapidly stretched its fingers out over the land. By consulting a map of forty-five years ago, it will be seen that the railroads of that time closely followed the banks of the rivers. They reached out, like the strands of a craftily laid net, to ensnare the business of the steamboats. In the face of such odds, defeat was inevitable. The river boats had to go, but the fight was an obstinate one. Says an old record:

"For ten long years the struggle between the railroads and steamboats went on; fierce and bitter for the first five, and, for the steamboats, vindictive and heroic to the last. Millions of dollars were invested in the great white vessels that glided up and down the Mississippi and its tributaries, but they dropped out of the race one by one, to be tied up to the bank and become the sport of time. Some far-seeing owners, knowing the fight lost for all time, dismantled their vessels and sold the fittings and machinery. Others, more obstinate or hopeful, kept their boats trim and clean, ready against the day when public sentiment and the flow of business should again come their way. Every spring they painted them, every day they polished the brasswork. Through the long idle summers, they would sit in the pilot-houses watching the railroad engines write, in letters of smoke, against the sky, the story of their doom. The hungry race for cargoes was responsible for more than one river tragedy, during the period of waning trade. Where, six years before, captains had haughtily steamed past landings, regardless of the frantic signals of planters whose cotton, wheat, or hemp was piled on the shore, they now found themselves driven to the humiliating expedient of arguing with shippers in favor of their boats, as against the railroads. Captains scented cargoes from afar. The wind seemed to carry news of a waiting shipment, and idle boats raced to the scene, like a school of sharks. The first to arrive nearly always secured the cargo."

In an address on the future prospects of the inland capital of Indiana, a pioneer orator dilated on its improved prospects owing to the new invention of the propelling power of steam on land which was to revolutionize the channels of commerce. About the same time, when Judge Test was running for Congress, he sought to attract popular approval by referring to the new steam roads: "I tell you, fellow-citizens, that in England they are now running the cars thirty miles an hour, and they will yet be run at a higher speed in America."[1] This was enough, said his competitor for the office, the crowd set up a loud laugh at the expense of the Judge. An old fellow standing by bawled out: "You are crazy, or do you think

[1] Test, Judge, *Campaign Address*.

we are all fools? a man could not live a moment at that speed." The Judge was lost. His successful opponent had reason to wish the trains were then running, as it took him seventeen days on horseback to reach Washington City. The people were so enthusiastic in projecting railroads, that in 1832 the legislature granted six charters in one day, but building them was quite another affair. The one from Madison to Indianapolis was the first one to be built in Indiana. It was constructed part of the way by the State, at a very gradual pace; and the remainder of the distance by private persons, enjoying a subsidy of land from the State. In 1839, this road had been completed twenty miles, to Vernon, and so deliberate was the extension that it did not reach Indianapolis until 1847! With the exception of the Madison road all of the first railways in Indiana, as in other States, were laid with "strap iron" on wooden rails. When other roads were being constructed, the Madison Railroad officials complained that their monopoly was being ruined by the competition of the other roads, since the State had passed a law granting charters to them! At first the railroads of Indiana were not parts of great through systems of transcontinental roads; but rather they radiated from the capital like the spokes of a wheel, connecting that city with river and lake ports. These roads traversed counties possessing wonderfully rich soil, and their agricultural products and live stock traffic enriched the companies that built them. The capitalists of each town imagined that they saw fortunes in railroad-building, and by 1853 there had been over fifteen opened to traffic. The mileage increased constantly. After the Civil War, on account of Indiana's geographical position, which made it necessary for the roads running east and west, north of the Ohio River, to pass across the State, her roads were made part of the great trunk systems. In a few years the surface of the commonwealth was a network of railroads. In 1907, there were 6976 miles of railways within the State. The development of Indiana attributable to steam roads is so in common with that of the whole country that it needs no special mention. The first telegraph line in the State was put up in 1848.

About the time that railroads were first penetrating the West, there arose a great craze for the building of "plank roads." This was in response to the urgent demand for better wagon roads whereon to reach the markets. Timber was plentiful and cheap, and this material seemed to offer a solution of the good roads question. By the year 1850, four hundred miles of planked roads, at a cost of twelve to fifteen hundred dollars a mile, had been completed in the State. But by that time the first roads constructed had begun to show the weak points of the method of paving. When new, these roads carried the traveller along swimmingly; but when the planks began to wear thin, and the sills to rot out, and the grading or foundation to sink away, they became justly called "corduroy" roads, and were certainly a weariness to the flesh. In some low places, the construction sank entirely out of sight. Many miles of the roads became so execrable that the farmers drove alongside in the mud rather than "jostle their bones" over the logs and ruts of the artificial road.

By the time the people were recovering from the great losses of money from this form of highway, and their discouragement about better roads, it was discovered that Nature had endowed the State in many districts with vast gravel beds, unsurpassed for the construction of turnpikes. Companies were chartered to build and operate toll roads. These proved very profitable, and were also a blessing to the farmers who used them for heavy traffic. They served their day, and passed into the free gravel roads now owned by the counties.

Mr. Riley represents his old pioneers as talking reminiscently [1]

"Of the times when we first settled here, and travel was
 so bad,
When we had to go on horseback, and sometimes on
 'shanks mare,'
And 'blaze' a road fer them behind that had to travel
 there.

"And now we go a-trotten' 'long a level gravel pike,
In a big two-hoss road-wagon, jest as easy as you like:
Two of us on the front seat, and our wimmen-folks behind,
A-settin' in theyr Winsor cheers in perfect peace of mind!"

The little toll-house at the side of the road with the superannuated couple on the front stoop has gone. The "pole and sweep" for closing the highway has disappeared. Better roads are still needed in most parts of the State, to bring it up to the high plane demanded for the truest economy and broadest civilization, but those advantages are surely, if slowly, becoming general in more neighborhoods. At the close of the year 1905, there were in Indiana 16,268 miles of gravel roads.

A new means of transportation has dawned on the

[1] Riley, James Whitcomb, *Neighborly Poems*, page 23. Indianapolis, 1891.

State, and is becoming a great social factor throughout Indiana. The interurban trolley roads are extending in all directions with astonishing rapidity. One corporation alone is operating over six hundred miles of electric lines and there are already thirteen hundred miles of electric roads within the bounds of the State and two thousand miles more projected. More than fifty millions have been invested. Indianapolis is the greatest electric railway centre in the world. Passengers are carried through the State for one half former railroad fares, and parcels at reasonable rates. What this pleasant and rapid transportation means to the rural population can hardly be realized by the denizens of cities. From a position of great social isolation, the farmer's family, along these routes, may come into close touch with near-by towns and cities.

Just now it seems hazardous to venture mention of the latest mode of locomotion in connection with the rural districts, but motor carriages have appeared upon the scene and are taking their place in both town and country. Progressive farmers are buying automobiles, many using them for power as well as for pleasure on the road. Motor wagons will still further eliminate distance between country and town.

With the national awakening to the vast opportunity for improving transportation facilities by utilizing the natural arteries of commerce to create deep waterways through the heart of the continent, Indiana must share in the benefits, not only because of her nearness to other great streams, but because of her geographical position, and by the development of her own tributaries to the Mississippi. When these new plans for inland navigation are developed to their consistent goal, the old "Appian Way" will again be dotted with the commerce of the East, on its journey from the Great Lakes to the Gulf. Through the Wabash route, the produce of a great interior will join the Mississippi deep waterway. Through the Ohio with its improved channel, which flows along the entire southern border of the State, the traffic of that district will be accommodated. The Calumet, deepened, will furnish an outlet for the regions about Chicago; while by a canal across the northern part of Indiana, from Lake Erie, by way of the Maumee, to Lake Michigan, the shipping between New York and Chicago may avoid the detour of five hundred miles of stormy lake travel, around the peninsula. Canals were once bankrupted by the incoming of railroads, and became obsolete; but with the enormous increase in the population and foreign commerce, the traffic of the country has outgrown the railroads; and, with the aid of electricity for rapid propelling power, canals must come into their own again. The shades of the early pioneers who worked so hard for improved transportation may hover over the fleets on their way across the State, and contemplate Indiana as a sea-going community!

We have travelled the centuries from pirogue to automobile and electric trolley; we have seen the first white man paddle his canoe to the trading-post; have jogged with the pioneer over muddy roads, and immigrated with the early settlers in the prairie schooner, or with them have poled their flatboats up the rivers. We have welcomed, with them, the little steamers and packets on the waterways; have seen steam applied to land locomotives, relegating all other modes of transportation to desuetude; and in turn have seen this, with all other methods, being surpassed by electricity. Before us has passed the panorama of the evolution of transportation, epitomizing the progress of civilization in Indiana.

As the quaint vehicles of the past roll slowly down the highways toward oblivion, we wave good-bye. With a sigh for the wearisome journeys they entailed, we look forward with wonder and interest to what the future has in store, in the development of the means of transportation.

CHAPTER XII

THE SOCIAL EXPERIMENTS AT NEW HARMONY

THOSE who are interested in the social problems of the day may wish to review the record of the experiments at New Harmony. They are an example of the failures in the establishment of socialistic communities, in a State where individualism is the pronounced belief of the whole people. Whether collectivism, in any form, will be congenial to the American spirit, it is too soon, perhaps, to declare. In that earlier day, however, the hardy frontiersmen looked upon the experiments of Owen and Rapp as a theory of social life which was in direct opposition to the independent freedom which they had come into the wilderness, at a great sacrifice, to secure. Individual initiative was the key to the character of the Westerner. He made it his creed. He was aroused to suspicion and antagonism by any encroachments of dictation regarding the forms of his religious belief, the family life, or contract for his labor. Hence the neighbors of the autocrat of Harmonie, and afterward the social reformer, David Owen, were lacking in sympathy and appreciation of the colossal efforts of the two great innovators. A few of the settlers sent their young people to the incomparable schools established by Owen. More of them bought articles that were manufactured by the Rappite community. Sympathy with the theories of the communists, they had none. A few visionaries, in different parts of the southern section of the State, and in other States, followed afar off, and made experiments of their own, lasting a few months, in community life. But the settlers, in general, combated the ideas promulgated at New Harmony.

This little village in southern Indiana will interest us by its unique history, two socialistic communes having succeeded each other on this attractive spot in the lower Wabash Valley. These communities, established in the early part of the nineteenth century, live only in history; but they brought to Indiana one of the most interesting phases of co-operative life known to the nation. Many volumes have been written on the history of the communities, the theories that they represented, and the lives of their founders and co-workers, but a brief account of their existence is necessary in any story of Indiana.

In the spring of 1815, George Rapp led his German peasant followers from their settlement in Pennsylvania to the wilderness of Territorial Indiana. They came down the Ohio River and fifty miles up the Wabash in flatboats laden with the community goods, implements of labor and manufacture, and landed at the beautiful location previously chosen by Frederick Rapp. In imagination we see the eight hundred men, women, and children, clad in the quaint costume of their native Würtemberg, kneeling on the bank of the forest stream, and joining with Father Rapp in dedicating "Harmonie" to the purposes of a primitive, Christian brotherhood. These people belonged to the stolid German peasant class, and joined their fortunes with George Rapp, to emigrate to a free country, and worship God according to their own peculiar beliefs, which were the teachings of Father Rapp. He was a strong-willed man, a very arbitrary over-lord, and the simple band implicitly followed where he guided them. The newly acquired estate comprised about thirty thousand acres, of the most fertile lands that bordered on the beautiful river. The tract was covered with the magnificent primeval forest usual in Indiana. The hillsides were suited to the planting of vineyards; and the river, as was foreseen, furnished a highway to the markets, and water-power for their various mills. A dozen years before this time, their autocratic leader had led his followers forth from the fatherland to the wilds of Pennsylvania, and had planted a wonderfully successful community there. They had labored with such industry and plodding faithfulness, under the wise management of George Rapp and his adopted son Frederick, that their common property was considered sacrificed, when it was sold for one hundred thousand dollars, upon their departure for Indiana. The Territory of Indiana at that time had but few settlers, and these were located through the southern tier of counties, on scattered clearings, and in tiny villages. There, the zealous Rappite community soon found that the opening up of the fertile acres exposed them to the prevailing malaria, which had proven so deadly to all the pioneers. The mortality among their membership, the first four or five years, appalled them, and, it is said, determined their resolution to sell the great plantation as soon as it could be made attractive to a purchaser. Gradually, however, as the lands were cultivated, the unhealthfulness dis-

Social Experiments at New Harmony 243

appeared; until, in the latest years of their sojourn, there were only two or three deaths a year. These thrifty people planted orchards, and vineyards, and broad acres of grain. Their gardens were models, and their flocks and herds multiplied in the meadows. After they had provided themselves with temporary cabins, they built a village of homes and community houses, a fort, a granary, saw-mill, woollen mill, brickyard, distillery, brewery, and a silk factory. Eventually, they built shops in the town for all the trades.

The homely buildings they erected are still in use, testifying to the integrity of their workmanship, if not to their artistic sense of design. One of the large community houses is now used as a tavern, another as a theatre, and one as a general store; and on the outer wall the same old sun-dial marks the hours for the twentieth century inhabitants, that served to assemble the plodding peasants for their march to the fields. The church in which all worshipped was built on the plan which Father Rapp claimed had come to him in a revelation. It was in the form of a Greek cross and was nearly one hundred and twenty feet in length. The roof was supported by twenty-eight pillars of walnut, cherry, and sassafras wood. The walnut logs measured six feet in circumference. The exterior of the church was not attractive architecturally, but an English traveller wrote that one could scarcely imagine himself in the wilds of Indiana, on the borders of the Wabash, while walking through the long resounding aisles and surveying the stately colonnades of this cathedral-like church.

During all their sojourn in the State, this peculiar people saw nothing of the outside world and its attractions. The adopted son, Frederick Rapp, was the business representative for the community. He it was that introduced any saving leaven of variety into their lives. Flower-gardens and a band of music were allowed them to relieve the dead monotony of the prescribed round of their existence. The people, both men and women, toiled in the shops and fields for the common treasury. Each day they rose before six o'clock, and after breakfasting went forth in a procession to the daily tasks. Marriage was not allowed, and the only increase in their numbers were the accessions from Germany. The squatters on the lands near the community were too fond of their free and independent life to be attracted to such an autocracy. The homely dress worn was all of their own manufacture; both men and women wore home-made straw hats, short jackets of coarse material, and a skirt or trousers of the same goods. There were flowers in the doorways, and there was a pleasant regulation which provided an excellent band of music that played in the public garden at sunset, and on the hillsides, when the peasants were laboring in the fields. The people were industrious, kind, strictly temperate—not even the use of tobacco being allowed. Their honest and upright dealing assured their communal success, everything that they sold being of excellent quality and strictly as they represented it to be. The trade of the community extended from Pittsburg to New Orleans, and they had branch stores at Vincennes and across the Illinois line.

In any estimate of the achievements of this experiment in community life, it must be remembered that the membership was united by a strong religious bond, that they were all producers, were all peasants who had been accustomed to being suppressed, and that they were ignorant of the language of America. They were from a dull and stolid social stratum, and had enjoyed little religious or political liberty in Germany, very meagre material comforts, and few pleasures, so that the lack of freedom of initiative in their restricted existence at Harmonie seemed, to most of them, offset by the creature comforts supplied to all of the commune.

The good business management of the leaders and the patient, plodding industry of the united membership, celibacy which restricted the increase of unproductive members, and their belief in the near approach of the judgment day which made them careless of owning private property, contributed toward the increase of community wealth. It was said that when the Harmonists left Indiana their funds amounted to a million dollars, which in that primitive time was a vast sum. "In May, 1824, we have departed," was scrawled under the stairway in one of the community houses. Back to Pennsylvania, this time on the borders of the Ohio River, eighteen miles below Pittsburg, George Rapp led his stolid followers to a new place which they named Economy. Was it to prevent any measure of rest being their portion, a fear that luxurious living might entice his flock from strict obedience? Or was it to be nearer the Eastern markets? No statement is left to tell why the autocrat sold Old Harmonie, and began the laborious task of creating a new settlement. Mrs. Blake, in her story of the commune, called *Heart's Haven*, gives a vivid impression of the life in that circumscribed community, with all of its suppressed emotions of mother love, and natural longing for separate homes, and a return to their marriage vows, and recognition of the family life.

When Richard Flower, a neighboring communist on the Illinois side of the Wabash, was going back to England, George Rapp commissioned him to sell the Harmonie estate, if possible, and Flower received $5000 for accomplishing the transfer. He made the sale to Robert Owen, a famous Scotch philanthropist, who had been conducting a successful commune in the manufacturing town of New Lanark. Mr. Owen took over the whole of the great property with its substantial improvements, paying about $150,000 for it. It is said that double the sum received would have been a modest estimate of the value of the princely estate and well-built town. When the faithful Rappists had settled in their new location in Pennsylvania, the same industry and capable leadership continued their material prosperity. George Rapp died in 1847. He was succeeded in command by Elders elected by the community. "These men were able and honorable, we are glad to know; for the sake of the quiet creatures drowsing away their remnant of life, fat and contented, or driving their plows through the fields, or sitting on the stoops of the village houses when evening comes."[1] In 1874, years after their exodus, the Rappists sent back to their old community in Indiana and repurchased the church edifice. They used part of the stone and brick for a wall about their ancient burying-ground; giving the lot and the wing of the building for the Working Men's Institute Library, in memory of the Harmonie Society founded by George Rapp in 1815.

The prosperity of the commune, in their new location,

[1] Lockwood, Geo. B., *The New Harmony Movement*, page 34.

was so great that in the seventies the wealth of the Rappists was estimated to be any sum from ten to thirty millions of dollars. These values dwindled with the passing of the membership by death and from the poor management of later leaders. The community ceased to exist, and became a corporation of individual holdings. From a material point of view it was one of the few successful communes, but Robert Owen saw wherein it was a failure. It contravened an important law of nature when it forbade family ties. The animal nature had been sufficiently cared for, they looked well fed and decently clothed and free from business anxieties, but Rapp's disciples had bought this immunity from bread-and-butter cares dearly—even at the expense of the heart and head. By the greatest imaginable contrast, the leaders of the new community, which entered into the possession of New Harmony, as they re-christened it, were assembled for the pursuit of the things of the spirit along intellectual paths—for culture for its own sake, for research in science, and particularly for educational advancement.

Robert Owen was a dreamer. He was of those who have visions of a better future for mankind. To obtain the right environment for instituting a new social system, on the community plan, he bought the magnificent estate of New Harmony. Of this selection he said:

"No site for a number of communities, in close union together, can be found finer than that which surrounds us. Its natural situation and the variety of its natural productions exceed anything I have seen in Europe or America; the rich land, intermixed with rivers, islands, woods, and hills in beautiful proportions to each other, presents a prospect which highly gratifies every intelligent beholder."[1]

The village on the domain, which had been built by the Rappites, the new commune diverted to the various needs of the different classes of inhabitants. The factories were retained, the community houses were used for the members and for the new boarding-schools. The vast church was converted into an assembly hall, for the town meetings, weekly concerts and balls, and the various lectures that were given. The second-story rooms in the wings were used for reading, debating, and music rooms. The frame church was retained for religious meetings, and day and night schools.

Of Robert Owen, the founder of New Harmony, his biographer, Lloyd Jones, tells us that the great reformer was born in Wales in 1771. After a few short years of schooling, which he appreciated so unusually, the lad, at the age of ten, went to London as a draper's apprentice. In the home of his employers he found a library, and read omnivorously during every leisure moment. After learning his trade, he worked at it until his eighteenth year, saving every cent possible; for in his whole life, it is said, he never indulged in an injurious or expensive habit. Starting in a manufacturing business with five hundred dollars capital, he went steadily onward, through various changes of partnerships, in the cotton spinning and allied trades, until he had accumulated a large fortune.

During these years of marked success in business, Robert Owen had constantly devoted much of his time and thought to the amelioration of the wretched

[1] Lockwood, Geo. B., page 70. New York, 1905.

condition of the laboring classes throughout the United Kingdom. After acquiring the factory town of New Lanark, which was typical in its drunkenness, squalor, and ignorance, he made that village renowned as a happy and orderly community of factory hands. At that time he met and was married to Miss Dale, whose name was coupled with that of Owen in naming each of their children. To New Lanark, it is said, came representatives of royalty, philanthropists, and educators from all parts of Europe, who journeyed thither to study the processes which Mr. Owen put in operation for the betterment of the working people in his mills, making them the most happy and orderly in all England. At the same time, in agitation and in national legislation, every social movement, every real advance in England on behalf of the workers, linked itself to the name of Robert Owen. He wrote voluminously, and labored unceasingly, for the reform of factory laws, for the establishment of cooperative societies, and for better conditions of living for the wage-earners. Frederick Engles has left the statement that as long as Robert Owen was merely a philanthropist he was rewarded with applause, wealth, honor, and glory. He was the most popular man in Europe, not only with men of his own class, but with statesmen and princes, who listened to him approvingly.

This was the man who entered into the project of establishing in Indiana a communistic colonization scheme which he had long advocated. His son has recorded that the offer of the Rappites to sell a village, already built on a vast tract of land capable of supporting tens of thousands of people, in a new and free country, was the determining cause of Mr. Owen's closing the purchase of Harmonie. He and his sons gave up every comfort and luxury in England that he might have a vast theatre in which to try his plans of social reform.

It was in 1825 that Mr. Owen came into possession of the thirty thousand acres of land, three thousand of which were under cultivation. Full of hope and noble enthusiasm, he inaugurated the plans for the "new moral world," which was to be an organization of society to rationally educate and employ all classes, giving a new existence to man by surrounding him with superior circumstances only. In contrast to the Rappite theory, education, pleasant environment, culture, and freedom of thought were to take the place of ignorance, an absence of amusements, and of an arbitrary ecclesiastical autocracy, to hold the band of people together.

Invitations to membership included all who were in sympathy with Robert Owen's belief in the need of a new form of society. In the course of his address in the halls of Congress at Washington, he said:

"In the heart of the United States, and almost in the centre of its unequalled internal navigation, that Power which governs and directs the universe, and every action of man, has arranged circumstances which were far beyond my control, and permits me to commence a new empire of peace and good-will to men, founded on other principles than those of the present or the past. I have, however, no wish to lead the way. I am desirous that governments should become masters of the subject, adopt the principles, encourage the practice, and thereby retain the direction of the public mind for their own benefit, and the benefit of the people. But as I have not the control of circumstances in this public course, I must show what private exertions, guided by these new principles, can accomplish at New Harmony, and these new proceedings will begin in April."[1]

During the year 1825, students of public questions in Europe and America were agog over the new project and visionaries of every description were attracted by the experiment. Mr. Owen was an extreme liberal in his religious views and many of those who drifted into the community were free-thinkers. Before he himself reached the scene there had swarmed into New Harmony so many eccentric and curious people, so many with hobbies to carry out and others who wished to attain a life where they would not have to labor, that Mr. Owen was deprived of a choice of inhabitants, upon whom to try the new social scheme. The first address of the great heart who founded the commune seems almost pathetic in the light of its brief history. His followers and the curious people from the country round about were assembled in the vast church, now rechristened the Hall of Harmony. "I am come to this country," he said, "to introduce an entire new system of society; to change it from an ignorant and selfish system to an enlightened social system which shall gradually unite all interests into one, and remove all causes for contest between individuals."[2] The change must be gradual, he explained, and after a sincere, candid, and hopeful explanation of the details of his plans, he laid the proposed constitution for the preliminary society before them. It was adopted four days later, and in it his purposes in founding the community were comprehensively stated.

[1] Lockwood, Geo. B., *The New Harmony Movement*, page 70. New York, 1905.
[2] *Ibid.*, page 75.

This document may be found in the old library of the village, or more conveniently consulted in the pages of Mr. George Lockwood's most interesting work on *The New Harmony Movement*. The points can only be touched upon here. The constitution is prefaced by the declaration that the society is instituted generally to promote the happiness of the world. It then sets forth that persons of all ages and descriptions may become members. Persons of color may be received as helpers, or for future colonization by themselves. No rank was to be recognized, no artificial inequality acknowledged. Precedence was to be given only to age, experience, and those chosen to office. As Mr. Owen, the founder, had purchased the property, paid for it, and furnished the capital to consummate the plans, it was modestly claimed that he should have the appointment of a committee of integrity and experience, to direct and arrange the affairs of the society. His expectation was announced that a sufficient number of trained members would be gathered to form an association, at the end of two or three years, who could establish an independent community of equality and self-rule. The formation of other societies of like order, it was hoped, would follow. Those who wished to become members were to sign the constitution, were to occupy dwellings assigned to them, provide their own household furniture and utensils. The society was not to be answerable for the debts of any of its members. They were to be temperate, regular and orderly in conduct, diligent in their employments, and were to apply themselves to acquire an occupation. They were to help protect the whole property from injury, and enter into the society with a determination to promote its peace, prosperity, harmony, and social equality. In return the members were to receive such advantages, living, comforts, and education for their children, as the present state of New Harmony afforded. In old age, in sickness, or when accident occurred, care was to be taken of all parties, medical aid afforded, and every attention shown to them that kindness could suggest. Each member should, within a fixed limit, have the free choice of food and clothing. Each family was to receive credits in proportion to the number of its useful members. Members were to have the privilege of receiving their friends to visit them, provided they be answerable for the conduct of such sojourners. The children were to be educated at the expense of the community. Parents that preferred placing their children in the boarding-school after they had attained two years of age could do so by special arrangement, week by week. Members were allowed complete liberty of conscience, and were afforded every facility for exercising those practices of religious worship which they preferred. They could quit the society on a week's notice, taking with them the productions of the establishment, to the value of what they brought. Families or members might be dismissed on the same terms, by the committee. Equality of rights and duties, community of property, co-operative union in business and amusements, freedom of speech and activity, acquisition of knowledge, obedience to the laws of the State and nation, preservation of health, courtesy in all intercourse, kindness in all actions—were declared to be the principles of New Harmony's foundation.

Proceeding upon this foundation, Robert Owen, assisted in his plans by his talented sons, and his enlightened co-worker William Maclure, went hopefully forward toward the establishment of the commune upon a substantial basis. Free schools for the youth, and all who wished for them, was the first care of the founders. Well regulated amusements were held to be a large part of the community's interest, and every Friday evening there were concerts. Tuesday evening was designated as the night for the weekly balls, for which an excellent band of music was supplied. Wednesday evening the public meetings of the society were held, for the discussion of all subjects relating to the well-being of the commune. In time these meetings must have come to be veritable fields of contest, when what has been described as the heterogeneous collection of radicals, enthusiastic devotees to peculiar principles, honest latitudinarians, and lazy theorists had assembled, and each wanted to put in practice his personal views. Thursday was officially a day of rest for the commune; some made it a day of recreation, also.   Permission to speak in the village church was given to any minister who asked it, his creed not being inquired into. *The New Harmony Gazette* was established as the official organ of the commune, with the beautiful motto, "If we cannot reconcile all opinions let us endeavor to unite all hearts."

By Christmas, eight months after the organization of the society, the *Gazette* announced that the population of the community numbered one thousand persons. The next month, on January 18, 1826, Robert Owen returned from Europe and a tour of the Atlantic cities, accompanied by the famous "boatload of knowledge." These were teachers, scientists, and eminent men who had been enlisted in the work of uplifting the world.

Social Experiments at New Harmony

Let us follow in a bare outline Mr. Lockwood's graphic summary of events and the characters that gave New Harmony its brilliant place in the dawn of the nineteenth century.[1]

"Notable as New Harmony was in its own time as the scene of an ambitious effort at social regeneration, the perspective of years is necessary to an adequate portrayal of its importance in American history." There the doctrine of universal elementary education at public expense, without regard to sex or sect, as a duty of the State, was first proclaimed in the Middle West, and equal educational privileges for the sexes established. There the Pestalozzian system of teaching, now so generally followed everywhere, was first successfully instituted in the United States. William Maclure's manual-training and industrial and trade school, in connection with regular school instruction, was the first of its kind in America. Through the prominent scientists who pursued their researches at New Harmony, it became the greatest scientific centre on this continent. It possessed a museum which contained the remarkable collections of Thomas Say, Maclure, and Owen, and a scientific library unexcelled in the New World. In New Harmony women were first given a voice and vote in the local legislative councils; and there the doctrine of equal political rights for all, without regard to sex or color, was first proclaimed by Frances Wright. Through this brilliant woman, too, New Harmony became one of the earliest centres of the Abolition movement, and by her was founded there what is known as the first woman's literary club in the United States. The

[1] Lockwood, Geo. B., *The New Harmony Movement*, page 3. New York, 1905.

community dramatic club, which endured from 1828 to 1875, was one of the earliest clubs of that kind that were organized in the country, and trained many actors for the profession. The first prohibition of the liquor traffic, by administrative edict, was made in this community in 1826. By William Maclure's provision, New Harmony gave to the State and to Illinois a system of mechanics' libraries for more than a hundred and fifty communities in those States. Josiah Warren of New Harmony originated a philosophy of individualism, which was a rebound from their own communism, and has impressed itself indelibly upon modern economic thought. And from the scheme of the "time store" and "labor notes," originated by that early philosopher and inventive genius, it is said Robert Owen derived the central idea of the great labor co-operative societies of Great Britain, which constituted the most successful labor movement of the last century. A leaven of liberality in religious thought was also introduced into the commonwealth which helped to dispel the narrow type of religion then so general.

Surely, if advanced thought and enlightenment could insure success, the great scheme should have attained it by the superior character of its leadership. By the October following the organization of the commune, the *Gazette* stated that every State in the Union with the exception of two and almost every country in the north of Europe had contributed to make up the population! What response was there to all of the endeavors for their welfare, by these adherents? What were the one thousand residents producing with all the grand equipment that had been provided, and how were they demeaning them-

Social Experiments at New Harmony 257

selves under the liberal rules passed for the control of the community? What activity had been shown in shop, factory, vineyard, and field? Alas! we read in their records that there were already those who felt that they performed more than their share of labor; that some of the great mills were idle for lack of workmen. Accessions of skilful hands in nearly all these branches of industry, as well as in some other departments, is still desirable, pleads the *Gazette*. Notwithstanding this poverty of laborers, and the surplus of idlers or incompetents, when Mr. Owen returned from England, with characteristic optimism, he proceeded to strike off two years from the three of the probation! He announced that he was so well pleased with the progress made that he would proceed to organize those of the society who wished it into a community of perfect equality! After a week of meetings for discussion and framing of the plans, a very comprehensive constitution and declaration of principles was framed, and adopted. This document is of too great length to reproduce here, but among other things, equal privileges and advantages, without regard to services, were assured to every member who should unite with the society. The son Robert Dale Owen afterwards wrote that it was liberty, equality, and fraternity in downright earnest, but that he made no opposition, for he had too much of his father's all-believing disposition to anticipate results which any shrewd, cool-headed business man might have predicted. How rapidly they came. One curious result of the adoption of the permanent constitution was the immediate defection of whole groups of persons, who formed societies of their own and were allowed to establish themselves on different parts of the domain. There seemed to be quantities of persons in the colony who, it has been said, discovering themselves out of place and at a discount in the world as it is, rashly concluded that they were exactly fitted for the world as it ought to be. No more convincing commentary on Robert Owen's freedom from commercially interested motives could be asked for than his pleasure at the increase of these detached communities. Not only to the offshoots that located on the estate, but to the other communities modelled on the New Harmony plan, he gave a gracious welcome and rejoiced at the spread of the ideas. No less than twenty communes sprang into existence in the country, twelve of which were in Indiana, three in New York, three in Ohio, one in Pennsylvania, and one in Tennessee. In five years they had all passed into oblivion, but Owen had given them every encouragement. He had a passion for the regeneration of society. His propaganda in the cities of both continents, and before the most illustrious people in public life, showed that it was a sublime interest in humanity, and not personal aggrandizement, that prompted his investment, and subsequent endeavors.

In establishing the educational departments of New Harmony, Robert Owen gave his co-worker William Maclure sole charge of that feature of the new reforms. Mr. Maclure had joined in the experiment, by investing a hundred and fifty thousand dollars and engaging to make the community the centre of his plans for educational work in America, according to the new Pestalozzian system of instruction. William Maclure was a Scotchman by birth, and had come to America to make a geological survey of the United States. On account of his invaluable services in this science,

Social Experiments at New Harmony

he is called the Father of American Geology. He was the principal founder of the Philadelphia Academy of Natural Sciences, and for twenty-three years its president. He was one of the first men to advocate industrial education, and had founded an agricultural school in Spain, on an estate of 10,000 acres, which he lost as the result of a political revolution. While visiting in Scotland, after he had retired from a successful mercantile career, William Maclure made the acquaintance of Robert Owen at New Lanark. He had gone there to study the model factory community, and especially the schools that Mr. Owen had established. The two men had many opinions and aspirations in common, and both were devoted to the cause of improving the conditions of existence for the lowly. It was natural that when Mr. Owen came to America, to establish the New Harmony commune, William Maclure should join him in the great enterprise. They brought out with them Thomas Say, the illustrious "Father of American Zoölogy," Dr. Gerard Troost, the geologist, and John Chapplesmith, the famous engraver. Those who were to be instructors in the great educational institutions planned were Professor Joseph Neef, Madam Frotageot, Phiquepal d'Arusmont, and their assistants. These teachers were trained in Pestalozzi's famous school in Switzerland. In taking so much care to establish a broad educational system at New Harmony, including industrial features, the founders were exemplifying their creed, that the formation of character was the chief end of all training, and that the school was the great means for social regeneration. The children were to be surrounded solely by circumstances favorable to their development. William

Maclure showed by his life-work that he believed that free, equal, and universal schools were the only means of raising the masses to the estate of comfort and enlightenment; and he addressed himself to that phase alone of the community life at New Harmony. He firmly believed the sensible doctrine that every child of the productive classes should be taught a trade, in order that he might be self-supporting when through with school.

The advanced section of the schools, numbering as many as eighty pupils, and called the school of adults, was also taught chemistry by the famous Dr. Troost, drawing by the French artist Lesseur, and natural history by Thomas Say—truly as brilliant a group of instructors as could have been found in any college, on either side of the water. In all of the departments, girls were received, and taught, on an equality with the boys, for the first time in the history of the country. Although the schools were established for the commune, they attracted pupils from every section of the country, from New Orleans to New York. It is pathetic to think that only three counties distant the lad Abraham Lincoln, hungering for knowledge, knew of these schools but had no possible means of availing himself of the great opportunity. Later Mr. Maclure attempted to maintain a seminary for young men and women, called an orphans' manual training school, and free of any expense to them; and still another was started called The School of Industry. We are told that when, one by one, his educational experiments, in each of which he placed such high hopes, came to naught, William Maclure, still eager to do something for the cause of education, and for the productive classes, directed his philanthropy toward the formation of an educational society for adults called The Society of Manual Instruction, which was really a mechanics' institute. This school, with all of the others, after failing health obliged Mr. Maclure to go to Mexico, went out of existence. Although the commune had failed and his earlier schools had passed into oblivion with it, Mr. Maclure in his closing hours provided for the widely known plan for the Working Men's Institute and Library.

Mr. Maclure was forced to leave his new work and go to Mexico; twelve years afterward he died on his way back to the village. In his will he had provided for a system of libraries for the working-people of the country. Hear from Mr. Dunn's article the foreign-sounding list of investments, that were to be devoted to the Hoosier libraries: Besides his property in New Harmony he set aside over a million *reals* in Spanish securities, his house in Alicante, his convent of St. Gives and accompanying estate of ten thousand acres in Valencia; his convent and estate at Grosmano; his estate of Carman de Croix; the valley of Murada; forty-one thousand francs in French securities; notes, and mortgages on properties scattered from Big Lick plantation in Virginia to various parts of England, France, and Spain; his vast collections of minerals and prints, and near two thousand copper plates of engravings and illustrations. By the provisions made in his will, and after legal vicissitudes and organization of many temporary societies, to fulfil the requirements before obtaining an interest in the bequest, one hundred and sixty libraries were created in as many different counties of Indiana and Illinois!

"Unfortunately there was nothing in their formation to insure, and but little to encourage, perpetuity. The preliminary library required, of one hundred volumes, as a nucleus, before the county could receive a donation of books, was often valueless; and after the little libraries were established it was a sad fact that there was neither a competent custodian nor suitable quarters; what with lack of supervision and rough usage, they melted away. And there was neither taxation nor endowment to replace them."[1]

The township libraries, organized by the State of Indiana in 1854, were often combined with what was left of the Maclure foundation. Memories of a dusty, musty attic, festooned with cobwebs and located over the dingy shop and office of the township trustee, caused a grateful sentiment in the heart of the writer toward that Maclure benefaction to Indiana. With her brother, in earliest childhood, the children, guided by a student father, found the forgotten heaps of books, and read with eager interest the classic juveniles and standard works included in that old collection. Nibbled by mice, mutilated by careless hands, many of the volumes lost, and more of them unreturned by previous readers, the old library was but a tattered ghost of William Maclure's intention; but, with other collections established by that bequest, it had been a means of inspiration and culture to many men and women in the frontier communities, who thirsted for knowledge. It is a pleasant relief, from this account of dispersed libraries, to record the faithful preservation and extension of the Maclure Working Men's Library at New Harmony itself. That village, aided by the Rappite memorial and the subsequent munificent bequest of Dr. Murphy, one of its own citizens, has built a handsome building, in

[1] Dunn, J. P., *Report on Public Libraries. Supt.'s Report*, 1904.

which are housed the library, a museum, an art gallery, and the village auditorium. The value of the library's holdings, since the bequest of Dr. Murphy, is estimated at two hundred thousand dollars; enabling the management to continually add books to the twenty thousand volumes now on the shelves. It has, also, the very important collection of the scientific works of its founders, and the records and publications regarding the unusual history of New Harmony and similar communes are carefully preserved. The library is of great interest to the student of history, or of sociology.

The cheap lands of the New World have attracted many dreamers of the possibility of community life solving the problems of existence, but few of them have had the element of persistence. Robert Owen's great plans for others failed to solve the riddle, and within three years the commune passed into oblivion! To the labors of this distinguished group of educators, who were a full half-century in advance of their time, Mr. Lockwood pays a beautiful tribute:

"Immediate results there were none—they were prophets and seers upon the mountain-top. But one 'cannot see 'neath winter's field of snow the silent harvest of the future grow.' For measured by its after effect the educational experiment at New Harmony deserves to rank among the most important educational movements in this country. The precious seed which was sown on frontier soil, after many days ripened into a golden harvest. When Owen's social system dissipated into thin air, there went forth from brief homes on the Wabash men and women who, scattering in every direction through the Ohio and Mississippi valleys, and becoming the instructors of the pioneer youth, sowed in almost every isolated hamlet the tenets of the educational creed which Pestalozzi and Neef and Maclure had espoused.

Coupled with the actual teaching influence was the presence of the eminent scientists who made New Harmony a rendezvous, and were themselves bearers of good seed and glad tidings. Their achievements and contributions drew renewed attention to the best features of the educational light that failed."[1]

Various reasons have been ventured as the cause of the failure of the vast, unselfish, philanthropic scheme. After all are recounted it seems attributable to selfishness and the perversity of human nature, and the previous living in competitive communities. No doubt a more gradual settlement of adherents, with Mr. Owen's presence constantly in command, would have prolonged the experiment. It was surely more benevolent than practical. Mr. McDonald, who studied the history of the undertaking, on the premises, a quarter of a century afterward, said that there were some noble characters among the membership who set examples of industry and self-denial worthy of a great cause. There were others who came and lived as long as they could get supplies for nothing, but had no conception of the sentiment of the community's foundations. It is touching to read how, when one theory failed, with cheerful optimism Mr. Owen would substitute another plan; not once or twice, but again and again, he would make new arrangements of the property, to suit new vagaries among groups of members.

"He seems to have forgotten that if one and all the thousand persons assembled there had possessed all the qualities which he wished them to possess, there would

[1] Lockwood, Geo. B., *The New Harmony Movement*, page 289. New York, 1905.

be no necessity for his vain exertions to found a community, because there would of necessity be brotherly love, charity, industry, and plenty; and all of their actions would be governed by nature and reason."[1]

By many persons, the entire freedom of opinion and absence of any religious bond or authority has been assigned as the reason of the dispersion at New Harmony. The partial severing of the family relation, by placing the children apart at school, was an element of disintegration. It is agreed that there was a deplorable lack of members who were skilful and industrious or who were willing to work. Years afterward, Robert Dale Owen gave the gist of the matter when he said that equal remuneration to the skilful and industrious and the ignorant and idle must work its own downfall. It must of necessity eliminate the valuable members who find their services reaped by the indigent, and retain only the improvident, unskilled, and vicious members. In confessing his defeat in the great hall at New Harmony in 1828, Robert Owen said:

"I had hoped that fifty years of political liberty had prepared the American people to govern themselves advantageously. I supplied houses, the use of capital, and I tried, each in their own way, the different parties who collected here, and experience proved that the attempt was premature. It all proves that families trained in the individual system have not acquired those moral characteristics of forbearance and charity necessary for confidence and harmony. I can only feel regret, instead of anger. My intention now is to form such arrangements on the estate as will enable those who desire to promote

[1] Lockwood, Geo. B., *The New Harmony Movement*, page 178. New York, 1905.

the practice of the social system to live in separate families and yet to unite their general labor, or to exchange labor for labor, on the most beneficial terms to all, or to do both or neither as their feelings or apparent interest may influence them; while the children shall be educated with a view to an establishment of the social system in the future. I will not be discouraged by any obstacle, but will persevere to the end."[1]

Many members of the commune, who took individual holdings, remained as residents of the beautiful valley, where their descendants still live. It is this remnant of former intelligence in the settlement that makes the community differ from other sections. At present, New Harmony is a little town with some commercial ambitions, and takes a pride in its historic past. If Robert Owen had done nothing more for the State than to bring within its borders his noble family, and the famous individuals whom we have mentioned as sojourning, at times, in New Harmony, he would still be the most valuable and distinguished pioneer of the commonwealth.

After the passing of the commune, Mr. Owen's sons, when not studying or writing elsewhere, remained as citizens of New Harmony, where he often came to visit them. Indeed the most brilliant period of New Harmony's history was after Mr. Owen's "splendid social bark went to wreck upon the rocks and shoals of human nature." Many of the eminent scientists continued to make the village their regular residence or rendezvous, and other scholars and travellers, attracted by the fame of the social experiment and the scientific researches, travelled thither

[1] Lockwood, Geo. B., *The New Harmony Movement*, page 174. New York, 1905.

on tours of investigation. From this centre, Thomas Say sent out his numerous scientific papers, his finished *American Entomology* and the *American Conchology*, for which his talented wife made the beautiful colored illustrations. The gray, gaunt figure of the picturesque Rafinesque roamed over the hills about New Harmony, collecting botanical specimens, and added his name to the illustrious roll of occasional residents. Thither came Prince Maximilian von Neuweid, accompanied by his taxidermist and illustrator, to preserve the results of his excursions into nature's virgin territory. He spent the winter of 1832 in making studies in natural history, in collecting valuable specimens, and having drawings executed. Sir Charles Lyell came to study the geological collection and library brought together by David Dale Owen. Audubon, the great ornithologist, visited the place. Charles Lesueur added lustre to the group of resident scientists by his publications and his explorations of the Indian mounds. It was he who painted the scenery for the community theatre, and taught drawing and the arts in the school. John Chapplesmith, the engraver, and his gifted wife lived in New Harmony the year they were making the illustrations for the United States Geological Reports, issued by David Dale Owen. Dr. Gerard Troost continued his researches in chemistry and mineralogy, until called to the University of Tennessee. Robert Fauntleroy, who married Jane Dale Owen, spent several years in New Harmony, making scientific experiments. The name is still one of the honored ones in the community. There was a whole group of brilliant men associated with David Dale Owen in his work as United States Geologist. It was in the museum at New Harmony that he treasured his valuable collections made during that survey. Another son, Richard Owen, devoted many years of useful labor to the State as State Geologist, served in the Mexican War, and as Colonel of the 60th Indiana regiment in the Civil War, and afterwards as Professor of Natural Sciences in Indiana University. Another son, William Owen, had taken an important part in the commune as trustee, as an editor of the *New Harmony Gazette*, and as head of their commercial relations. Of the most widely known of Robert Owen's useful sons, Robert Dale Owen, it has been said, in connection with the socialistic community, that he was the embodiment of the spirit of his father and William Maclure. He believed in its mission, was an enthusiastic helper in its maintenance, and regretful over its failure. After his labors, he was in New York for a time, as associate editor of the *Free Enquirer*. But it is in connection with his work in his adopted State of Indiana that Robert Dale Owen's life of usefulness became so illustrious. As Mr. John Holliday once wrote of him:

"In scholarship, general attainment, varied achievements as author, statesman, politician, and leader of a new religious faith, he was unquestionably the most prominent man Indiana ever owned. Others may fill now, or may have filled, a larger place in public interest or curiosity for a time, but no Hoosier was ever so widely known, or so likely to do the State credit by being known, and no other has ever before held so prominent a place, so long, with a history so unspotted by selfishness, duplicity, or injustice." [1]

Mr. Owen began his political career as a member of

[1] Holliday, J. H., *Indianapolis News*.

the State Legislature of 1836, and was also an Elector that year, and one of the most desired speakers of the campaign, being a most logical reasoner and rising above the rancor and personal attacks of the stump speaker. Afterwards he served two terms in Congress, and while there was instrumental in passing the bill founding the Smithsonian Institute, and, as a member of the first Board of Regents, largely guided the nature of the work it was to undertake. In 1851, Mr. Owen became the most efficient member of the Constitutional Convention of Indiana; and in that convention and the following Legislature he merited the reputation for unselfish and far-seeing statesmanship. Again it should be remembered that while he was in the Legislature his conscientious and persistent efforts advanced legislation for women, until he procured the enactment of the laws securing their right to own and control their separate property during marriage, and the right to their own earnings; laws which abolished the simple dower of the common law, and procured for widows the absolute ownership of one third of the deceased husband's property. He modified the divorce laws of the State so as to enable a married woman to secure a relief from habitual drunkenness and cruelty. The women of the country owe Robert Dale Owen recognition for his successful efforts to establish equitable property rights in one State as a pattern for others. In 1851, a group of Indiana women presented him with a testimonial of their esteem and appreciation of his services to their sex; and the State Federation of Clubs is to place a portrait bust of the distinguished man in the halls of the State-house. Of Mr. Owen's labors for the nation, during the Civil War, it would require volumes to recount in detail, when only a passing mention can be made here. He was Governor Morton's most valued co-worker. He procured arms and supplies to equip the troops hurriedly sent to the front, and looked after the men on the field. His stirring appeal to President Lincoln, so the President averred, helped nerve that great Executive to the issuing of the Emancipation Proclamation. Mr. Owen served as head of the Freedman's Bureau, and he issued a strong protest to the Northwest against the proposed compromise with the South. He opposed extending the suffrage to the blacks, but labored for years as the efficient friend of the freedmen. He served as *Chargé d'Affaires* at Naples for six years, and wrote with conviction in advocacy of spiritualism. Robert Dale Owen died in 1877. In his death "the last of the great figures conspicuous in the New Harmony communes passed away, but the great movements to which they had given origin and direction still sweep onward in an ever widening current,—the failure of George Rapp's success standing out in vivid contrast to the success of Robert Owen's failure." [1]

Groups of men have impoverished themselves in their efforts to alleviate human misery, and for the advancement of their fellow-men on the community plan; but there is no nobler example than that of Robert Owen and his co-workers at New Harmony, in their groping toward the light, in the endeavor to emancipate humanity from ignorance and poverty. This group of illustrious men conferred great honors on Indiana.

[1] Lockwood, Geo. B., *The New Harmony Movement*, p. 377. New York, 1905.

CHAPTER XIII

IN THE FORTIES AND FIFTIES

NOT the least merit of Mr. Tarkington's story of the *Vanrevels* is the passing glance it gives into the social life of the Indiana villages some fifty years ago. He embodied in the atmosphere of the story, memories of his grandmother's days, and the life and hospitalities on the Wabash of which her family and their neighbors were representative. This phase of the past is apt to escape us. In placing the period of Indiana's civilization, we are apt to carry forward the pioneer times equally in all districts; whereas the southern inland and river towns were quite old settlements, before the aborigines were banished from the northern third of the State.

As the Indians were pushed back, the State gradually emerged from frontier conditions, and the little towns in the southern tier of counties took on themselves the pleasures and gayeties of high-life in a provincial way. The present generation knows little of this charming social life which prevailed in the days before the Civil War. As Edward Eggleston said of the town of Madison when he first knew it, life took an aspect of ease and serenity nowhere shabby, new, or raw. It is true the life was simple, as it was elsewhere in youthful America, and there was little difference between the material conditions of the classes, for none were vastly rich; but the tone of society was the same as in Carolina and Virginia from whence so many families had come, and the infusion of Eastern blood added to the sterling qualities of citizenship. The mellowing grace of family traditions, and past history to be lived up to, marked the intercourse of these people. Many of the joys were almost rural, and there was a mingling of the home-made appointments with imported luxuries in household articles and furniture. But the personal demeanor and punctilious manners of the period were far more stately and formal than those of the present. The language of correspondence, of public addresses, and of personal salutation was more elaborate. The style of oratory then in vogue may be recognized in this opening of a patriotic address on the Fourth of July in 1843, by the orator of the day:

"Once more my countrymen, we are permitted gratefully to behold the Anniversary sun of American Independence. Once more we salute the Star Spangled Banner, and rejoice that the cherished emblem of our Union and liberty, spotless and peerless as ever, still waves over a land and nation. All this assembling of beauty and chivalry and intelligence and piety, with religous rites and martial music, announce the virtuous emotions over this patriotic celebration."

In the days when such speeches were the custom, correspondence was made a fine art. People composed letters then. Men of political life wrote as if for biographical purposes. The belles of the towns were constantly receiving and sending scented *billets-doux*, sealed with the little glazed wafers or sealing-wax. Girls were taught letter-writing and the proper way of composing, signing, and addressing letters. The swain addressing the fair object of his affections in verse or prose, wrote with a quill, inditing flowery paragraphs descriptive of the beauty and grace of the object of his gallantry, to whom he prayed to be permitted to pay his respects.

"I am alone and have been gazing upon the mild and peaceful moon gliding with majesty through the deep blue expanse," writes Almira to her "shining specimen of perfection." Continuing, she says that "this ever inclines me to sadness more than formerly and is a pleasing contemplation in which I love to indulge. Perhaps at this moment one that I admire at West Point is gazing on the same lovely orb, perhaps in the same train of thought. How delightful the idea." These elaborate effusions made the greetings and communication among young people much more dignified than the modern "hello!" over the telephone, or "so long" in closing a letter. At the same time "keeping company" was a very informal proceeding. No chaperone was thought of and a gentleman's intentions were not sought, until he was ready they should be known.

The service at table was simpler, in that time, and the present fashion of serving food had not come in, but the quality of the viands in these homes was delicious. Housekeepers vied with each other in culinary skill. The storeroom and cellar of a householder, in those bountiful times, would provision a half-dozen families of the present day. The "festal board"—as it was termed in the poetry of the time— fairly groaned with the prodigal variety of dishes. The log cabin of pioneer times had been succeeded by more spacious colonial homes. George Cary Eggleston said, reminiscently, that in the early forties the thrift and ambition among the well-to-do landowners had dotted the region along the Ohio with spacious brick dwellings—most of them with stately colonnaded porticos in front and ornamented lawns surrounding them. Wealth abounded in the towns and luxury was there also. Some of the residences would be accounted fine in our large cities of to-day. Speaking of Madison, which was, during the Crimean War, the most important pork-packing centre in all the world, and consequently amassed wealth, he said that the city was beautiful, with its broad, well-shaded, and smoothly gravelled streets, and ornamented grounds surrounding all of the best houses. Of Vevay it was said that "the town is the most beautiful one I have anywhere seen in America." A hint of the style of some of these homes may be seen in a description of an old one which was being advertised as a young ladies' seminary. It was an old residence in 1843, but "its large halls, commodious drawing-room and parlors, airy galleries and unusual number of bedrooms rendered it especially adapted to the needs of a female seminary"; which occupied it for a long and flourishing term of years.

The drinking of wines and whiskies was almost universal before the temperance waves passed over the country. Many of the wines and fine brandies were imported and came up the river from New Orleans. But the home-made cherry bounce and peach brandy were offered everywhere. In the taverns and on the boats where men of the world congregated, it often happened that drink was deep and play was high. In those days, gentlemen prided themselves

Old Mahogany Furniture Brought to the Wabash by River and Canal.
From a photograph.

on their own cure of hams, venison, and beef. Game was plentiful at all times, and poultry, cream, butter, and fruits were abundant and cheap. Chickens could be bought for six cents each and turkeys for twenty-five cents. Entertaining was not costly, the people were heartily hospitable, and the lack of other amusements made them largely dependent on one another's society. Social visiting seemed to be going on every day, in the forenoon as well as in the afternoon and evening. In these hospitable homes, large families were reared, filling them with gayety and life. To them young gallants brought home their blooming brides, by stage-coach or steamboat, or mayhap on horseback, from the neighboring towns or States. When these happy events occurred, a week of village festivities set in, always beginning with the "infair"—which was the name of the reception given by the parents of the groom, and was an invariable custom.

In some of these homes you would find heavy old mahogany furniture, and silver, glass, and "sprigged" or gold-band china, which had been brought out the long weary way from the East, or up from New Orleans. Every spinnet, piano, hauteboy, or four-poster made of mahogany which is inherited by the present generation represents what was then a treasure, brought out West with toil, and patience over long delays. Local cabinet-makers skilfully made sideboards, bureaus, and cupboards of the native cherry wood, which ranked next to mahogany in beauty; and these pieces are worthy of preservation, as examples of good handicraft.

The fashions for a gentleman were much more elaborate at that time than now. His waist must be of the hour-glass form. He wore a colored broadcloth, claw-hammer coat, finished with a low velvet collar and brass buttons, over a buff waistcoat. A black satin stock or flowered neckerchief, with flowing ends, was worn about the extremely high collar. He wore pointed shoes, and the hat that he carried in his hand, as he swept a low bow of salutation, was a bell-crowned beaver made of white fur. A long camlet cloak and gold-headed cane finished the toilet of the gentleman on the Wabash in the early forties.

The manners of the old school went well with the picturesque costume of the period. The gentleman who flourished his cane as he walked, was much puffed out above the waistcoat, by the plaited or ruffled shirt-front, and had a fashion of swearing and b'godding for emphasis.

The ladies wore stiff brocades, shining taffetas, and peau de soie of quaint designs. If these garments had to do duty many more seasons than the frail chiffons of the present day, still the material was elegant, the style formal, and the gowns were worn with the grand dame air of the time. Our modern belles still like to reproduce the costumes worn in the forties. Capes, mantles, and shawls were the outside wraps then in vogue. To obtain the stately silks they bartered eighty bushels of corn in New Orleans for a single yard, and my gentleman gave in exchange, one hundred bushels for a yard of broadcloth, and eight bushels for a single yard of cotton print. Most beautiful furs were worn in that day. The trappers of the West were still sending their pelts to the markets, and one of Mr. Astor's agents, who had gathered wealth in the fur-trade—one doubloon for John Jacob, and two for himself, making him a man of importance by 1840—dressed his wife in

The Dress of the Forties.
From a photograph of the period.

furs that were fit for a queen and they were copied by every land speculator's and pork packer's wife on the Wabash.

The universal fashion of that day prescribed very full dress skirts, much be-flounced, and worn over a large hoop. From the sloping shoulders of the tight "basque" a shawl was draped—lace in summer and broché in winter. The muffs were enormous, measuring eighteen to twenty-two inches in length, and a deep "perline' was worn about the shoulders. Bonnets were universal for old and young, and their large round fronts were filled with a garden of flowers for "face trimmings." Men and women travelled about everywhere, on stage-coach and steamboat, in these showy toilets. For evening, garlands of flowers were worn in the hair and around the low neck and skirt of the gown, and curls were worn so universally that one wonders if fashion has changed the nature of locks since then.

The girls of the little towns were educated at the Academy, or had been away to some Young Ladies Seminary to be "finished" in music and French. Those who went to St. Mary's Convent learned to embroider in chenilles, to make wax flowers, and do the old masters in cross-stitch. They attempted the harp and guitar, and most of them "took piano lessons."

A description of one of these Indiana schools, by Mrs. Carleton, gives an excellent idea of most of them.

"In addition to solid attainments, the young women were taught French and German with piano, guitar, and harp lessons, vocal music, drawing, and painting in oil and water. Piano and guitar-lessons were twenty-five cents each, while French, and lessons in painting and drawing were ten cents each, and vocal music at two cents per lesson! From North and South, East and West came young women to this noted classical school for girls. Many of the instructors were from New York State, and the pupils were on the records from Oswego and Saratoga, from Mobile and New Orleans."

Ballads were in vogue, and many a sweet girl sang in simple style but with fresh young voice, "Shepherds have you seen my love?" "The harp that once through Tara's halls," and other forgotten airs. "Manners" were also taught in every good school, including the curtsy and the dance. The dancing masters of that day still wore the ruffled shirt, knee breeches, and buckled shoes of the colonial period.

The curriculum of many of the schools was not very serious; was generally finished in a couple of years and girls married while yet in their teens. When the young ladies had finished their schooling, they came home bearing their worsted flowers, and were welcomed with a June party, while the garden roses and honeysuckles made a bower of the porches and strawberries were plentiful. A bountiful supper followed by cake and ice-cream, mint-julip and punch, were the refreshments served in that day. Young and old were bidden together and the gentlemen were not too *blasé* to enjoy the festivities. When once a belle was out of school there were informal gayeties going on constantly. Though informal, the dancing parties were called balls, and the figures of the lancers and quadrilles were as stately as their name implied. The ladies in stiff brocades or flounced muslins glided through the dance and curtsied deeply with due appreciation of their grace and dignity.

Their partners never slurred the music nor hurried the low bow. Nothing but the after-supper frolic through Tucker ever approached the romp of a modern two-step.

Horseback riding continued to be a very general pleasure, long after the pioneer paths through the wilderness had broadened into roads. The lady's riding-habit of that day had a long flowing skirt, sweeping almost to the ground, the gloves worn were deep gauntlets, and for gala occasions a plume was worn in the hat; at other times a veil floated out behind the fair equestrienne. Gay cavalcades of the young people attended country parties or a neighboring village festival. The carriage of the period was a large capacious affair, fashioned like a landeau, which had an aristocratic rumble as it bowled along the shaded streets. The ponderous steps let down with a rattle as the barouche drew up at the curbstone and the door was opened for my much-furbelowed lady to alight. These carriages have entirely disappeared and nothing quite so impressive in style has taken their place.

In all Indiana households "before the war," and especially in the many homes where dancing was not approved of, the favorite entertainment was the tea-party, sometimes followed by kissing games. At early candle-light, a hostess would assemble her guests, young and old, around her table, ladened with everything the culinary skill of the time produced. The substantial dishes were flanked by pickles, "jells," preserves, hot rolls, the feast culminating in that pride of the village, "at least three kinds of cake." As one of these very hospitable ladies said in her old age, "In my time we had a roast turkey at each end of the table and mashed potatoes in the middle and when you sat down you could know there was really going to be something to eat." For these occasions the treasured silver and egg-shell china were brought forth, and home-made ice-cream, then a luxury, crowned the feast. It was during this decade that the thrifty housewives learned the art of canning fruits, and they vied with each other in friendly rivalry which could only be decided at the County Fair.

By this time spinning and weaving were practised only in backwoods homes, but sewing-machines were not yet introduced and when ladies went to "spend the day," they always carried their stint of sewing or eyelet embroidery. Spending the day meant a bountiful noon dinner and they went at eleven o'clock and stayed until five. While they stitched wristbands or worked buttonholes, they gossipped of neighborhood doings, went over the church troubles, and settled affairs of state. These women were as alert, intelligent, and interested in questions of the day as their descendants of present club-land. In the scarcity of literature, books and journals were freely loaned and one's volumes sometimes travelled far and wide. A copy of Scott, or *The Children of the Abbey*, or *Scottish Chiefs*, or Moore's *Poems* sometimes wandered so far by horseback, or stage-coach, that they never returned to their owners again. There was not so much literature published every year, in those days, but the English classics and standard Reviews were familiar to Indiana men and women and there was, perhaps, more time for reflection upon what they did read. *Godey's Ladies' Book* and *Peterson's Magazine* were the fashion plates, universally consulted by Hoosier ladies for styles and patterns.

In the social life "before the war," there was much more light-heartedness and gayety than in the present time. The country was in its youth. Communities had not plunged into the seething turmoil of social unrest. Literature and the drama were not depressed by morbid introspection and joyless disillusionment. Few were richer than they needed to be, and not many more were poorer than they should have been. There was little misery to depress the fortunate that could not be relieved by my Lady Bountiful sending her basket of provisions and necessities to the needy. Each neighborhood took care of its own unfortunate and shiftless.

"This gay insouciance, this forgetfulness that the world existed for any but a single class," says Lowell, "has been impossible of late years. Perhaps opportunity for all was the touchstone of blithe spirits. There was a cheerfulness and contentment with things as they were, which is no unsound philosophy for the mass of mankind. It certainly was a comfortable time. If there was discontent, it was individual, and not in the air; sporadic, not epidemic. Responsibility for the universe had not yet been invented. Post and telegraph were not so importunate as now. Now all the ologies follow us in our newspapers to our burrows and crowd upon us with the pertinacious benevolence of subscription books. Even the right of sanctuary is denied. One has a notion that in those old times the days were longer than now, that a man called to-day his own, by a securer title, and held his hours with a sense of divine right, now obsolete."

The West being detached from great cities and their depressing poverty, led this unharassed life, and it was reflected in the simple joys of their social intercourse. Indiana towns had few idle persons, work was a necessity for all; but there was time for rest as well as for toil; and there was a rural freedom to pursue one's bent.

Hospitality toward incoming settlers was proverbial. If a desirable family came into a neighborhood, the very fact that it was to cast in its lot with the town was enough to warrant a welcome. Naturally, society was provincial. In the community all knew each other, and felt at liberty to follow their impulses. As Mr. Tarkington says, they were a natural people who had not learned to be self-conscious enough to fear doing a pretty thing openly, without mocking themselves for it.

An ever-present interest in Indiana was politics, and that question certainly absorbed the attention of all classes in 1840. The principal events of the year, both social and political, clustered about the campaign of William Henry Harrison for the Presidency, against Martin Van Buren, who was then the incumbent. Harrison had not only been famous on this frontier as an Indian fighter and shrewd in management, but had been appointed Governor of Indiana while it was yet a Territory, and also was the hero of the battle of Tippecanoe. Naturally his party, in the State where he had dwelt so long, rallied with great enthusiasm to his support. Very spectacular mass meetings, barbecues, celebrations, and processions were a part of the means to keep up the excitement of the time. One Indiana celebration is still recalled as the most unique of its day. That was the great gathering on the scene of General Harrison's victory at Battle Ground. From far and near, even from New York State to Illinois, the Whigs came in long processions to the event. There were wagons with log cabins on them. Standing in the door, men served hard cider from barrels, with a long-handled gourd, to the throng as they passed along. Other wagons held great canoes filled with young ladies who were dressed in white, with sashes of the national colors. There were great "floats," made to represent the conditions of frontier life when Harrison began his career in Indiana; and on these wagons were glee clubs singing the lately improvised campaign songs. One very popular topical song began:

"What has caused this great commotion, motion, motion
　　the Country through?
　It is the ball a rolling on, for Tippecanoe and Tyler too.
　With them we 'll beat little Van,
　Van, Van is a used up man.

　Farewell, dear Van,
　You 're not our man,
　To guide the ship of state."

Owing to this enthusiasm, and the "hard times" cry which made the masses demand a change, the Whigs swept the country when election day arrived. Indiana was jubilant over the election to the Presidency of her favorite candidate.

About 1840, a very tragic phase in the history of the country vitally affected the States along the Ohio River. The anti-slavery sentiment, which each year had grown more intense, crystallized into organized societies, advocating the emancipation of the slaves, and rendering assistance to those who stole away from their masters and made a break for freedom. Although four fifths of the people in the southern counties were in sympathy with the South still,

Indiana had many ardent spirits who entered into this opposition to slavery. After the passage of the Fugitive Slave Law, fourteen Northern States practically nullified the national statute, by enacting State legislation for the protection of runaway slaves. Zealous opponents of the traffic sometimes advocated armed resistance to the slave-owner seeking to reclaim his human chattels. Abolitionists despaired of a remedy by law, and gradually worked out a system of friendly routes and welcoming stations for fugitive slaves, which came to be known as the "Underground Railway." The league had boats in which they transported the negroes across the Ohio River at five or six points, and started them northward. The homes that would aid the runaways formed many routes in the chain from Dixie to Canada, where the slave reached foreign territory and freedom. Solitary and in groups, the negroes came trembling across the Ohio in the dead of night, shoeless and ill-clad, to the homes of free negroes or of their white deliverers. The women maintained sewing-circles to prepare clothing for these fugitives, and the men carried them forward in wagons to the next resident who was known as a member of the Underground Railway. In the course of a year, thousands of blacks made this effort to escape and were helped along the Indiana routes toward freedom. Mr. Hanover, the chief of the workers, assured Colonel Cockrum that for seven years more than an average of four thousand fugitive slaves passed, each year, through the hands of the men who were on duty in the Indiana district. Not forgetting other humanitarians who labored in this cause, it is conceded that the members of the Society of Friends were among the foremost in acting upon their convictions

LIBERTY LINE.

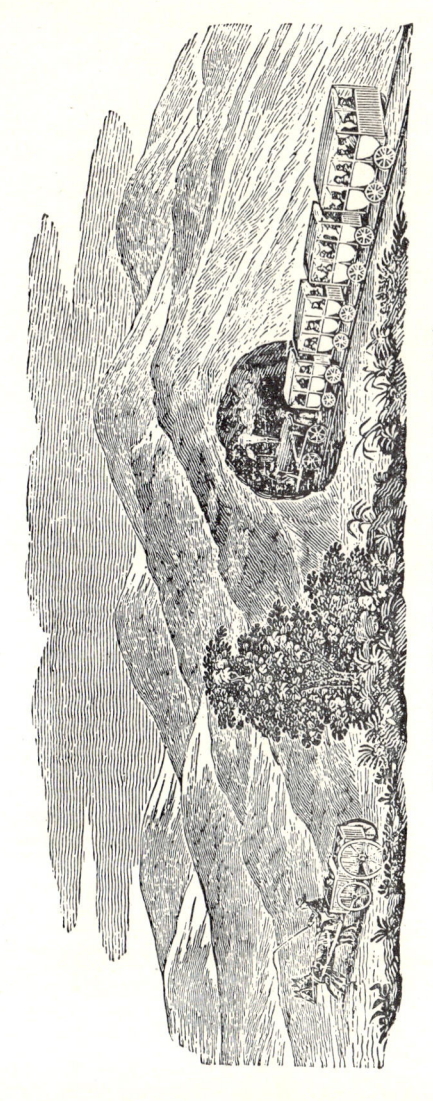

NEW ARRANGEMENT---NIGHT AND DAY.

The improved and splendid Locomotives, Clatksoft and Lundy, with their trains fitted up in the best style of accommodation for passengers, will run their regular trips during the present season, between the borders of the Patriarchal Dominion and Libertyville, Upper Canada. Gentlemen and Ladies, who may wish to improve their health or circumstances, by a northern tour, are respectfully invited to give us their patronage.

SEATS FREE, *irrespective of color.*

Necessary Clothing furnished gratuitously to such as have *"fallen among thieves."*

"Hide the outcasts—let the oppressed go free."—*Bible.*

☞ For seats apply at any of the trap doors, or to the conductor of the train.

J. CROSS, *Proprietor.*

N. B. For the special benefit of Pro-Slavery Police Officers, an extra heavy wagon for Texas, will be furnished, whenever it may be necessary, in which they will be forwarded as dead freight, to the "Valley of Rascals," always at the risk of the owners.

☞ Extra Overcoats provided for such of them as are afflicted with protracted *chilly-phobia.*

An Advertisement of the Underground Railway.
(From *The Western Citizen*, Published July, 1844.)

against the traffic in human beings. Benjamin Thomas gave a farm at Spartansburg, for a school for the fugitives; Benjamin Stanton, Pusey Graves, and others published an anti-slavery paper, without profit, for the promulgation of anti-slavery ideas. William Lacey, who rescued Eliza, of *Uncle Tom's Cabin* fame, and sent her by the Indiana route to Canada, was one of the secret-service band that patrolled the banks of the Ohio watching for escaping slaves, and directing them where they might find protection. Levi Coffin's house is said to have afforded shelter for thousands of fugitives. Joel Parker and Nathan Thomas not only expended untiring energy in helping slaves on their way, but they also conducted free-labor stores for the many citizens who, at great inconvenience to themselves, would not use the products of slave labor. Dr. Posey used his coal mines to secrete the travellers; and a lumber barque was maintained on Lake Michigan to carry fugitive slaves across to foreign territory. Orators like Dr. Bennett and Mr. Graves lectured throughout the State, and elsewhere, amidst great persecution and contumely. One of the songs sung at this period to arouse enthusiasm for the wronged began:

> "Ho the car Emancipation
> Moves majestic through the nation."

Colored men who were natural orators spoke at these meetings, telling their experiences and struggles to gain freedom, making stirring appeals for their race, that moved the people to sympathy and action in their behalf. The self-sacrificing labors of the anti-slavery people, throughout all of those dark years, was not undergone for any pleasure there was in it. Their endeavor came from deep convictions prompting them to the performance of hazardous duties and distasteful ministrations. The Fugitive Slave Law made it a crime to aid escaping slaves, and the masters, following close upon the trail of their "property," searched houses and caused arrests of suspected citizens. Neighbors who sympathized with the Southern section scorned the acquaintance of the "black abolitionists." Through danger of arrest and social ostracism these single-hearted people heroically maintained their unceasing efforts for the freedom of the slaves, during the forties and fifties; until the Emancipation Proclamation removed the necessity for their efforts, and the shadow of slavery from the land.

In 1844, the electric telegraph was invented, and an Indiana lady, Miss Annie Ellsworth, dictated the first message ever transmitted: "Behold what hath God wrought."

An amusing phase of village life at that time in Indiana were the primitive appliances for protection against fire. Mr. Condit's droll description of the conditions at Terre Haute shows them to be typical of the other towns of the State:

"In the early history of the village, the first organization of a fire company was, in a sense, no organization, that is, the Village Bucket-line brigade was a voluntary affair. By common consent, every villager, old and young, was a member. Next to the ringing of the bell of the public crier and his loud cry, 'A child lost!' nothing appealed to the sympathies of the community so strongly as the midnight cry of, 'Fire! fire! fire!' The words were taken up by every villager as he issued from his gate, bucket in hand, on the run, guided by the light of the blazing building. At the fire every man was his own chief, and with a quick eye was called to see, and to do, the most needful thing. So each one quickly found his place either in rescuing the sick and helpless; in carrying out furniture; in manning the pumps or wells; in falling into lines for passing the full buckets of water and returning the empty ones to be again refilled; or it may be in standing upon the roof and fighting the flames with the buckets of water as they were passed up to him. The fiercer the fire the harder the fight, in which every volunteer was enthusiastic; knowing that his work was important though his place was only in the bucket-line. The Village Bucket-line brigade held sway till 1838; when by action of the Common Council the first hand engine was purchased. This was a real live engine, to be worked and pulled by hand, yet it was worthy of having a house and a special keeper. In 1839, the Council ordered the following premiums to be awarded. For the first hogshead of water delivered at the fire, three dollars; for the second, two dollars; and for the third, one dollar; and after that, for every hogshead, till the fire was extinguished, twenty-five cents. When a fire alarm came, every drayman in town started on a mad race to the fire; but first it was helter-skelter for the river, where his hogshead was quickly filled. It was a wild and exciting scramble of odd-looking men, and old drays and spavined horses."[1]

Indiana people were greatly disturbed over the sudden death of President William Henry Harrison, whom they regarded as their own representative; and events did not reconcile them to his successor. Naturally the Whig element in the State became greatly disgruntled with Vice-President Tyler's policy during the remaining four years of the term, but the State was largely Democratic, and sided with him regarding the annex-

[1] Condit, B., *Early History of Terre Haute*, page 168. New York, 1900.

ation of Texas. There was, also, much bluster throughout the West during President Polk's campaign, over the claims of Great Britain regarding Oregon. With the other States west of the Alleghanies, Indiana joined in the cry of her own United States Senator, Edward Hannegan, of "Fifty-four forty or fight." But when the boundary line was peaceably settled, by treaty, on the 49th parallel, the South and West accepted that solution of the question, and resumed the agitation over Mexico's denial of our claims regarding the Rio Grande, as the boundary line between the two countries. Indiana being largely settled by people of Southern birth, who scoffed at any fears of slavery extension, the State fell in line with the prevailing sentiment of the South, and West, as against the East, and favored a war with Mexico. Indiana village life was greatly excited over the issue. There was much speech-making, and "resolving" that Texas was in the right.

When it was declared by the government on May 15, 1846, that "War existed by the act of Mexico"—when she was but defending her own territory—the State of Indiana was "roused to arms." In the approaching conflict with Mexico, Indiana was ready for her part. New England was declaring that the South had incited the war, to increase slave territory. The majority in Indiana asserted, with the South, that Texas was already independent of Mexico; that the Republic had asked for annexation, and if it was persistently refused admission into the Union, might form European alliances which the United States would, in the end, have to destroy for her own safety. Better an immediate war with Mexico, declared the statesmen, than to leave Texas in nominal independence, to involve us in ultimate war with France and England. Whatever justice there was in the arguments of the factions, it ended in the American army of occupation moving towards the border, and when the Mexican troops crossed the Rio Grande, volunteers were called for amidst the greatest enthusiasm in Indiana. Bells were rung, mass meetings were called, and enlistment was so vigorous that eight regiments of Indiana infantry responded to the call. The services of five regiments were accepted by the War Department. All of these passed through many of the trials and dangers of the war; many companies were decimated by disease on the scorched plains and the low river banks. Others were fortunate enough to be ordered forward, and distinguished themselves in action. The First Indiana regiment was left by General Zachary Taylor, the commanding General, to languish in the miasma at the mouth of the Rio, until, as General Patterson said twenty years later, while he knew his action in sending the troops on was without authority, still it was a venture with humanity at the bottom, for such a want of wholesome food, such hopelessness in suffering, such wholesale dying, he had never thought to see in an American camp. The gallant Third Indiana regiment had a more brilliant opportunity to make a record at the front. The Second regiment suffered from unjust military reports of General Taylor and Jefferson Davis, regarding an unequal engagement, at Buena Vista; where, fighting a force of Mexicans, eighteen to their one, they were called by their mistaken Colonel to retreat. In surprise and panic they obeyed; but not before they had left ninety of their three hundred and sixty men dead or wounded on the field. Afterward, the remaining troops rallied without the Colonel, and fought bravely to the end. It is to the honor of the State, that Indiana did not give her electoral vote for President to General Taylor after his unwarranted report regarding the Second regiment; and the enduring enmity of the people followed Jefferson Davis for his unfair criticisms. Many of the volunteers from Indiana, in this unholy war, as General Grant always called it, learned the arts of war in these campaigns, only to use their knowledge in the greater civil conflict, a few years later on.

When the treaty of peace was signed in 1848, and General Taylor was elected President on the glory gained at Buena Vista, the Indiana troops returned to their homes, the heroes of their generation. Peace celebrations were held in every district, and "Remember the Alamo" was heard on every tongue. There are many people still living who recall the fervor of the welcome home to the sun-bronzed soldiers from the Mexican plains. Many of these volunteers, said Judge Ristine, in a touching memorial of his old neighbors, sleep their last sleep on the plains of Mexico; others returned to die at home; a few are with us yet. Among the settlers of that rude frontier of Texas, were Hoosier soldiers who remained to enter lands in the new domain. Many of the men who served on the long marches over those southwestern plains, and the trail to the Pacific, returned in the following year on the pilgrimage for the quest of gold. They had secured the California country to the United States, and explorations had begun immediately; gold was discovered and the craze of '49 swept the country. Most of the people who went out to the coast from Indiana journeyed overland in the long

One of the Old Colonial Homes Long Since Passed into Other Uses.

trains. The gold-seekers travelled in company as a protection against the Indians. Besides the dangers from the savages, many other hardships were endured by the emigrants. Burning deserts were traversed, where only alkaline waters were to be found. Six months was not an unusual time for the long journey. The pace was necessarily snail-like. They travelled in covered wagons drawn by horses or oxen. Slowly these great caravans plodded the weary way toward the Pacific. Indiana women who had been gently reared died of sickness and exposure on the way. Children were born to them out on the great solitary plains, and husbands felt their hold on life slip from them, and said farewell to their helpless families, as they closed their eyes in death beneath the stars on the mountain heights. A few of the Hoosier gold-hunters found paying mines; many others, as the chances for fortunes disappeared, straggled back to old Indiana as to an Eldorado. Some remained and prospered in commercial or professional life. This excitement over California gold absorbed the attention of the nation from '49 to '53, but nowhere did it enlist more interest than among the enterprising and venturesome Hoosiers.

Along in the fifties, the agitation regarding slavery swayed and rocked the nation, and Indiana was a storm centre. As General Wallace has said:

"The whole North was alive with 'isms,' some purely sentimental, some sound in morals, each one, however an army of zealots. These, it is to be added, all had in their organization men of far sight, scheming and struggling to bring about a general coalition, without which there could be no effective opposition to the Democratic party. It was from these nebulous conditions that the new Republican party was formed. Old party lines were broken up and many life-long Democrats found themselves aligned with Whigs whom they had combated in many a previous campaign."[1]

Indiana had been regarded as safely Democratic, in the all-powerful grasp of Senators Bright, Thomas A. Hendricks, and Joseph E. McDonald, but the Whigs, and one wing of the Democratic party, gradually joined forces to make up the working staff of the Republican party in Indiana. They had, as leaders, such men as Henry S. Lane, John Defress, Schuyler Colfax, George W. Julian, Owen, Allen, and Morton. Through great tribulation and the weighing of principles on the slavery question against a possible national conflict, came these thousands of men into the ranks of a new political party; and the fifties passed out of the calendar of years, in Indiana, amidst sharp political divisions between old neighbors; and as the decade closed, there were ominous signs of the strife which broke upon the country in 1861.

[1] Wallace, Lew, *Autobiography*.

CHAPTER XIV

INDIANA AS AFFECTED BY THE CIVIL WAR

TO trace Indiana's part in the Civil War would be to write her history during that period, for Indiana lived the war, and scarcely anything else for four years. But many of the happenings within her borders, during that time, differed from some of the Northern States and resulted from the character of her early settlement. Governor Morton expressed a truth when he wrote to President Lincoln that "the case of Indiana was peculiar in that it had, probably, a larger proportion of inhabitants of Southern birth or parentage—many of these, of course, with Southern proclivities—than any other free State." Indeed, southern Indiana was considered one of the outlying provinces of the empire of slavery. When we recall that, as a territory, she was almost rent asunder over the question of entering the Union as a free State; that the State was admitted with slaves still in the possession of a part of the settlers; that all of the fourteen counties which comprised the new State were mainly settled from slave States, and that south of the National Road the Southern sympathizers had a controlling political majority; that in 1840, when William Henry Harrison was elected President, but one vote was recorded for the abolitionist candidate; that in 1851, when Indiana's new constitution was adopted, it included a provision for the exclusion and colonization of negroes and mulattoes and that this article was submitted, as a distinct proposition, to the people of the State for their approval, and was adopted by a vote of 109,976 to 21,066; again that for forty-four years after the admission of the State—that is, from 1816 to the election of Lincoln in 1860—the electoral vote of Indiana was given to the Democratic party, with the exception of two campaigns when William Henry Harrison was the candidate of the Whigs in 1836 and 1840;—recalling these significant facts in the history of Indiana, it will be easy to picture the state of mind which prevailed at the approach of the war with their Southern neighbors, and during that struggle; for all of the citizens were not pro-slave in sentiment.

A visitor to the State a dozen years before the war, in commenting on an ordinary national election, as he saw it in Indiana, said that a stranger to our government, looking on, would naturally suppose that it was the last night we were to enjoy our Union; would think that the excited parties would never be reconciled to the success of their opponents, but rally under their leaders and contest their power at the point of the sword. It is not difficult to imagine the strained relations existing between such violently opposed factions, and the result of such sentiments during the deplorable conflict. Ties of kindred were severed, neighborhoods became divided, the bitter dissensions knew no sex, no church, no age. Ministers of the gospel took sides, and found Bible texts for either side of the question. Newspapers were full of incendiary utterances. Orators fulminated and people wrangled and argued as they never have since.

"Ef dey's one thing topper God's worl yo' pa do despi'cibly and contestibly despise, hate, cuss, an' outrageously 'bominate, it are a Ab'litionist, an' dey's a considabul sprinklin' erroun' 'bout de kentry," said a knowing Indiana servant before the war. This was true of a vast number of the residents who were of Southern extraction,—they had a violent hatred of abolitionists. On the other hand many of these same abolitionists, defiantly if secretly, allied themselves with the "Underground Railway." Slavery was just over the border. In their opinion that institution was mortally wicked. Danger did not deter them from aiding the slave to escape from his master, and gain freedom in Canada. Earnest men and women in Indiana secretly helped Sambo and Chloe along another stage in their journey. The true story of the efforts of that secret band—it can hardly be termed an organization—would be a thrilling tale. Before day dawn, the hunted slave or groups of slaves would tremblingly approach a homestead, be quietly given a day's rest, shelter, food, fresh clothing, and then at night passed on to the next station of the Underground Railway. In a few hours more if hunters from the South came for their "property," they also must be fed, and *detained* as long as possible. No record, perhaps, exists of the members of this society or of the unfortunates whom they helped. It was against the Fugitive Slave Law and only justified by the greater law of humanity. Suspicion often prompted espionage, and this engendered hate and recrimination. Householders were sometimes imprisoned for helping slaves to escape and then it became known that their neighbors had informed against them. It was not a happy time, either North or South, those anti-bellum days; and the border States were in a very unhappy position which is now fortunately at an end. Composed of this divided population, Indiana heard the news of April 12, 1861: "Sumter has fallen." An Indiana woman who lived and labored through those thrilling times afterwards wrote:

"No man living within the limits of America will ever forget that despatch. The old earth itself seemed to reel under a blow, and no longer to afford a sure foothold. Through the long Saturday, business was at a stand. That night, from the banks of the Ohio to the sand-hills of Lake Michigan, from the Quaker towns on the eastern border to the prairie farms on the western line, the streets of Indiana towns were black with breathless people, still awaiting tidings of the loyal men in the unfinished Fort Sumter, bombarded by the thousands of raging rebels. When the banner was unfurled—the banner which within the memory of the present generation had only idly fluttered in holiday breezes—a new meaning seemed to stream from its folds. At ten o'clock a despatch announced, Sumter has fallen, and another, President Lincoln will issue a Proclamation to-morrow calling for 75,000 volunteers. Governor Morton's proclamation followed the President's. It was as the blast of a war trumpet. Indiana's quota of the 75,000 troops was six thousand. Fifteen thousand men answered the call. Eight thousand came up to the Capital. The clerk dropped his pen, the woodsman his axe, the machinist his tools, and more than all in numbers, the farmers left their ploughs in the furrows and came to their country's call. By dint of coloring his hair and beard, an old soldier of 1812 found his way into the ranks. 'If I were only four years younger,' sighed Major Whittock, the contemporary of William Henry Harrison; 'ninety is not too old in such a cause, and the young people know nothing of war. Fifty years of peace have made no soldiers.'"[1]

Men who had scarcely opened a book since leaving school became attentive students of tactics. It is averred that for the military terms "right and left" it was necessary to substitute "gee and haw" to the farmers' boys. In some cases, it is said, officers ordered whisps of straw wound round one foot and hay about the other, and the drilling began easily with, "hayfoot!" "straw-foot!" Of these new recruits, in their first engagement, a Confederate General said, "Can't make me believe that volunteers stand fire that way," and thus Hoosiers entered the four years' contest.

We cannot follow these troops beyond the bounds of the State. They placed their own names in the temple of fame. It is a matter of record that an Indiana soldier was the first to yield his life on the battlefield, and that the last battle of the war was fought by Indiana troops. The last Union soldier killed in battle was John J. Williams of the Thirty-fourth Indiana regiment. Indiana left her dead in seventeen States and Territories. Ere the war closed the Hoosier state with 246,000 voters had furnished over 259,000 troops. Three hundred and ninety-five men, only, served as conscripts; and that was after the State had furnished 8000 men in excess of her quota, the draft being the result of an erroneous computation of the muster rolls at Washington. The Indiana soldiers were the tallest men in the army, and were noted for their droll humor. The first men responded from the principle of patriotism and the fire of enthusiasm.

[1] Merrill, Catherine, *The Man Shakespeare and other Essays*. Indianapolis, 1902.

Some joined the army from love of adventure or expected glory. Not all that stayed in the service were heroes; but "there was no stain upon a single regiment or battery of all those sent out by Indiana." They bore themselves heroically and no State's soldiers won a prouder position. "We now occupy, alone, the proud position," said the *Journal*, "of offering volunteers to the government in advance of any call, while many of the other States are still behind, even with the draft."

No State could possibly have found herself, on the eve of a great war at her very threshold, in a more hopeless state of unpreparedness. Indiana had officials known as Quartermaster and Adjutant Generals, but they were undoubtedly on a peace footing with the world. It is doubtful if the whole State could have furnished arms for two regiments and the militia would not have supplied a half dozen regiments. The munitions of war were absolutely lacking. The department had no knapsacks, no canteens, no tents, and there was no money. It was a fact that members of the legislature and other State officers had been paid from the school fund, so empty was the treasury! Fortunately in this crisis Indiana had a great man for Governor.

Many a time has been recalled to memory the explanation which the wise old Quaker gave Oliver P. Morton of the reason why he was not to be elected United States Senator. Mr. Foulke tells the circumstances of Mr. Morton having expressed his preference for the Senatorship, when the Friend said, "Oliver, we cannot let thee go to the Senate." "Why not?" asked Morton. "Because thee is a good man for either of these places, and Henry Lane would make a good Senator but he would not make a good Governor. So he must go to the Senate and thee must stay and be Governor"; and Mr. Foulke very truly says that if Mr. Morton could have looked into the future and seen the career which opened before him, he would have valued the place given him more highly even than the Senatorship which he was not to have (until in later years), for the very reason that his abilities fitted him for the other place. How great these abilities were was gradually revealed in every pressing need and crisis of the next four years. Loyalty, foresight, fearless courage, tireless industry, resourcefulness in extremities, tenderness for his soldiers, influence over his people, political sagacity, business ability, and an intuitive knowledge of men; these were the traits of character which Governor Morton developed and which made him so successful in his administration.

It may be of interest to younger readers, who have come upon the scene since the Civil War, to recall the different party elements in the commonwealth and the opinions they held at the opening of that conflict. The war was not a sudden calamity. Forebodings of the disaster had been felt in all sections of the nation for more than a decade, and party lines were drawn on the questions involved in the struggle over slavery. In Indiana, at the beginning of the war, there were two elements in the new Republican party. A large number who had come into its ranks from the Democratic party, and others who were conservative, were disposed to conduct the war strictly for the preservation of the Union and the maintenance of the Constitution as it was, and an early pacification of the South. The other wing of the Republican party, chief of whom in Indiana were those illustrious men, George W. Julian and his co-workers, stood resolutely and uncompromisingly for the abolition of slavery, come what might. They felt that Lincoln had expressed a vital truth when he declared that there could be no lasting peace with a nation half slave and half free and they held that the sooner the question was settled forever, the better it would be for the whole country. Both of these classes of Republicans came up unitedly and inflexibly to the support of President Lincoln and Governor Morton in the prosecution of the war until the Union should be restored. In the Democratic party there were three divisions in the national campaign preceding the war. In Indiana, twelve thousand of the party had voted for Breckenridge, and were known as the nucleus of the party of the anti-war Democrats. Five thousand had voted for Bell, the constitutional candidate, and Douglas had a following of one hundred and ten thousand; most of whom gradually came to be known as war Democrats, and were staunchly loyal. These men joined in the plans for a vigorous prosecution of the war, and many of them served in the army. They held that all party strife should be put aside, until the federal authority was again established in every State. The anti-war Democrats, called derisively Copper-heads, were opposed to coercing the Southern States in any way, made a bogy of race equality, asserted States' rights, and were openly in sympathy with the Confederates. United States Senator Bright from Indiana, who belonged to this branch of the party, was expelled from the Senate for alleged complicity with the rebellion. Many of his associates engaged in secret treasonable organizations, and some of them were arrested for attempting warlike preparations for resistance to government. From this political alignment of the inhabitants of the State, it can be imagined that the division of sentiment caused much excitement. Present discussions, rancor, and political dissensions pale into personal pleasantries when compared with the rending of life and limb in those combats. It was not all a battle of words. In the history of the world, there cannot be found a more loyal people than the patriotic population of Indiana was. They not only rallied at once to the support of the government by sending more troops than were called for, but among those who did not go to the line of battle there was a great loyal majority who upheld the hands of the Governor.

Business men subscribed money, forwarded supplies, and went to the front with goods and provisions for the soldiers. Indiana men organized the first Sanitary Commission, and the people supplied the funds for it to furnish the comforts and necessities which the government could not. Citizens served on this Commission without pay, and followed the soldiers on the march, in camp, and in the hospital, with everything needed for the sick or wounded. Governor Morton took special pride in the Commission's work and was never tired of devising ways and means of improving its efficiency. Four hundred and fifty thousand dollars' worth of supplies was donated by private contribution through this channel by the people of the State. Nor were the women of the State backward in patriotic endeavor. They toiled unremittingly during the entire war. In October of the first year of the struggle, Governor Morton issued an appeal to the patriotic women of the State, calling their attention to the approach of winter and the possibilities of suffering which the troops would undergo unless help from other sources than the government should reach them. He asked for blankets, knit gloves, socks, and hospital supplies. The response to this suggestion was so liberal that, in the latter part of the winter, the Quartermaster-General issued a letter stating that there were already enough contributions to supply the needs. What was sent? Necessities, comforts, and luxuries. Women canned fruit for the soldiers; they knit stockings and mittens for them. Aid societies made great bales of hospital shirts and warm underwear; children spent their Saturdays and holidays in scraping lint and rolling bandages. They wrote kindly letters and placed them in the useful "house-wife," which was a bag made with pockets and filled with needles, buttons, and patches for the soldiers' use. Each company that started for the front was accompanied to the station or boat-landing by the whole village, cheering them on to duty, and lading them with good things to eat. Every passing regiment was hurriedly given a feast in the court-house or station. As one of these noble helpers wrote: "And people did not tire of liberality. Hands, houses, and hearts were open to our soldiers. The war was no sixty-day affair, as had been promised. It went on and on, and recruiting went steadily on. The troops in the capital, though always changing, were never gone." Many Indiana mothers saw every son march away to the army. Tenderly reared women went as hospital nurses. Brides of an hour said good-bye to their soldier lovers, and old gray-haired fathers went into the harvest fields that the sons might serve at the front.

Robert Dale Owen, who himself stood next to the War Governor in tireless labors for the soldiers, was appointed by the Executive as agent, and purchased all the arms and equipment for the State with honorable and efficient ability. From some of the colleges of Indiana every man went that was able to go to war. Several of these schools closed for want of students until after the struggle was over. In any estimate of the progress made by Indiana, it must always be borne in mind that the State lost a valuable element of her population in the men who died during those four years, which detracted greatly from her future greatness.

At the opening of the war, not only individual citizens but the State, through its Legislature, responded to the call of the War Governor. Later, as we shall see, the Executive had to meet a newly elected Legislature which tried his soul to the last extremity, by their lack of loyalty, but the men who were assembled in extra session in April, 1861, voted and placed under the control of Governor Morton, within a fortnight after the fall of Fort Sumter, a half million dollars for arms and ammunition, and one hundred thousand for military contingencies. They also voted a million dollars for enlisting, maintaining, and subsisting troops. Responding with vigor to the sentiment of the people of Indiana, the Legislature (then in office) sustained the Governor in his arduous task. With all of this great patriotism on the part of the large majority of the people of Indiana, there was a minority whose acts afforded some reason for the Confederate General Morgan supposing that his invasion of the State in 1863 would be welcome to a larger following than he found. As there were Union people within the Southern

States, there were also Secessionists in the North, and, so far as they could, and dared, the Southern sympathizers in Indiana plotted and conspired against the Executive and endeavored to thwart his plans for the defence of the nation. To-day we can afford to forgive, but mention of the proceedings of this minority in Indiana, during the war, is necessarily a part of its history. Steadily but secretly the leaven of disloyalty to the government and its policies permeated one section of the conservative party. In several counties of the State, secret organizations were effected, and conspiracies against the government were planned. Military drill was a part of the business of the regular meetings of the "Knights of the Golden Circle" and the "Sons of Liberty," as these secret societies called themselves. The Union neighbors and old friends of the men in these bands debated with and counselled them in vain, on the futility and wrong of their plans. When the war had gone on through two years they became bolder in their teachings and movements.

There had been disastrous battles at the front, the Emancipation Proclamation had been issued, there were large numbers of Union men absent serving in the army, and treasonable sentiments grew more outspoken. Owing to these circumstances it had come about that at the Congressional elections of 1862 many of the returns went against the administration, and, excepting the Governor, all of the State officers and a majority of the Legislature who were elected were Democrats and many of these were anti-war men. The Legislature sought to enact laws tying Governor Morton's hands in enlisting troops and raising militia. To prevent the passage of such a law the Union legislators withdrew from the sessions until the term closed by limitation. Governor Morton said, in his carefully prepared message to this seditious Legislature: "I believe that the masses of men of all parties are loyal and are united in their determination to maintain our government, however much they may differ upon other points; and I do sincerely hope that all will be willing to subordinate their peculiar opinions to the great cause of preserving our national law and existence." Even after this appeal secessionist sympathizers of this Legislature continued throughout the session to oppose, obstruct, and misrepresent the acts of the Executive and the Federal officials. Mr. Foulke says in his biography of Governor Morton:

"Scores of grotesque and preposterous resolutions were tossed into the seething cauldron. There were propositions for an armistice, for a withdrawal of the Emancipation Proclamation, for peace conventions to consider impossible compromises. There were dismal wailings at the calamities of war, at the overthrow of 'sacred rights and liberties' by 'tyrants and usurpers,'— incoherent ravings against the President, the Governor, the Abolitionists, the Negroes, the 'Massachusetts Yankees,'—a great tumult of words and dissonant eloquence."[1]

But Mr. Foulke goes on to show what a stinging rebuke was administered to this misguided Legislature, by the letters and resolutions from the army of 60,000 soldiers in the field, who were naturally enraged and indignant over these stabs in the back. Their protests became general, and on the twenty-third of January resolutions adopted by the officers of twenty-two regiments and

[1] Foulke, William Dudley, *Life of O. P. Morton.* New York, 1904.

four batteries and approved by the soldiers were sent from the Indiana troops at Murfreesboro. These protests were followed by similar representations from the soldiers at Corinth, in Arkansas, and from the Army of the Cumberland. Said this remonstrance from the soldiers to the Assembly:

"We have watched the traitorous conduct of those members of the Legislature, who, misrepresenting their constituencies, have been proposing a suspension of hostilities, plotting to divest Governor Morton of the rights vested in him by our State Constitution and laws, and we calmly and firmly say: 'Beware of the terrible retribution that is falling upon your coadjutors at the South, which, as your crime is tenfold blacker, will swiftly smite you with tenfold more horror should you persist in your damnable deeds of treason.'"

To be fair, it must be borne in mind that Indiana was not alone in having Southern sympathizers within its borders. All of the Northern States had this to contend with; but these communications, coming directly to the Legislature from the army, were marvellously efficacious in clearing the atmosphere about the Statehouse. They enabled the legislators, at least, to see national patriotism in its true perspective, and modest resolutions were passed protesting against being misunderstood.

Encouraged by the evil example of their lawmakers, the Southern sympathizers in the State grew more bold and insolent. Secret societies, with disloyal intent, multiplied; and leaders were found who endeavored to alienate the people from their loyalty and to organize the disloyal element. Cheers were heard for Jeff Davis, and there was always some one ready to respond "a rope to hang him with." Peace at any

Indiana as Affected by the Civil War 307

price, even the recognition of the Southern independence, was the purpose of those in control of the Legislature, and of those who were members of these societies. Assassination of the Governor was openly threatened. In the back districts men and women wore homespun clothes dyed with butternut juice; and in the towns many of them wore brooches made of the shell of a butternut, to denote their sympathy with the South.

A conspiracy to overthrow the State government was planned. And this too at a time when our national existence hovered between life and death. In the words of Mr. Foulke:

"At other periods it would have been only a subject for scornful jest, but at that time was dangerous, and demanded additional energy from those who had already expended the strength of Hercules in the efforts to subdue an armed rebellion. It was fortunate that there was at this time at the head of affairs in Indiana a man whose resources were equal to every emergency, whose autocratic will supplied everything there was lacking in a disloyal Legislature and a partisan judiciary."[1]

Governor Morton said of this period, a dozen years afterwards in the United States Senate, that the State was honeycombed with secret societies formerly known as the Knights of the Golden Circle and later as the Sons of Liberty. They claimed to have 40,000 members in the State; they were lawless, defiant, plotting treason against the United States and the overthrow of the State government. In some counties their operations were so formidable as to require the militia to be kept on a war footing, and throughout 1863 and until the final explosion of the organization in 1864

[1] Foulke, William Dudley, *Life of O. P. Morton*. New York, 1904.

they kept the whole State in agitation and alarm. Certain leaders of the Democratic party felt themselves handicapped in their ambitions by these organizations. So bold were they in the summer of 1863 that General John Morgan of Kentucky was encouraged to invade the State with his forces, in the belief there would be a general uprising in his support. In 1864, so numerous were these organizations and so confident were they of their strength, that they matured a plan for a general uprising in the city of Indianapolis on the sixteenth of August. The plan that was discovered, as shown by the subsequent confession of some of the leading conspirators, was to march on the capital city, release on that day about 7000 Confederate prisoners confined at Camp Morton, seize the Arsenal and arm these prisoners, overturn the State government, and take possession of the State. The arrival of a detail of infantry hastily broke up the mass meeting.

"Some of the more frantic climbed on the shoulders of those in the rear in their efforts to escape. The order was given to search every man attempting to leave the city. Three hundred revolvers were taken from the passengers on one train. Hundreds of them were thrown through the windows by their owners, into Pogue's Run. Pistols were given to women, believing that they would not be searched. Seven were found on one woman. Thus ended the farcical Battle of Pogue's Run, whose waters were filled not with the blood of combatants, but with firearms prudently cast away."[1]

The whole plan having been discovered, was abandoned and denied by the leaders, three of whom were State

[1] Griffith, Frank. Detailed for this duty from 83d Regiment. *Indianapolis Star*, August 23, 1908.

Indiana as Affected by the Civil War

officers! They quickly sent out orders countermanding the march of the forces on Indianapolis. In a short time the seizure of arms and ammunition collected at Indianapolis for treasonable purposes (some of them labelled Sunday-school books) and the capture of the records and the rituals of the Sons of Liberty, as well as the arrest of eighty of the ringleaders, gradually caused the breaking up of organizations in the more remote neighborhoods. By actual invoice it was learned that in two of the preceding months nearly 30,000 guns and revolvers had been brought into the State, followed at later times by larger quantities of arms for the bands amounting to 60,000 revolvers and 6000 muskets. The Southern records show that these organizations and the leaders of the Confederacy were in constant correspondence and negotiation by a cipher code. Later when the tide of war was turning against the South, in 1864, the greatest hope of succor of Jefferson Davis's Cabinet was from the treasonable societies of the North, and the States which bordered on the Ohio River were depended upon for an uprising against Federal control.

While the administration was struggling with treasonable legislators and bands within its borders, the whole Commonwealth was startled by a raid upon its own soil. There had been two scares previous to this, but on July 8, 1863, there occurred one of the most daring, most spectacular events of the war. This was the invasion of Federal territory along the Ohio River, with the avowed purpose of bringing the war home to the Northern States, and giving the Southern sympathizers an opportunity to show their colors and join their friends from the South. There had never been any arrests of Southern sympathizers up to this time and no tests were made of their courage. General John Morgan, commanding between two or three thousand Confederate cavalry, was cut off from Bragg and Buckner's army and determined to carry the war into the enemy's country, make an "astounding diversion" that would call off some of the Federal forces that were pursuing his chief. Probably six hundred adventurers bent on plunder were with this troop. It was a brilliant cavalry manœuvre, from a military standpoint. War is no holiday play, and the raid won lasting notoriety for its commander, but he was disappointed in its results; for few if any Northern secessionists joined him. He found that all the men he added to his numbers, he was obliged to capture.

It is said that riding at the head of his troops to the Kentucky shore, General Morgan dramatically pointed to the northern bank of the Ohio River and said, "Boys, over there is Yankee land, we will cross over and possess it"; and that after they were safely over, he ordered the boats burned, denoting no intention of a return and no chance of being followed by the Federal troops who were close upon their heels; so near, in fact, that the Johnny Rebs in the boats called back to some of them, "Got any word want sent your ma?"

The present generation can make a very fair estimate of this "secesh" element of the Indiana backwoods population, from a little lifelike sketch by George S. Cottman. He introduces it with a description of a "Dixie" neighborhood where these poor whites lived in their log cabins in the woods. Isolated not only by location but by nature these squatters remained Southern in sentiment and sympathy.

"Stray newspapers, carried in like bones into a den, to be read at leisure, passed from hand to hand and so kept them apprised of the doings of the outside world. Suddenly the news came that John Morgan was invading the state and the squatters in 'Dixie' settlement met to consider the question of joining him.

"One day Mr. Jabez Baughman issues a call for all Dixieites to convene at his cabin that evening to discuss questions of moment. Of the resultant meeting no minutes were preserved; you will find no mention of it in the Adjutant-General's reports, nor elsewhere, and the only authority I can claim for it is the oral account of Mr. Andrew Jackson Strickler, a member of the convention, who afterwards became reconstructed and reconciled to the Government. As faithfully as I can quote him here he is, Tennessee dialect and all: 'It was,' said Mr. Strickler, 'in July of '63. I disremember adzactly the date, but it was after the hayin' was done an' the wheat harvest about over. We heerd tel' o' John Morgan crossin' the river an' headin' our way, an' was consid'ble intrusted like, an' so w'en Jabe Baughman's boys went eroun' the settlement tellin' all the men folks their pap wanted us to meet at their house late that night, we jest natchally fell in with it, kase we knowed from the sly way it 'as done thar was somepin' up. None of us was to come till after ord'nary bed-time, an' none of us was to carry 'ary light, an' that putt ginger in it, see? Well, w'en night fell the weather got ugly, and I mind, way about ten o'clock, as I felt my way through the thickets, how everlastin' black it was, an' how the wind rasseled the trees erbout, roarin' like a hungry lion seekin' who he may devour. It made me feel kind o' creepy, kase it 'peared like the elerments an' man an' everything was erbout to do somepin'—kinder like the bottom was goin' to drap out o' things, y' understand.

"'Well, the fellers come steerin' into Jabe's one by one, an' by 'leven o' the clock ever' man in Dixie was thar.

Jabe's young 'uns an' womern folks hed been sent out in the stable to sleep, an' so ever'thing was clair fer business, but we all sat eround talkin' hogs for a spell, kase we felt a mite unsartin; but by-m-by Baughman, says he: "Gent'l'men, I call this meetin' to order." Then my oldest boy whose name was Andy, too, and who'd been to two or three public meetin's before an' felt kind o' biggoty over it, he hollers out; "I second the motion." Then young Jerry Stimson says; "I move that Mr. Baughman take the cheer," an' my boy seconded that, too, an' it was so ordered. Then Baughman riz an' said he hadn't hardly expected that honor (which was a lie), but sence they had putt it on him he'd try to discharge his duties to the meetin'.

"'After that we made young Stimson secatary, seein' he was somepin' of a scholard, an' then Jabe he made us a speech sayin' as how we'd orto stick by the grand old South, w'at was even now sendin' her conquerin' hosts to our doors, an' how we'uns should be ready to receive her to our buzzums. It wa'nt all quite clear to me, an' I ast how we was goin' to take her to our buzzums. "W'y, give her our moral s'port," says Jabe. "How'll we give our moral s'port," says I, an' then says Jabe slow an' solemn like: "Gent'l'men," says he, "w'en our sister States found it was time fer 'em to be up an' adoin'— w'en they found the Union wa'nt the place fer 'em, w'at did they do?" Here Jabe helt his fire, an' ever'thing was stock-still fer a spell, w'ile the wind howled outside. It 'peared like no one hadn't the grit to tackle the question, an' Jabe had to do it hisself. "Gent'l'men," says he, "air we men enough to run risks for our kentry? W'en John Morgan's histes the flag of the grand ol' Confede'cy over the Injeany State House who's goin' to come to their reward, them as helt back skeert, or them as give him their moral s'port?"

"'At this my boy Andy who was gettin' all het up like with the idee o' doin' somepin', bellers out: "Mr. Cheer-man, I move 'at we air all men, an' 'at we ain't afeerd to give the South our moral s'port." Then Jabe grabbed the cow by the tail an' w'ipped her up. "Do I understand the gentl'man to mean," says he, "that we'd orto do w'at our sister States hez done, an' draw out o' this yere Union, an' ef so, will he put a movement to that effeck before the House?" "I make a move then," says Andy again, as bold as Davy Crockett, "that we don't whip the devil eround the stump no more, but that we git out o' the Union an' we git out a-flyin'." I was right proud o' the boy, not kase I thought he had a durn bit o' sense, but kase he went at it with his coat off like a man bound to make his mark. That got all of us spunky like an' nigh ever' one in the house seconded the move. Then says Jabe: "Gen'l'men, the question is before you, whether we will lend the Southern Confeder'cy our moral s'port an' foller our sister states out'n the Union. All in favor of this yere motion signify the same by sayin' 'aye.'" "Aye," says ever' livin' soul with a whoop, fer by that time we shore was all runnin' in a flock. "All contrary-wise say no," says Jabe, an' we all waited quiet fer a minute, kase that 'as the proper way, y' know, w'en all of a sudden, above the roar o' the wind outside, thar was a screech an' a tremenjus racket; the ol' house shuk like it was comin' down; the daubin' flew from the chinks, an' overhead it 'peared like the ol' Scratch was clawin' his way through the clabboards. Next he came a-tearin' at the floor of the loft above us, an' a loose board swingin' down hit Jabe a whack an' knocked the candle off'n the table, an' the next thing it was black as yer hat. Jabe I reckon, was consid'able flustered, kase he gathered, hisself up an' yelled: "The Devil's after us—git out o' here, fellers!" An' you bet we got.

"'It tuck me a full hour to find my way home through the bresh, an' w'en I did git thar, at last, an' was tryin' to tell w'ich side o' the house the door was on, I bumped up, agin Andy groopin' his way too. "Andy," says I,

"I move we git in jest as quick as the Lord 'll let us," an' says Andy, "I second the motion."

" 'The next day w'ens we went back to Baughman's to see w'at we c'ud larn we found a good-sized ellum had keeled over again the roof-poles an' poked a limb down through the clabboards. It 'as never settled among us jest w'at it meant. Some said it 'as the Lord's way of votin' no again our goin' out o' the Union, an' others allowed it was the Lord's way o' savin' us from our brashness, kase, as ever' one knows, John Morgan did n't git to Injunoplis after all, an' as things turned out it wa'nt jest best fer us ti be seced, y' know.' "[1]

It was this sort of disloyalty, north of the river, that all unwittingly, the dashing cavalrymen were depending upon. Crossing the Ohio River General Morgan entered Harrison County in Indiana and passed eastward across the entire river districts and on into the adjoining State of Ohio. His plans were well laid and he was extremely bold in action. Through farm and village they swept capturing and paroling prisoners, appropriating the finest horses as they went, helping themselves to the fat of the land, as is the wont of military raiders. Out through every town in the State alarm bells were rung and the Governor's call for troops was sounded. The response was magical. Within forty-eight hours sixty-five thousand men had tendered their services, and were on their way to report for duty. Within three days, thirty thousand men, fully armed and organized had taken the field at various points to meet the enemy. Not being expected, on first landing Morgan's men found only a handful of troops to oppose them, and

[1] Cottman, George S., *Indiana Magazine of History*, page 52, vol. i., number 1.

Indiana as Affected by the Civil War 315

these were driven back; but within twenty-four hours, when attempting to penetrate into the interior of the State and afterwards to retire across the river, they were confronted in both attempts by bodies of armed men. Soon their march was quickened into a flight which in five days, carried them across the eastern border into Ohio and on over that State. Those were five exciting days in Indiana and the other border States. Frantic telegrams for help from raided towns, and daring dispatches from the invaders, wherever they had tapped the telegraph lines, located the raiders now here, now there. The Confederate general was so rapid and sudden in his movements as frequently to confound both friends and enemies. Morgan's army was reported as ten, twenty, and thirty thousand strong. The atmosphere was rife with excitement. Unharvested fields of over-ripe wheat stood golden in the sun. No raid had been believed possible by the farmers. Burning barns was fun as well as policy to this band. As they went they emptied ovens and pantries. Money and horses were gathered in as necessities of war. The banks throughout the State sent their gold and most of their currency to New York. People concealed their valuables and men hurried to enlist. Cold shivers reached even to the Capital. The damages in the raided States, to railroads, steamboats, bridges, and public stores was not less than ten millions of dollars. The troops plundered private properties, burned all bridges to prevent pursuit, detached parties right and left to cut off communication and destroy stores.

And what of the invaders? It was an adventurous band. From an interesting note-book of one of the troop we learn their feelings when two broad States lay between them and their comrades.

"Kentucky grew too warm for us and we determined to cross over into Indiana and try to stir up the Copperheads. We had no trouble in supplying provision. The chickens strolled before the doors with a confidence that was touching but misplaced. The good women baked wheaten bread in large quantities twice a week and we took the whole baking. The raw militia that was encountered were badly armed and had had no drill. A great fear seemed to have fallen upon that part of Indiana and they acted as if stunned. Often our men would throw away plunder to pillage afresh, generally without method or reason. A horn, seven pairs of skates, a bird cage, and cards of horn buttons would dangle from one man's saddle. The disposition for wholesale plunder exceeded anything that any one had ever seen. The men seemed actuated by a desire to pay off in the enemy's country, all the old scores that the Federal Army had chalked up in the South. The fatigue of the marches was tremendous. We often averaged twenty-one hours in the saddle. There was battle and death and destruction, but many ludicrous things happened during our raid. We rode into Salem and a small swivel gun, used by the younger population, four days before, for the Fourth of July Celebration, had been planted to obstruct our way. It was about eighteen inches long, loaded to the muzzle and mounted in the public square, by being propped against a log of fire wood. It was not fired for the man deputed to perform that important duty, somewhat astounded by our sudden dash into the town, dropped the coal of fire with which he should have touched it off, and before he could get another the 'rebels' captured the piece."

At Vernon, the Confederates were confronted by

several hundred hastily gathered militiamen. To Morgan's demand for their surrender the raw troops replied, "Come and take us"—but the enemy moved off toward Dupont.

Sometimes a mischievous cavalryman would coerce a farmer's daughter into riding a part of the way with the troop, and then set her down at a farmhouse far away from home. Often a whole squad would occupy the front porch while waiting for the good dinner they had compelled the household to cook for them. A favorite trick of the raiders was to send alarming messages to the towns farther north that they were at their doors; and another was to "cut in" and take messages and orders that were intended for the Federal officers who were after them; or listen to the news of the panic they were causing in the State. All this frolic, and many dark and terrible experiences fell to the lot of the invaders as well as to the residents of the river counties. The loss of life on either side was not great, perhaps, but all too many when it is remembered the combatants were from sister States. Some of the raiders crossed to Kentucky. Over in Ohio the commander, and those who had not been killed or wounded, were captured. An amusing story is told of an Irish Quartermaster who was captured by Morgan on one of these forays.

"Lieut. Igoe had a horror of regulations. Monthly, quarterly, and semi-annual reports, required by the department, were treated with easy neglect; not that the eccentric Quartermaster did not honestly discharge his duties; but because he regarded all such reports as 'a piece of magnificent tomfoolery.' A twelvemonth went by, and no report had been received at Washington of the state of affairs in the Quartermaster's department of the Irish Regiment. A note from headquarters to the Colonel brought the report question to a head. Igoe at once gathered up all his receipts, vouchers, and loose papers, and putting them carefully in a keg, headed up the concern, and respectfully forwarded them to Washington, with a note, stating that as the clerks in the department had more time than he had, they could assort and arrange the papers to suit themselves; remarking, too, that if they could make anything out of them, it was more than he could do himself. The reply from Washington was what might have been expected. Notice was served, that if he did not make out a report in full form, he would be sent for. Nothing disconcerted, the subject of our sketch sat down, and, as report goes, wrote the following exceedingly polite letter:

"'Headquarters Irish Regiment,
"' Quartermaster's Department.

"'DEAR SIR:—Your kind and friendly note of the —— inst. is before me. I regret exceedingly you can not make anything out of the keg-full of papers forwarded some two months ago. In order to facilitate the solution of the difficulty, I take pleasure in sending another box-full. I have long contemplated a visit to the capital of this mighty nation; but my finances being in such a dilapidated condition, I have been forced to forego that pleasure. I will be pleased to make a visit to your, I am told, delightful city, under the auspices, and at the expense, of our much afflicted Government.

"'Accept the assurance of my most distinguished consideration.

"'M. IGOE,
"'Lieut. & A. Q. M.'

"Of course the bureau of 'Contracts and Quartermasters' was not satisfied; but John Morgan, having a short time afterwards captured the hero, with his books, papers (all not 'kegged up'), and wagons, Igoe made a final statement, and a satisfactory settlement, by stating in

Indiana as Affected by the Civil War

a humorous way the facts and incidents of his capture. It has been his boast ever since that John Morgan kindly settled all his affairs, with the big 'conostrophies' at Washington."

A Confederate who was with General Morgan thus describes the end of the raid.

"Straight ahead he rode, passing the Indiana border and thundering desperately on upon the highways of Ohio. On he swept, brushing aside one foe, eluding another, and defying the telegraph, the steam-cars, the Generals, the swarming Militia. No time for the rest nor to replace the vitality that was constantly being expended. . . He baffled his enemies in three states. From day to day his men were killed or captured, singly or in groups. Another Sunday dawned, the 26th of July. There were left only three hundred of the three thousand troops who had crossed less than a month before. Many of the men, feverish almost to delirium from wounds received in fights on previous days, reeled in their saddles as they went. About two hundred of his command crossed the river and escaped. General Morgan and a few hundred men were finally driven to a bluff from which there was no escape, except by fighting their way through or leaping from a cliff. Finding themselves thus cooped Morgan's command surrendered. The gray fox was cornered at last in the open, but he had led a long chase."

The five hundred miles and more that they had traversed had been a succession of sudden encounters, skirmishes, and battles. Fire, panic, terror, and sorrow followed in their wake. The same Confederate asks, "Was anything accomplished by them save their own destruction?" I will answer, "Yes: the victory six weeks later by Bragg's Confederate Army in the great battle of Chickamauga. Of the forty thousand Northerners that we were led to believe would join us not one rose up to help." The Confederate troopers taunted the inhabitants of the region openly, with being a pack of cowardly curs, who could plot in secret, and stab in the dark, and curse the Government, but when it comes to fighting like men would not come out in the open. By superior numbers and equal bravery, the hastily assembled Northern volunteers had hedged in the raiders, defended assailed points, repulsed attacks, fought many skirmishes, and finally captured or dispersed the whole command. They had been greatly delayed in accomplishing their task by the bridges being destroyed, roads obstructed, and an utterly unprepared state of defence. It had taken several days to assemble volunteers and start in pursuit. Some of the Commands rode for a fortnight with only four hours' rest in the twenty-four. One hundred miles were sometimes covered in thirty hours by the fugitives. The inhabitants on the last stretch of the raid barricaded the highways to hinder their progress. There was no hesitancy among the war recruits in meeting the foe, when they could overtake them.

General Morgan's hotly pursued forces were overtaken in the valley near Buffington Island, where they were waiting for the dawn to clear the fog, so that they might cross the Ohio River at the ford and escape into West Virginia. The Federal troop came into the valley on the rear of the raiders; and fresh re-enforcements landing from the steamboats on the river, approached about the same time. All hope for escape, by fording the shallow place in the Ohio was gone. The one desperate chance was by the road leading out of the upper end of the valley; and toward this outlet Morgan's confused troopers swept through the standing grain fields of the fertile farms,

Soldiers' and Sailors' Monument.

"And the answer came: 'We would build it
   Out of our hopes made sure,
And out of our purest prayers and tears,
   And out of our faith secure."
  . . . .

"And see that ye build it stately,
   In pillar and niche and gate,
And high in pose as the souls of those
   It would commemorate."
             JAMES WHITCOMB RILEY.

the Federals following in hot pursuit. Immediately after the stampede began, said one of the Union officers who was present, each one of Morgan's troopers began to unload the plunder carried on his horse. Boots, shoes, stockings, corsets, gloves, skates, sleigh-bells, bird cages, were scattered to the winds. Then the flying horsemen let loose their bolts of muslin and calico, holding one end, and each cavalryman let the whole hundred yards stream out behind him. Instantly we found ourselves to be rainbow chasers. No road could accommodate such a confused mass of flying horsemen, and they spread across the valley. In the gorge and on the hills beyond many were captured. Here the Indiana–Ohio raid practically ended although Morgan himself was not captured here, but, with a small part of his men, escaped and fled nearly to Lake Erie, being captured at New Lisbon. Colonel Allen tells of an amusing incident which happened with his detail of prisoners, immediately after their capture, which illustrates the fraternal feeling which manifested itself numberless times during the Civil War.

"The prisoners and guards rested for a few minutes on the river bank, all gazing wistfully at the water. It must be borne in mind that both Morgan's and Hobson's command had been in the saddle for about three weeks, during all of which time we had ridden in the clouds of dust which our thousands of horses raised on the country roads in midsummer, and these dust clouds were so dense that at times it was impossible for the rider to see his horse's ears. It can readily be understood that under these circumstances a bath would be most desirable.

"As we sat on the river bank, first one man, then another, asked permission to go to the water's edge and wash his face, till soon about one-half of the men, both

Union and Confederates, were at the river's edge washing their faces and digging dust out of their eyes, ears, and nostrils. This proved to be such a half-way sort of business, and so unsatisfactory, that the men asked permission to go in swimming. Recognizing the merit of this request, I gave permission for one-half the prisoners and one-half the guards to go in swimming together, the other half to stand by and take their turn. Soon both 'Yankees' and 'Johnnies' were splashing in the water together, enjoying the most necessary bath they ever had in all their lives. The first detachment having completed their scrubbing, the second detachment took their turn. While the men were bathing, one of the Confederate officers turned to me, and pointing to the naked soldiers in the water said, 'It is difficult to tell t'other from which.' I quickly agreed with him as I was at that moment debating in my mind whether there was any danger of 'getting the babies mixed,' but a glance at the line of men in dusty blue on the shore with their Spencer carbines reassured me and I permitted the boys to gambol in the water to their heart's content.

"After the baths the guards shared the fried chicken in their haversacks with the prisoners, and we spread ourselves out on the grass under the shade of the trees, in regular picnic fashion, resting and waiting for orders."[1]

During the raid General Morgan's losses in killed and wounded were two hundred and fifty men, and twenty-eight commissioned officers killed and thirty-five wounded. The loss on the Union side was two hundred killed and three hundred wounded. The raid had lasted but a few days, leaving a blackened, devastated trail across the summer landscape and across the hearts of loving friends North and South whose

[1] Allen, Col. T. F., "A Thousand-Mile Horse Race," *Trottwood's Monthly*, 1907.

Indiana as Affected by the Civil War 323

dear ones fell in the fight for the invasion of the enemy's country or the defence and protection of their homes.

After this invasion, the men of Indiana who were called out for the little brush, as the raiders called it, returned to their homes and the Governor directed a more permanent and effective organization of the militia, especially along the Ohio River. There, business places were to be closed after three o'clock, so that able-bodied citizens might meet and drill, for not less than two hours each day, to be prepared for any further raid.

It seems strange that in this late war the question of navigation on the Mississippi River should again come up, after a quietude of sixty years, but it certainly was a disturbing feature in 1864. The sympathizers with the South, living in the Northwest, had encouraged the emissaries from the South to think that those States might join with the Confederacy. Overtures to this effect had passed between them. The control of the mouth of the Mississippi River was in the hands of the Confederates. Railroads were not yet universal and this was used by the disaffected element as an argument that the interests of the Northwest were identified with those of the South. Governor Morton recognized this influence on political opinion in Indiana and the conquest of the Mississippi became, in his eyes, a matter of supreme importance. This conquest was accomplished by Grant's campaign at Vicksburg, and the ultimate extinction of the Confederate control of the Mississippi. The gaining control of that highway of commerce, the banishment of Morgan's raiders, and the breaking up of the treasonable organization of Sons of Liberty were the closing scenes of the drama of internal dissensions in Indiana.

The war was prosecuted to its close beyond the borders of the State. The remainder of the struggle meant a consuming anxiety on the part of those who awaited tidings of battle, the sorrow for lost ones, the prayers for the absent, and the joys of victory. When peace was declared in June, 1865, the Indiana boys in blue began returning to Indianapolis to be mustered out of service. Loving parents and wives came up to the capital to welcome them home. The clouds of war were lifted and bells rang out in jubilee over the return of peace. As the long lines of soldiers marched up the streets, tears of joy and shouts of pride greeted the battered battle flags; but always, among the throng, silent and pathetic in their black robes of woe, were they who mourned for their loved ones who never would return. "Deaf to the welcoming shouts, blind to the rejoicing crowd, they saw shadowy figures following the flag, and dim faces that would smile no more." The living were welcomed home with universal joy, the dead were remembered with unspeakable sorrow. But the sorrow was individual; the joy was general, for the country was saved!—the country that above all others was the hope, and is the hope, of the world. No more South, no more North, no more bickering about slavery. An undivided country, and in time a united country. In a third of a century the scars of dissension had healed even in Indiana.

CHAPTER XV

PICTURESQUE INDIANA

TO the traveller who sees Indiana from the car window only, the State may seem uninteresting. Railways run along the lines of least resistance and through the most productive but not the most picturesque regions, and the endless stretches of waving corn grow monotonous to the tourist; but there is another point of view. Should you journey about the state with a naturalist, in each neighborhood you would find attractive places worthy of a special excursion. There is natural beauty of scenery hidden away in many sequestered spots only short drives from the main line of travel. There is hardly a spot in the State, says Mr. Nicholson, that touches the imagination with a sense of power or grandeur, and yet there are countless scenes of quiet beauty. The early writers of Indiana all sang of the beauty of forest and stream, of the birds and flowers that surrounded them.

In the northern tier of counties, toward Lake Michigan, or bordering on the sinuous Kankakee, over a thousand little lakes are nestled among the farms of that region. For many years sportsmen and summer tourists, from far and near, have frequented these waters for pleasure and sport. Vast herds of wild game and birds, and shoals of fish, have been taken from these haunts.

The topography of the middle and southern counties differs from the lake districts, and there are many picturesque places along the watercourses of these sections. The rivers of Indiana have ceased to be used for commerce, since railroads usurped transportation, but a boating trip on any of the beautiful streams repays one during a summer holiday. Along their banks the enormous soft maples, elms, and sycamores stand like giant sentinels white and far reaching, casting long afternoon shadows over the shallow waters. In no other way can one realize the wild beauty of the Tippecanoe, the Mississinewa, the Whitewater, the Wabash, or the countless small creeks and streams which flow into that river and the Ohio. The English cover the placid Thames with pleasure craft, and write verses to the gentle stream that they prize so dearly; but the Hoosiers have a world of sylvan beauty lying within their domain unexplored, save by the immediate neighborhood people. There are no less than a hundred and thirty named creeks flowing into the twelve rivers of Indiana; besides many smaller streams which feed these creeks. All of these waters, somewhere in their course, flow through picturesque ravines, and gorges hung with vines and ferns. Wild flowers cluster along the banks and, as has been pictured, all about the splendid elm trees stand, and stately green thorn trees fling their delicate fern-like foliage athwart the gray and white spotted boles of the tall leaning sycamores. Many of these streams rush along stony rapids, and plunge over cliffs, making waterfalls imposing in their grandeur. The banks are miniature canyons, which

A View on One of the Beautiful River Roads of Indiana.

astonish one who approaches them from the level farms above.

> "A hidden host of chiming springs
> Like countless harps with silver strings
> Are singing songs eternal.
> Like clustered chords of sweeping sound
> Adown the pebbly ledges
> The loosened waters laugh and bound
> To splash the swaying sedges."[1]

These living springs were known and frequented by the Indians, when the wilderness was theirs. Around the sparkling pools were the trading-points where groups of red men and white traders met to barter skins of fur-bearing animals for ammunition and trinkets. The aborigines are gone from their old haunts, but the beautiful springs of water still flow for the traveller. An old settler revisits his native State and rejoices that now as of old the banks of the Wabash are lined with the richest verdure, wild flowers intermingle with the tall grass. Blossoms of wild plum, hawthorn, dogwood, and red-bud make the air redolent with their familiar perfume. The prairies, rich beyond belief, for which the speech of England has no name—gardens of the desert—the unshorn fields, are still boundless and beautiful.

Some of the beauty of southern Indiana clusters about the entrances to numerous caves, to be found in a half-dozen counties in the limestone area. Here numberless sink-holes occur; through the fissures of many of them, adventurers have penetrated into the underground caverns beneath. Doubtless there are undiscovered caves throughout that region; some that

---

[1] Stein, Evaleen, *Fugitive Pieces*.

are known are unexplored. The entrances to some of the larger caves are wildly beautiful. The rugged vine-wreathed approaches to their mysterious cavernous depths are framed in a jungle of evergreens and ferns. Of the picturesque opening into Porter's cave in Owen County, which makes it, alone, reason for a pilgrimage to the place, the State geologist says that it is the most beautiful of any that he has visited in his journeys through the State. It is in the side of a hill at the head of a narrow canyon, which has been eroded by the stream which flows from the cavern. This stream falls perpendicularly thirty feet from the floor of the cave to the bottom of the gulch. "The rock down which the water flows is covered with moss, and in the early morn, when the sunbeams light up the interior of the cave for a distance of seventy-five or more feet and the waters glisten and sparkle from the background, the scene is a most entrancing one."[1] This cave may be traversed eight or nine hundred feet. The entrance to Shawnee cave, located in Lawrence County, is also surrounded by scenery of marvellous beauty. In Crawford County, among the rugged hills between the Ohio and Blue rivers, are Marengo and Wyandotte caves, which are natural caverns of immense dimensions; the latter second only to Mammoth cave in extent and beauty. Marengo was discovered in 1883, is nearly four thousand feet in extent, and is noted, as also is Shiloh cave, for the number and brilliancy of the interior chambers, glittering with myriads of beautiful stalactites. Wyandotte may have been the resort of the natives during the stone age, and was well known

[1] Blatchley, W. S., *Gleanings from Nature*, page 105. Indianapolis, 1899.

The Mouth of Donnehue's Cave in Lawrence County, Southern Indiana.
From a photograph loaned by W. S. Blatchly.

to the later Indians, who used some of the large dry chambers in which to store their seed corn. The vaulted domes and great apartments, vast in size and colossal in height, its fluted columns supporting the arched roof, give the interior the appearance of an immense cathedral. It contains large deposits of satin-spar, nitre, epsom salts, and plaster of paris. The running streams and dry tortuous paths, the enormous stalactites and stalagmites, crystal and glittering, sometimes reaching seventy feet in circumference, make scenes of wondrous beauty quite unsuspected from the surface above. A description of one of the Indiana caves would not answer for all. They vary in extent, in the loftiness of their interiors, and in brilliancy; but in most of them, we are told, the roof and sides of the chambers are studded with pendants of glittering water-tipped carbonate of lime, that flash in the light of a torch like jewels of crystal. As with many other things in Indiana the caves have not been exploited and advertised to attract tourists.

The mineral springs of Orange, Martin, Morgan, Warren, Owen, and other counties of Indiana are well worth a journey for the enjoyment of their environment. These "licks" were well known to the Indians, and the waters have long been regarded as valuable for their medicinal qualities. Indeed, as cures, the Indiana springs are only on the threshold of their history; they are steadily becoming celebrated spas.

The Switzerland of Indiana is in the country along the Ohio River. In that part of the State the scenery is, in many localities, wildly beautiful. The drives and walks about Madison, Hanover College, Vevay, and other southern towns are unsurpassed in the

Middle West. In all of these counties, there are picturesque retreats worth a journey to see them.

Among the pleasures of driving in different parts of the State, is the coming upon the old mills which were such an essential feature of the early settlement. Many of these old buildings still stand between the placid mill-race and the necessary stream, which winds about through the hills, and is crossed by the picturesque bridges. These old mills are tucked away in the valleys, or hang over the falls, where one comes upon them unexpectedly at a turn in the road. They are set amidst the most charming scenery, making one long to stop and stay through the golden October days. Nowhere else may the beauty and gorgeousness of the forest trees in their autumn foliage be so intimately known and enjoyed, as around these old mill sites. Here the stream makes its tortuous windings, past steep bluffs and sloping banks, covered with primeval oaks, maples, and walnut trees, clothed in their scarlet and gold. To the busy man who has known these nooks in childhood days, there is no greater joy than to return from life's round of cares and renew his youth in the old valley. The mystical haze of autumn mellows the brilliant sunshine and gaudy coloring of the foliage. The squirrel still scolds him, as in days of yore, for gathering the nuts on his preserves. He browses on the wild grapes and black haws, and thinks with Mr. Howells who recalled years afterward in historic old Venice, when he heard the market boy cry his wares 'neath the Rialto Bridge,

" ' Mulberries! fine mulberries here.' "
Though I hardly should count these mulberries dear
If I paid three times the price for my pleasure.

The Clifty Falls, near Madison, Indiana.

For you know, old friend, I have n't eaten
A mulberry, since the ignorant joy
Of anything sweet in the mouth could sweeten
All this bitter world for a boy." [1]

Native Hoosiers love their woods and wild flowers and gentle streams, as the old salt loves the sea. None of Whitcomb Riley's poems express the feelings of his people more truly than do the verses about the banks of the creeks, the fields and farms, and the old swimming-hole. Evaleen Stein—who is preeminently the Hoosier poet of the green meadows, the grassy road-sides, the shimmering streams, the mysterious marshes, the beautiful birds and the dim forests which she claims as "the sweet familiar things of the ever dearest home-lands," voices the feelings of the true Indianian, in the next line, "I think those fields are fairer than any anywhere." [2]

From any one of the towns it is not far to the woods, and it has always been part of the life of the children to wander forth on holidays and get into the real country; gathering wild flowers or nuts, as the season happens to afford; exploring the old rail fence corners, where the wild cherry and the elder bushes grow, where the ground-cherries and the sassafras are found, under the wild-rose tangle; and a boy may be sure of arousing a rabbit or a Bob-white. Sitting on the old worm-fence, watching the wrens and thrushes flitting in and out, intent on family cares, many a Hoosier youth has planned the career that he determined, then, should be his. Many a comely maiden has dreamed of the future awaiting her, as she filled her basket with blackberries, where the vines had clam-

[1] Howells, Wm. D., *Poems*.
[2] Stein, Evaleen, *Among the Trees Again*. Indianapolis, 1902.

bered over the old "stake and riders." This home of the golden-rod and sumach is fast passing from the roadsides; but the picturesque fences, with their neglected corners of lovely wild things, will live in the memory of the native of the West. It is the same with the great forests, and the love they inspire in the Hoosier breast: as Miss Dunn felt marooned in a bleak prairie town she fell to dreaming of an Indiana woodland, musical with birds and the singing of a pebbly brook; arrow-grass edged the bank; yellow, waxen buttercups gleamed near. A great mottled sycamore leaned over a deep pool splendid with shiners. Some frogs croaked farther down the bank, and opposite, a billow of ferns were reflected daintily on the surface. Some magnificent beeches and splendid oaks, on a little knoll beyond, threw deep shadows that called to comfort on the mossy beds and leafy carpets of the natural groves of old Indiana. It is the beauty of these woodland scenes that looks forth from the canvases of artists like Bundy, and there is little wonder that the impression of the forests and fields is present in the writings of Hoosiers. Surely nowhere outside of the tropics was there a greater profusion of wild flowers, ferns, and trees than on the hills and valleys and over the plains of this State. The magnificence of the primeval forests of Indiana is a matter of history. The present "dweller in the land" cannot fully realize their vastness, well wooded as it still may seem to them.

As the State slopes toward Lake Michigan the forests grow light, until there are only straggling oaks, and undergrowth; but other beauties of nature compensate here for the products of a more fertile soil. It is a peculiar country,—a succession of shel-

One of the Gorges of Montgomery County.

tered prairies, rounded sand hills and reedy marshes, interspersed with quiet lakes and by a net-work of sluggish streams. The lakes in northern Indiana, writes Mr. Blatchley, are the brightest gems in the corona of the State. They are the most beautiful and expressive features of the landscape, in the region wherein they abound. Numbered by hundreds, they range in size from an area of half an acre up to five and a half square miles. The whole number of these pretty lakes cannot be less than one thousand. They were caused by glacial action and are scattered over the fourteen or fifteen northern counties. Their depth varies in different localities from five to one hundred and twenty feet. Many of these charming lakes have groups of cottages, hotels, and club-houses around their shores. Some are still without settlements. On their banks, adds Mr. Blatchley, one can pitch his tent with no fear of invading the privacy of some cottage. Over its deeper pools he can troll or cast for black bass, with the assurance that he will cause that gamy denizen to rise and strike, or alongside the weed-covered bars he can at times pull in bluegill, catfish, ringed perch, and warmouth as fast as he can bait his hooks. Still farther in the northwestern part of the State, the swamps that are tributary to the Kankakee River, covered half a million acres before the modern scheme of drainage was begun. These swamps have been the paradise of the sportsman, and are still visited by hundreds of hunters in the duck-shooting season. Most of the hunting is done in boats poled along in the current, or pushed about among the reeds. If approached from the plain, the huntsman is in danger of losing his way in the interminable swamp, or of getting in beyond his depth, in the soft ooze of the marsh. It is a weird landscape of vast stretches of land, covered with tall grass and prairie flowers, almost impenetrable because the soil is like a sponge. Through this great area of lowland the beautiful little river bends about as it winds its slender way through the wide marsh. A river is known to be there, writes Mr. Ball—the blue lines of trees marking its course can be discerned from the prairie heights; but only occasionally in mid-winter or in a time of great drought can one come near its water channel. So far as any ordinary access to it from Lake County is concerned, it is like a fabulous river, or one the existence of which we take on trust.

> "Ah, surely one would never guess
> That through that tangled wilderness,
> Through those far forest depths remote,
> Lay any smallest path, much less
> A way wherein to guide a boat."[1]

The banks of the river itself are bordered by beautiful trees, hung with vines and filled with singing birds. Floating dreamily down the sluggish stream, under the depths of its summer shade the idle angler looks through the trees and across the marsh, and recalls Evaleen Stein's beautiful description of the scene:

> "And now and then a wild bird flies
> From hidden haunts among the reeds;
> Or, faintly heard, a bittern cries
> Across the tasselled water-weeds;
> Or floating upward from the green
> Young willow wands, with sunny sheen
> On pearly breast, and wings outspread,
> A white crane journeys overhead.

[1] Stein, Evaleen, *One Way to the Woods*, page 21. Boston, 1898.

An Old Mill.

One comes upon these old mills unexpectedly at a turn of the road, set amidst the most charming scenery. From a photograph.

> For leagues on leagues no sign is there
>   Of any snare
> For human toil, nor grief nor care;
>   The fields for bread lie other-where.
> Only the wild rice, straight and tall,
>   The wild race waving over all." [1]

The lover of solitude and sylvan joys may set his canoe on the shaded waters of the Mississinewa, or drop down the shallow sparkling Tippecanoe, or hunt the course of Lost River, for pleasures unalloyed by sound of trade. He may take a tramp over the rugged hills of Brown, or ramble along the route of the old canal, the while he recalls the vanished travellers who once glided past the woodland beauty that still borders the old towpath. If in search of the grandeur of nature, he may rove through the stretches of primeval forest in Montgomery County, misnamed the Shades of Death. There naught but a feeling of exultation in the mysterious beauty comes to the beholder; may within the boundaries of his own State enjoy tranquil sojourns made interesting in the exploration of hidden nooks of untold beauty. He may renew his youth by long tramps through the fields of waving grain or under the shadows of great trees, where the singing of innumerable birds invites to joys undreamed of by the tourist who knows Indiana scenery only from the highways of travel.

[1] Stein, Evaleen, *One Way to the Woods*—poem, "The Marshes." Boston, 1898.

CHAPTER XVI

AN INDIANA TYPE

A BIOGRAPHICAL sketch of a native Indianian, who was representative of a class of citizens in that State, is given here to show another element that entered into the settlement of the commonwealth. The typical Hoosier of dialect stories is known to all. Among those who were born amid the crude conditions of frontier life, there was another class of men and women. These people maintained the traditions of their ancestry amidst the rude surroundings and scarce educational advantages. They grew up in the wilderness, but became the public-spirited citizens who stood not only for law and order on the border, but for the gentle graces of social life, when the neighborhoods developed into villages and cities.

The characteristics of this type of Americans, wherever found, were the love of country and of religious liberty, a deep pervading sense of the priceless value of education and every means of culture; with the desire to establish equal opportunity for all. There was about them a true knightly quality of *noblesse oblige*. They were reformers without being visionary, for they were the active men of affairs. The frank manner, erect figure, sterling integrity, betokened the

An Indiana Type

high-bred gentleman and decisive man of action. This type had representatives in every section.

The number of these citizens in Indiana was not small, but even smallness of number never deterred such men and women from initiative in movements of progress toward their high ideal for the individual and the country. Unfettered by Old World conditions, they saw the opportunity of the New World, and each bore his personal part of the responsibilities. It was of such that Lowell said in his immortal ode concerning Lincoln:

> " For him her Old-World moulds aside she threw,
>   And, choosing sweet clay from the breast
>   Of the unexhausted West,
>   With stuff untainted shaped a hero new,
>   Wise, steadfast in the strength of God, and true.
>   . . . .
>   The kindly-earnest, brave, foreseeing man,
>   Sagacious, patient, dreading praise, not blame,
>   New birth of our new soil, the first American."

Albert Henderson was one of this class who wrought without thought of rewards or honors. He was born within the territory on the tenth of January, the year before it was admitted into the Union. His father was of Carolina Quaker stock; and his mother came of Southern blood, tracing their ancestry through colonial service back to Scotch-Irish distinction in past history. Albert Henderson embodied the elements of this combination of lineage, and showed it throughout his life. The Quaker grandparents had come to the new territory because of their convictions in opposition to slavery, but they were possessed of lands and chattels as that frugal people is apt to be. His mother's family had always owned slaves, but came away from their kindred and people for the same reason. Her forefather, Robert Orr, the founder of the American line, had served as a colonel in the Revolutionary War, with seven sons in the service, and the little grandson, who afterward emigrated to Indiana, was a powder-maker to the Carolina forces.

In 1811, this branch of the family left South Carolina with a party of relatives and neighbors, who had determined to cast in their lot with a free State. After the long journey over mountains and down the rivers, they settled in the Whitewater Valley. Here they took up tracts of fine forest lands, and here, a little later, one daughter married the Quaker John Henderson, who had been suspended "from meeting" for serving in the War of 1812, but whose family life, and training, continued in that simple faith.

It was easy to trace the heritage of such antecedents in the character and bearing of their son, Albert. His simple tastes, his courtly old-time manner, his ardent patriotism, his craving for knowledge, his own correct life, with its gentle tolerance of others' shortcomings, all told plainly of the combination of the proud Southern blood with the Quaker strain, and he was as attached to the one family history as to the other.

Mr. Henderson's life may be considered as representative of the careers of those Western men who were his contemporaries. At sixteen years of age he was apprenticed, and learned to be a "master builder." He built many of the important buildings, and residences, in his part of the State. He drew his own plans and made the specifications. He moulded the brick in his own brick-yards, and burned the lime in his own lime-kilns. His own workmen reared the

Albert Henderson.

walls, plastered the interior, and put on the carpenter's finish. Complete from "plans to occupancy" was his enterprising announcement. The construction was sound and meant to last. Many of those buildings are still standing, a monument to honest work. In later life he took up the stone and granite business, but at all times he was a farmer. The love of the soil, a passion for seeing things grow, a knowledge of rearing live stock, and the Anglo-Saxon wish for lands made him a persistent farmer, although he never lived on a farm after his childhood days. Covington, in Fountain County, was one of the rising river towns, before the railroad innovation, when Mr. Henderson settled there, and his early manhood was identified with that section, and he was a member of the first Town Council of Covington after its incorporation. There he married a wife from the Ristine family, who came into the State with the earliest settlers. Her useful life closed within a few years.

Mr. Henderson was a man of indomitable energy, great initiative, and extremely enterprising for the times. Old settlers are fond of telling how he and his workmen built a house for a farmer near the Wabash while obliged to wait for the river to rise, so they could proceed on their journey to New Orleans with a flotilla of lime boats and lumber with which they had started to market.

He was a man of commanding presence, and noble bearing, with the manners of the old time. He had a very keen sense of humor, without any of the buffoonery of the border. While making no pretensions to oratory he was an excellent speaker and presiding officer, to which duty he was often called in his community.

In 1844, he married Lorana, the daughter of Dr. John Lambert Richmond, one of the pioneer surgeons of Indianapolis. Dr. Richmond was a very original man, of great talent, and possessed a mind enriched by years of study and investigation. In this union of Southern and Northern families, on Indiana soil, the life of Mr. Henderson is again typical of the West. Lorana Richmond was of New England-New York parentage, and of English descent, with an historic ancestry from the days of the Conqueror to colonial settlement, and through Revolutionary service in Massachusetts and New York. The marriage was an ideal one, uniting two persons who had the same noble aspirations and aims in life. She was a woman of rare judgment, wide reading, conservative temperament, and graciously hospitable. The home which these young people set up was ever full of good cheer and hospitality. Visitors from far and near, relatives, pensioners, ministers, educators, and lecturers of note filled the house at different seasons and on various occasions. In the town, Albert Henderson and his helpmeet were always identified with the charities and philanthropic endeavors. By her kindly ministrations, her baskets of food, and beautiful flowers, and the sheltering home offered in time of need or sorrow, his wife was as his other self in helpfulness in this community.

In the church it was Deacon Henderson, and he was ever the "right-hand man" to the minister. Educational advantages for every child was his life maxim. He maintained a private school for his own family and the immediate neighborhood. While he was a young man, and before he had children of his own, the great struggle for free public schools throughout the State came up, and Mr. Henderson was one of the staunchest supporters of Caleb Mills and his coterie of helpers, in their long agitation for enactments to further universal education. These friends of free schools, in his district, called conventions, and organized a circuit of county meetings, over which he presided and which he also addressed. This group of men won their victory with the adoption of the new State Constitution in 1851, and continued to agitate for increased facilities.

In the early days the use of alcoholic drinks in the West was very general and was clearly leading into widespread drunkenness, most threateningly disastrous it seemed to the minds of temperate citizens. From this foreboding sprang the "Washingtonian movement," which swept the country. Mr. Henderson cast his influence with the movement and, being a staunch teetotaler during his life, always co-operated fearlessly with the temperance work.

Covington was a very thriving town in those days, with the lively commerce of the new canal and river, and far eclipsed the capital of the State in business prospects. In the village there was a brilliant coterie of young men, who had settled there because of the flattering business outlook. Many of them became famous afterwards in State and national politics. Such men as Senator Edward Hannegan, Judge Ristine, Daniel Voorhees, David Briar, Daniel Mace, and Lew Wallace resided in the town, with many others equally honorable, but who attained less fame. Mr. Henderson was associated with these men in a lyceum and literary club, with the object of sharpening their own wits, in tilts against each other, and for the purpose of bringing noted lecturers to the town for the benefit of the general public, and to sustain a town library. Like other pioneers he was deprived of early advantages, except for the winter term of the district school, but he never lost a moment's opportunity to improve himself. He kept up his studies until long past middle life; poring over books of history, biography, travel, mathematics, philosophy, and science, making his own crude experiments in physics and chemistry by improvised methods, like Isaac Watts with his teakettle. He was up before daylight, for the real study was during the morning hour. His children never remember having seen him abed, in all their earlier years. The training which this kind of thoughtful struggle for knowledge gave him was a thoroughness of education seldom attained in the schools. As was said of another, "he himself disclaimed credit for being what is called a self-made man. It is true that he had his own way to make, but he began with all the benefits of good ancestry, and he was, in his phrase, born into an intellectual atmosphere." His family on both sides had cared for the things of the spirit, and for learning. Their advantages were only those of the frontier, but the love of nature and of books was their continuous heritage in each generation.

There was something almost pathetic in the quenchless thirst for learning and vast respect for education which this man and others of his type had throughout life. Judge Darrow says of his own father, in his great solicitude for the education of his children: "I could not know why my father took all this trouble for me to learn my Latin grammar, but I know to-day. I know that it was the blind persistent effort of the parent to resurrect his own buried hopes in the greater opportunities and broader life that he would give his child."

The early and continued care of others hampered Mr. Henderson's personal undertakings. Throughout life, he kept his own ambitions within possible attainment, consistent with his duties to those in his care; but for his children and his wards, his own sacrifices made it possible for them to have advantages that he had missed. He carried his youngest brother and five other youths in a wagon, overland, to Franklin College, and installed them there for their "schooling," the best to be had in that day. For many years he contributed to this school, and was a member of the Board of Trustees until his death.

Like many of the pioneer boys brought up in the country, he had a knowledge of trees and woodcraft, all sorts of wise intimacies with nature, a practical knowledge of live stock and crops, which made him a successful farmer, although an "absentee." He had a genuine love of the soil and all growing things. Until his last days he took great pleasure in making children acquainted with trees and shrubs, with the flavor of wild strawberries and the tang of the wild grapes. To take a group of little ones to the woods for a nutting expedition, or for spring flowers, to show them where to find paw-paws and his favorite black haws, to let them wade in the creek, and learn the habits of birds—all this was a perennial source of joy to him and to them. He could not bear to have them grow up without the close contact with nature which had been the joy of his youth.

Next to his care for his father's and afterwards his own family, and wards, Mr. Henderson took a most vital interest in civic and state affairs and was a man who made known his convictions by his efforts to better things always. He exerted his energies to influence others, who were bound by narrow views, prejudices, and indifference in educational and civic affairs. He was of Southern family and their dislike of slavery, which had impelled them to leave that environment, and journey to free soil, had descended to him; but in early life he was a Democrat in politics. The struggle over the extension of slavery was approaching. His father-in-law, Dr. Richmond, who had retired from his medical practice at Indianapolis, and was living with him, was an ardent colonizationist, and a member of the circle who carried on the "underground railway." He would often say, after reading the discussions in Congress, "I shall not live to see it, but the storm will be upon us soon." It came within a half-dozen years. Together, the old and the young man discerned the cloud that was settling over the nation. In the new alignment of forces, those Democrats who regarded slavery with horror joined the new Republican party, as did Governor Morton and many leaders of men. Sorrowfully Mr. Henderson left the party of his youth, and voted with the new one looking towards the abolition of slavery. By this time national events moved rapidly towards the crisis of '61, and the future confirmed him in the stand he had taken.

From the time Sumter was fired upon, through all the years of that sad war, Mr. Henderson, with the men and women who held to the staunch principles of universal rights, saw troublous times in Indiana. These men who held for the Union were the strength and support of their great war governor. They were tireless in their efforts to uphold his hands and give him the encouragement he so much needed. These citizens gave their personal services, forwarded supplies, donated quantities of food, clothing, delicacies for the sick, books, and hospital necessities. Every passing regiment on its way to the war was fed; and men went to the front to bring back the wounded to be cared for at home. The largest part of this labor of love was done at the capital, but every county and town constantly contributed men, women, and funds for the work. In the central and southern districts of Indiana many of the people were of Southern extraction, and, naturally perhaps, sided with the South. Loyal men, who had been lifelong Democrats, like Mr. Henderson, now devoted much of their energies towards reclaiming this element to loyalty. Knowing many of them personally, their family history, and their previous record, he went to scores of them during the darkest days of the war, trying to persuade them to see the right, denouncing their disloyalty and dispersing their mistaken following. Mr. Henderson, and the men of like convictions, would ride all night to disband a traitorous organization. No complete roll of honor has been kept of those noble men and women who helped the cause at home. Their name was legion. In every village, hamlet, and town, both North and South, the people who waited and watched at home worked and suffered for the firing line. Their reward had to be a consciousness of duty performed, as they could reach it; and (in the North) the triumph of the cause they held to be just and right. The Sanitary Commission aids, the hospital supply workers, sewing societies, and the men who quietly aided Governor Morton, were effective forces which he felt were backing him in the struggle at home and in the field. Of this element were Albert Henderson and his wife. With their neighbors they spared neither labor, funds, nor time. This whole group of citizens devoted the years to continuous service for the troops and the cause.

During the anxious war time, financial disaster had come to the subject of our sketch. Not from personal failure, but from "going surety for others." It was before the day of bond companies, and every land-holder was apt to be asked to go on paper. As John Clay said in his father's biography, "one helped another, and this man backed many a worthless note. He took his losses good-naturedly and the friendship continued." So with Albert Henderson—it was his one vice. He was always helping some one else to his own inconvenience, and the failing he never overcame. In the sixties it caused the crowning regret of his life. He had sacrificed the accumulated property of years of labor to cancel these security accounts, and in justice to those dependent upon him, he could not enlist in the army. Not to go to the front during the war caused his patriotic heart many sorrowful and weary nights. Because of these losses he declined to represent his district in Congress, saying that if he could leave home it must be for the "line of battle."

Although faithful at the primaries, and conscientious about his ballot, he never held political office. Near the close of the war, after paying his large indebtedness, and readjusting his financial affairs, he moved to Lafayette and henceforth his life was passed in that community, where he and his wife started anew in life with limited means, but with the same ideals and earnest purposes. They went on performing the duties of the hour as the days brought them forth.

The hopefulness of their youthful start in life could not be repeated; but the years that followed were years of usefulness and full of quiet pleasures, of books, of friendships, and family life.

Mr. Henderson's interest in civic affairs, in educational movements, and public questions continued unabated during life, and he was always abreast of the times. Besides many benefactions, he was a "building and loan association" to all of his steadily employed workmen. By his accommodation and foresight for them, they all built homes for themselves.

When Mr. Henderson was over seventy years of age he wrote: "I have enjoyed my reveries of silent planning for the wrong-doer, for the homeless, and the enforced idleness of those who say, 'because no man hath hired us'; in planning for co-operative labor, as a cure for the cry against monopolies and capital, and sometimes in directing spiritual work. But having no time to spare, and not being inclined to leadership, I have tried to content myself by advising individuals as they come in my way; starting and encouraging young people to qualify for business, by a word, or the small loan of means for a beginning." This "small loan of means" meant a hearthstone and home for many an employee.

Mr. Henderson was for a number of years president of the Tippecanoe Fair Association and took an active part in the development of farming and live-stock interests.

During the last years of his life a rash young clergyman, with the instincts of a pope, proposed to the congregation of the Baptist church, of which Mr. Henderson was a member, that they adopt a written creed; which was thereupon produced. The " church meeting" had taken it up and were discussing the proposition, to which Mr. Henderson listened until all were through, and the young minister asked, "Are you ready for the question?" Here Deacon Henderson, for whose opinions all had such respect, arose and gravely said:

"My young brother and friends, in these days when the whole religious world is 'groaning and travailling in pain' trying to rend asunder the bands of their creeds, which are their heritage of the past, and an incubus to their present life and growth, it impresses me as a very dangerous and unnecessary proceeding for a congregation in a denomination which has always boasted freedom from any creed, save the New Testament, to foist upon itself and load itself down with one, at this late day. Brethren, I move that the proposition be laid upon the table, and that we adjourn with the singing of 'Praise God from whom all blessings flow.'" In which all joined, and went out wiser and better for his clear vision and foresight.

At the last week-night meeting of the church that he was ever able to attend, he arose and spoke of "two articles which have come to my notice during the last fortnight. One is the account in a current magazine of the great work being accomplished by the Salvation Army under General Booth and the vast good being done by that noble band, whose work at first was like our Saviour's, so 'despised and rejected of men.' The other is a little book on charity, or love, written by Henry Drummond, and called *The Greatest Thing in the World*. I have not strength to comment on their usefulness to you, but I commend them to you for your careful and prayerful reading."

In closing this sketch of the everyday career of a

representative Western man, who was a type of the best citizenship of Indiana, no tribute could have been especially written of Albert Henderson more fitting than the following words of Mr. Howells written about a man of similar character:

"He had all the distinctive American interest in public affairs. He was in full sympathy with the best spirit of his time. His conscience was as sensitive to public wrongs and perilous tendencies as to private and personal conduct. He voted with strong convictions and labored with tender love for all. It was a life beneficent to every other life that it touched, and of the most essential human worth, charm of character, and truest manhood. His admirable mind, the natural loftiness of his aims, his instinctive sympathy with every noble impulse and human endeavor, his fine intellectual grasp of every question, all made for him friends of the best men and women of his time and neighborhood."

CHAPTER XVII

LETTERS AND ART IN INDIANA

THE prevalence of authorship in the Hoosier State has occasioned one of its prominent writers to remark that one is distinguished in Indiana if he has not appeared in print. Recognizing the fact of this phase in the development of Indiana's people, no sketch of the State's growth would be complete without some notice of the manifestation of their interest in letters and the arts.

When it is remembered that Hoosiers have hitherto been of necessity hewers of wood and drawers of water, that only within the last generation have they emerged from actual frontier conditions, it will be evident, to the most casual thinker, that there has been scant time for artistic development. Mr. Riley felt and expressed this when he said that our brief history as a nation, and our finding and founding and maintaining of it, left our forefathers little time, indeed, for the delicate cultivation of the arts and graces of refined and scholarly attainments. Their attention was absorbed looking toward the protection of their rude farmhouses and their meagre harvests from the dread invasion of the Indians. When William Coggeshall published his Anthology of Western poets in 1860, he called attention to the short time which his collection of verses covered, and said that it had been a period significant for perilous wars, for hard work, for amazing enterprises; all of which furnished materials for literature, but, until the mellowing influences of time have long been hung over their history, repel poetry. Very few of these early singers made literature a profession. It has been noted that the poets of the West have been lawyers, doctors, teachers, preachers, mechanics, farmers, editors, printers, and housekeepers. They have written at intervals of leisure snatched from engrossing cares and exacting duties. Their story is touching. The author of *Ben Hur* had made his difficult way in the world as a lawyer, had fought gallantly in two wars, served as governor of a territory, and given much attention to politics, before he found time to complete his *Tale of the Christ*, begun so many years before. Maurice Thompson wrote his stories between times, while doing his work in the world as a soldier, civil engineer, and lawyer. Benjamin Parker was surprised that the personal experiences in his poems about *The Log Cabin in the Clearing*, and other pioneer scenes, had found readers to exhaust the first edition within sixty days.

The material development and vast natural resources of the West have been exploited until, as an observer said, there is little wonder if the world has come to think of that section's ambition as bounded by acres and bushels and dollars. It is another kind of wealth and attainment that now arrests attention. In the individual expression of thought and fancy, on the canvas and in literature, Indiana is manifesting the effects of the dawn of more leisure for study, and what has been termed comparative freedom from worry about crops and clients. It has been truly said that an era of business prosperity in the Middle West means a succeeding era of intellectual activity, more attention to higher education, more search for culture, and higher standards of intellectual ability.

Mr. Maurice Thompson calls attention to the youth of the commonwealth, when comparing her production to those of older literary centres. He reminds us that Indiana was only eighty years a State when *Old Glory* was written, where New England was two hundred when Bryant produced *Thanatopsis;* that *Ben Hur* was given to the world less than a century after Clarke captured Vincennes in the howling wilderness.

It is significant of the extent of the attempt at literary expression that a sufficient number of talented people could be assembled within the first half-century of its settlement to form so flourishing a society for the advancement of general culture as the Association of Western Writers. Mr. Hamilton has collected a full volume, giving only a page to each author, of the fugitive pieces of Indiana writers; making it seem that the State had sprung full-handed from pioneer conditions into literary work. Remembering, then, the newness of habitation and the dearth of advantages for culture and instruction in art, the world is prepared to forgive any lack of constructive skill, of delicacy of style, of notable development of character, and of extraordinary literary achievement.

A poem published in 1787 lays claim to being the first Indiana production, and by the early date of 1827 a writer acknowledged that "we are a scribbling and forth-putting people." The most noticeable characteristic of the earliest writers in Indiana is their response to the charms of nature lying all about them.

The Early Poets all Sang of the Beauties of Forests and Streams.

In William Coggeshall's collection, he assembles twenty-three writers of poetry, from the earliest Indiana scribblers. Their verses are full of the love of nature and of sentiment—many of them sentimental. They are idyllic songs of the forest home and experiences of frontier life. The rhetoric is rosy and they indulge in rhapsodical flights. Their chief claim on our interest is the reflection of the times in which they were written. The spell cast on poetic souls by forest and stream breathes through all of them. In the "Poet's Corner" of the newspapers of the time, in the *Ladies' Repository*, in the *Literary Messenger*, or in Mr. Prentice's encouraging columns, these poets presented their songs to the Western world. One wrote of how she

> "Loved the thoughtful hour when sinks
> The burning sun to rest,
> And spreads a sea of flowing gold
> Along the illumined west."

A poet then very famous pictured the setting for her story, out

> "In a green meadow, laced by a silvery stream,
> Where the lilies all day seem to float in a dream
> On the soft gurgling waves in their bright pebbled bed,
> Where the emerald turf springs up light from the tread."

Another poet, in time of grief, expressed the wish that the fair loved one might be buried

> "In the vale where the willow and cypress weep;
> Where the wind of the West breathes its softest sigh;
> Where the silvery stream is flowing nigh."

Sarah T. Bolton, who was one of these pioneer writers that lived on into the nineties, voices this feeling of response to their environment, in the lines:

" I learned to sing in nature's solitude,
   Among the free wild birds and antlered deer;
In the primeval forest and the rude
   Log cabin of the Western pioneer.

" They loved the whisper of the leaves, the breeze,
   The scent of rivulets, the trill of birds,
And my poor songs were echoes caught from these
   Voices of Nature set to rhythmic words."

In the later collection of *Poets and Poetry of Indiana*, made by Benjamin Parker and E. Hiney, we find that they have included one hundred and forty-six writers of verse, and the same pleasure in the fields, flowers, and forests is shown in all of the selections. Many of these poets are now known only by being preserved in these collections, but, like the local painters of those times, they were the pride of their village, in their day.

In the earliest times, when there were fewer periodicals and books published, oratory, in the most ponderous and lofty style, and the addresses framed in sonorous periods with soaring flights of eloquence, beyond what would be acceptable now, took the place of printed composition. The oration had then a real literary influence. In this form of expression Indiana has always occupied a position of prominence. Her public men have enjoyed a national reputation for eloquence, both at the bar and in political life.

Another form of writing, among the very earliest publications which emanated from the State, were the contributions of the group of scientific men in the New Harmony community, mentioned elsewhere. The collections of William Coggeshall, of Benjamin Parker and E. Hiney, coupled with Meredith Nicholson's very interesting book on the literary performances of Indiana, entitled *Hoosiers*, makes any detailed mention of particular writers and their books unnecessary, except as illustrating the development of authorship within the State. Continuing to be a "scribbling and forth-putting people," so many authors have appeared that Wilbur Nesbit facetiously declared at the Sons of Indiana dinner in Chicago that "envious outsiders look up from their Hoosier books long enough to speak satirically of Indiana as the literary belt. They mention the dialect-poetry regions, and the historical-novel districts, and the counties wherein the ballad and rondeau flourish with the prodigality of commerce. They have even prepared maps showing by means of shaded and unshaded portions where the traveller must strike in order to find or avoid certain brands of literature."

It has been said that none of the literary work yet done in Indiana rises to the first magnitude; none has achieved the highest eminence; that no "greatest American author" may be claimed by that State. If this be true, it must be admitted that the average attained by the group has been high, and that the books published by the State's coterie of writers compare favorably with contemporaneous American literature. It might be asked, What other State, at the present time, can claim a poet who surpasses James Whitcomb Riley in expression of the humor, pathos, and experience of the lives about him? Who has written more interestingly and with more information on foreign affairs than John W. Foster or Alpheus H. Snow? Who tells a finer story than *Beaucaire*, or excels Evaleen Stein in delicacy of feeling and sentiment in the description of wood, river, and sky?

What American has written more interesting essays and biography than Dudley Foulke or more convincing addresses than George W. Julian? What juveniles are awaited more eagerly by the children than the tales by Mrs. Catherwood, Evaleen Stein, or Annie Fellows Johnston?

While loyally enjoying the successes of its literary guild, the people of literary taste, within the State, have not lost their discrimination, and scarcely set too high a valuation on these publications. They are fully conscious that the work done by their neighbors must be measured by universal standards and not by current popularity. Ignoring then the recent trade announcement that "of the six best-selling novels of the season three of them were written by Indiana authors," it may still be claimed that where there are so many readers some measure of approval must be granted. A wit has termed the commonwealth "a state of mind," but sometimes the facetiousness regarding the Hoosier's reputation of having a "monopoly of gray matter" turns out very droll. George Ade tells the story of meeting in New York a gentleman who said: "At last we have found here in New York a native humorist who is just as keen as any of those fellows out West. He is as droll as Riley, as quaint as Mark Twain, and as fanciful as Bill Nye. You ought to meet Simeon Ford." A short time after that I had the pleasure of meeting Mr. Ford, and during the conversation I referred to him as an Eastern man, whereupon he said: "I am living here because I have interests in New York City, but as a matter of fact I was born in Lafayette, Indiana." "So what's the use?" inquires Mr. Ade. A New York wag was provoked into saying that the Boston pundits' plaint that "somebody somewhere was writing good literature which never gets into print," might be true, but not of Indiana.

People of culture within the State would be the last ones, simply from local pride, to blindly give promiscuous praise to everything that is published from their State. They would be much more apt to say of any poor writing, as Sidney Lanier once wrote of a very popular Southern novel emanating from his own section:

"From all I can hear 't is a most villainous, poor, pitiful piece of work, and so far from endeavoring to serve the South by blindly plastering it with absurd praises, I think all true patriots ought to unite in redeeming the land from the imputation that such books are regarded as casting honor upon the section. God forbid we should really be brought so low as that we must perforce brag of such works; and God be merciful to that man who boasted that sixteen thousand of these books have been sold in the South."

An Eastern reviewer has said: "Whether Hoosiers have or have not a right to set up as literateurs, a lusty lot of them have successfully assumed the responsibility and against the tide of adverse influence made their way to distinguished recognition." Maurice Thompson, in writing of this development, said that

"the preposterous legend which somehow has linked Indiana's name with illiteracy and ill-breeding is a legend, and nothing more. The fact is that Indiana has always been a leader in literature among the Middle West States, just as she is now, and her literary people have won recognition strictly on the merits of their work. We have the best schools in the world—not universities and great colleges indeed, but schools for the people in which our entire population is trained to love books. We create a demand for all sorts of good literary wares. As Indiana goes, so goes the Union, may yet be as true in literature as in politics—time alone is the arbiter of quality in all book-making. Even the Indianians themselves, in their pitch of honest pride, are not yet venturing to boast that this remarkable vogue of their local writers has drawn around Indianapolis the sacred circle of literary primacy, or that their capital dome is the axis of the universe."

On the contrary, most of the men and women of Indiana who have published are students with an ever-receding ideal, to which they never attain, thinking lightly of what they have produced, in comparison to that which they have in mind.

When Edward Eggleston wrote his stories of Indiana in 1871, portraying the Hoosiers of the backwoods district, in the southern counties, as he had known them "back in the fifties," many people in the State resented their publication. They declared that the life delineated, and the local coloring of the tales, was a libel on the community. Even at that time, which was more than thirty-five years ago, many native-born Hoosiers had never seen the type of squatters that Eggleston depicted, had never even heard the dialect spoken, and in long residence within the towns had not encountered the lean, gaunt type of people who had come thither and squatted on lands in the back districts of Indiana. These citizens felt that outrageous grammar and a drawling dialect would be eternally associated, in the minds of the outsiders, with their State, and that it would bring discredit upon all the people. They maintained that it misrepresented the large contingent of its educated population.

As Mr. Nicholson says, "this criticism has come

largely from a new generation that does not view these tales as instructive foot-notes to the history of education in Indiana."[1] It is true that outside people did come to associate the dialect with the State. This is unfortunate; but they may learn that the class of people delineated in those stories was never large, and has diminished before the illuminating influence of public schools. The dialect bears the same relation to the speech of educated Hoosiers that Yorkshire or Cockney dialects do to the language of educated English residents of Great Britain. At all events, the lives of these settlers afforded picturesque material for verse and story, and it is a fact that such people were in the State, although never much wanted. The backwardness and inertia of these people was an element which always had to be contended with, in every progressive movement in southern Indiana in the last century.

This class was made up of three streams of immigration: the mountain whites from the South; the well born, but uneducated frontiersmen from the same sections; and people of foreign parentage, from east of the Alleghanies. The first of these three classes and its presence in Indiana makes a study of its origin interesting. The peculiar character and speech of these poor whites, and the taint of their illiteracy within the State, make a passing mention necessary.

Three or four generations before the first settlement of southern Indiana, there had been brought into the tide-water colonies, from England, a class of debtors, derelicts, and political offenders. It was before the days of negro slavery. These people were indentured for service to the planters, and after a few years of

[1] Nicholson, Meredith, *Hoosiers*. New York, 1900.

labor they were freed and many drifted to the western frontiers, belonging to Virginia. Convicted criminals were sent over in great numbers. Kidnapped boys and girls from the streets of London, Bristol, and other seaports were huddled on board ship and brought to the Southern colonies to work as house servants and on the farms. There was also a fair proportion of white servants there, who had sold themselves into slavery for a brief term, to defray the expense of the voyage over. The latter were known as redemptioners and many of them became the respectable small farmers of Virginia.

Among the transported persons there were those who had been guilty of trivial offences, only; many were political offenders and prisoners of war. Cromwell ordered no less than two thousand over, and in turn the monarchists sold so many Nonconformists into servitude that it created an insurrection in England, in 1663. From which it follows that among all of the indentured whites who were "involuntary emigrants," many were upright and valuable settlers. After the general introduction of negro slavery, manual labor became a mark of servitude. As a consequence of this, there came to be a class of shiftless white people, who must either move on or starve. In time, many of these withdrew from the settlements, and drifted to the frontier. Here in their mountain fastnesses they became a peculiar people. Of unmixed English blood, retaining many of the forms of speech of the seventeenth-century British, gradually becoming a law unto themselves, bereft of all educational advantages, they became half savage in their customs and passions. Their descendants may still be found, and are known as "moonshiners" in the mountains of Kentucky and Tennessee; as "corn-crackers" in Georgia, and in Florida they are "clay-eaters." All of the lowlanders seem to be of a lower type, morally, and were probably of a lower origin, than the mountaineers. All are of the same gaunt, shiftless type; living on corn, pork, wild fruits, and crude whiskey. It is estimated that there are more than three millions of them in the Southern sections at the present time. Into these same mountainous districts there drifted nomadic characters, adventurers, hunters, escaped criminals, and stranded unfortunates, who joined their fortunes with the early immigration. A hardly credible isolation from all civilizing contact with the world has made this marooned element of the population, what we find them to-day, the most distinct and neglected people in the States.

We do not associate this tribe of Ishmaelites with the section north of the Ohio, and there were comparatively few of them that settled there permanently; but we know that many of these "movers," as they were called, did abide for a time in Indiana, and some stayed on after the others had journeyed toward the Missouri. These itinerant whites used to pass along the Kentucky roads toward the north in a listless way. They were lank, cadaverous, clay-colored vagabonds, going overland in rickety wagons, drawn by raw-boned horses, and a raft of unkempt children and mongrel dogs were their only possessions. They were clad in homespun and wore dun-colored hats, that matched their visages. North they went in springtime to "Indeanny," and very often back to the South in winter.

It was these descendants of the "poor whites" of the South who brought into the North the language of the mountaineers of Tennessee, the Carolinas, and Kentucky. When they emigrated to the West, they seemed incapable of change and improvement. In Indiana they were known as renters, seldom acquiring land of their own, though there were rich acres all about them. Their methods of cultivation were shambling and haphazard; they neglected their meagre crops for hunting and fishing, in which they were tirelessly occupied. The tale of more game beyond would lure them from the clearing they had begun, and they would sell out for a pittance, and move on into the vanishing wilderness. They were a silent people unless they drank too much cheap whiskey, and then they were apt to be quarrelsome, but they were honest and generally inoffensive. Their language was that of the common people of England, which had been astray on the heights for generations. They were hopelessly superstitious, a characteristic so well depicted in Dr. Taylor's very dramatic dialect verses entitled *The Theng*. This emigrant drift was densely ignorant. Their democracy was absolute, and they were loyal to the Federal Government. These people have been strangely persistent in type wherever found, perpetuating the more than conservative, the really negative qualities of their peculiar class.

Their history has been traced here, because, in accounting for the dialect found in the non-progressive districts of Indiana, these people must have first place. They were the people who tainted the language of the trans-Alleghany pioneers, from Tennessee to the Lakes. Besides these vagabond immigrants, there came into the new State decidedly larger numbers of people from the South who were descended from far better stock, but whose families had migrated westward each time new territory had been opened up, without waiting to teach their children to read. They were often persons of estate and substance at home, but it is to be remembered that educational opportunities for the English settlers on the Atlantic coast, in the seventeenth century, were meagre in the extreme. When we recall that the members of these families, however well born, journeyed over the mountains and settled in solitary clearings in Kentucky and Tennessee, and that their sons moved on to Indiana Territory, always seeing other frontier peoples, we can easily imagine that superior English speech was hardly more than a tradition by the time the third generation is encountered along the Ohio Valley. Most of the men could read and write, and their minds were keen, but they were not cultured. Many of these hardy pioneers settled in Indiana. As late as the end of the nineteenth century, fully 70,000 residents gave Kentucky as their place of birth, not to mention Virginia. North Carolina sent a large contingent, not only of good Huguenot and Quaker stock, but also the Hoosier dialect class. These Southerners were patriotic, hospitable people; but in letters they had the disadvantage of three generations of poverty of learning. These were the Hoosiers who had that sense of humor and dry philosophy still so characteristic of Indianians. In severing the ties binding them to the home communities, the better Southerners often threw off the family traditions of culture and gentle life. Many a pioneer has retrograded on the frontier. Most of these last-mentioned people were of the slave-holding class, and had the Southern accent. The sayings, superstitions, and omens, as well as the expression and speech current among them, had been acquired by contact with the colored race, in infancy. The religion of these Southerners was largely Old School Presbyterian and "Hard Shell Baptist," and in politics they were with the South.

Besides these two classes of settlers from the South, who influenced the speech of Indiana, and the Scotch-Irish people, there was another vein of immigration. In the uncultured strata of the State there were people of foreign descent who came over the Alleghanies into the richer lands of the Ohio Valley, within the three States of Ohio, Indiana, and Illinois. They made good settlers for the border States, because they were laborious and dependable, but they spoke the English language in a most barbarous way; much of it incorrectly bunched together by American people as Pennsylvania Dutch. Large numbers of the early settlers, also, had the broad Scotch-Irish dialect. These foreign people added another element to the "folk-speech" of the new West, and a few of them came into Indiana. It was the opinion and prejudices of some of these classes which it was so difficult to counterbalance, by the efforts of the educated people of clear English descent, who came into the State from the East and South. As late as 1850, there were fifty thousand of them who voted against free schools.

It was the speech of these people which came to be known as the Hoosier dialect and it vitiated the English of those about them. They had little learning and scarcely knew how little. They all came from other States and brought their characteristics of speech with them; few, if any, were coined on Indiana soil.

Mr. Hayworth and his collaborator O. G. S., writing in the *Indianapolis News*, five or six years ago, and discussing folk-speech in Indiana in the most interesting manner, said many true things, from which we make the following extracts:

"Not only has folk-speech never been uniform throughout Indiana, but exact geographical bounds cannot be given to the Hoosier dialect. The fact is, it has always been true, and never more so than in these days of rapid communication and shifting population, that in nothing is the student of folk-speech so liable to error as in assigning geographical limits to a phrase or word. Our local dialects, as well as the local English dialects from which we get many of our folk words and phrases, are pretty thoroughly mixed. Probably some if not all of the following words and phrases are more frequently used in the benighted regions of Indiana than elsewhere: 'Heap-sight,' as in 'more ground by a heap-sight'; 'juberous,' as in 'I felt mighty juberous about crossin' the river'; 'jamberee,' in the sense of a 'big time'; 'flabbergasted,' *i. e.*, exhausted; 'gangling,' *i. e.*, awkward; 'I mind that,' for 'I remember that.' But the individuality of a dialect is, in fact, far more a result of accent, or of pronunciation, than of the possession of expressions peculiar to itself. As has just been pointed out, Indiana has but few provincialisms that are peculiarly her own. But where else than among these settlers would one hear the long-drawn flatness of the 'a' in such words as 'sasser,' 'saft,' 'pasnips,' etc.? . . . One would hear such a sentence as 'I swum straight acrost the crick, an' kep' agoin' right ahead through the paster, an' clim plum to the top of yan ridge over yander, an' wus consid'rable tired-like comin' down t'other side, but at last got to that air road,' pronounced as a citizen of 'Hoopole kyounty, Injeanny,' would have pronounced it forty years ago. 'Between you and me and the gate-post' is a formula used in impressing the necessity of secrecy. 'When he gits a dollar it's got home' is an admirable description of a stingy man. An old woman from the hills of Brown County once expressively described to one of the writers the feelings experienced after a night spent in dancing by saying, 'When I 'us goin' home in the mornin' both sides of the road 'ud belong to me." [1]

Mr. Nicholson very truthfully observes that

"it may be fairly questioned whether, properly speaking, there ever existed a Hoosier dialect. A book of colloquial terms could hardly be compiled for Indiana without infringing upon prior claims of other and older States, and the peculiarities that were carried westward from tidewater early in the century. The distinctive Indiana countryman, the real Hoosier, who has been little in contact with the people of cities, speaks a good deal as his Pennsylvania or North Carolina or Kentucky grandparents did before him, and has created nothing new. His speech contains comparatively few words that are peculiar to the State." [2]

The origin of the very name of Hoosier, as applied to the settlers of Indiana, is lost in the twilight of the wilderness. Whether it came from a drawling pronunciation of "who 's-heyer?" or was a corruption of "Hussar," as applied to deserters from the ranks of the hirelings in the British army of the Revolution, is not known. At all events the word has always been used by trans-Alleghany pioneers as a general term to designate a verdant or uncouth person, and later to the outlanders, living across the Ohio River. In time it became attached to the extreme border territory of that period; which happening to be Indiana and Southern Illinois, it clung to that section. The dialect by that name was used by the border

[1] Hayworth, Paul L., and O. G. S. *Indianapolis News*, Aug. 15, 1900.
[2] Nicholson, Meredith, *Hoosiers*. New York, 1900.

people generally, not alone by the few of them who became residents of Indiana.

After this digression to determine the sources of the backwoods use of English as it was practised in Indiana, and allied districts, we return to the statement that the preservation of this passing form of speech, in story and verse, should not be resented by Indianians. The thought, the sentiments, and the environment of the early settlers had been embodied by them in the verses written, in more classic English, by many of the contributors to the "Poet's Corner" in the local papers, and have since been included in permanent collections; but none of them wrote in dialect. In fact, these very earliest writers used Addisonian phrases—the best of evidence that the Hoosier dialect was not universal.

The stories of Mr. Eggleston were the first to fully delineate the life in the hill districts. The dialect in Mr. Eggleston's tales was not so true to life as is that in Mr. Riley's poems, but he gave the true frontier setting in which it occurred, and his characterizations are generally faithful. The actual personalities of the backwoodsmen stand before you. Sometimes he verges on caricature, but in the main, he is true to the life that he is trying to portray. The schoolhouse with its puncheon floor and great fireplace, the scarcity of schoolbooks, the rough, unruly, uncouth boys, were the very scenes to which the barefooted pupils went for instruction in the three R's. Mr. Eggleston reproduces vividly the superstitiously religious life of part of the people, as contrasted with the rude roystering of their drinking neighbors, of whom they heartily disapproved. He pictures the drawbacks of the bad roads, and the poverty of life's conveniences, and necessities as well. He depicts the sensational exhortations of the itinerant preachers, and the effect of their hell-and-damnation preaching on their ignorant hearers. He shows the grovelling materialism of the toothless old crone as she smokes her cob pipe by the fireplace and reiterates, "While yur gitten git a plenty, sez I"; pictures the easy-going husband, chopping a handful of wood out in the weather, until the old cracker reappears in all his hereditary shiftlessness. Among these life-like reproductions, he does not neglect to bring out the occasional poetic soul, always found amongst the rudest people—a young girl, or youth, born amid such discouraging surroundings, trying to develop according to the longings within their isolated natures. All these are actual pictures of real neighborhoods, happily passing into oblivion, and even now only history.

"I call him the first of the Hoosiers," writes George Cary Eggleston, of his older brother, "because he was the first to perceive and utilize in literature the picturesqueness of the Hoosier life and character, to appreciate the poetic and romantic possibilities of that life, and invite others to share with him his enjoyment of its humor and his admiration for its sturdy manliness."[1] It may be regretted that untravelled people take Eggleston's stories of backwoods life, nearly extinct a half-century ago, as a reflection of present conditions in Indiana cities, just as Europeans do Fenimore Cooper's Indian stories of New York State—but that must pass. The grammar, the quaint terms, the peculiar pronunciations, the nasal drawl of all the dialect stories seem picturesque to a new generation, but that dialect was a menace to the speech

[1] Eggleston, Geo. Cary, *The First of the Hoosiers*. Ferno, 1903.

of the early settlers and unconsciously affected the English of whole neighborhoods of people who were of widely different birth. In the crude conditions of living and the democratic mingling of all classes on the frontier, children drifted into lax habits of speech and constantly borrowed words and prhases from illiterate neighbors, farm-hands, or the household help. In the third generation, graduates of a college, with an advanced degree from a German university, have been guilty of lapses into this primitive speech, still clinging to them from their early environment. None will say that the speech was not delightfully full of surprises in the phrasing, in the rural comparisons, now nearly obsolete, and in the quaint humor, the stoical philosophy, and droll illiteracy of a frontier people. "The material waited only for the creative mind and sympathetic intelligence," and again found a faithful interpreter in James Whitcomb Riley.

As an evidence of the integrity of his portraiture and characterizations, it is noted that these very people enjoy hearing his verses read, as much as any city audience. They feel the genuineness of his sympathetic acquaintance, recognize his types of character, his love of nature, enjoy the humor of the situations, the drollery of the talk, and are touched by the pathos of the stories. Mr. Riley tells most entertaining stories of his acquaintance with these people:

"Sometimes some real country boy gives me the round turn on some farm points. For instance here comes one stepping up to me,—'You never lived on a farm,' he says. 'Why not?' says I. 'Well,' says he, 'a turkey-cock gobbles, but he don't ky-ouck, as your poetry says.' He had me right there. It's the turkey-hen that ky-oucks. 'Well, you'll never hear another turkey-cock of mine ky-ouckin,' says I."

Naturally, Mr. Riley finds it difficult to get the present-day illustrators to seize his idea of the characters he is trying to portray. Mr. Christie got *That Old Sweetheart of Mine* through school, in a real log schoolhouse, with sun-bonnet on her tangled curls, and bare feet going along the meadow paths, but when grown to womanhood he painted her in city garb with city airs and graces. In speaking of this difficulty, Mr. Riley said:

"I do not undertake to edit nature, either physical or human. I can't get an artist to see I'm not making fun. They seem to think if a man is out of plumb in his language, he must be in his morals. Now old Benjamin looks queer, I'll admit. His clothes don't fit him. He's bent and awkward; but that don't prevent him from having a fine head and deep tender eyes, and a soul in him you can recommend."

These countrymen drive miles to an evening entertainment at some schoolhouse or church to hear recitations from Riley's pages. If loaned a copy of his verses, they will ask for everything else that he has written. They feel, as one of his biographers has remarked, that Mr. Riley never satirizes, never ridicules his creations; his attitude is always that of a kindly and admiring advocate. The countrymen also appreciate his poems of correct literature, not written in dialect. Outside of these native admirers, Mr. Riley was soon received with universal enthusiasm. Mr. Garland wrote of him several years ago that no poet in the United States has the same hold upon the minds of the people as Riley. He is absolutely American in every line he writes. His work is irresistibly comic, or tender, or pathetic. In this reviewer's estimation, the man is the most remarkable exemplification of the power of genius to transmute plain clods into gold, that we have seen since the time of Burns. Of himself, he has said, "I'm only the 'willer' through which the whistle comes." Mr. Riley's inimitable readings from his own composition testify that he is a natural actor; this is the verdict of every audience. Amy Leslie, the dramatic critic, wrote when she heard him years ago in Chicago:

"To hear Riley recite his own poems is a treat to remember an entire life. He has the oddest, most gray and toneless face. There is a three-cornered smile and a two-edged glance which illuminates his face like a shower of stars. Tears come at the call of words so simple as to have a tinge of comedy, where the softest minor chords tremble. All that is quaint and humorous ignites the pleasantries within him, all that is true and innocent inspires him. He never broods, nor rails, nor chants ecstasies, but laughs and weeps and ties brave old-fashioned true love-knots. I imagine he may not read at all well as elocution is accounted. I do not know, except that it is the loveliest reading I have ever heard, and the sweetest poetry."

Mr. Garland quotes him as saying, of himself, "I'm so blamed imitative, I don't dare to read everything." His ability to imitate was fully established when he published on a wager, and in a newspaper, lines entitled *Leonanie* which trapped England and America into treasuring them as Poe's verses.

A critical reviewer said of the Hoosier poet that the qualities which secure his poetry a wider reading and heartier appreciation than any other living American are wholesome common-sense, and a steady cheerfulness, freedom from dejection and cynicism and doubt, and untainted by the mould of sensuality. At his best he is original and sane, full of the sweetest vitality and soundest merriment. His poetry neither argues, nor stimulates, nor denounces, nor exhorts; it only touches and entertains us.

"While his poems in dialect gained him a hearing," says Mr. Nicholson, "Mr. Riley strove earnestly for excellence in the use of literary English. His touch grew steadily finer. He had begun to write because he felt the impulse and not because he breathed a literary atmosphere or looked forward to a literary career." [1] Lacking the advantages of an earlier training in the schools, and having a natural appreciation of the best in literature, he formed his style by private study without losing his individuality, his humor, and his inimitable sense of character and situation, which make him a natural writer of comedy. Apparently, he can dramatize a scene almost instantaneously, as the *personæ* assemble themselves in the fancy. After years of recognition by the public and many tokens of their appreciation, he was invited by one of the oldest universities to accept an honorary degree. At the Yale convocation in 1902 that university conferred the degree of Master of Arts upon James Whitcomb Riley. In receiving the candidate, President Hadley spoke of Mr. Riley as an exponent in poetic art of the joy and pathos of American country life. When the hood was placed on his shoulders, the prolonged applause of the vast throng assembled made that scholar's emblem as a crown of laurel.

[1] Nicholson, Meredith, *Hoosiers*. New York, 1900.

Old alumni and undergraduates joined in giving the Hoosier poet a great ovation, and felt that old Yale honored itself in honoring him. The graduating class of that June day loves to claim that James Whitcomb Riley was of their class of '02.

> "Thou gavest thy gifts to make life sweet;
> There shall be flowers about thy feet."

Primitive living and frontier environment have seldom prompted the subjects of the later Hoosier writings. Showing not the faintest resemblance, in either literary style or subject, to the preceding writers who have preserved the earlier Hoosier life in their pages, another loyal Indianian, with a widely different temperament from theirs, has written in the West his stories of the Orient. General Lew Wallace was born and reared in Indiana when it was actually a Western frontier, but his books are about ancient peoples; one concerned with the Aztec civilization, and the rest Asiatic tales. Nothing in his youthful life could have suggested the themes which his talent developed into the *Prince of India* and *Ben Hur*. That General Wallace has told an interesting tale is shown by the fact that a million and a half copies of *Ben Hur* have sold in the English version and it has also been translated into every language of Europe, into Arabic, and Japanese, and printed in raised-letter for the blind. This *Tale of the Christ*, so guardedly received at first, has grown steadily in the favor of the people until, in presentation in a dramatized form upon the stage, the story met with a sensational reception. *Ben Hur* and his other books brought great distinction to the author. That General Wallace was, above all things, a writer who could enlist the interest of the reader is shown in the Autobiography published since his death. Surely his native commonwealth could show no greater honor to a son than Indiana has in placing General Wallace's statue in the Hall of Fame.

Mrs. Wallace shared her husband's triumphs and had honors of her own, from her writings regarding the Pueblos, some early poems, *The Repose in Egypt*, and *The Storied Sea*. Mrs. Wallace was also a native of Indiana, born in the literary atmosphere of Crawfordsville, and one of the Elston family, all of whom were known as interesting conversationists. Hon. Henry S. Lane married into this family, and added to the brilliancy of the reputation of the college town for its leadership in culture during those early days.

Within this same town, the scholarly Maurice Thompson, another prolific writer, and native Indianian, passed most of his life, after the Civil War. Without once dreaming the dreams that came to his neighbors, the Wallaces, Mr. Thompson wrote charming novels, a widely known book on *Archery*, and beautiful out-of-door poems. His story entitled the *Banker of Bankersville*, (unfortunately, for it has little to do with either, and does not distinguish it as it deserves), is an excellent picture of village life in Indiana; not the backwoods, but the average small towns. His essay on *Ethics of Literary Art* deserves embodiment in every course in English literature. Although a civil engineer, and a lawyer, Mr. Thompson's later life was more constantly devoted to literary work than any of the other Indiana writers up to his time. In the closing days of his career, he enjoyed the triumph, if he cared for popular favor, of having his name on every tongue, for his sweet story of *Alice of Old Vincennes* captured the people.

Will H. Thompson, brother of Maurice, was also born in Indiana and practised law in Crawfordsville for many years. While living in the State he wrote that great war poem *High Tide at Gettysburg* and also the *Bond of Blood*.

The Soldier of Indiana in the War for the Union, by Catherine Merrill, is a record of the part performed by individual soldiers who went out from this commonwealth. It was written soon after that war, and the purpose of the author was the patriotic one of commemorating the sacrifice and heroism of the ordinary soldier. She knew the reality of that which she penned, for she served many months as a nurse in the hospitals during the war. Without any noise or announcement she had intense patriotism, both civic and for her country.

"She was far from being an organizer of movements, or a trampler of platforms. She cared neither to agitate nor to fulminate [says her biographer]. All of the civic and social betterment, in which she engaged so much of her strength and vitality, came from her great love of our neighbor, and from the impulse toward action, help, beneficence, the desire for removing human error, clearing human confusion, and demolishing human misery, the noble aspiration to leave the world better and happier than she found it." [1]

This memorial to the soldiers was written in her earlier years, by the woman who probably led more families along the paths towards real culture than

[1] Merrill, Catherine, Memoir in *The Man Shakespeare and Other Essays*. Indianapolis, 1867.

any other Indiana woman. Catherine Merrill "inculcated in the minds of three generations a discriminating taste for literature," and what Matthew Arnold calls a liberal and intelligent eagerness about the things of the mind. Miss Merrill's printed work includes this war record of the troops for whom she worked so nobly in her early womanhood, a series of literary criticisms given to the press, and a slender volume of essays selected by the literary club which bore her name. These essays were included by them with biographical sketches from her friends Professor Melville B. Anderson and the naturalist Mr. John Muir. The volume is entitled *The Man Shakespeare and Other Essays*. Although Miss Merrill left so little published writing, no story of Indiana's development would be complete without a reckoning of the impression which her life made on all those with whom she came in contact. Other notable teachers of the State have faithfully instructed more pupils in the schools, and added to the usefulness and enlightenment of their students; but it has fallen to the lot of few people to have formed a literary taste and deepened the moral insight of the youth of one generation, to execute the same loving task for their children, and to perform a like service for their grandchildren.

Miss Merrill was a daughter of the pioneer State Treasurer, Samuel Merrill, whose influence and that of his descendants has stood for the value of culture and literary training as a means of creating a cultivated citizenship. During all of her professorship at Butler University, and later when she held private classes, Miss Merrill found time to take part as a valuable member in the literary clubs of Indianapolis, to prepare addresses for other circles, and to conduct classes at the earnest solicitation of old pupils, in neighboring cities.

Professor Anderson's sketch of Miss Merrill places before us a correct valuation of her career. Among other things he says that her life teaches us we should bear in mind particularly that Catherine Merrill's fine wide culture offers the most signal and cheering example of the educative power of English literature. With her beloved sister they made their own home the centre of humanizing culture and elevated thought, seemingly unconscious of the joy it was to every one to come within the charm of their presence, "preaching without sermons, informal as sunshine." Mr. Muir, appreciating the great points in Miss Merrill's character, adds, "Nothing in all her noble love-ladened life was more characteristic than its serenity," and an equally strong habit of her mind was "tracing the springs of action through all concealment. She never left herself in doubt as to motives, rejoicing in all truth, especially happy when she discovered something to praise."[1]

From this slight sketch of Miss Merrill, a dim idea may be gained of the reasons for her influence over the large number of persons in Indiana who came under her guidance. It follows that "those who had the good fortune to know a human being so large and excellent should take pious care that her memory does not fade with the passing of the lives she immediately touches."[2] Perhaps the greatest value of the publication of the little memorial volume is its power to recall to minds of her old pupils the teachings

[1] Muir, John, Memoir of Miss Merrill in introduction to *The Man Shakespeare and Other Essays*. Indianapolis, 1900.
[2] *Ibid.*

of that voice they shall never hear again. Reading these pages one may experience the conviction, the exaltation, the enthusiasm of the classroom under that severe but impressive teacher. Calmly she again reminds them through the printed pages that

" 'Superficial judgment, hasty and ill-formed opinion, blunt the power of discrimination and dull the sense of right.' 'Slovenly and false work of any kind tells on character.' 'Prejudice is twin sister of ignorance and is a stupendous bulwark against knowledge.' 'The individual preserves his mental integrity by doing his own thinking and maintaining a sense of justice and candor.' 'We hold in grateful remembrance the hand that planted the tree that shades our door, and we owe grateful reverence and love to him who made for us a good book, who gave us nobler loves and nobler cares. We owe nothing for the books that are no better than wolves in sheep's clothing. We owe it to none to call ugliness beauty, awkwardness grace, falsehood truth, or wrong, in any way, right. Black is black, crooked is crooked, wrong is wrong, whatever the reason, wherever the place.' "

In inculcating a love for books she would say:

"It is true that the best society and the most accessible may be found in the library. Here the solitary and the sorrowful, the disappointed and the erring, the betrayed and the deserted, the unthanked benefactor, the young who are sensitive as to the limitations of poverty, the old who have neglected to repair their friendship, the slow who have been left behind, the weary, the over-burdened may find company, solace, stimulus, and the happy and strong may find increase of happiness and strength." [1]

Passing to another writer who was also greatly

[1] Merrill, Catherine, *The Man Shakespeare and Other Essays*. Indianapolis, 1902.

revered, we are reminded that Indiana has been honored by her historians. To Mr. John Dillon the State owes a lasting debt, for his conscientious history of the territorial period and his monographs on different phases of its development. Mr. Dillon was an earnest student and painstaking historian. His methods were the modern scientific ones. His facts were gleaned from State archives, from private sources, and from territorial records. His histories must live, for the account of the transactions in the periods covered by his writings may only be added to; everything that he committed to paper is of value. "He had certain noble ideals, severe and simple, as to the office of historian, and no artist was truer to his art than he to this ideal."

As General Coburn has said, Mr. Dillon knew that his work would endure. He had no profession but letters, and in the solid result of his best labors neither money nor applause added to his satisfaction. No library in America can be considered complete without his histories. He was a noble example of integrity, modesty, industry, and purity of character. Mr. Dillon wrote some verses, but it is from his *History of Territorial Indiana* and the monographs on the same subject that his place as an author is assured.

"Forty years of honest, conscientious devotion, four books that people would not buy, in his life-time, and death in a lonely garret, face to face with grim poverty, because he wrought for the love of truth, and not for dollars [says Mr. Cottman] this is the life story of John B. Dillon. He is buried in Crown Hill, next to the soldiers' graves, and the friends who were kind to him in life have erected a fitting monument to his memory. That he lies beside the heroic dead is well, for he, too, gave his life to a cause and did his country a service."[1]

The vogue of Indiana novels has not, very naturally, been accorded to her historians, but their work will live. It has been thorough, scientific, and conscientious. Mr. Jacob P. Dunn's *History of Territorial Indiana*, and her redemption from slavery, and his monographs on different periods of the history of the State are enduring contributions to the records of the West. Mr. Dunn goes to original sources for his information. He is a tireless student of documents, records, and official papers, and restates the whole story in an interesting style. He has the ability, none too common, said a critic, to write history attractively, without imperilling his authority. No tribute from the writer could add to the importance attached to Mr. Dunn's work as authoritative, than the presence in this volume of extended quotations from his histories and monographs.

In a similar manner has Mr. Dudley Foulke's *Biography of Governor Morton, and his Times*, served as an accepted authority on that most interesting period the Civil War. The students of Indiana's part in the great struggle must go to that biography for light on the inside history of the troubled times, and for a knowledge of both the well known and the obscure facts of the history of those years.

Mr. John L. Griffith's *Biography of President Benjamin Harrison* will be of importance for the same reason. Aside from its interest as literature it deals with the career of a great figure in national history. It is written by a resident of Indiana, of an Indiana

[1] Cottman, Geo. S., in *Indiana Magazine of History*, vol. i., No. 1.

man who also became the State's most noted citizen and renowned statesman.

Hon. John W. Foster's *Twenty Years of Diplomacy* is an interesting book, written by one who has taken a brilliant and valued part in the department of the government service of which this volume and others by the same author treat.

The historical writings of Professor John Clark Ridpath, while not pertaining to the State, in particular, are of importance in this sketch because he was a native of Indiana, was educated in one of her universities, and was afterwards a member of the faculty of Asbury for a number of years. His historical work was voluminous, and was both national and general in its scope. His career as a professor with his alma mater formed a valuable element in the educational work in Indiana. Other teachers in the various Indiana colleges, as Professor Ogg, Professor Moran, and many others have contributed valuable special studies in history, but they cannot be enumerated as native Hoosiers.

The famous Scotch philosopher and teacher Thomas Davidson has said of another Indiana book, originally written for the State Teachers' Reading Circle: "I hoped to satisfy the desire, evinced by so many of the young people, to discuss social problems, and took for the basis a single book, Charles Richmond Henderson's *Social Elements*, which I hoped to have discussed chapter by chapter. The book was well adapted for our purpose, offering a comprehensive view of the whole field of sociology, and treating every part with simplicity and good judgment." [1]

[1] Davidson, Thomas, *The Education of the Wage-Earners.* Boston, 1904.

This book has been translated into Japanese under the direction of Professor Takebe of Tokio University.

The student of Indiana's history will find invaluable information in the histories, biographies, reminiscences, and historical papers by George W. Julian, William Henry Smith, Augustus L. Mason, Julia S. Conklin, William W. Woolen, Captain J. A. Lemcke, William H. English, W. W. Thornton, Richard G. Boone, Timothy E. Howard, Colonel Cockrum, David Turpie, M. M. Pershing, Professor Rawles, Judge Howe, and Rev. T. H. Ball. Each of these has occupied a prominent place in the districts of the State in which they lived, and they knew whereof they wrote. The books and monographs by W. F. Harding, Frederick Bartel, and George B. Lockwood are full of information on local or special phases of Indiana history, and the interest they enlist in historical subjects is enhanced by their literary style. W. S. Blatchley, W. W. Woolen, and others have written charming nature studies, attractive to the young and old. The Hon. Hugh McCulloch, during a brilliant career as a financier and cabinet officer, wrote authoritatively on financial subjects and left a volume on *Men and Measures of Half a Century*. Colonel Richard Thompson not only served his State and nation long and nobly, in military and political life, but closed his career with his very interesting *Recollections of Sixteen Presidents*. The annalists have performed a service in preserving local history by their records and reminiscences. Sanford Cox's *Recollections of the Wabash Valley*, Rev. Thomas Goodwin's *Reminiscences*, Blackford Condit's *Recollections of Early Terre Haute* are most entertaining. County histories, the published addresses of Wayne and other county celebrations, the Hon. William

Holloway's and Mr. Berry Sulgrove's histories of Indianapolis are valuable contributions to the State's records of the past.

Mr. Sulgrove was also a brilliant journalist, and exerted a wide influence through his writings for the press, extending over a number of years. He was the close friend and adviser of Governor Morton during the Civil War. His judgment was excellent and his opinions reliable. It is said that he possessed a marvellous memory, and that, his mind being stored with vast information, he was an unusually interesting conversationist. In 1866, when Mr. Sulgrove was in Paris with Governor Morton in a company of distinguished men, one evening a discussion arose between two gentlemen present about a quotation from Horace. When the debate between the British guests seemed hopeless of decision, Mr. Sulgrove modestly begged leave to give the quotation and also added a half-page or more of the context, to the wonderment of the learned gentlemen, who marvelled at his memory and scholarship. The story is told of Mr. Sulgrove that in his later years he was in London with a friend from Indianapolis. This friend was invited to dine with the Lord Chief Justice and declined the honor, saying that he had a friend with him whom he could not very well leave. Lord Coleridge would not let the gentleman off and stipulated that he should bring his friend, Mr. Sulgrove, with him. After the dinner there was brilliant talk of affairs, of the world's happenings, of literature, science, and travel, in all of which Mr. Sulgrove joined with the brilliancy which a lively interchange of thought provokes in the responsive American. The next day the host called on his guest and inquired who this friend from Indiana was; said that after they had said good-night, he and his guests had declared they had never heard such an interesting talker and they had searched in every encyclopedia, biographical dictionary, and list of people in the United States on the shelves of the library, to learn who B. Sulgrove was; for they were sure they could not be ignorant of the career of such a brilliant man.

Very naturally the period of stress and storm which Indiana passed in common with the rest of the States during the Civil War gave rise to stanzas of more heroic measure than the earlier wildwood poems. These were the years when Forsythe Willson wrote *The Old Sergeant*, and Will H. Thompson gave out his *High Tide at Gettysburg*. There were other hearts that found a place in the "Poet's Corner" for their expression of patriotism, and pent-up sorrows over those lost on the field of battle. The fugitive writings of Ben D. House, Daniel L. Paine, Lee O. Harris, and others who wrote then, have been collected by appreciative friends and published.

In the years since the war, Indiana has produced Maurice Thompson, James Whitcomb Riley, Meredith Nicholson, Wm. Vaughn Moody, Evaleen Stein, Elizabeth Conwell, the Fellows sisters, and others, all of whom have written in both poetry and prose, to the great pleasure of thousands of readers. The same note of enjoyment in all of nature's charm, the breath of out-of-doors, still rings through the Hoosier verse, but it is coupled with human interests and the style of composition conforms to modern forms. There is a facility, a grace, and strength unknown to the earlier period.

It is interesting to note how many of the poems

that have become familiar household words were penned by Hoosier writers. There are *Little Brown Hands, Six Little Feet on the Fender, Paddle Your Own Canoe, The Patter of Little Feet, Better Late than Never, Some Say This World is an Old, Old World; Yes, the Smiling Clouds are Angels; Papa, What Would you Take for Me?; Sleep, Little Sweetheart, Sleep; Love Came to Me in a Life so Late; The Curfew Shall Not Ring To-Night,* and many others too well known to need recall.

Mr. Meredith Nicholson had secured a hearing by his journalistic work before he published either story or verse. Few lines by present-day poets, in this country, have the charm of some of his late poems. His fiction seems less analytical, less reflective than his friends would have expected from him, perhaps, but his stories seized upon popular approval at once. In *The House of a Thousand Candles* he has created an exciting plot-story, with a series of startling episodes, crowding one upon another. The interest is sustained throughout, as it also is in his later and better story *The Port of Missing Men*. Mr. Nicholson's essays contributed to the various periodicals, and his book on Indiana entitled *Hoosiers*, have received their meed of commendation from the writer, in the liberal quotations from their pages in this volume.

"Is the novel destined to devour all other forms of literature?" asks a critic; certainly its prevalence would seem to indicate the sweep of a wide and powerful imagination, but very much of current fiction produced everywhere is crude, and still less clever. Imaginative writing requires more art than is frequently accorded it, and few are free from the imputation of hurried work. The large number of Indiana writers at the present day, who have attracted attention by their great popularity, is indicative of this wide interest in fiction. Evidently the public, as Mr. Riley said of his own leisure hours, "read a good deal of chop-food fiction and browse with relish." It is a matter of congratulation that the Hoosier writers in general have given out healthy, wholesome stories, devoid of morbid sentiments and taint of moral decadence.

The variety of subjects that interest Indiana authors is also to be remarked. Scarcely any two have written upon the same theme. Within one family, we have John A. Wilstach devoting his years to classical studies and publishing his translations, with voluminous critical notes, of Virgil and Dante; his son, Walter Wilstach, writing a charming biographical sketch of *Montalembert*, and another son, Paul, issuing a manual on *The Game of Solitaire*, some short stories, several acting plays, and a notable work of dramatic review in his *Biography of Richard Mansfield*.

In another instance we have Mr. Beveridge writing a homily entitled *The Everyday Life of a Young Man*, and again he appears as the prophet of the *Russian Advance*. Environment and nature's charms suggested subjects to the earlier writers, but General Wallace dwelt on Oriental themes, in far-away lands. Robert Dale Owen, who was of Scotch birth, but one whose life was passed in Indiana, wrote a spiritualistic book, *On the Boundaries of Another World*, a volume of fiction, many vigorous state papers and public addresses. William Dudley Foulke urged civil service reform, wrote a biography of absorbing interest, and published a translation, with scholarly notes, of Paul the Deacon's *History of the Longobards*.

Again, an Indiana lawyer turns back the hands

of time to the days *When Knighthood Was in Flower.* His are no problem novels. Charles Major knows that the average reader wants sensation; wants scenes and circumstances depicted with which he is not familiar; wants something that will take him out of the daily round of everyday life. Mr. Major has supplied tales of the days of chivalry, and the public has rewarded his efforts.

Another story by an Indianian carries us back to the seventeenth century, in Dutch New York, Professor Henry T. Stephenson's *Patroon Von Falkonburg* being a charming tale of that period. George Barr McCutcheon, within a half-dozen years, has dashed off a stream of stories of adventure, written in a popular vein, that has given him a multitude of readers. His stories have had a wide vogue, and he seems to agree with a pronouncement of Sir Leslie Stephen's, that the author of the future may give up bothering himself about posterity, and be content with writing for his contemporaries, and the immediate present.

The Gentleman from Indiana has gone far and wide for material, since his first Hoosier stories, and his style improves with time. The lightness and delicacy of *Beaucaire* would be difficult to surpass, but *In the Arena*, *Hector*, *His Own People*, and the longer novel *The Conquest of Canaan*, are original, spirited stories that show keen discernment and an intimate knowledge of Americans, their characteristics, and their life. Mr. Tarkington has the gift of expression, an artistic touch, and a sense of character that is most satisfactory. Some of his first novels were crude in their development, but they are prettily set in their proper environment, the people are natural in the life in which he places them, and he knew how to tell a story interestingly. Is it not to Booth Tarkington that the people of the State are looking to write of the real gentleman from Indiana? Mr. Eggleston, Mr. Riley, and others have given the Hoosier with the dialect; but the native-born Hoosier of straight English descent, with his perfectly natural manners, and decided individuality, has not yet "been put in a book." Mr. Tarkington knows him. He will be recognized by his droll humor, his keenness for knowledge, without great learning—generally a "fresh water" college man, if a college man at all. In physique he will be tall and sinewy; unconventional in dress. Not at all peculiar in character, but indefinably a Westerner. Earnest, but self-controlled, full of ideas and not afraid to mention them, and, as was said of John DeFrees, with a courage that seemed to have no weak side, mental, moral, or physical. He will be moral and religious, but one will hardly call him pious; he will be patriotic, fond of his family and home, and generally possessing both; insistent upon having good schools; a regular newspaper-reader, interested in every subject, and always interested in politics. Being fond of travel, he and his family are to be met in any quarter of the globe. In all his characteristics the typical Indianian awaits portrayal in literature.

A new author, who has written sympathetically and with appreciation of the early people in Indiana, is Miss Alexander. In a story by this journalist of *Candle Lit Days*, which she calls *Judith*, there is a reminiscent strain which will help to preserve memories of that past.

Without previous announcement or heralding of literary skill, Elizabeth Miller issued the story of *The Yoke*. The book differs entirely from the others produced by Indiana authors, and is another illustration of the variety of subjects chosen by this group. The scenes in *The Yoke* were of the Orient and life of the Nile. It at once created a stir and arrested attention. The same region and people are delineated in her latest drama, *The City of Delight*, a tale of the siege of Jerusalem.

Besides the stories of Indiana already mentioned, there are Millard Cox's *The Legionaries* and Miss Krout's *Knights in Fustian*, which are both interesting tales of the Civil War as it affected Indiana. In both stories, there are correct pictures of the localities involved in the struggle, and the incidents are true to history.

Enoch Willoughby, by Mr. Wickersham, is a novel of decided interest. Lucy Furman's *Leadings* and *A Sanctified Town* and Anna Nicholas's *An Idyl of the Wabash* are stories of provincial characters and village life. They are more analytical than the stories of some of the writers mentioned and show an observation and knowledge of character, and of the people and places depicted, that is inimitable. They write sympathetically, and show a touch of the characteristic Hoosier humor.

Indianapolis has produced many volumes of interest by authors who have written only occasionally. It would be impossible to name all of them deservedly in a chapter like this, but sketches and stories from Mrs. Judah, Mrs. Alice Woods Ulman, Mrs. Locke, Mrs. Eaglesfield, and others have interested many readers, and the same may be said of occasional authors in Bloomington, Fort Wayne, Evansville, and other Indiana cities. It has been claimed that Richmond alone offers one hundred!

It is no part of the intention of this chapter to give extended mention of each individual author who has written on Hoosier soil. Only enough are mentioned to illustrate in part, the development in this direction and the reason for the fame that the State has acquired in authorship.

Some of the most famous writers of Indiana, in history and fiction, have passed from the scene, and their place is secured by the work they have left. The young novelists who occupy the stage have the assurance of a sympathetic appreciation by the public. Conscientious work will improve their art, and the style will be more finished when there is less haste to publish. Psychological insight, more intense inner life, finer artistic conscience, less materialism will appear in their writings as character is deepened by culture and the experiences of life.

There is a dramatic quality in the stories by Hoosiers which has been very successfully utilized in the reproduction of these romances on the stage. *Ben Hur, Beaucaire, The House of a Thousand Candles, Alice of Old Vincennes, Brewster's Millions,* and *When Knighthood Was in Flower* may be cited as examples of this adaptability. In a greater degree this dramatic talent is shown in the plays produced by William Vaughn Moody, Booth Tarkington, Wilbur Nesbit, and George Ade, which have delighted audiences in England and America season after season.

If the novels produced by Indianians have shown little of the keen sense of humor which is characteristic of the native Hoosier, that trait has certainly appeared in Lincoln's drolleries, in Riley's dialect stories, in McCutcheon's cartoons, in George Ade's satires, and in the prose comedies of Hermann Viele. The native

Hoosier cannot be called vivacious or joyous in temperament, but for whimsical humor, and a keen enjoyment of by-play and anecdote, he has always been noted. All of these humorists show the particular kind of dry wit, told with a long face, and told on one's self rather than miss a joke, that is so characteristic of Hoosierdom. Odd characters, the weaknesses of a local capitalist or political celebrity, a "greenie from the New Purchase," have always been touched off by the wag of the town. And now this same droll way of putting things has come into print from this group of native Indianians. In Ben McCutcheon's newspaper stories, in Wilbur Nesbit's verses, in the late John DeFrees's editorials and Orth Stein's fanciful sketches, in Simeon Ford's drollery, in George Ade's fables, in James Whitcomb Riley's poetry, in Gillilan's tales and in John McCutcheon's cartoons, with their explanatory foot-notes, we see the gentle cynicism, the naturalness, the freshness which belongs to youth and to life, in communities where opportunity is unhampered and impulses are spontaneous; where there is a sense of sheer fun, and a wholesome ironic way of dealing with the faults and frailities of the people. We see the quick observation of passing events, the knowledge of human nature—especially of American people—that was demanded of stump speakers in the backwoods times, and of which the early preachers were not guiltless. When kindly Mr. Howells, who knows his American so well, and who has a keen scent for everything of every sort in literature, came upon George Ade's first productions he recognized at once, through all of the slang, that a new spice had been added to life. In an extended review he declared this conviction, and said:

"Both Mr. Ade's touch and material are authentic and genuine. The sense of character which so richly abounds, without passing into caricature, in these pictures of unerringly ascertained, average American life, has enabled him to go straighter to the heart than any former humorist. In Mr. Ade the American spirit arrives, puts down its grip, looks around, takes a chair, and makes itself at home. It has no question to ask, none to answer. There it is, with its hat pushed back, its hands in its pockets, and at its feet the whole American world. The author posts his varying people in their varying situations without a word of excuse or palliation for either, in the full confidence that so far as you truly are American you will know them. He is without any sort of literary pose, and his sarcasm is of the frankest sort." [1]

The plays by this author fill the same position; indeed, *The County Chairman* and his other comedies surpass any of the *Fables* which won Mr. Ade's audience for him. This same droll way of looking at life's frailties, and showing the peculiarities and failings of the people and parties, which we have noticed as being so characteristically Western, finds another exemplification in cartoonist McCutcheon. Of his work it may be truly said as was remarked of *Punch* that his aim was to provide relaxation for all, fun for all, without a spice of malice or a suspicion of vulgarity, humor without a flavor of bitterness, satire without reckless severity, and nonsense so laughter-compelling as to be absolutely irresistible from its very absurdity. It may be an humbler mission to tickle the midriffs of men than to labor for the salvation of their souls. But both are legitimate vocations. The world laughs too little anyway, and

[1] Howells, William D.

when we consider the vast influence of the pictured lesson, in catching the attention and driving home a truth, when an editorial is skipped, we realize the mission of the cartoonist in fashioning opinion and the importance of such a career. "You have a great teacher out here," said a New York divine of this cartoonist, "a militant force against sham, hypocrisy, pretence, and folly." John McCutcheon shows ready invention, vigorous if not careful drawing, and odd conceits, with an intelligent grasp of facts and events; all infused with conviction, and rich humor, which makes him a great power against dishonesty, social pettiness, and demagogy. "Never malicious or brutal, he hits hard but always fair." This group of young men have always been accorded attention not only because of their Hoosier drollery, but because they know their clientele, and the people respond to their portrayals.

More than a passing mention must be made of another form of expression of thought. As we have noticed, public speaking, in an early day on the frontier, was the easiest way of reaching the public. Before there were many books issued, oratory was cultivated as an art, among people of Southern extraction, who were the first settlers in Indiana. Stories are told of young attorneys and politicians rehearsing their speeches in the forests, and learning to round their periods as they journeyed on horseback from one court town to another. The backwoods voters were fond of pitting one political candidate against another, while they sat about on newly felled logs. There were no canvasses or nominating conventions in those days; candidates brought themselves out, and the settlers voted for the man who captured their ballot by his off-hand oratory. Public debate on religious and political questions would draw the people from twenty miles around.

Indiana's famous political leaders were all orators, each possessing his own personal style. Vice-President Hendricks, Henry S. Lane, Vice-President Colfax, Governor Morton, Daniel Voorhees, were representative of the different types of effective speakers during the Civil War period.

Commenting on the little that President Benjamin Harrison has published, it was very justly remarked by a critic that "the most finished orator in American political life to-day is not dependent upon book-writing for a literary reputation." Mr. Harrison's oratory was, no doubt, the model of the best form in public speaking of his time. Thoughtful, logical, clear, unimpassioned, and convincing, his addresses may be read now with an interest second only to hearing them delivered.

In discussing modern political orators, Mr. Reeser said in an interview: "I have reported the speeches of most of the representative men and feel entitled to write of present-day speakers, and I must say of another Hoosier, in the language of a New York journalist, that 'as a picturesque, rapid-fire orator, the East has nothing to compare with John L. Griffiths of Indiana.'"

Some of the literary addresses prepared for public occasions by men and women of Indiana in recent years, and many of the club papers, deserve to rank with the published essays of the country. As the essay is pre-eminently the product of meditation and leisure, it could hardly be expected that the industrial State of Indiana should up to this time

Benjamin Harrison.
From a photograph by Clark, Indianapolis.

excel in that form of literary expression. Nevertheless, the work of Arthur Middleton Reeves, Oliver T. Morton, Judge Baldwin, Charles R. Williams, and others, with a number of papers by members unknown to fame, give such evidence of a just regard for literary values, a skilful use of language, a play of imagination, and withal a vigorous way of setting things forth, that their publication would add more to Indiana's claim for recognition in real literature than her score of popular novels. No one, unfamiliar with this class of productions in the State of Indiana, can rightly estimate the degree of virile, thoughtful study and discussion which goes on among the people. This certainly prepares the men and women of the commonwealth for authoritative opinions of affairs and an enjoyment of the literary productions of others. As Lowell has said, "their *obiter dicta* have the weight of wide reading, and much reflection, by people of delicate apprehension, and tenacious memory for principles."

It is interesting to recall in this connection that there were clubs in Indiana before it was a State; not, perhaps, in their present-day form, but men on the frontier who had literary taste, or those with wishes for intellectual improvement, banded themselves together for an interchange of thought, and to practise the expression of opinions. Evidence of the existence of these primitive clubs is found in an old record that in a diminutive cross-roads hamlet, which never even attained the size of a village, "a polemic society was organized which was strongly attended by debaters from Weaver's neighborhood east of the river, and Judge Clark's neighborhood in Warren County. At one time there appeared to be a strong probability of a lyceum and academy being established there, but a few cabins and a small frame house soon brought the village to its culminating point, and it was in a few years entirely gone."[1] A half-century ago, clubs took the form of debating societies, mock legislatures, and lyceums.

The members of these imitative assemblies assigned themselves counties and discussed the measures that came before real legislatures, and not infrequently with more intelligence and spirit than the august body that they represented. It is said that they elected a governor as often as they wanted to hear an inaugural address, which was sure to be humorous and full of local hits and personalities. These sham legislatures were in vogue from 1824 to 1836, and were revived again in '42 and '43.

A form of literary endeavor customary during the middle of the century was the lyceum. Besides the papers and addresses by the members there was generally maintained a lecture course. During the succeeding period came the rise of the modern club. The writer has never belonged to a club, but feels assured, from an interested observation of others' enjoyment of such associations, that in Hoosierdom at least they have been a decided impulse in letters, art, and music. Many of these organizations have inaugurated movements for local improvements, for general culture, the spread of an interest in art, for historical remembrance, and for civic reform.

In Indiana, it is claimed, was formed the first woman's literary club in the United States. It was founded at New Harmony by the brilliant Frances Wright. The satirist may throw his little shaft of

[1] Cox, Sanford C., *Recollections of the Wabash Valley*, chapter xxv.

wit at clubdom, and at these satires the members themselves may laugh, even more heartily than the uninitiated, for they know all the vulnerable points in such associations; but the truth still remains, that the interchange of thought, the intellectual stimulus from such contact of mind with mind, has proved itself desirable and valuable, and worthy of wider adoption, rather than of lessening the number.

Within later years there were created in Indiana two State federations of these clubs, which have now, very happily, been consolidated. This union has endeavored to assist in many different measures of progress within the State. It has advanced legislation and influenced public sentiment toward civic improvement, for the establishing a juvenile court, for the child labor laws, for pure food regulations, and home economics. The Federation is a real dynamic force in the commonwealth. Among other measures emanating from the union of literary clubs, none have proven more encouraging to the whole people than the passage of the law in 1899 creating the Library Commission to promote the development of public libraries in all of the towns. This commission is also to help in the organization, give training to library workers, supply lists of desirable books, and secure statistics from all the libraries. Since the creation of this valuable commission, libraries have more than doubled in numbers, and, what is encouraging to future efforts, they are all on a permanent basis. The board has established a system of travelling libraries for the districts where there are no local ones, or where students need books on special subjects. Indiana has reason to pride herself on the awakening of interest in the library movement. Over fifty towns have shared in the Carnegie fund for the buildings, while other cities have built for themselves beautiful homes for the books which are provided by public assessment.

Whether as a medium of literary expression or as representing the personal political interests, the newspapers of Indiana have always had a large circulation and commanded an influence not easily overestimated, when considering the development of the State. The most influential journalists have helped to mould public opinion; nor have these men and women held their mission in light esteem. In addition to presenting the current events, the editors of Indiana's best papers have striven to make their publications representative of the best writing available to the State. In all the years that are past, local literary talent has found the columns of the newspapers open to its efforts. Editors have also shown a belief in the truth that a man who maintains a wholesome tone in the daily press serves his country well; hence the moral tone has been conserved. Editorial writing certainly exhausts a disproportionate amount of energy for the ephemeral fame it secures, as compared with other forms of literary labor. As the veteran editor Mr. Samuel Morse expressed it, at the close of a nonsense rhyme:

"And thus for more than thirty years I worked
  But all was written for the day,
  And ere the day was done
  It found its straight and certain way into oblivion."

Elihu Stout is credited with establishing the first newspaper in Indiana Territory, in the year 1804, at Vincennes, which was then the capital. It was called the *Indiana Gazette* and, after many vicissitudes, still flourishes under the name of the *Western Sun*. Through his publications, his public spirit, and his fine character, Mr. Stout wielded a wide influence for half a century.

The number of newspapers increased slowly, as new counties were organized. The story is told of one of the earliest sheets that it was printed with swamp mud used for ink, and run off on a cider press. The editor complained that the lack of *mails* made it difficult to gather enough news to issue a newsy paper! The paper on which the earliest journal was printed was often brown wrapping paper. Sometimes it was printed only on one side of the sheet. After it had been read, the subscriber would return his sheet and have it printed on the reverse side the next issue. There was little currency in those days, and the editors often advertised that they would forgive debts if produce was brought to the sanctum. Maple sugar, jeans, tow-linen, oats, chickens, corn meal, firewood, and coon skins or deer hides were solicited in payment of arrears, "before winter set in." Articles advertised in these early newspapers included knee-buckles, spinning-wheels, flint rifles, buckskin and saddle-bag locks. Notices of murders and kidnapping by the Indians were among the local items of the day.

Besides the usual titles of *Journal, Times, Register,* or *Express,* some of the names given to the weekly papers published in wilderness towns had the flavor of frontier life. *The Broad Axe of Freedom, The Whig Rifle, The Coon-Skinner, The Pottawattomie,* and *Miami Times* live only in the treasured files of public libraries, but they once passed current as regularly as the uncertain mails would permit.

In his reminiscences of Brookville, Mr. Johnson tells

this story of early journalism: The newspaper then published in the town was called the *Brookville Enquirer*. Robert John was the editor, and subsequently there was associated with him I. N. Hanna, a sprightly and talented young man. The editors, however, soon got at loggerheads. During the ensuing Presidential campaign, Robert John was for John Quincy Adams and I. N. Hanna was for Henry Clay. An editorial would, therefore, come out for Adams, followed by another signed "Junior Editor" for Clay, creating considerable sensation among the politicians of Brookville—and indeed all the citizens were politicians.

If one is tempted to feel that a difference of opinion on political subjects is eternal, he should contemplate the peaceful demise, within a short period of each other, of the great newspaper combatants at the capital, the *Journal* and *Sentinel*. Both were historic organs, dating from older papers established in the '20's, and representative of their respective parties. For many decades they were ably edited, and were a reflection of the sentiments and principles of the two great political parties that formed their constituency. For years they fought the party battles with energy and virulence. The Sunday edition of the *Journal*, under the editorship of Miss Anna Nicholas of late years, was a model family paper. The cause of the passing of the *Sentinel* and *Journal* is perhaps not obscure, and is certainly an interesting indication of a new phase of party politics in the State. The notable editors had passed from control. The Democratic party has for several years been divided in its convictions on public policies, and probably did not sustain a party organ. The Republicans have grown more independent of party control and they

The Daughter of Chief Massaw.
From a sketch from life by William Winter on the Miami Reservation.

read independent papers. How much personal indifference of candidates and private financial reasons mingled in allowing the two journals to be submerged, is not told, but, as the Lafayette *Courier* said in its requiem,

"It is impossible to note the passing of the old-timers without regret, for they recall a vigorous journalism and bring back the days of intense political rivalry, when loyalty to party was second only to loyalty to country. Times have changed, and doubtless for the better. We have more independence now in the newspapers, but there is no gain-saying the statement that the old days were interesting."

The record of brilliant talent which has been employed in Indiana journalism would make a long roll of distinction. Journalists received due honors in their day, and their interesting careers form part of the history of their respective fields of labor. There is a great temptation to make personal mention of individuals, but their life's story should have a volume to itself. Nor is there a dearth of good work through the State at present. At the capital, the literary ability of those regularly engaged on some of the papers has never been excelled.

The State takes a commendable pride in its writers on scientific subjects. Beginning with the scientists at New Harmony, who joined David Owen in his community experiment in the wilderness, and since then, there have always been scientific men in Indiana who have made valuable contributions to the literature of their especial branches. Some of these men were born in the State, and others, coming from elsewhere, have identified themselves with the history of Indiana.

Their useful labors have been within the State, and their national recognition located them in this commonwealth, and has reflected honor upon it. Most of these scientists were members of the faculty of some of the colleges. Indeed by far the largest part of the intellectual development of the State has been through the labors of its teachers in the schools and colleges. Many of these men and women have published critical and historical works, and others the results of their original investigations. It could only be a list if all these books were mentioned, but they represent the patient research, the scholarship, and literary skill of the best trained minds in the State. They are honored and honorable within its borders.

The monographs published by the State Historical Society, the scientific societies, and the educational bodies are of a high order of literary merit, sound scholarship, and of national importance in the knowledge they impart on the subjects treated.

Hoosier books may be more widely known than the pictures painted by Indiana artists, but there has been no literary work done that is better than the artistic work done by the present-day "Hoosier Group" of painters. The efforts of the pioneers were naturally directed to perpetuating the features of their loved ones; consequently the early artists of Indiana devoted their talents to portrait-painting. Later an occasional one, like George Winter, or Jacob Cox, ventured into the delineation of Indian life, or the landscapes about them. In the frontier life, the painter was a person apart from the everyday world. It was regarded as little short of lunacy for a man to attempt to live by art, but if he would, then the neighbors pointed him out as a celebrity; even if lack of patronage kept him indigent. General Wallace tells us in his *Autobiography* of his father's commands, when he showed an early predilection for art, which the family feared would become a passion:

"'You must give up this drawing. I will not have it. If you are thinking of becoming an artist, listen to me: In our country art is to have its day. The day may not come in your time. To give yourself up to the pursuit means starvation.' 'But Mr. Cox'—'Oh, yes,' he replied, 'Mr. Cox is a good man, but he had a trade to fall back upon—a shop to help him make ends meet. I suppose you do not want to be a poor artist—poor in the sense of inability as well as poverty. To be a great painter two things have always been necessary—a people of cultivated taste, and education for the man himself. You have neither.'" [1]

The extinguishment of the beautiful dream left him disconsolate. And thus the artistic yearnings of the youthful Lew Wallace, like those of many another frontier boy, were quenched by his discouraging environment. "I resolved to give up the dream," he says, "still it haunts me. At this day even, I cannot look at a great picture without envying its creator the delight he must have had the while it was in evolution." [1]

In this story we have revealed to us the repression of the artistic temperament in the life of many a frontier youth. The early painters had only self-training, and it may be said felt their way toward the light. The pathos of the isolated artistic nature, far away from any atmosphere of encouragement, could

[1] Wallace, Lew, *Autobiography*, page 50. New York, 1906.

scarcely be depicted by brush and pencil. The work of these men, and those who immediately followed them, is interesting as a portraiture of the times, and as examples of the state of art "before the war."

After the painters of pioneer days, the Munich and Paris schools were attended by students from different towns in Indiana. Some of them remained abroad, and others settled where there was more encouragement and patronage. They reflected credit on the State of their birth wherever they were, by the quality of their productions. To those who came back to Indiana, well trained in their art, the commonwealth is now indebted for its enviable position in the Association of Western Artists. They are known throughout the country as the Hoosier Group, and, while differing individually, there is a certain kinship in the products of their brush. They paint the things about them, the hills of Brown, the citizens of the towns, the drooping beeches of the wood, the bit of upland from their own studio window, a homelike landscape just out of town, or the gray beach in front of their summer cottage. The Hoosier Group have succeeded too. They have maintained their ideals for the encouragement of art within the State; they have secured an appreciative patronage, and they command the attention of students who are to become the painters of the future.

Indianapolis, being the capital and the centre of things in many ways, has always had successful artists who have led in the effort to create a distinct opportunity for the development of the talent about them. A very interesting fact in connection with the growth of art in Indiana has been the occurrence of little detached groups of men, outside of the capital, as

A Miami Indian.
Sketched from life by William Winter on the Miami Reservation.

in Madison, in Muncie, and in Richmond, who have worked along their own lines, and have come into an appreciative recognition, wherever their canvases have been shown. These men paint scenes which have the very breath of the woods; and the coloring in their pictures is a joy to the possessor. In the blending of realism and idealism, they are very happy. They feel and express the sentiment of their own beloved landscapes. An instance of the art impulse occurring in the solitary individual in the provinces is in the career of Amelia Kusner Coudert, the noted miniature-painter. Born in Terre Haute, with no primary teaching to guide her impulse, she felt, as she said, that she could paint. While studying in New York, she produced some extraordinary work, which afterwards attracted attention in London, when exhibited there under the patronage of Sir John Millais. Immediately the young artist's success was assured, until now it may be said that Mrs. Kusner Coudert has painted miniatures of most of the crowned heads and celebrities of Europe.

In a notice of Western artists by Mr. Dickerson it was very correctly stated that the late Chicago exhibition revealed the fact that, if one were to omit the work of the women painters, he would deprive the exhibition of some of its best art. Indeed, what some have regarded as the best painting would be omitted; for *In an Old Gown*, by Miss Martha S. Baker of Indiana, not only received an honorable mention at the recent Carnegie exhibition, but was purchased by the Municipal Art League of Chicago for its permanent collection. The same statement regarding women's work was made at Indianapolis exhibitions. The paintings in oil and water-color by artists whose names we recall at random, as Izor, Steele, Woods-Ulman, Hendricks, Goldsworth, Robinson, Comingore, Rehling, Birge, King, Morlan, Wilson, and many others equally good, show evidence of real talent. The illustrated parchments by Evaleen Stein, the illustrations by Virginia Keep and others, the modelling by Helen Hibben and Clara Barth Leonard, give evidence of serious work being done by the young women in Indiana.

Public taste in the West, art critics say, is growing appreciably discerning. Picture-buyers are slowly being educated to confidence in Western picture-makers. They are learning to regard what an artist creates, not where he creates it. This growth in creative power, accompanied as it is by the increasing self-confidence of the possible purchaser, encourages the Western artist.

Most of the exhibitions of art in Indiana towns have been the results of the efforts of the women in those communities. These collections were intended to stimulate the latent artistic talents of students, and for the general pleasure and information of the public. They also afford an opportunity for possible purchasers to show their appreciation of the work exhibited. There is scarcely a city in the State but has its circle for the study of the literature of art, and that study is carried on by the local literary clubs. The town of Richmond has a popular organization, with three thousand members, whose membership fee of fifty cents each sustains an annual loan exhibition of great merit. At a late exhibition, Otto Stark won the Foulke prize with a beautiful landscape, and Justin Gruelle and Dorothy Morlan received honorable mention. In the prize offered by the famous "Richmond Group," Anna Newman was first, and

Girardin and Holly had honorable mention. Raymond White received recognition for his portrait carved in ivory, and Miss Overback for excellence in design. This association is given as an example of the forces that are working for the elevation of the whole people, in matters relating to art, and for the encouragement of local artists.

In the spring of 1903, the Hoosier Group of artists assembled an exhibit in Indianapolis consisting solely of the work of Indiana painters "contemporary and retrospective." This collection made it very evident to the visitor that the springtime of art had already dawned upon the State; that the patient, persistent work done by the men born within its bounds had nursed the feeble impulse toward artistic expression, by brush and pencil, until the State could now take an honorable place in the field of art.

While this exhibit may not have been so stirring as a military review, it was a greater source of pride and congratulation. The gentle arts of peace had brought honors to the State, not attainable by war. It was a noticeable fact that there were so many canvases that one would like to live with. The subjects chosen were never morbid, or the inspiration of a degenerate nature. The coloring was pleasing, natural, and there was little straining after sensationalism. Lovely woods were pictured by Bundy and Conner and Girardin and Ball and Nordyke. There were great portraits by William M. Chase, T. C. Steele, and others; marines by the illustrious Richards; sea pictures and landscapes by such favorites as Forsythe, Gruelle, Adams, Stark, Forkner, and Love; genre and figure paintings by Henry Mosler, Stark, and many others whose gentle scenes and charming coloring live in the memory when the name of the artist has slipped from recollection. The water-colorists and illustrators also made a most interesting contribution. As noted in the catalogue, "the point of great interest in the exhibition was this: that the body of this work was done by the natives of Indiana in Indiana, who love the State and love art, and who feel and know that here as well as anywhere art can be created; and they venture this ambitious effort to, as far as possible, prove the fact." Mr. Steele continues to preach this truth, by the beautiful pictures which he brings up from his summer studio in Brown County, and J. Otis Adams sends his canvases from Brookville to take first prizes at the Exhibition of the Western Society of Artists. The names of Vance, Weisenberger, Wheeler, Walker, Reeves, Riess appear on the lists among the resident artists who are showing new canvases, and winning new laurels as the seasons go by.

Indianapolis is easy of access from all parts of the State and if an endowment should be given to the Art School at the capital, which would enable the directors to offer scholarships to young students who would be attracted to such a centre, it would give a helpful impetus to the study throughout Indiana.

The books that have been written by Indiana authors have attained greater fame, perhaps, than the pictures of her painters, because the printed form of expression is more easily disseminated to the multitude. But it is very certain that the Hoosier painters have produced beautiful work, and have fully shown the development of the artistic impulse in the commonwealth.

CHAPTER XVIII

EDUCATION IN INDIANA

IN the very earliest dawn of Indiana's history, when there were only a few families at each of the scattered French military posts, the only instruction given was by the French priests. In 1719, Father Marest wrote back to his superior, "as these people have no books and are naturally indolent, they would shortly forget the principles of religion, if the remembrance of them was not recalled by these continued instructions. We collect the whole community in the chapel and after answering the questions put by the missionary, to each one without distinction of rank and age, prayers are heard and hymns are sung." In after years when there was a resident priest, an effort was made to teach the children to read and write, but the happy-go-lucky frontier Frenchman resisted mental effort even more than he avoided physical toil. We are told that their written language was much worse than their speech (which was tolerable French). All that they knew was handed down from father to son. They had no education. There never was a school in the territory until during the American occupation. In 1793, Father Rivet held what was probably the first regular school in Indiana; it was in Vincennes. There is record of a little school in a settlement in Dearborn County three years later. After the Americans gained control of the territory, and settlers began to come in from the East and South, the children were at first taught in the homes. Colonel Cockrum recalls, in his *Pioneer History of Indiana*, that in the very first years of settlement, when there was such great danger from Indians and wild beasts, the teacher was employed to go to the houses and spend about one third of the day with the family instructing the children. In this way, with six families he could give three lessons each week to all of the children. These circulating teachers, as they were called, did a good work. When it became less dangerous for the children to pass through the forests they would congregate at the home of the family most centrally located in the neighborhood, in a lean-to built at the side or end of the pioneer's cabin. Here if there were enough families within reach of each other, one of the mothers or an older sister would collect the children of the scattered families together and teach them to read and write and "cipher." As soon as possible the neighborhood would get together and build a log cabin in which to hold the school, and a "master" would be "hired" for three months of the year. A site was selected near a living spring, if possible; and the memory of drinking the cool sparkling waters from the long-handled gourd which always hung by the spring brings back one of the joys of childhood.

Judge Banta tells us in his interesting recollections, published in the *Indianapolis News*, of the old school-houses and the buildings which were made to do duty as such; he speaks of a school that was taught in 1808, in the dwelling-house of John Widner, which house was almost a fort, having been constructed with special reference to making resistance against attacks of Indians.

"Indeed, there is direct authority for the statement, that schoolhouses were constructed in Washington County with port-holes, for shooting at the Indians, and if in Washington County, we have good reason to suppose that they were likewise so constructed elsewhere at the same time. The first school in Martinsville was a summer school on a gentleman's porch taught by Dr. John Morrison. Barns were given up during part of the temperate season to the pedagogue and his pupils. Mills were also utilized on occasions. The first school ever taught in the English language in the town of Vevay was by John Wilson, a Baptist minister, in a horse mill. An early school in Waynesville, Bartholomew County, was taught by a retired distiller, in a blacksmith shop, which school, for reasons not stated, was attended by young men and boys only. In Spencer County a deserted tannery was utilized. In Knox, in Jackson, and perhaps elsewhere, the old forts, after the close of the Indian wars, were turned into schoolhouses."[1]

Old settlers give graphic pictures of their schooldays, in these surroundings. "Pleasing reminiscences come before me," said Barnabas Hobbs, "when I think of the pioneer schoolhouses. They were made of hewed logs and had puncheon floors and capacious mud and stick chimneys with great fire-places. They had benches without backs or desks, and there were two long wooden pins above the teacher's desk on which his whips were laid. These were generally well-trimmed beech or hazel rods, from two to six feet in length—some well worn and others kept in reserve. Teachers were expected to govern on the home plan—

[1] Banta, D. D., in *Indianapolis News*, 1892.

'spare the rod and spoil the child.'" They believed the rod had a twofold virtue. It was not only a terror to evil-doers but was a specific against stupidity. Beech and hazel rods had a wonderful stirring effect on both mind and body. The State at this time had no school revenue to distribute, so each voter must become a builder. By common consent the voters divided themselves into choppers, hewers, carpenters, and masons. If any could not report for duty on the schoolhouse, they might pay an equivalent for work in nails, glass, or boards for the roof. If they neither worked nor paid, they could be fined thirty-seven and one half cents a day. These school buildings were well ventilated, not only by the great open fire but from the chinks between the logs.

Whence came the pioneer teachers? They were generally adventurers from the East, or from England, Scotland, or Ireland who sought temporary employment during the winter, while waiting for an opening for business. Some of these were first-class men, and they left a lasting impression on the communities.

Schools commenced then at seven in the summer and half-past seven in the winter. There was one hour at noon and five-minute recesses; fully ten hours in school in summer. In the pioneer period "loud schools" were in universal esteem. By this is meant, that all of the pupils studied out loud. The theory was that sound intensified the memory. Boys and girls were taught to think in the midst of noisy surroundings. In those ungraded district schools the younger pupils listened to the instructions and recitations of the older ones and bright pupils stepped from one class to another as rapidly as they were able to progress. The geography lessons were taught to

Young's Chapel, Consolidated School, Union Township, Montgomery County, Indiana. Hacks ready to start home.

the whole school at one time in concert. Many an old timer can recall his States and capitals to this day, better than his grandson, by humming over "Maine—Augusta on the Kennebec River," etc. Manual labor was also a part of the school life, for the great open fire-places must be kept replenished with logs and these must be chopped by the older boys of the school who rather enjoyed the reprieve from study.

Mr. Hobbs said: A very accomplished lady teacher who came from a bright centre in North Carolina taught a summer school in southern Indiana in the early days. Many had doubts about her success. It was not considered possible for a woman to govern a school. She had read much and had a happy way of illustrating prose and poetry by anecdotes of history and biography. She stirred within the pupils a love for classic literature, history, and art, and the question was settled that a lady could teach school as well as a man. The compensation received by the early pedagogues was not such as to encourage an over-supply of teachers. Judge Banta says in his reminiscences that seventy-five cents per quarter was a price quite commonly met with as late as 1825, or even later, but the price varied. In some sections $1 per scholar seems to have been the ruling price, in others $1.50, while in a very few instances $2 was paid. Some teachers eked out their earnings by chopping timber at night and on Saturdays. In many cases, probably a majority, the teacher was obliged to take part of his pay in produce. Wheat, corn, bacon, venison hams, dried pumpkins, flour, buckwheat flour, whiskey, leather, coon skins, and other articles are mentioned as things given in exchange for teaching. At the expiration of the three-months term, says one old settler, the teacher would collect the tuition in wheat, corn, pork, or furs, and take a wagon-load to the nearest market, and exchange it for such articles as he needed. Very little tuition was paid in cash. One schoolmaster of the time contracted to receive his entire pay in corn, which, when delivered, he sent in a flat-boat to the New Orleans market. Another, an Orange County schoolmaster, of a somewhat later period, arranged to teach a three-months school for $36.50, to be paid as follows: $25 in State scrip, $2 in Illinois money, and $9.50 in currency. This was as late as 1842, and there were seventy school children in his district. A large per cent. of the unmarried teachers "boarded around," and thus took part of their pay in board. The custom in such cases was for the teachers to ascertain by computation the time he was entitled to board for each scholar, and usually he selected his own time for quartering himself on the family. In most instances it is believed that the teacher's presence in the family was very acceptable, for the isolation was always felt in the wilderness, and as books and papers were scarce the conversation of an intelligent teacher was very welcome. Later it became quite common to have a schoolmaster's house erected by the district, hard by the schoolhouse, for the use of the married masters.

"A few years ago," continues Judge Banta, "I had occasion to look into the standing and qualifications of the early teachers of my own county, and on looking over my notes I find this statement: 'All sorts of teachers were employed in Johnson County. There was the "one-eyed teacher," the "one-legged teacher," the "lame teacher," the "teacher who had fits," the "teacher who had been educated for the ministry but, owing to his habits of hard drink, had turned pedagogue," and the "teacher who got drunk on Saturday and whipped the entire school on Monday."' A paragraph something like this might be truthfully written of every county south of the National road, and doubtless of every one north of it. The lesson this paragraph points to is that whenever a man was rendered unfit for making his living any other way, he took to teaching. The first schoolmaster of Vanderburg County lived the life of a hermit; and is described as a rude, eccentric individual who lived alone and gained a subsistence by hunting, trapping, and trading. John Malone, a Jackson County schoolmaster, was given to tippling to such excess that he could not restrain himself from drinking ardent spirits during school hours. He carried his bottle with him to school but he seems to have had regard enough for the proprieties not to take it into the schoolhouse, but hid it outside. Wesley Hopkins, a Warrick County teacher, carried his whiskey to school in a jug. Owen Davis, a Spencer County teacher, took to the fiddle. He taught what was known as a 'loud school,' and while his scholars roared at the top of their voices the gentle pedagogue drew forth his trusty fiddle and played *Old Zip Coon, The Devil's Dream*, and other inspiring profane airs, with all the might and main that was in him. Thomas Ayres, a Revolutionary veteran, who taught in Switzerland County, regularly took his afternoon nap during school hours, 'while his pupils,' says the historian, 'were supposed to be preparing their lessons, but in reality were amusing themselves by catching flies.' One of Orange County's early schoolmasters was an old sailor who had wandered out to the Indiana woods. Under his encouragement his pupils, it is said, 'spent a large part of their time roasting potatoes.' "[1]

[1] Banta, D. D., "Early Schools of Indiana." Articles in the *Indianapolis News*, 1892.

Thus we see that an odd character who had a little learning, or a lame soldier who "had seen some schoolin'" in his mother country, or a Yankee tinker who could combine some useful trade with a few months' teaching the three R's to the frontier children, were generally the teachers found in the cabin schools. They solicited their pupils from house to house, telling or submitting in writing, to the parents, where they would hold the school, that they would teach spelling, reading, writing, and arithmetic as far as the single rule of three. They announced what their charges would be, and sometimes added, the discipline would be, for being idle, two lashes with a beech switch, for whispering, three lashes, for fighting, six lashes. The text-books used were not closely graded: as may be imagined. The children learned to read from whatever book the family happened to possess, the Bible, *Gulliver's Travels*, *Pilgrim's Progress*, a dream book, or the moral maxims at the foot of the page in the old blue speller. Colonel Cockrum tells a touching story of this dearth of text-books, when parents were obliged to cut up a volume and paste the parts on boards for the different children of the family. A pointed goose-quill was used for the pen and the ink for "copy-book work" was manufactured from oak balls saturated in vinegar.

The children walked miles through the forest to gain the meagre rudiments of knowledge these eccentric masters might impart to them. This poverty of advantage in youth was another pathetic phase of the tragedy of the frontier. From Georgia to Michigan, we may picture to our minds these eager, intelligent youths, rising in the gray winter dawn to "do the chores" about the farm and chop the wood for the cavernous fire-places which required cords of wood a day to warm the open house. After their early breakfast they trudged through the woods with dinner-basket on arm to the little log schoolhouse. "In imagination I can still hear the squish, squish of water-soaked shoes as their wearers crossed the puncheon floors to repeat their lessons," writes a pioneer. Many a time these pioneer children encountered the skulking savages, the wild beasts, or were terrorized by snakes, on the way to school. Colonel Cockrum relates a true incident in the school-days of Mrs. Nancy Gulick, who lived near where the town of Hazleton now stands. One of the patrons of the school near White River had started out hunting and gone by the school to see one of his boys. While there the hunter's dogs treed a young panther, not far from the schoolhouse. The children went out to see what the dog was barking at, and the hunter, on coming up, shot it, and told his boy to drag it to the schoolhouse and when he went home to take it with him and save the hide. A short time after "books were taken up," the teacher and pupils were startled by the awful scream of the old mother panther, as she came bounding along the way the young one had been dragged. They had forethought enough to close the door and put the window-bench in place and fasten it there. The furious animal rushed up to the carcass of her kitten and when she found that it was dead she broke forth in terrible screams and howls of lamentation. Looking around for something on which to avenge its death, she made a rush for the schoolhouse, ran two or three times around it, and then leaped on top of it and commenced tearing across the roof from side to side, as if hunting some place where she could get in to the imprisoned teacher and scholars. After a while she gave three or four most terrible screams; presently the answering screams of another panther were heard some distance off. It was but a short time before her mate came rushing up; they gave several screams, one after another, and made a rush for the building, bounded on the top of it, and for the next half-hour kept up a screaming such as the helpless scholars and frightened teacher had never heard before. Major Robb had several men working for him at that time. They heard the fearful noise, and by the direction were sure it came from the schoolhouse. Three men took their rifles and hurried to the rescue. Several dogs had followed the men, and they set up a loud barking, which frightened the panthers into a tree which stood near the schoolhouse and they were soon shot to death by the hunters.

At night the school children studied their lessons and "worked their sums" by the firelight, or the feeble flame of a "tallow-dip." This is not alone the picture of the conditions which surrounded Abraham Lincoln's childhood and others known to fame; but it was the common lot of all the children in the early Indiana settlements, whose lives afterward went into the foundation of the sturdy commonwealth. They were the men and women who so conscientiously laid the foundation for better conditions of instruction for later generations of Indiana children. Nor did these men and women in after days claim that their early years were a time of woe, unmixed with rural pleasure. The privations and dangers became in memory partly offset by the joys of a vigorous childhood in close contact with nature. They had found pleasure in the long walks to and from school. They had gathered nuts, berries, and acorns by the way. The hunting of May-apples, paw-paws, calamus-root, or blackberries had often beguiled their footsteps from the direct path, to where they knew the biggest and best fruits to be lurking.

> "In the fields we set our guileless snares
> For rabbits and pigeons and wary quails,
> Content with the vaguest feathers and hairs
> From doubtful wings and vanished tails."[1]

Thus, in later life, reminiscences of early trials and pleasures seemed almost balanced; and "the good old times" became a term of reproach to modern degeneracy.

When the "man teacher" was found to be unnecessary to cope with the muscle and brawn of hardy overgrown boys who came for the three months' schooling, and the power of personality and gentleness was found to be a more efficient civilizer, then women often became the instructors. Some of these women had a talent for inspiring their pupils with a love of learning which made them invaluable instruments of progress and culture in those crude surroundings. Many of them were of New England birth, and had been thoroughly taught. Often they had received their training from a clergyman father whose classical scholarship and general culture moulded most excellent instructors for the frontier. Some of these intelligent women married soon after coming out West and their descendants were among the especially enlightened citizens of the State. Sometimes the women continued to teach after their marriage, owing to the scarcity of good instructors. The little libraries

[1] Howells, Wm. D., *Poems*.

they brought with them were loaned far and wide to eager readers, who were starved for good literature, just as the people on the frontier are now.

Although the earliest schools in Indiana were started and maintained by the parents who were anxious for the development of their own children, the demand for *popular* education was included in the very first ordinance for the formation of the Territory. In 1785, and in 1787, the famous laws passed for the government of the Northwest Territory declared that "religion, morality, and knowledge being necessary to a good government and the happiness of mankind, schools and the means of education shall forever be encouraged," and provisions were incorporated in that ordinance, setting aside a thirty-sixth part of all lands for the maintenance of public schools for all the people. This provision was a wise one. By the year 1825, it was estimated that the common school fund consisted of 680,207 acres valued at $2.00 an acre. These lands formed the endowment for the future means of maintaining common schools, but for many years there were no available funds, until the broad acres could be sold or a revenue could be obtained from them. It was during this period that the little "entry" schools, with paid tuition, of which we have been speaking, performed their mission for the straggling settlements.

In 1807, the Territorial Legislature passed an act incorporating the Vincennes University, originating the first of those weak academies with the high-sounding titles. This "University," according to the language of the bill, was to be for the instruction of youth in the Latin, Greek, French, and English languages; mathematics, natural philosophy, logic, rhetoric, and the laws of nature and of nations! Special provision was made, in the charter, for the education of the Indians. The University was to provide all expenses for them, including maintenance and clothing, to induce them to embrace the opportunity for an education. At the same time, the frontier was so constantly threatened that Governor Harrison, at a later session, earnestly recommended a military branch in every school to instruct the youth in defence against the savage. Only one Indian is said ever to have availed himself of the opportunity of an education at Vincennes University! At the time of granting its charter, the Legislature gave it authority to raise $20,000 by lottery for its establishment. And this privilege was used for the next sixty years to maintain the school!

When the first constitution was formulated for the new State government in 1816, it included provision for township schools, for county seminaries, and a State university, ascending in regular order, with free tuition and open to all who wished an education. None of the lands that had been granted to the State, by the Federal Government, for school purposes, could be sold before 1820; and actually none were sold until eight years later. The legislation from time to time for public schools was as advanced as in any of the States, but there were no funds to maintain the authorized schools. There were many reasons for this,—the sparseness of population, slender school revenues from taxation, lack of qualified teachers, "opposition of the few and indifference of the many," who needed their children to work at the clearing of the forest and the planting and gathering of crops. Superintendent Cotton reminds us that "the settlers were busy felling the forest, draining swamps, and making homes. They exhausted their time and energies, in providing for their families the necessities of life, and in baffling malaria. They had no leisure for the contemplation of educational problems, and the spiritual life had to wait. The day of free schools was afar off and illiteracy grew apace."[1] Even the elementary schools were left to private enterprise.

At this very early point in the history of the educational affairs in Indiana there occurred within the borders of the State the most brilliant experiment that could be found on the national soil; that is, the schools established at New Harmony, by David Owen and William Maclure, which are described in the chapter on that socialistic community. From those short-lived schools, there went out teachers over the whole West, whose influence on education cannot be calculated.

In 1824, a law was passed providing for county seminaries and about fifty counties availed themselves of the provision, but the schools were all supported by private tuition fees, and money was so scarce that many of the children were not able to attend. The prevailing theory of that time, all over the country, was that parents alone were responsible for the education of their children; the rights of a *child* and the necessity of the *State* requiring and providing elementary education in its own defence had not yet been accepted. It was during this period of half a century before the full inauguration of public schools over the State that private citizens established those academies and denominational colleges which dotted

[1] Cotton, Fassett S., *Report of Supt. of Public Instruction*, 1904. Indianapolis.

all of the districts then populated. These schools must be borne in mind, by the student of the State's history. They are an enduring testimony to the intelligence of the pioneer settlers. They were determined that their children should have the advantages of which they had been deprived, and for which they had hungered in their youth, and tried to supplement by solitary studies. While the conviction necessary to the establishment of public schools, for all of the youth, was slowly coming to the people, the more enlightened men and women subscribed the funds necessary to establish what were known as "pay schools." There were fully seventy of these seminaries opened before the middle of the century.

It was commonly held, that the various religious denominations should undertake the higher education of the young and each sect tried to provide a school for its own following. Many of these institutions did good work for their time, and have passed into oblivion with their founders. They served the purpose of their day and generation, and deserve honorable remembrance. They were a large part of the uplifting influences of the frontier, and were built and supported at great sacrifices on the part of the parents of two generations ago. As they have so entirely passed beyond the ken of the present generation, they must be embodied in every history of the State, or due justice will not be rendered to the pioneers' intelligence, and the wise provision for their children.

These schools educated the men and women who, in their turn, established the State universities, the public school system, and provided for the denominational colleges. In that early time many a towhaired youth, barefooted, and with his scanty outfit tied up in a "meal-poke," kissed his mother good-bye and walked the distance to the seminary. In his ears rung his mother's benediction, and the father's urgent counsel to "get learning while he had the chance." At home the father chopped and tilled, and the mother spun and wove, to pay the slender price charged at these academies for board and tuition. The principals and teachers who supplied the thorough, if limited, instruction have long since gone to their reward, but their place in the annals of the States, and in the esteem of posterity, is by the side of the self-sacrificing parents. As General Wallace intones, for many others, the praise of one, in his autobiography:

"Step by step Prof. Hoshouer led me into and out of depths I never dreamed of and through tangles and appreciations which proved his mind as thoroughly as they tried mine. That year was the turning point in my life, and out of my old age and across his grave, I send him, Gentle Master, hail, and all sweet rest! Now I know wherein I am most obliged to you—unconsciously, perhaps, but certainly you taught me how to educate myself up to every practical need."[1]

Several of those early foundations have survived. Vincennes University, which was the first college established in the Territory, has suffered throughout its history on account of its endowment. First because its wild lands were unremunerative, and later because of the lottery feature, which hurt it when that form of raising funds was no longer approved of; then in 1830 the Legislature assumed control, sold the land grants, and put the proceeds into the general treasury of the State! Thirteen years later the trustees brought

[1] Wallace, Lew, *Autobiography*, page 58. New York, 1906.

A Scene near Hanover College.
From a photograph.

suit to recover their rights, in hopes of resuscitating the school; and after years of litigation and at a cost of one third of the sum in attorney's fees, they gained their suit, and the school was reopened with the good wishes of all who recall its ancient foundation that the new century may be kinder to Vincennes University and bring it greater prosperity. If it were called an academy it then might live up to its name.

The State was still in its infancy and the material resources for maintaining the population still undeveloped, when the first settled district along the Ohio River began to establish advantages for higher education. In 1827, the Presbyterians, who always stood for an educated ministry, made the beginning of Hanover College, in a little log cabin at Hanover village, on the Ohio River, near Madison. The college has continued its existence through a most honorable history; and in the present day attracts many students on account of its excellent instruction, high standards of scholarship, healthful location, and the marvellous beauty of the incomparable scenery which surrounds it. Only five years after establishing the college, on the southern line of the State, the Presbyterians started another school at Crawfordsville. This little town was then on the very edge of civilization; but Wabash College has had a continuous existence, in the little city which has always been known as a centre of culture. This school on its beautiful woodland campus welcomed its first students under the guidance of Caleb Mills, the man who afterward did so much for the cause of public schools in Indiana. Wabash College has been most fortunate in its presidents and through the poverty of the pioneer days, the vicissitudes incident to the Civil War, and the later competition with more richly endowed schools has been known as a strong institution sending out useful men. It is hoped that the new course to be offered in pedagogy will help to raise the standard of teaching in the State.

The Society of Friends, which was always foremost in the agitation against slavery, and against oppression and ignorance, was among the first to aid in the cause of education in the State. Being opposed to the support of schools from the military fines from the enforced militia system of that day, they established schools of their own immediately. Settled in large numbers in the southeastern part of Indiana, they established many minor schools as well as Spiceland Academy in 1834, the Bloomingdale Manual Labor School in 1845, and the well-known Earlham College, for both men and women, which was opened at Richmond in 1847, and has always stood in the front rank. The graduates of this school have been a valuable teaching force in many other institutions. All these schools, and other seminaries founded by the Friends in other localities, at later times, are recognized as giving practical and thorough educational facilities.

In 1834, the Baptists founded Franklin College under the leadership of such representative members as Henry Bradley, Reverends Eliphalet Williams, Reuben Coffey, Ezra Fisher, Moses Jeffries, William Rees, J. V. A. Woods, and the two brothers, Reverend Nathaniel Richmond and Dr. John L. Richmond— the latter had already, on his way toward the West, lived long enough in Ohio to help establish Dennison University. Franklin College was organized as a manual labor institute; and fulfilled that provision

Consolidated School in Union Township.
From a photograph.

many years, for most of the students supported themselves by real toil. In an old letter written by a student at Franklin in 1842, we get a real breath of the primitive conditions surrounding the student as he wrote:

"**Dear Brother:**
"I found I could earn 40 cents a day by chopping beech timber at 20 cents a cord. So I rolled up my sleeves and went at it. I walked two and a half miles to the place and every Saturday I earn that much. I want to stay on for another term if possible. I never felt the importance of trying to get an education before. My landlord offers to board me for fifty cents a week, and find everything and candles in the bargain. I can get shoes for $1.50 a pair and Mr. Lancherson will make a coat for me for $3.75 and take it in old scrip. A cloth coat will not cost any more than a jange coat which I am now wearing. I want to go to school as long as I can and if you can send me the cloth for a coat instead of the money, you can send it by the stage coach. I must close now as it is after ten o'clock and I have 21 pages to commit for to-morrow."

This letter, yellow with time and sealed with wafers, reflects many of the phases of frontier life and the early college environment. During the Civil War the patriotic body of students at Franklin responded so universally to the call for troops that the college was closed for lack of students. Only two pupils, sad and regretful, remained within its halls, and they were both lame. It was at this time that Dr. Silas Bailey, that great man and great educator, resigned the presidency. After the war closed, classes were resumed and Franklin College is still living and only needs larger endowment to make its usefulness commensurate with the hopes and sacrifices of the long roll of good Baptists who have fostered the institution.

The Methodists laid the corner-stone of Asbury— now Depauw—University in 1837. Through varying fortunes but "all leading to ultimate victories" this school still lives. Its influence has been vast within the Methodist Church. Like the other denominational colleges of the State it is "rich in traditions and in the sacrifices that have been made for it, and is firm in faith for the coming years."

As early as 1846 the Fort Wayne Female College was opened, but later it became a co-educational school and still flourishes at Upland as Taylor University.

Moore's Hill College is another of the early schools established for both sexes, that still maintains its useful corps of instructors and still sends out its army of graduates. The Methodists have reason to be proud of the history of this school that they founded in pioneer times and have continued until now.

Indianapolis being an inland town was settled later than the section where these other schools are located and has no college extant that was organized before Butler University; which was founded in 1850, by the Church of the Disciples. This school, so beautifully located in the environs of the rapidly growing capital of the State, and with the record it bears of a useful past and vigorous present management, only needs the personal interest and an endowment from the citizens of Indianapolis to make it one of the leading colleges of the West.

In 1840, six brave Sisters of Providence came out from France and established the Convent School, at Terre Haute, of St. Mary's of the Woods. This school has attracted pupils from all classes and many of the young ladies of the earlier time went there to

From the Stately Entrance you Look out over the Beautiful Campus of "St. Mary's of the Woods."

secure the accomplishments not elsewhere obtainable, and they still revisit their loved alma mater. The school has grown to be a little world within itself, and is nestled in the lovely park which gives it its name.

Terre Haute is also the home of the State Normal School and Rose Polytechnic Institute; giving that city three influential educational centres. The Polytechnic was opened in 1883, and is intended for the higher education of young men, especially for the profession of engineering. There are over two hundred students enrolled. They come from all parts of the country and are offered excellent advantages under a fine corps of instructors.

The growth of the Roman Catholic college at Notre Dame would read like a fairy story to the members across the sea of the order which founded that school. No longer ago than 1842, its founder, Father Sorin, arrived from France. On a bleak November day a boy, who two years later entered as the first student, guided the stranger through an unbroken forest to the shores of the lake, where there stood a lone cabin surmounted by a cross. In sixty-six years, this Old World religious society, transplanted to virgin soil and adapting itself to new conditions, and the New World demands of its following, has planted in northern Indiana a vast establishment. This community includes a primary school for children, an academy for youth, St. Mary's Convent School for girls, a theological seminary, and a university; all of which are flourishing, and their facilities must be constantly increased to meet the demands of the people. The university comprises schools of letters, science, laws, and engineering. Notre Dame is also a church publishing centre, for various influential church journals and books. Learned writers dwell within its walls and the influence of its journalists is international. The head of the Order of the Holy Cross has now moved the headquarters from France to this point. If one is seeking for a marked example of the rapid strides made by American institutions, and at the same time an instance of how a conservative Old World congregation may adapt itself to the spirit and progressiveness of the New World, no more striking instance could be found than the vast Roman Catholic school at Notre Dame.

Most interesting educational influences have been inaugurated at beautiful Lake Winona; not only the Chautauqua summer classes, but the Technical Institute at Indianapolis, governed by the same people, has a most useful field before it as a much needed trade school, if its fine location is used as it should be.

The old Lutheran Concordia School transferred to Indiana soil at Fort Wayne, and the Merom College in its beautiful surroundings, were both founded before the Civil War. There are many schools all over the State, such as Culver Military School at Lake Maxincuckie—the largest school of that kind in the country,—the immense schools at Valparaiso, at North Manchester, Oakland City, and elsewhere, that are doing excellent work, but have been established in later times than the pioneer schools of which we are speaking. Those mentioned will show the character of the work done by the early settlers in the foundations they laid for the future generations. In the history of both the early and later schools established, "each educational institution is replete with examples of heroism and self-sacrifice on the part of many faithful friends."

Of the State schools, Bloomington University was

the first one established after the State was organized. The constitution provided for such a college and the Legislature authorized its organization. Bloomington opened its doors in 1824, with ten pupils and President Hall as the only teacher, serving at a salary of $250.00 a year. He constituted the whole faculty, and if we may believe his reminiscences of *The New Purchase or Seven and a half Years in the West*, he felt that a Princeton graduate was lost to the world while teaching in the wild West. Those were the days when the classics were insisted upon, and Greek and Latin were the only branches taught there for the first three years! To this some of the practical frontier people very naturally objected. State politicians were as vague in their standards of culture at that time as they are still accused, at times, of being. One is quoted as declaring that "it was a right smart chance better to have no college at all, nohow, if all folks had'ent equal rights to larn what they most liked best." The common branches were soon added to the schedule of dead languages and the institution grew apace. Later it became co-educational, added an efficient school of pedagogy, was chartered as a university, and it has attained a most honorable position among the State schools of the Union. It now has nineteen departments, an enrolment of over fifteen hundred students, and a brilliant faculty of instructors. The members of the faculty of Indiana University have made notable contributions to our national literature in history, criticism, and science.

In addition to the establishment of the denominational schools and the State University, there were always far-sighted men of broad views, who saw that many children were unprovided for. Looking into the future, they maintained with Caleb Mills that in a government like ours, the State ought to provide *free* education for every child, sufficient to enable him to become an intelligent citizen. This seems self-evident truth now, but the movement for common schools, supported by taxation, had to be worked out in each State separately, and each State in turn has had to meet the same objections and the obstructive tactics of those who opposed the movement. Massachusetts went into the campaign for universal education very early in the history of the nation, and other sections followed. But after all these years, there are still neglected districts where the instruction within the grasp of the youth is meagre in the extreme, with a corresponding benighted condition of the population. In our day, we cannot imagine the warfare waged in the different States against free schools in the last century. All the objections now used against forward movements like taxation for public libraries, or old age pensions, were then in vogue against public schools. Some of the arguments were that the industrious should not be taxed to support the indolent; that free schools would pauperize the poor and make them depend entirely upon government help; that people who had no children should not be taxed for those who had more than they could bring up; that paternalism was in danger of creeping in; that free schools would make education too common! And some objected to people being made benevolent by law. These and other arguments were brought forward by short-sighted people in each State, as it swung into the line of progress. It seems strange now to read of mass meetings being held to oppose the movement, but they were, and speakers harangued the

Student Building, Indiana University, Bloomington, Indiana.
From a photograph.

crowds with all these arguments to try and stem the tide of opinion which had set in so strongly favorable to general education. For years pamphlets were circulated and long newspaper editorials were written against the proposition. Indiana was no worse than many other sections of the Union. Indeed she was in advance, for from Territorial times there had been statutes anticipating the future needs of the West. The Ordinance of 1787, Territorial laws, and the first State Constitution, as we have seen, provided for township schools, seminaries, and colleges, but there being no revenue from taxation the schools during all these years and for many years longer depended wholly on the sentiment of the community. Notwithstanding the advanced citizens had established such numbers of "pay schools" there were so many children growing up in ignorance, whose parents either could not or did not send them for instruction, that the agitation for the tax levy was begun. It was claimed by careful investigators in 1834, that only one child in eight between five and fifteen years of age was able to read. Even the capital did not have a free school until 1853, and that one was kept open only two months, and this in spite of many noble characters in different parts of the State, working for a change. At many places these men and women were seeking to awaken public sentiment in favor of free schools. The laws were on the books but the masses were very slow, as in all the States, in taxing themselves for the laws' fulfilment.

While affairs were at this stage, a New England settler, Caleb Mills, who had come out to act as a professor at Wabash College, became the grand leader of the forces who were agitating for effectual legislation. Over the signature, "One of the People," he addressed a series of six most urgent and convincing messages, directly to the Legislature, under the heading, *Read, Circulate, and Discuss.* These pamphlets were issued four years in succession. Mr. Mills set forth earnestly and plainly in the most pungent and telling manner, the illiteracy prevalent, because of the lack of common schools, and the responsibility of the legislators to formulate plans for their organization. He reminded them that to attend the schools then extant, it was necessary to pay tuition, which many were utterly unable to do. That owing to this fact only one in three of the children of school age attends any school, "that the constitution has committed to your charge the primary schools, the only institution to which nine tenths of the rising generation will ever have access." Like other legislative bodies they were slow to act on self-evident propositions. Friends of general education in different sections of the State rallied to the cause, and common school conventions were held in many localities. In almost every county the newspapers published communications from local leaders, presenting the arguments in favor of free schools. Many pamphlets on the subject were circulated for the general enlightenment of the people and to enlist more ardent interest in the immediate attention to the question. One of these circular letters, issued in 1847, expressed the hope that the free common school system may throw its broad mantle over the thousands of children of the poor—a helpless class of innocent sufferers—to shield them from infamy.

As a result of these combined influences, after two years of further delay, a referendum was ordered by the Legislature. The records tell us that at the fall election of 1848, after a voter had deposited his ballot, he was asked by the judge of the election, *viva voce*, "Are you in favor of free schools?" When the vote was counted it was found that 78,523 had voted for free schools, and 61,887 against them! Notwithstanding this opposition of the short-sighted element, the voters of Indiana had endorsed free schools, by a majority of 16,636. But the 60,000 non-progressives must be kept in mind, if we are to appreciate the heroic work done by the really active friends of universal opportunity. This element was a dead weight that the more intelligent portion of the community carried, until they had succeeded in elevating Indiana to her present educational eminence; and are still carrying while combating the inertia of the ignorant and indifferent. Since the victory for no slavery in the new State had been won, when Indiana came into the Union, this triumph for free schools was the most important result reached at the polls by the commonwealth.

Even after this popular endorsement another session of the Legislature passed without that body devising any measures for relief! In 1849, the campaign was renewed. Again Caleb Mills addressed the Assembly, urging the members to have the independence to enact, and the wisdom to devise, a system that would be an example to the sister States, adding further valuable statistics of the prevailing conditions and outlining a remedy.

Following all these efforts of educators and citizens, the Legislature, guided by Governor Whitcomb, passed an act, giving the people of the State power to call a convention, to draft a new constitution. Robert Dale Owen, both as member of this convention and afterwards as a member of the State Legislature, was efficient in promoting the legislation. Professor John Q. Morrison, as a member of this convention, and an enlightened educator, proved to be a guiding hand in the educational provisions secured to the people in that instrument.

The new constitution, after being submitted to the people, went into operation in 1852. It contained the long desired authority for the actual establishment of a free school system, and the necessary enactments followed. This blessing had not fallen easily into the lap of the State. Detailed mention of the battle for popular education is made, that the present generation may not forget that their present extensive privileges did not come to them without a struggle. The lesson of this phase of the State's history may be a warning against obstructing future progressive measures for the general advancement of the whole people, as they arise. The labors of Mr. Mills, Mr. Owen, Mr. Morrison, and the liberal thinkers who worked with them for the great educational system have enabled Indiana to take rank among the very foremost States in the Union. Under the new law if the local tax was too meagre to supply funds, it was augmented from the State fund. The township became the political and social unit, a fact of the largest significance in the school system; and of equal importance was the fact that a head had been provided for administering the law in the State, a Superintendent of Public Instruction, under whom the work of intelligent organization has been carried forward from that time. Step by step Indiana has developed a most admirable free school system, that is comprehensive and, in time, will be adequate. New provisions are annually suggested for its betterment, from kindergarten to university. Industrial instruction is yet to be made an integral part of all schools. Some of the country districts still need more school days and the advantages of centralization, which it is hoped may become universal. One of the chief factors in the development of opportunities for all the children of the State, has been the high grade of service that Indiana has enjoyed in her State Superintendents of Public Instruction. If one is skeptical regarding the sum of good citizenship he should feel encouraged by the records of the incumbents of this position. Notwithstanding it is an elective office, and the candidate changes with the political party in power, as a matter of fact, each of the parties has from the beginning nominated good men. After these men are elected, however much the individuals differed in their ideas of what was most needed, it is noted that each superintendent has stood for progress in general and each has emphasized some great idea in particular and our present system is in this way the work of our successive State Superintendents and State Boards of Education.

In reporting on her inspection of the Indiana schools, Miss Shaw says that there is a general level of excellence. The average rural school is far above the visitor's expectation. They are better than others because most of the teachers are better. And why? The State Superintendent neglects no one. The monthly letter to each teacher keeps them alert. There are uniform examinations and teachers are encouraged and invigorated by the system of teachers' meetings. Under the very representative State Board, and the Superintendent of Public Instruction in Indiana, the plans are laid for the expenditure of over ten millions and a half of money annually. The Superintendent must study the problems to be solved for the best advantages of the schools all over the State. The Monthly Bulletins, a system originated by Superintendent Cotton and issued from his office to the teachers, are intended for their inspiration and encouragement, and are alone invaluable to the upbuilding of the school system.

As the public schools developed, means of making them more and more adequate to the growing demands of the people gradually caused the organization of Teachers' Institutes, Reading Circles, Associations, and Normal Schools. *For the better training of teachers was, and still is, the greatest need felt in making common schools effective.*

In 1870, the State Normal School at Terre Haute was opened and there are a large number of independent normal schools, at Danville, at Angola, Marion, Rochester, and elsewhere, established for training teachers, which have a long enrolment of attendants. Many of the colleges also have included pedagogy in their curriculum. At Valparaiso the normal school has been merged into a college which attracts vast numbers. There are now over four thousand students, it being one of the busiest centres of young life in the West. An improvement in these schools is assured by the enactment of a law empowering the State Board of Education to act as a teachers' training board, regulating the system of normal school instruction and determining what schools shall be accredited a place in the system. The Superintendent says that there are more than eight thousand students now in normal schools and colleges, preparing to hasten better schools. In the cities, training schools are conducted in connection with the high schools. The Indiana Kindergarten Training School at Indianapolis does invaluable work for the training of teachers for primary work, and they, in turn, are missionaries for the extension of better preparation of teachers.

Indiana takes the enlightened position that the special State schools for the blind, deaf and dumb, feeble-minded, and soldiers' orphans are to be on the same plane as for the other children of the State; they have been instituted, not as charities, but as parts of the great scheme of public education. Industrial training is combined in all of these institutions with the regular school work.

The developments of the school system to meet the needs of the people are most interesting. Among the most important innovations is the consolidation of the weak country schools into strong central ones. The little red schoolhouse at the crossroads makes a sentimental picture in verses about old school-days, or in the biographies of aspiring politicians; but it has always been a sorry substitute for the advantages supplied by the city schools. The tax affording only six months of schooling with one lone teacher trying to instruct twenty or thirty classes—very often there being but one pupil in a class; the single, ungraded school held in an uncomfortable room, remote from any one home, has always been the real truth about the condition of educational surroundings in the solitary schoolhouses. These isolated buildings with their poverty of equipment, and limited advantages of instruction, long seemed to the patrons the only possible way of managing district schools; but the leaders in educational matters had visions of better ways. The disadvantages under which the small isolated rural schools labor were recognized in the earliest days and were set forth by William Maclure as early as 1827, and again by Caleb Mills when he was the State Superintendent in 1856. The attention of the Legislature was called to this handicap of the country pupils, by State Superintendents Geeting and Jones. Finally in 1899, the General Assembly passed a law, recognizing the right of township trustees to transport pupils at public expense to a stronger central school. But it was soon seen that trustees must be required by law to do this, if the cause is to advance rapidly; for the backward districts, which need it most, will always have those who oppose any innovations. This was accomplished in 1907, when the Legislature *required* the township trustee to discontinue weak schools averaging twelve pupils or less, and permitting it when there were fifteen or less; and when a school was thus abandoned, made it his duty to provide means of transportation for the pupils to a central school. Superintendent Cotton is largely responsible for the present flourishing state of this beneficent arrangement; and it is greatly due to his influence that so many pupils now enjoy the advantages of better school surroundings. Statistics of the results of these efforts for consolidated schools are most encouraging, but the figures are misleading; for they are outgrown before they can be published. At present over seventeen thousand children of the State are transported to better equipped schools than could be maintained in the little crossroads schoolhouse, attended by less than a dozen pupils. Nearly one thousand wagons are used for the purpose of carrying the pupils, the daily cost amounting to one dollar

Industrial Training in the Public Schools,
Photograph by Miner.

and eighty-four cents per wagon. Over thirteen hundred small schools have been combined into five hundred consolidated schools, with the number always increasing. Seventy-five counties of the State have tried the plan to their satisfaction. These children, thus transplanted, find themselves in better buildings, under better teachers, longer terms of schooling are possible, and the tax rate is no higher. "Being a farmer myself," said one trustee, "I believed that centralization was the farmer's opportunity to get as good schools as the village and towns have." Said another, "it is cheaper to run the hacks than it is to run the abandoned schools, and the educational advantages are many times greater in the central school."

One of the greatest advantages of consolidation to the country pupils is the possibility of industrial training, of laboratory work, of access to a library, and of instruction in music, drawing, and nature study. Special teachers may be employed in those subjects. The plan has been tried long enough, says the State Superintendent, to prove that a township school at one central point affords an opportunity for thorough work in these desirable branches. The elevating influence of such a school is felt to the very extremities of the township. It awakens educational aspirations of no mean power, stimulates efforts, and arouses mental energies and capacities. Such work is impossible in small isolated schools. The object toward which the friends of improved rural educational advantages are working is, that each township in Indiana shall finally have a complete system of schools, centrally located, with kindergarten, primary, and grammar grades capped by a four years' high school. In these schools industrial training, which includes agriculture, manual training, cooking, and sewing, is to be coupled with the regular literary course. This reasonable plan will equalize the advantages for education between the city and country youth; and there will be less incentive for them to desert the farm for the towns and better results at less cost surely will follow the centralization of rural schools for which Indiana educators are now contending. If instruction in agriculture and home economics is given in the schools, the youth who are to be the farmers and homemakers can afford to remain longer in attendance at school. Technical instruction in their home school for the practical work which is to be their career will retain them in the country where they may be growing more proficient in their vocation instead of drifting into the forlorn ranks of unskilled labor.

For many years after free schools were fully installed throughout the State, there was no law making attendance compulsory, and truancy, or very indifferent regularity was common, as in other States. In 1897 and 1901, laws were enacted compelling attendance at school until the age of fourteen; and the same law provided that books and clothing should be furnished when there was necessity. Only one written notice of habitual truancy to the parent or guardian of a child is required in any one year. The parent who violates the requirements of the law may be fined or imprisoned. "Truancy being the primary school of crime," the State recognizes that it is the part of wisdom to demand the regular attendance of the twenty-five thousand children who have been gathered in by the truant officers, and still greater vigilance in carrying out these laws is of imperative

Cabinet Work Done in the Public Schools of Bluffton.

importance to the State. As manual training and industrial instruction become multiplied there will be less work for the truant officer, less crime to be punished. When the schools have trained enthusiastic teachers, and are equipped to fit their pupils for the active duties of life, while pursuing their regular school course, then it may be said of the boys and girls in country and town, as it was said of the little Graysville, Indiana, school, "All of the children in this community attend school regularly—boys and girls who are far beyond the compulsory age limit. Not only so but they dispense with their recess and part of their noon hour and devote that time to hand work, and the children in this school passed the strongest examination in the regular lessons of any children in the country." Leaders of the educational work in Indiana are working for a time when in all of the high schools there will be commercial, industrial, or agricultural courses coupled with the academic studies; then the State may expect the other half of its boys who enter, not to drop out of high school as they now do; and the girls to "dignify the office" of housewife, when domestic economy is required for graduation along with history and political economy. Moving steadily, if slowly, along these lines, the Indiana schools are advancing in practical utility. Between sixty and seventy-five towns have already instituted manual training and domestic instruction. Beautiful equipment produces most gratifying results at Fort Wayne, Madison, Indianapolis, Greensburg, Richmond, and other cities.

The county schools have made even greater strides, proportionately. In an agricultural State like Indiana, industrial training will, in the very nature of things, be very largely instruction in agriculture; this should lead the children back to rural employment and ambitions. It is interesting to note the efforts that are being put forth by educators to enlist the interest of the youth in the principles of agriculture. In presenting a course for teachers to pursue, State Superintendent Cotton clearly showed the object of this training when he said that the course will direct the boys and girls to an intelligent study of agriculture which will inspire in them a respect for honest labor, and show them there is a demand for brains on the farm. The country schools are clearly combining artistic, scientific, and manual training in a most practical and attractive way. The average layman in the cities, who has not had his attention called to the progress being made, would be surprised and delighted with a walk around the school garden at Delphi, in Carroll County, where each pupil is given six feet of mother earth to plant and cultivate in a practical way; where an orchard affords practical lessons in fruit raising, a tiny plantation of nut trees an experiment in forestry, and the ornamental grounds an example of landscape gardening. An inspection of the laboratory work in the county schools of Randolph, Henry, Johnson, and other counties would awaken the citizens to the studies that are being carried on regarding soils, seeds, injurious insects, and processes of cultivation. A visit to the centralized schools in Wells County at Bluffton, Lima, and in scores of other centres would surprise the visitor who sees for the first time the bench work, cabinet pieces, and pottery made by the industrial classes; and learns how number work, language lessons, and nature study are taught from the practical experiences in the garden plot.

The enthusiasm in the corn clubs has been mentioned in the chapter on agriculture. The local trustees in the townships and instructors from Purdue University have given their assistance in encouraging these innovations, and in helping the teachers.

School gardens and lawns have been introduced in some town schools, giving great pleasure, and are instructive in homemaking and a decided impulse to civic improvements.

If the study of elementary agriculture, in the schools, is in its infancy, advanced instruction in that science, and all of the others, has been well provided for in the great State Agricultural University at La Fayette. Instruction was begun at Purdue University in 1874. It was founded as Indiana's land-grant college, authorized by Congress in 1862, when thirteen million acres of government land were set aside for the establishment of industrial colleges throughout the Union. The act stated that the schools to be organized were for the promotion of agriculture and the mechanic arts, without excluding other scientific and classical studies. Purdue is one of sixty-five institutions which have been organized in different States and Territories. Purdue University at present has an annual enrolment of about fifteen hundred students with a faculty numbering over a hundred. The experimental farm and campus comprises one hundred and eighty acres of beautiful land with about twenty-five buildings crowded for room to accommodate their students. The equipment is constantly being added to, in the effort to keep pace with the demands of the times. Scientific and agricultural progress, in this day, advances by leaps and bounds, so that these schools are always in urgent need of facilities. The legislatures of adjacent States have provided much more bountifully for their colleges affording similar lines of instruction. This parsimony has handicapped every State college in Indiana. Private bequests and endowment is the only way in which Purdue University can be kept up to date, if the General Assembly of Indiana does not assume a more vigorous support of the institution. The United States Experiment Station for Indiana is an organic part of Purdue University, and the very important Farmers' Institutes of the State are conducted by the board and faculty of this college. The different engineering departments are attended by students from every part of the nation. The Mechanical Engineering School has attained an international reputation as one of the foremost schools of its kind in our time.

The lives of the teachers of Indiana, past and present, in the schools and colleges of the State, would be an interesting history of the culture and progress of thought in the commonwealth. The men and women of this profession have been the greatest factors in the State's advance, the most important element in training its citizenship.

In tracing the history of Indiana's schools from the wilderness cabin through the days when all instruction was by paid tuition in private schools and seminaries and when this period was followed by the brave struggle of the more enlightened for a system of free public schools, we have arrived at the summit. In the two State universities the Indiana public school system is logically rounded out. In three quarters of a century, a complete chain of progressive departments of instruction from kindergarten to universities were established. The State may well claim that it

Mechanical Engineering at Purdue University.

has not worked in vain. The outline for the necessary system to be maintained and strengthened has been established. Indiana has taken her place among the foremost States in her provision for popular education. In time the backward districts will be brought up to the general standard; and supplementary legislation will increase the efficiency of the laws for all of the communities. A union of councils between legislators and educators, and harmony between the academic and technical universities should keep Indiana steadily in the front rank of educational affairs.

Owing to the central location of the commonwealth, Indiana colleges should play an important part in the development of interstate community of interests. In speaking of the value, to an Eastern man, of taking a part of his schooling in the middle West, that astute observer, Edward S. Martin, recently said: "The West can make a strong claim to be the most instructive section of our country. It can be argued with much force that the ideas that are most potent in our national life come from there, that the spirit of the West is the dominating American spirit, and that to comprehend the West and live in fellowship with it, is an immensely valuable detail of American education."[1]

[1] Martin, Edward S., in an editorial article in *Harper's Weekly*.

CHAPTER XIX

THE QUALITY OF THE PEOPLE

"WHAT do you value most of all that you have won?" was asked of a frontier woman. Without an instant's hesitation she replied, "The standards by which generations of my family were bred." The ruling class among the early settlers of Indiana were of this mind. It was the severing of these ties, as well as personal loneliness, that added to the pathos of their isolation on the frontier.

No one regrets the extreme democracy of the West. This social freedom, permitting superior individuals no matter what their ancestry was, to rise to their appropriate level, infuses hope into the soul of both the humble of native birth and the Old World immigrant. It develops a vigorous, efficient, and capable population, but it inevitably brings down the average of culture, for several generations. Social conditions in Indiana are typical of the Republic. New people of varying traditions have come into all the States, faster than they could be assimilated and at the same time the general tone of information and culture be kept up to the standard of the most enlightened.

Of this better class are the people who are recognized as being the responsible, representative citizens, who have been the leaders of thought and action in the first century of Indiana's history. No one has given

The Quality of the People

more fitting recognition of this element, which has controlled the State in its short past, than the editor of the *Dial* when he said:

"There is in the middle West, indubitably, a social temper which seeks the best in things of the mind and of the spirit. We have fallen heir—legitimately enough, surely—to the idealism of the New Englander. Perhaps the twin spirits of idealism and shrewd utilitarianism which were pretty clearly to be distinguished in our Yankee forebears have fused in some degree in us, so that at one angle we seem to have lost one, and at another angle the other. Yet they both remain, modified but active, and the result is a social life in reality finer, stronger, more wholesome, at least more vitalized, one may say without offence, than in that older region. Nowhere in America are ideas more welcome. Nowhere are they examined with more self-control. We are the most teachable of communities and we are, beneath everything, the most aspiring. If we are naïve, if we lack urbanity, finish, it is because we are fresh, exuberant, and very young. But those who come to know the life of the West come to realize that its humanity is large and deep, and that its grave and kindly spirit will bear us far. The quality of moral and intellectual earnestness, that is, the main current of the life of our region, is pretty generally underestimated. Yet it is the factor, one believes, of greatest importance in the life of America to-day. It is well for the West to recognize this, not boastfully, but with a sense of all it involves."

To say that Indiana differs in enlightenment in any respect from the other States is not in accordance with the facts. The dominant race, the master force in its civilization, has remained the Anglo-Saxon strain which was attracted by the fertile acres. They came over the mountains from the English families settled in the sea-coast colonies and later from the other States. Colonel Cockrum, who knew so many of the old settlers, says: "As a whole the people who were the pioneers of this State were from the best families of the countries from which they moved; intelligent, brave, hearty, and honest." The change of habits, the new environment, the very fertility of the soil, the remoteness from older civilizations, the untrammelled spirit of the frontier, produced a variant of the type, without doubt; but the racial characteristics, and relative social position, have been maintained. Indiana, like the other States, has had her share of immigration from foreign countries. There was the handful of French who were left of the settlements at the posts on the Wabash, the early accessions of Scotch-Irish, the Swiss vineyard-planters who settled along the Ohio, and a wave of European refugees, fleeing from the ill-fated conditions in their fatherlands during the Napoleonic wars. Later there were hordes of Irish and German laborers, who were imported into the central counties to work on the canals and other internal improvements. Then gradually, as the years passed, and factories were established, and the coal mines were developed, all nationalities joined the original population; but there has been comparatively little intermarriage between the educated people of the English strain and later arrivals. They were welcomed and they prospered, but they became one with the communities without these alliances. It has required all of the energies of the progressive citizenship to assimilate these accessions. Ere the whole population could become enlightened, self-controlled, and delicately considerate of others, there was a new immigration at hand.

In Indiana, education was early regarded as the "deepest hope of all ultimate, attainable qualities," and the public school and university system was established. There are few congested centres of population in the commonwealth, and there is work for all who are able to do manual labor, but it is a slow process to bring these accessions up to the average. The cause of backward conditions in *material improvements* which are the *outward manifestation of progressive people* seems to be the *force of inertia* in these uncultured classes. This inertia also reaches into the class elected to office, and prevents desirable State and municipal legislation. The shiftlessness and ignorance of this minority are what hampers the progress toward well-kept cities and farms, but this fact is common to all of the States.

Formerly, the term *Hoosier* meant a backwoodsman, to a resident on the Atlantic coast. As late as the Centennial exhibition in Philadelphia, two gentlemen of birth and lineage from the Wabash, both descended from old colonial stock, and both of commanding presence, personally, overheard an Eastern woman say: "Well, I've seen the glories of the earth here. I've seemed to travel from the Occident to the Orient, but before I go home I should like to see a genuine Hoosier." The humor of the situation was too much for our unintentional eavesdroppers. The two gentlemen, with habitual courtly grace, turned, and bowing said, "By your leave, madam, we present ourselves as humble citizens of Indiana." Disillusioned, one more denizen of the East went home after a friendly interstate chat with the gentlemen—with a fairer appreciation of Hoosierdom.

By the part played in the Civil War, Indiana placed herself, as it were, among the States. The gallant record of her troops, and the conspicuous ability of her war governor and citizens, revealed to the East the position the State had gradually grown to occupy, while they had still been thinking of the Wabash as the frontier, and Hoosiers as benighted. In 1906, the New York *Sun* called attention to the fact that Indiana was the only State which had a solid delegation of college-bred men in the two houses of Congress. Massachusetts had theretofore ranked highest in this particular. The Indiana men, however, have an unbroken record of collegiate education.

It is admitted that the West in general has "contributed to manners a certain frankness of demeanor, a certain unquestioning sincerity in the attitude of man to man, which has a beauty, no less than moral value, quite beyond appraisal. In course of time the manner developed from this fundamental trait of frankness, and coupled with real refinement, should become the most gracious and altogether charming that American life has yet evolved." Nevertheless, "vulgarity is an eighth deadly sin," as Lowell says, "and worse than all the others put together since it perils your salvation in this world." But Europeans and Chinese criticise the manners of our older States, with condescension; and mayhap it will always be that the older civilizations will be critical of the younger.

Indiana people of culture especially resent the pronouncement of one of their prominent politicians, that "Indiana achieves the true meaning of the common people. It is the home of the average American." They claim that such a statement belies history, that such an assertion proceeds from the demagogue who is fond of referring to the people, but never claims to belong to them unless he is running for office. Gentle birth has been the heritage of the real leaders of thought and life in the Hoosier State from its beginning. It is interesting to note in Oliver Smith's reminiscences how many gentlemen with talents and manners he found among the pioneers who continued in public life until his time. Speaking of some, he tells of their "energy that never slumbered, their integrity that was never questioned, their high conception of morality and religion, coupled with social qualities of the first order." Again he introduces to us a group of which one was "a courteous and polished gentleman," another "is a fine scholar and well-read man," and another "a distinguished specimen of the last generation."

General Lew Wallace says of his father, who was one of the pioneers of the State:

"Added to the graces, he had a pleasant voice and manner more stately and gracious than we meet to-day; the urbane sweetness to which we give the name of high breeding. There were fewer books then, and they were of the best, and constant familiarity with them gave a stateliness of speech and a certain dignity that comes of keeping good company. They dined with Horace and supped with Plutarch, and were scholars without knowing it."[1]

An early settler tells of a new book that was reported in a neighboring settlement: "At last there came a day when my father could spare a horse from the plow, and I went in quest of the book, which was

[1] Wallace, Lew, *Autobiography*. New York, 1906.

found, borrowed, and read with a zest now unknown, for it was one of Sir Walter Scott's immortal stories." The gentle influence of these cultured families was a welcome leaven in frontier neighborhoods; and later, as Mr. Nicholson has said, "the older Indiana towns enjoyed in their beginning all the benefits that may be bestowed upon new communities by a people of good social antecedents. In no old community of the seaboard had loftier dignity been conferred by long residence or pioneer ancestry, than in Indiana."[1] Hon. Hugh McCulloch came out from New England and settled in Indiana in 1833, and knew the whole State well; of it he says:

"Indianapolis was fortunate in the character of its early settlement. Such men are rarely found in any place. Their superiors in intelligence, in enterprise, and moral worth can be found nowhere. What was true in regard to the early settlers of Indianapolis was also true of those in many other Indiana towns. Nor have their successors been degenerate. No State has been more prolific of superior men than Indiana."[2]

Writing of one of the older towns, George Cary Eggleston said: "I have before me a long list, which I forbear to copy, of men who made Madison, or its near neighborhood, their home at that time, and who were conspicuously distinguished in State and nation for their intellectual achievements."[3]

The careers of public men who have place in the pages of history cannot be touched upon in a volume

[1] Nicholson, Meredith, *Hoosiers*. New York, 1900.
[2] McCulloch, Hugh, *Men and Measures of Half a Century*, page 72. New York, 1888.
[3] Eggleston, George Cary, *First of the Hoosiers*. Fenno, New York, 1903.

"Often from morning until night there was a continual rumble of wheels, and when the rush was greatest there never was a minute that wagons were not in sight."
From an old print.

like this, but their abilities and their attainments must be considered in any estimate of the State's average of citizenship. Running over the list of governors, senators, and congressmen from the earliest time, the Indiana officials will be found representative of American ability, occupying those positions in each decade. A State which has furnished a President and three Vice-Presidents to the United States, who have all "magnified the office," and done honor to the commonwealth in those exalted positions, may lay claim to sending out representative men. The numerous Cabinet officers called from Indiana, in the course of the history of the country, have shown the quality of the State's public men, one of whom served as Secretary of the Treasury for three different Presidents. The rank of Indiana diplomatists at foreign courts and consulates has been second to none, and they have rendered distinguished service to the nation in these positions. As naval and military commanders, of high and low degree, no State has surpassed the officers of Indiana. Nor were any men braver fighters than the Hoosier regiments.

In letters and the arts there are men whom all delight to honor, and her faithful educators compare with any other section of the country. Scientists she has the results of whose investigations are watched for all over the world. It may be safely claimed that there is not a capital city of any other State in the Union whose citizens have maintained, through a quarter of a century, a club of representative men that could surpass the well-known Gentlemen's Literary Club of Indianapolis. In the national fame of its membership, the interest of the papers and discussions, the quality of its literary work, and the breadth of view and wide reading of the men who for many years past have served on its programs, there is no commonwealth but would be honored in possessing such a circle. The same might be claimed for similar circles in the other cities of Indiana.

It is not alone the men and women who have remained and labored within the State that show the quality of its people. The men who were born there, but who have gone out from Indiana, in earlier or mature years, also denote the character of her settlement. John Hay, one of the greatest premiers the United States has had, was born at Salem, Indiana, and his writings and great diplomatic career reflect credit on the State of his birth. John B. Eads, the civil engineer of the Mississippi jetties and constructor of St. Louis bridge, came from the Hoosier State. Joaquin Miller, the poet of the Sierras, first looked upon nature from the hills of southern Indiana, and the young poet William Vaughn Moody was born in New Albany. Dr. Billings, who manages the libraries of all Manhattan Island, was born at Rising Sun, Indiana. Hiram Powers, the sculptor, was from this State, and William M. Chase, the noted painter, who encourages and inspires, aids and cheers, the rising artists who come up to New York, was born in Johnson County, and began his art work in Indianapolis. Henry Mosler, the talented genre painter, now claimed by Cincinnati, is a native of Indiana. General Joseph E. Johnston, Generals Carrington and Burnside of great military fame, and Admiral Glisson and Commander Herndon were born in the Whitewater Valley. General Lawton has added laurels to his name and that of the State; and Erasmus Weaver serves the nation, as well as his native commonwealth, in the councils of war and defence. Robert U. Johnson, long the editor of the *Century Magazine*, was born in Indiana, and Mr. Roswell-Smith went from the State to found that periodical. Another editor who honors the field of Eastern journalism is George Cary Eggleston, also from the Hoosier State. Charles Denby gave the most valuable years of his life to the service of the nation as its representative during those trying years in the Orient. John W. Foster, though living in Washington, keeps closely in sympathy with his native State, and no man of the present day has rendered more brilliant service to his country in diplomacy. George B. Williams of Washington, now interested in international shipping contracts, went from Indiana to formulate Japan's revenue system. The work of Harvey W. Wiley in the United States Agricultural Department, for pure foods and the advance of science, reflects great credit on the Hoosier State, of which he is a native. Judge Landis of the Federal Court is a member of a large family who have served Indiana. International recognition of Charles R. Henderson as an authority on measures for social betterment, in charities and corrections and kindred works, is also a recognition of an Indiana man, and the State's interest in those matters. Professor John W. Coulter's pre-eminence in botanical research means a credit mark to an Indiana family, as well as the work in the same line done within the State by Dean Stanley Coulter. Professor Charles Barnes has distinguished himself in the same science, and the Director of Dresden's great orchestra is Clark of Indiana.

The membership of the "Indiana Society of Chicago" shows that the Hoosier State has contributed judges, authors, poets, artists, bankers, journalists, and engineers of note and signal ability, to Chicago's commercial and intellectual life. Those of Hoosier birth in that city are too many to enumerate; but they are known to all, as now occupying places of honor and great responsibility in that busy centre of the nation.

The list of past and living Hoosiers who have added to the history of achievement throughout the Republic might be lengthened indefinitely. But enough have been mentioned to emphasize the statement that the character of the population of the State, however plain and simple, is not the "common people." Indiana produces men and women of marked ability, who, whether they go out from her borders to do their life-work or remain identified with the history of the State, show that they are more than the "average American."

In writing of his exhaustive and analytical search into the origin of the term *Hoosier*, Mr. Dunn very truly says: "The essential point is, that Indiana and her people had nothing whatever to do with its origin or significance. It was applied to us in raillery, and our only connection with it is that we have borne it meekly for some three score years and ten, and have made it widely recognized as a badge of honor, rather than a term of reproach." In the language of Mr. Maurice Thompson, "Say Hoosier, if you like, but say it with admiration and pride."

CHAPTER XX

AGRICULTURE IN INDIANA

IN the very opening of the history of Indiana, the French settlers did little in agriculture beyond cultivating, in communistic fashion, the gardens and fields about the forts, under the encouragement of the priests. The French trader opposed agricultural settlements, because they destroyed his trade in peltries, and the Jesuit was sometimes hostile to them, because they dispersed the Indians and removed his mission field. The French Government gave no land grants, at many of the posts, hence there was no permanency of settlements as where some system of land-holding prevailed. When the American settlers came out from the Eastern coast, it was to make homes and cultivate the land.

Marquis Duquesne himself had shown the Indians, before he left in 1754, the difference there would be to them between the English and French colonization: reminded them that the Frenchman was not a menace to their game areas, that they could hunt to the very walls of the French forts, and that those forts were placed conveniently for trading-stations with the natives; that the inhabitants were only a garrison; and they had their lands as tenants of the crown. On the other hand, the English moved the frontier forward, only to possess the land. They felled the forests, planted the ground, and the game disappeared. Congregations and communities were established at every favorable landing where the products of the soil might be shipped to the markets of the world. They grew steadily into independent States, instead of remaining dependent colonies that had to be fed from over seas. The magnificent forests that were found growing over a large part of Indiana indicated an exceedingly rich soil, more productive than any State east of it, and from the time of the first clearings it has been pre-eminently an agricultural State, there being but few acres of its twenty-three million that cannot be cultivated.

"After a personal inspection of a great part of the United States, I have seen no portion of the Union more beautiful in appearance or one combining so many advantages as that which is watered by the Wabash River," wrote Henry L. Ellsworth when he was Land Commissioner at Washington, and he took up great tracts of land in the valley of that river. In 1843, in his message Governor Whitcomb said: "Our position, soil, and climate point to that branch of labor devoted to agriculture as our chief reliance for lasting wealth and prosperity. This calling should rank first in respectability as it is unquestionably the first in importance to the State."

An old settler, speaking of Indiana's geographical position as a great factor in her future prosperity, said that "lying directly across the track, for all time, of all the great artificial improvements that can ever be made connecting the East with the Pacific, over the valley of the Mississippi, coupled with the fact that she is so highly favored in climate, soil, mineral,

The Entrance to School Garden, Delphi, Indiana.

wood, water, and rock, we can see that Indiana combines all of the elements of a great and growing State."

Into this territory, where the aborigines had raised their crops by making holes in the ground with bone hoes and dropping in a seed, to come up without further cultivation than scratching the soil a little, the first farmers came. They began their primitive culture by cutting down or girdling the forest trees, and cultivated their first crops between the stumps. Generally they paid for their lands by selling the pelts of the wild animals which they had shot in the woods. Often the ploughshare was the only piece of iron in their equipment. The rest of that implement was made by the farmer himself from white oak; as also was made his harrow, both timbers and teeth. All of the farmer's implements were well pinned together with hickory pins, through holes that were burned out, for he had no auger. In winter rudely fashioned sleds, hauled by plodding oxen, carried the farmer's crops and timber to market. Wooden rakes were universal, and pitch-forks were made from the forked boughs of a tree, or the antlers of an elk. The cabin of the settler, the mortar for grinding grain, the cider press, the tannery, the implements of toil, were all made at home, and without nails, screws, or bolts.

Comfortable homes, great granaries, and barns have long ago displaced these primitive surroundings. It is interesting to recount the various movements and influences that have contributed to the rapid progress of the farming community. First, because earliest and most continuous, must be accounted the rural churches and Sabbath-schools, with the social assembling of all ages for worship and friendly intercourse, as the greatest means of the development in Indiana farm life.

Next to the church gatherings, the earliest stimulus the farmer had to do better things, materially, was the organization of the State and county fairs. There had been several successful county fairs held in Indiana before the first State fair occurred in 1852, and Governor Wright urged the people to organize a State institution for the promotion of friendly rivalry in agriculture. It was a new idea in the Western States and the first exhibition was a success. The records show that the first Indiana State fair lasted through three days, each one of which was marked by the balmy sunshine of Indian summer; over thirty thousand Indiana people were on the fair grounds during the three days, and this first State fair was a successful one for the times, in a financial way, in exhibits, and in attendance. It called together town and country men from remote sections of the State. People started from home days before the fair opened, some driving horses, and others being content with the slow pace of oxen that drew their wagons. It was the first general exhibit of the products of the labor and skill of the people. The stock-raisers of Indiana sent their sleekest cattle to the fair in 1852, as they have done every year since. They also sent their largest and finest horses, the fattest from their herds, the best products from the field and orchard, and the best from their looms.

There were plowing contests between farmer boys, who drove either horses or oxen. There were exhibits of many new inventions in farm machinery, very helpful in informing the farmer. The new art of taking daguerreotypes claimed many patrons. Staves cut by machinery collected a crowd of sight-seers. Homespun fabrics and spinning-wheels were shown side by side with the recently introduced invention called sewing-machines, which enlisted the greatest curiosity, because of their novelty. There were half a dozen railroads in operation in the State by that time, and they carried in thousands of people to the fair who had never been on a train before! The plank roads passed animals free of toll, and the roads were lined with exhibits going into town. One newspaper contained the editorial announcement that it was sure the State fair would infuse into the farmers a just pride in the utility and greatness of their pursuits, and "that a laudable ambition to have the mantel decorated with a silver cup will actuate all, and, thus feeling and acting, who can calculate the ultimate result?"

In the earlier years of the State fair, energy was directed to building up public interest in the enterprise, and with this purpose in view the fair was held at various points in the State. The chief reason for this was to bring it within reach of all the people, and to maintain the interest that the first fair had won. The other reason was, the State Board of Agriculture was in its infancy; its treasury had nothing behind it but the faith and good-will of the people. It had no permanent home. The State Board borrowed from county fair associations the use of their grounds in these earlier years. In 1853, the second State fair was held, at Lafayette. Horace Greeley delivered the speech, which was made one of the chief attractions. The next season the State fair was held at Madison. Until 1868, the fair was migratory. In 1861, the strife of war cast a gloom over its career. Soldiers were camping on the grounds, and no exhibition could be held that year. The misfortunes of the war followed the fair through the years of 1862 and 1863, when the institution lost money. In 1868, the fair came back to Indianapolis, to wander no more from county to county. The attendance has increased since its salad days with the growth of the population, until now fully 164,000 people are in attendance.

The social side of all of the agricultural fairs cannot be overlooked in estimating the benefits derived from them. The people come up to their county exhibitions, renew old friendships, and make new acquaintances, which is a most wholesome variation of the daily treadmill of their isolated existence. The people have been loyal to these local institutions too; one prosperous farmer's wife, who was going for a tour of Europe, said, "I shall not go until after our county fair; my husband and I have not missed a session since its organization." Lectures and demonstrations in agriculture and domestic science are generally held on the grounds in connection with the exhibition. These advantages contribute to their educational value.

The fairs have always been the largest means of making known improvements in farm machinery, which has manifolded the labors of each man on the farm. To appreciate the lightening of toil by invention applied to farm implements, we only need to recall that until 1840 grain was mown with scythe and sickle; and great bands of reapers were necessary to gather the golden crop. These troops of men went from the southern to the northern part of the State, garnering the harvest as it ripened in each district. After the grain-cradle was introduced, a man could reap the great area of two acres a day! In those

Children Crating their Tomato Crop in the School Garden at Delphi, Indiana.

times the grain was threshed out with a flail or tramped out by horses and winnowed through sieves. The first crude threshing-machines had a capacity of thirty to sixty bushels of wheat a day, and the chaff must be separated by men using wooden rakes and forks in the choking dust. Afterwards they must drop the grain from an elevation, at the same time dexterously fanning it with a tow sheet. Lieutenant Governor Cumback used to be fond of telling that when his father bought an improvement for this labor, in the form of a fanning-mill, he was taken to task by a devout neighbor, who maintained that, as it was a "wind contrary to nature," it must be displeasing to the Almighty. Soon there were travelling threshers, with six horses and twice as many men, who astonished the agricultural world by threshing two hundred bushels a day! Later steam machines appeared and two thousand bushels were threshed out, and the dust blown far from the sweltering laborers. The improvement in farm machinery for other purposes was equally startling. Indiana now stands near the head of the line in the manufacture of these implements and vehicles.

The introduction of machinery was the greatest factor in the increase of the comforts of living and the efficiency of labor on the farm, in Indiana, as elsewhere. When we remember the primitive implements of the past, we think with patience of the boys who left the farm. The future before the Hoosier on the farm is the ideal life, where the work is to be done by the combined use of brains and machines, when electricity from the streams will perform the toil, and science will have added to the productiveness of the acres.

The first Governor of the infant commonwealth, Jonathan Jennings, was a farmer and deserves the honor of being the man who introduced clover into the State. He imported the seed from England in 1832, paying thirty-five dollars a bushel for it.

In 1862, President Lincoln gave his approval to the bills creating the Agricultural Commission, and to the land grant act, establishing colleges of agriculture in all the States, which Buchanan had vetoed two sessions before. This grant was the largest ever made to education, and was the foundation of industrial education in America, which is to revolutionize methods of higher instruction. In Indiana, the results of this act, and a further one of the State Legislature taking advantage of it, was the establishment of Purdue University at Lafayette in 1874. The value of the agricultural department of this school to the State is only limited by the appropriations made by the Legislature for its further upbuilding. Other States should not be allowed to outstrip it, either in the initiative of its management or in its equipment, if Indiana is to keep pace with its neighbors on every side. Indiana's agricultural university gave instruction to more than one hundred thousand people of the State in 1907. This multitude was reached through the regular college course, the short course in agriculture, the Farmers' Institutes, and that popular form of instruction of sending out corn and fruit excursion trains through the counties. These trains carry valuable exhibits of superior products of the soil, and specimens showing the ravages made by insects. Lecturers from the staff of the university accompany the train, and instruct the assembled farmers.

Besides the agricultural fairs, and the establishment

of a great university as the fountain head of all progressive work, the Farmers' Institute, promoted by that university, and conducted by its staff of teachers, is one of the most broadening influences in the rural life of Indiana. It is recognized that the Farmers' Institute is to the adult farmer what the agricultural school is to his son. Through the papers read at these meetings, and the discussions which ensue, the farmer receives the benefit of years of study and investigation by scientific men. Another very practical mission is performed by the university in connection with its "short course in agriculture," which is held in January each year; that is, the assembling of the Corn School, and other agricultural organizations, within the very walls of the university. These sessions are attended by enthusiastic farmers, numbering over a thousand, who are intent on learning better methods. Scores of their wives and daughters are enrolled in the courses of domestic science, poultry-raising, dairy work, and horticulture. The faculty of the university, speakers from the Agricultural Department at Washington, and practical growers and agriculturists, give the lectures. Competent judges pass upon the prizes to be awarded to youths, who are entered for practice in judging exhibits. These annual meetings at the college have double the value of conventions held elsewhere; for the members receive definite scientific instruction. They also have the advantage of practical demonstrations in the raising of stock, grain, and fruits, coupled with strict judging of the products displayed. The close examination of 2025 exhibits of the best seed that can be raised in Indiana, and 133 different exhibits of fruits as well as prize cattle and dairy products, were among the practical object lessons of the 1908 session.

The grange, as now organized and conducted, is one of the important steps for improvement instituted by the agricultural classes. Being on a co-operative and educational basis, and non-political, it can work for the betterment of conditions in rural life along so many lines that its influence in the future should be vast. In Indiana its membership is growing steadily. As it is a "family club" and holds county, State, and national meetings, it necessarily follows that when the grange chooses to address itself to vital questions it can sway a multitude of opinions, and be a great force in the commonwealth.

Agricultural and live-stock journals, and kindred departments in the regular newspapers, have been a most potent influence in the history of Indiana farm life. They bring inspiration, information, and entertainment into the farmer's home. The ability and knowledge engaged in this editorial work is commensurate with the wide influence of their pages. Perhaps the periodicals of no other trade or calling have more attractive pages than those published for country life. Not only the useful reading matter is valuable, but the illustrations are surpassingly beautiful. To be a progressive farmer in this day, without the agricultural and live-stock periodicals, is not to be imagined. The State publications and all other journals of merit have their hosts of subscribers in rural Indiana. It requires but a glance over the papers on the table of a representative farmer to estimate their usefulness to him.

Indiana is showing the results of all these influences in the increased productiveness of her areas, the extension of good roads, the comfort of the farm-houses, and barns for cattle, and the improvement

Prize Crop Raised by a Member of the Boys' Corn Club in Laporte County, Indiana.

in schools. These all demonstrate the progressive spirit of the agricultural communities. At the National Corn Show of 1907 out of eight thousand exhibits, shown from all of the corn-growing States, those from Indiana were declared superior. A single first-prize ear of Johnson County White Dent corn, raised by a gentleman from Franklin, Indiana, sold for $250.00. Twenty-five other prizes were taken by Indiana farmers, which shows what intelligent growers can do, with this soil and climate. Indiana also won "every blue ribbon" in some classes of horses and cattle at the live-stock shows of the same year. That there is large room for further improvement must be admitted, when the claim is conceded that the present population may increase fourfold and still get its living from the soil that is now in cultivation; that the resources of the country, in unimproved areas, will admit an increase of population twice that amount with scientific, intensive farming!

Probably nothing of more importance has been inaugurated on Hoosier soil than the movement to introduce elementary study of agriculture into the free public schools, to which we have alluded in the chapter on Education. In time this work should revolutionize farm life in Indiana. It gives an ideal education for the average farmer's sons and daughters, and turns the attention of town youths toward the country. In speaking upon this important innovation, a lecturer from the university said truly: "The study of agriculture in country schools, in most of its ramifications, is of perennial and universal interest. It sustains a vital relation to the life and well-being of the individual, and of the community. The subject is not only interesting and inspiring, but it is also definitely practical. It has to do with the problem of bread and butter. It deals with the here and now." Another reason for the study of elementary agriculture, which applies particularly to the rural schools, is the right of the country children to a school training which will specially prepare them for life on the farm. The great majority of these children do not attend school beyond the eighth grade. If special instruction in the elements of agriculture is denied them before that grade is finished they must be greatly handicapped in their efforts to win success and become useful citizens. An agricultural high school, supported by a group of counties, which would give a sound industrial training for the boys and girls who are not to go further, with the agricultural university maintained as the pinnacle of the educational scheme, is the intention of Indiana educators. In a most interesting paper, Professor Hays has outlined the plan of the high school as suited to the agricultural districts, in which he says that the course covers three winters of six months each, leaving the student on the home farm during the six crop months, where the industrial, business, and social position is retained unbroken. With this arrangement eighty-two per cent. of the graduates remain in agriculture, seventy per cent. actually return to the farm! In the history of agricultural Indiana this is a most important step in advance. Evidence of the wonderful interest inspired by these elementary lessons in agriculture in the district schools is given in the displays of results already achieved by the pupils. Many counties have organized clubs for the study of the problems of tillage, soil, and seeds. Any pupil, boy or girl, who is regularly enrolled in the school and doing creditable work may enter the contest. Seed is distributed to them after preliminary instructions have been given; and bulletins on corn-growing, issued by the university, are distributed to the members. Prizes are offered, and experienced judges are provided when the crop is exhibited. During the season of growth of the little plantations, the pupils are expected to keep notes of the kind of soil, amount of moisture, cultivation, drainage, and yield from their individual plot. When the date arrives for the display of the products it is made a gala time. In some districts there is a procession, headed by a band of music. Often there is a corn dinner, cooked and served by the girls of the club. Some organizations have given trolley excursions to visit Purdue University, where they view other exhibits.

Most of the boys of the clubs have been reported as very successful growers. Some of the plots of ground planted by them have produced at the rate of a hundred bushels to the acre. When sold for seed the prize packages in many places sold for $2.00, and none of the corn brought in to the contest sold for less than $2.00 a bushel.

The influence of these clubs reaches out over the whole country where they are organized, provoking rivalry among the farmers too, and arousing their attention to the importance of careful selection of seed, and the scientific cultivation of the crops. This extended mention of the school clubs is justified in a sketch of agriculture in Indiana, because it is the most practical progressive step in the history of farming, and shows what advancement the whole State may make in productive wealth, when the work of the county schools is based on the dominant interest of the community.

The history of the agricultural districts in Indiana shows that they have steadily endeavored to throw off the yoke of intemperance, which hampers prosperity in the cities and reaches out for the countryman. Three fourths of the townships of the State now prohibit the sale of liquor, and every year the list of "dry" townships, and even counties, grows longer. This movement against the liquor traffic in the country districts is full of hope for the future, and will prove of priceless value to the commonwealth.

When factories superseded, to a certain extent, the home-made productions, agricultural Indiana added a new industry in the form of truck farming. The canning establishments which have sprung up within the factory era have provided an enlarged market for the produce of the small farmer living near these enterprises. Several hundred thousand acres in the State are now devoted to this purpose, and it gives a greater chance for variety of crops. Probably 2,900,000 bushels of tomatoes alone are now produced annually.

The labor of woman on the farms, in the raising of poultry and fruits and the making of butter, has become an enormous economic factor in rural commerce. In Indiana the greater part of poultry and eggs is raised by the women; and the value of this product in the last year reached over fifteen and a quarter millions of dollars. The influence of women in the agricultural communities of Indiana does not stop with the commercial side. Her part in the Farmers' Institutes, Sunday-school conventions, church meetings, sessions of the grange, in the day schools, and the county and State fairs is fully equal to that

The Entrance to Purdue University.

of the men. Mrs. Virginia Meredith of Indiana is a well known exponent of agricultural instruction and progress, in theory and practice; but she can call to her aid scores of efficient workers, from every part of the State, in all forward movements for the rural communities.

With a soil so rich as that in Indiana, good roads were felt, from the very dawn of her history, to be a vital necessity, as there seemed to be no bottom to the trail through the forests. The early settlers were ever floundering through mud-holes, fording streams, and helping one another's teams out of a quagmire. The improvement of the highways has been steady but very deliberate. Some districts are still far in advance of others, with a consequent effect on their prosperity. Wells County built one hundred and two miles of gravel roads last year, while another county built but one. The constant agitation of the subject by a few enterprising men in each district has added a thousand miles a year since 1900 to the sum total of good roads, which now reaches the number of 16,268 miles. Shades of the forefathers, who had to travel on horseback through the mud, bear witness and hope for more! Indiana may take pattern from the interesting story told by Joseph Brown, apropos of better roads, and how one neighborhood attained them. His story goes that

"After John Tyler retired from the presidency of the United States, his neighbors of the other party, as a sort of a practical joke, and also perhaps to show their opinion of his capacity, got together and elected him roadmaster, but they wot not that they were casting a boomerang. John accepted the office. The Virginia law gives this functionary almost unlimited power in calling out citizens for road service, and the distinguished roadmaster made the most of his privilege. For about three months that year, in season and out of season, he worked his constituency on the public highways, till they wished they had n't done it. Tyler stood the joke better than they did, and the travelling public got the benefits."

Purdue University authorities have for some time been making a careful study of the good roads question in the State, and received reports from hundreds of farmers, some of whom live on good roads once bad, and others on roads still bad. From these reports they have computed statistics, showing that the difference between good and bad roads amounts to seventy-eight cents an acre annually on the farms. Multiplying this amount by the entire State—23,264,000 acres—we have the sum of $18,145,920. Of this amount, fully two thirds is wasted every year in the State in the loss of time, and in the loss of opportunity in securing the best market for the produce of the farm. As State Geologist Blatchley points out, Indiana is rich in clay suitable for vitrified brick, rich in gravel, rich in stone for macadam roads. There are plenty of convicts needing the exercise, who could manufacture these products in private. There is no reason, therefore, why every public road of any importance in the State should not be improved, so that it can be travelled with ease any day in the year.

Rural mail delivery, where the roads warrant it, has added more to the convenience and pleasure of country life than any provision of the government since regular mail service was first provided.

Another event in rural Indiana's history was the building of electric roads which have been extended across the State. Over thirteen hundred miles of these rapid transit conveniences now pass the doors of Indiana farmers, bringing them in close communication with town and market. Telephones and automobiles have also added to the luxury of living. Land values are increased by the combined agencies of these modern conveniences; and the isolation which causes so many to desert the farm, and makes labor so scarce, will be largely overcome by rapid transit.

The greatest single instrument of progress in agriculture in Indiana has been the progressive spirit of individuals. In the century of Indiana's history, from territorial days onward, there have been so many men who have led their immediate district into more progressive agricultural practices, that any personal mention would leave out great numbers who have been a blessing to the State by improving the conditions in their own neighborhoods. Biographies of statesmen, politicians, and military men figure largely in history, but the available "short and simple annals" of farmers are so scarce that it is almost necessary to treat of them as a group. To improve the quality of seed corn or potatoes, or to import better live-stock into a region, deserves the commendation of him who "makes two blades of grass grow where one grew before." Some of these progressive residents of the State were individuals whose business did not permit them to live in the country, but who had such a genuine love for the soil that they have always been farmers in addition to their other duties, and have found pleasure and profit to themselves and their neighbors in practical agriculture. These men have helped to inspire their farmer acquaintances with increased pleasure in country life, and enthusasm in tilling the soil. They have encouraged road-building, and better rural schools, introduced new fruits, poultry, and grain, and raised the grade of cattle and horses.

Among the first registered live stock in Indiana, it is said, were the pure-bred short-horn cattle brought into the State in 1825 by Edward Talbott. Since that time, the values in live-stock farming have been immensely increased by the interests maintained in Indiana on the special breeding farms. The cattle and horses shown every year by experienced and enterprising men in Indiana have commanded prizes in State and international exhibitions. These leaders have stood for high standards in pure breeding. The value of their famous herds of cattle, and breeding farms of horses, sheep, and swine, to the general farming interests of Indiana, is not to be calculated by their own financial returns.

"We have a self-satisfied way of considering [says the *Gazette*] that all the pioneering has been done in the work of live-stock improvements in America. We could not think farther off the true line. The whole rural community must be brought forward. It is easy enough to have faith in that which is demonstrated before our eyes by these breeders of pedigreed stock; and we may go ahead along a line marked out by a neighbor, when we hear the clink of the golden coin as it jingles in his pocket."

The National Registry Associations, which maintain the "strict letter of the law" in live-stock pedigrees, have always had Indiana men identified with their management. The active secretaries have given many years to the supervision of correct registry of live stock, as a means of keeping up the standards to the highest grade, and these citizens must be enrolled among the vital influences of progress in the industry.

Regarding the outlook for the future of agriculture in Indiana, the following statements in the *Indiana Farmer* regarding farming in the middle West are very pertinent.

"The writer moved five hundred miles east, to his present location, because of the rapid division of Western ranges and ranches into small farms. By thus increasing the value of the arid lands they place the East on a fair competing basis with the far West. Western ranges which formerly yielded unlimited free grass to all comers are now on an acre basis; it must be seen that the middle West is now able to compete fairly with the far West in cattle-raising."

Another reason for expecting continued prosperity in the profession of farming is that Indiana's field crops are fairly divided into the great staple products of wheat, oats, timothy, and clover, averaging between one and two million acres of each; all of which are in steady demand. For corn the average runs over four million acres.

Dairy farming in Indiana has been very largely confined to the northern counties, and near the capital. But her geographical position seems to indicate a sustained future demand for this industry. Indeed, Indiana farmers are fortunate in being about the centre of things, for markets, temperate climate, fertility of soil, and transportation. Under these favorable conditions, intensive farming is an assurance of increased income in the future.

In closing a sketch of Indiana's progress in agriculture, it is not amiss to recall again that, owing to her geographical position, the State is spread before the eyes of the travelling world. If she has shiftless farms and untidy villages, they are " seen of all men." More thrift is desirable, not only for increased revenues to individuals, but for the good name of the State. The following thoughtful suggestion from a Winona Agricultural Institute address is most invaluable to rural Indiana:

"During the next few years we may be sure that lawn-planting, as an art, will develop into a most important feature of home life of the humblest owner of a spot of ground. An abundant variety of trees, blooming plants, ferns, and trailing vines may be found hidden and unseen by the man that owns them. What a wealth of education and enjoyment they would bring into everyday life, if a goodly portion of them were placed near the house; such decoration would be a source of pleasure to those doing the work, and to all the occupants of the home."

Most farmers try to cultivate too much land, and they would in many cases grow rich faster if they cultivated less land and planted the less productive places, the odd bits, the rough stony fields, and abrupt slopes, the small irregular lots in the angles, with trees, that would beautify their place and in time add value to the property. In the future, the home garden and dooryard, well kept, as part of the real farm work, is to be the distinguishing mark of the domain of the enlightened farmer.

CHAPTER XXI

NATURAL RESOURCES

MOST of the natural products necessary for modern existence may be found within the limits of the State of Indiana. Without surpassing States that have a larger area, she comes within the first ten in the development of a large range of products and deposits. This makes residence within her borders far more desirable than if she possessed in abundance any one of the precious metals, to the exclusion of necessities. The variety of the agricultural resources of the State has been considered elsewhere. They have always been counted as her chief source of wealth, but the geographical position of the State, and the development of the deposits in the geological strata underneath the surface, make manufacturing also a great source of profit. Most of the natural resources of Indiana lie undeveloped, and none of them has been exhausted. The maximum of agricultural crops has not been approached; the mineral deposits await the demands of the future. The uses to be made of Indiana's limited lake shore is an undeveloped feature of the great commercial life that is only dawning upon its business world. Already great manufacturing interests have recognized the availability of combined harbor and railway facilities possessed by the extreme northwestern portion of the State. This district formerly had no inhabitants but huntsmen in quest of game. Now, vast industries, which will require a great population to carry them on, are being established, making the whilom sand dunes and marshes of great commercial importance.

Of the wealth of timber once possessed by the State there is but a fraction remaining. Statistics show that more than four-fifths of the area, at its settlement, was heavily timbered with the most valuable varieties of forest growth. There were the many varieties of oaks, walnut, ash, cherry, poplar, elm, maples, hickories, beech, cottonwood, sycamore, and more than one hundred other varieties. Much of this timber was very large; an early explorer left a memorandum of blazing a sycamore that was forty feet around. The official measurements of the State Statistician gives authentic record of oaks—black, white, burr, and scarlet varieties—that were six and seven feet in diameter and a hundred and ninety feet in height. This fine timber was an encumbrance to the early settler, who had no market for it and must raise breadstuffs. What would now be worth billions of dollars was rolled into great piles and burned, when there was more than could be used for fences and fuel, in order to clear the land for cultivation of crops. For many years the corn raised on these same lands would not sell for more than ten cents a bushel. As lumber came into demand, later on, Indiana was almost devastated of hard-wood timber. Her forests furnished enormous amounts of the hard woods used in the manufactories of the country. In the early days, there were great areas covered with sugar-maple trees, which served the settlers as "sugar orchards," and sugar-making time was a season of harvesting the annual sweets. The Indians were as fond of maple sugar as the white man. One red chief, who had been sent west of the Mississippi to a reservation with his tribe, stole off and wandered back to his old haunts in Indiana, grunting "must have maple sugar." Most of the present timber areas are second growth, except in the hill regions of the southern counties. The statistics of 1905 report that there were still a million three hundred and seventy thousand acres of timber land in Indiana, but probably not more than half a million acres that could be called merchantable for manufacturing purposes. Professor Stanley Coulter, than whom there is no greater authority on the flora and forests of Indiana, says, that, originally, seven-eighths of the 21,673,760 acres, comprising the area of the State, was covered with a dense growth of timber. Many of the most valuable hard-wood forms reached their maximum development, both as regards size and number, within the bounds of this State; what remains can but little more than remind us of the wealth of the past. Of the one hundred and thirteen species of trees found within the State, seventy-five were in use in manufactures, and hence had a market value. Professor Coulter makes an eloquent plea for a systematic reforestation of untillable lands.

"It was of course necessary to reduce the original timber lands in order to gain agricultural areas; but the demand for crop areas being satisfied, the remaining timber lands should be so treated as to secure their constant reproduction and betterment. The present impoverished condition of the forests is very largely the result of the neglect of such precautions on the part of the preceding generation of landowners." [1]

The day is coming when timber will be a more paying crop on some lands than corn. Systematic and scientific reforestation should be the watchword of enlightened landholders in a State where the native forests indicate exceptionally superior natural adaptability of soil and climate for tree-growing. That growth showed what the results of planting may insure in the future. There is no æsthetic and merchantable future for denuded hillsides, made barren of verdure by the removal of trees and incapable of producing crops. The lowlands are the natural home of the nut trees, and a little attention to forestry will again make both hills and valleys a source of profit and beauty.

The coal deposits of Indiana form one of her greatest resources. Eighteen counties contribute to the total production. Some of the mines produce block and others bituminous coal, making it possible for the State to furnish both superior and cheap grades of fuel. The better grades have great heat, steam, and gas properties. The production of coal has increased rapidly and uninterruptedly during the last dozen years, having trebled, in that period from 3,905,779 short tons in 1896 until in 1907 it reached 12,492,255 tons. Coal is at present the greatest tonnage of any commodity moved in the State. Fifty million tons, annually, could be produced from her own mines if there was a demand; nearly ten million dollars are paid in wages to miners of this product each year.

[1] Coulter, Stanley, "Flowering Plants, Ferns, etc., Indigenous to Indiana," *24th Annual Report of Dept. of Geology and Natural Resources*, 1899, page 574.

The Picturesque Sand Dunes Cast up by the Great Lakes.

Natural Resources 483

The State Geologist shows that no State in the Union, except Pennsylvania, possesses a better and cheaper supply of fuels than Indiana. The coal is used to great advantage in the creation of "producer gas," which is largely used for manufacturing purposes, since the failure of natural gas.

Indiana has developed oil fields in four different sections of the State, and in as many different geological strata, varying in depth from 100 to 1350 feet, with an annual output, in late years, of from eight to eleven million barrels annually. The Trenton rock area, covers portions of nine counties, in the central northeastern part of the State, and belongs to the same field as the Lima–Ohio oil and gas. A smaller field, in the region of Terre Haute, produces petroleum from the Corniferous limestone, and there is an almost abandoned field in the same formation in Jasper County. The Princeton field, in the southwestern part of the State, near the Illinois line, has developed deposits of oil in the Huron sandstone strata, after disclosing five different veins of coal in boring the wells, but the region about Princeton has been very superficially tested, and further development will probably reveal greater deposits. There is no way of determining, in Indiana, by any surface indications, whether petroleum or gas may be found. Both lie in pockets, and may be developed in remunerative quantities for years to come, one well being no test for any location even a few feet away. No doubt oil exists beneath many localities where there has never been any prospecting, and where the exploration has been too shallow to reach the great depth at which the deposits are found in this State. In the future, when there is greater scarcity elsewhere, the fields within the State will be more carefully developed.

An interesting revelation is that the clays of Indiana rank in value next to coal and petroleum. The State Geologist demonstrates that Indiana has within her counties the raw material in abundance for making every kind of clay product used within her borders. Kaolin of the purest quality occurs in vast quantities, the veins extending through miles of territory where outcroppings reveal deposits that have never been uncovered. "There it lies," writes Mr. Blatchley, "a great mineral resource of untold value, unworked, unutilized, awaiting only the coming of energy and capital to make it up into many kinds of products which are now brought into the State from distant lands."[1] Fire-clays of fine quality also await the manufacturer. In many different counties there are small industries engaged in the manufacture of building brick, paving brick, encaustic tile, terra-cotta, drain tile, stoneware, and some white wares. These factories increase annually, and those already established find it profitable to increase their capacities. The materials for road construction have been revealed in inexhaustible quantities. The stone for macadam, the gravel deposit, and clays for brick are unsurpassed. Of the deposits of shale, so available in Indiana, the State Geologist says that a dozen years ago those great soft beds of soft blue-gray, thin-layered rock, which occur over vast areas in the coal-bearing counties, were looked upon as a wholly valueless nuisance, which had to be removed or tunnelled through before the underlying veins of coal could be reached. To-day

[1] Blatchley, William S., *State Geological Report*, 1906. Indianapolis.

the smoke is pouring forth from hundreds of kilns where these shales are being burned into paving brick, sewer pipe, hollow brick, conduits, drain tile, pressed front, and ordinary building brick. Not only have the carboniferous shales been proven in the highest degree suitable for the best of such products, but the knob-stone shales, which were accounted even more valueless, are now being utilized for vitrified and pressed brick as well as the clay ingredient of Portland cement. These knob-stone shales are very available, lying, as they do, close to the surface, over an area three to forty miles wide and extending from Jasper County to the Ohio River. Allied to these industries is the very interesting development of making superior building brick from the white sands of the lake counties, where clays are scarce. Combined with eight to twelve per cent. of unslacked lime, and moulded under steam pressure, a cream-colored building brick is manufactured. Unlimited quantities may be made from the mountains of sand cast up by the great lake.

Lying near the great Chicago market for building material are the extensive deposits of marly clay, excellent for the manufacture of a terra-cotta fireproof material for building purposes. These marl beds in the lake counties of Indiana are also suitable for the making of Portland cement. This greatest of modern commodities may also be created from the limitless quantities of limestone found in all sections of the State. The growth of the values of concrete for the manufacture of structural materials, and the use of the clay products in Indiana for those purposes, show that capital is awakening to the resources immediately at the door of the great markets, and their availability on account of the State's central location and transportation facilities.

Indiana has become justly famous for her quarries of unrivalled building stone, outranking any other State in the desirability and variety of stone for purposes of construction. Twenty-three counties have working quarries in operation. The Oolitic limestone, known to commerce as the Bedford stone, which possesses so many qualities of excellence for great architectural monuments, is only on the threshold of its development. The formation stretches from Putnam County to the Ohio River, in a tract from two to fourteen miles in width; and occurs in a stratum near the surface and varying from twenty-five to one hundred feet in thickness. This stone is easily carved when first quarried, has beauty of color, great fire-resisting properties, and the stratum is so massive that the size of the blocks quarried need only be limited by the facilities for its transportation. Its availability is further enhanced by its immediate location along the lines of railways. Perhaps the building stone which ranks next in importance in the State is the Niagara limestone, which also occurs over a wide area and in very accessible localities. It is found lying in natural seams, making it easily quarried without blasting. It is handsome in color and very durable. There are also beautiful sandstones for building purposes, in great abundance along the lower western border of the State. Stones adapted to paving, the manufacture of concrete, macadam, ballast, flagging, and other purposes are found in all sections of the State; the formations used in the manufacture of lime have been notable since the first settlement of this State, as have also the grind-

and whetstone. The interesting Madison County limestones, showing a fibrous quality in the process of manufacture, are being converted into a superior mineral wool for building and refrigerating purposes.

The discovery and the waste of natural gas has a lesson which should not go unheeded. The finding of natural-gas deposits was a most important factor in the development of the eastern-central part of Indiana. This gas and petroleum area covers four thousand-square miles, with its centre about Anderson. In Indiana, gas is found in Trenton rock or sand, and then only when the formation is very porous, which accounts for the borings that have failed to be productive. The first well that was really utilized was drilled in March, 1886, and for ten or twelve years there was the most phenomenal development of the fields, attracting a vast number of industries. The finding of gas and the development of the facilities of transportation increased the value of the manufactured products of Indiana three hundred and sixty million dollars in the last half century, placing her eighth in rank in the Union as a manufacturing State. Manufactories of all sorts flocked to a territory where free fuel was offered to all comers. The population increased enormously. Great factories were built, towns arose where there had been fields of grain, and little hamlets grew into cities. Seventeen counties produced gas in paying quantities. In a dozen years four of these quiet agricultural counties increased their assessed valuation fifty-eight million dollars; by 1893, over three hundred million dollars had been invested in Indiana factories, and substantial and permanent properties were established throughout the region. The gas field in Indiana was larger than that of any other State. If this great natural product, so bountifully stored away by nature, had been properly conserved, it might have continued to enrich the State for years to come. Never have ignorance, wastefulness, and oblivious carelessness of fast-passing resources, freely bestowed and vastly valuable, been more surely shown, than in the almost criminal waste of natural gas in the central States. All through the fields in Indiana and Ohio, if a "gusher" came in suddenly, it was allowed to run for days without capping, merely for advertising purposes. There was a great waste of gas from wells used for obtaining oil. Pipe lines were crude and wasteful, their disjointed condition causing great leakage. Factories wasted it like water and great flambeaux flared unextinguished, night and day, at every farm gate on the highway. In the zenith of production, 100,000,000 cubic feet of this valuable fuel was wasted in every twenty-four hours. The farmers claimed the right to waste all they pleased, as it came from their own wells! The law of '91, forbidding this wanton exhaustion was not enforced for five years after its passage. Then the authorities made strenuous efforts to regulate the gas wells. On account of this prodigal shiftlessness, there was a gradual exhaustion of the pockets, in which the gas is supposed to be stored, and the supply has diminished, although other wells may be developed in after years. Many cities have ceased to be supplied. Some factories have moved to other localities within the gas belt. Some have resorted to the use of other fuel, but the extensive coal-fields are near, and at a very low price other fuel is available. The factories are so advantageously located with regard to markets and the transportation facilities in Indiana are so exceptional that most of the factories have continued where they were established.

The passing of natural gas is a sad commentary on the lack of foresight and thrift, even in a material age, and a striking example of the vast carelessness of nature's benefactions in a country so gloriously endowed. The waste of introducing "civilization" on a continent may be traced in the sacrifice of the timber and the waste of natural gas within the bounds of Indiana. The Indians only destroyed each other and such game as they could consume. The white man came, and, as we have seen, billions of dollars' worth of timber was sacrificed. The whole aboriginal race was swept from the face of the country. The greatest variety of game found in any region was annihilated. Beautiful lakes have been drained to enlarge farm areas, and myriads of fish in all the waters have been ruthlessly exhausted before there was any care taken toward replenishing the stream. Whole species of beautiful birds have become extinct. Something may be done to redeem the waste by reforestation and restocking the streams with fish in the immediate future. These are not only possibilities, but economic necessities. Sentiment awaits a recompense for the devastations.

In the earlier days, Indiana was considered an iron-producing State; there were a dozen blast furnaces, and ore has been mined in a score of counties. With the building of the largest steel mills in the United States on her northern border, the deposits of iron will, doubtless, again be found worth developing. Mineral paints, partaking of the nature of iron oxide, and many ferruginous clays are found in great quantities in southern Indiana, sufficient to make them a valuable commercial commodity.

Very interesting deposits of peat and muck are found in the lake counties of Indiana. By a wise provision of nature, in the 7500 square miles of the northern part of the State, where there is no coal or wood, there were found great beds of peat, which is only less valuable than coal when dried or pressed into form for fuel. When made into coke or charcoal, it has a high commercial value; and by changing it into producer gas, peat will be a most valuable fuel for the future throughout the region where the formation occurs.

The muck fields, which formerly were considered worthless spots on the farm, are now being burned over or mixed with clay or sand and planted to vast fields of vegetables; these lands, when brought under cultivation, bringing three or four times the price per acre of the surrounding ground.

This chapter cannot serve the purpose of a complete report of the natural resources of Indiana, but may give a slight idea of the wealth stored beneath the surface which is being constantly revealed. Very few acres of the State will be found worthless. There are no great stretches of wholly unproductive land to be traversed before paying areas can be reached; all are near transportation. Either from the soil or beneath the surface the landholder may find a reward for his investment. What were regarded as waste places at one time, it is being demonstrated by the geologists is invaluable territory.

In utilizing the natural resources of the Commonwealth, no gift of nature has been more neglected than the waters of Indiana. The beautiful lakes

Lower Falls Cataract, Styner's Falls.

Such falls as Styner's Cataract await their development as generators of electric power.

that dot the northern counties, the rivers, the gushing springs, the flowing wells, and the limpid streams which flow through the central and southern districts have yet to be made a great factor of wealth and pleasure. Nothing has been done toward irrigation, and with very few exceptions the farmers have not begun to appreciate the value of stocking the waters, bordering on their lands, with fish. An intelligent co-operation of State and landholder will, in the future, render these bodies of water a perennial source of food to the whole population. Another vast source of wealth and lightening of labor flows all undreamed of past village and farm. The sparkling waterfalls in the streams and woodland brooks, and the hundreds of turbulent rapids in the placid rivers, await their development as generators of electric power. As the waters slip past farm and town they murmur of energy that they might lend to the overworked farmer and his tired wife; how light, heat, and power could be taken from the rippling streams. They invite the village factory and mill to expand, by the use of little wires connecting their dynamos with a turbine in the waterfall. Independent of coal mines or syndicate power-houses, the power is theirs right at hand. Nor is it necessary to dwell on the banks of the streams, for the power may be transmitted far and wide. Twenty counties might have electricity by water-power generated by the Wabash; White River and its tributaries could serve as many more. Such falls as those at Pendleton, at Shields, at Flat Rock, at Styner's cataract, and the great rapids in the Ohio River could furnish light, heat, and motive power for all of the factories, interurban lines, farms, and homes in Indiana. Italy calls this water-power, which she is turning to such vast economic advantage, her white coal, and uses it to turn wheels, spindles, and trolley lines many miles from the torrent's source. The graduating engineers from Purdue and Rose Polytechnic have at hand a brilliant career, in the conservation of such a force within the State. "Tomorrow, the day's fuel may be dipped from the brook," if the waters of Indiana are utilized, and the forests about their sources are preserved.

CHAPTER XXII

THE STATE OF CIVILIZATION IN INDIANA AS SHOWN BY HER LAWS

THE public sentiment and the legislation of a state define her status in civilization. The provisions made for equal opportunity for all of the people is a test of enlightenment. Indiana must measure herself by these standards. With the passing of pioneer conditions, when our country lived the untrammelled life of a backwoods boy, when there was much more than room enough for all, and a struggle to live meant manual labor at the very most, when no one was very rich or very poor, when there was no clashing of class interests, for all might rise by their own efforts; with the passing of that time when all planted and built and prospered, we have come to the time when, with the increase of population and the narrowing of opportunity, the State must often intervene for the protection of the individual and for the good of society. In Indiana, as in other States, when new laws for the Commonwealth are necessary, there is often a long striving after righteousness by the elect, before party strife and narrow-mindedness will permit disinterested legislation. Indiana has not been exempt from this handicap, and in any estimate of public sentiment due allowance must be made for this baleful influence in delaying legislation. It is necessary to remember that after 1872, when the reaction of the patriotic fervor of the Civil War period had passed, neither party carried the State at two consecutive Presidential elections for a quarter of a century. When there is this marked conflict of political opinion, the men who gain office, in any State, are not always those who are enlightened enough to lend their efforts to the broadest measures, and the legislation accomplished represents compromise rather than the very best thought of its citizenship. Step by step, only, may its ideals be realized. Bearing these facts in mind, it will be recognized that Indiana has embodied enough advanced plans in her statutes to place her among the foremost States in the Union in enlightened provisions for her population. More than forty years ago, in commenting on Robert Dale Owen's part in successfully inaugurating all of the pioneer legislation for the advancement of woman's control and equitable rights over her own property, the London *Times* said that "Indiana has attained by this step the highest civilization of any State in the Union," and in all of the years since, few States have approached her position on this question. The common-law dower was abolished, and absolute ownership of one third of the whole of the deceased husband's estate is conferred upon the widow. Women can own and control their own separate property during marriage, have a right to their own earnings, and can contract every legal obligation that men can, except to become security for another person.

In the chapter on Education, an outline is given of the legislation which has been enacted founding a comprehensive system for universal instruction of all the youth of Indiana. It is shown that a most admirable State school system has been developed, beginning with compulsory attendance through the primary and grammar grades until a child is fourteen years old, from thence he may pass into the high schools, which are gradually adding industrial and manual training. Following this, there is the provision for higher learning, in the normal schools and great State universities. Opportunities which are unsurpassed in possibilities for general culture of all her communities are thus afforded, if future legislatures do not deprive the system of the necessary appropriations to maintain the structure built on the broad foundations already established.

Coupled with this educational plan, are the enactments authorizing tax levies to promote the formation of public libraries in the towns, and the creation of a commission to supervise that work, and also to have charge of a system of travelling libraries, which are furnished by the State for small villages and the rural districts. This legislation enables every school, every reading-circle or club, where five persons will join together in requesting the service, to have these collections of books sent for their use, making it unnecessary for the most isolated persons in Indiana to be deprived of good literature.

The temperance laws of Indiana have shown a steady advance, of late years, towards the regulation of the liquor traffic. This control has been assumed through the form of regulation by local option rather than by a sweeping State prohibition. The laws have been secured as a result of the gradual conviction in the minds of an ever-increasing number of citizens that the habit of drinking intoxicants was growing and that its effects were ruinous to the people. By far the larger portion of the inmates of the penal and correctional institutions and asylums, and the recipients of out-door relief come upon the State for maintenance, through the effects of intemperance. Aside from the misery and unhappiness entailed, it was recognized as a bad business proposition, when the total license fees from the sale of liquors brought into the treasury less than a million and a half dollars and at the same time the Commonwealth was expending twice that sum in caring for the wrecks of humanity caused by drink. After enacting numerous laws by great effort and ceaseless agitation, from year to year, defining who should be granted license to sell; stipulating that they should not sell to minors, to habitual drunkards, to prisoners, to intoxicated persons; that liquors should not be sold near schools, churches, soldiers' homes, nor in rooms not on the ground floor, nor in drug stores except by a physician's prescription, nor on Sundays and election days, nor in a "blind tiger"; and after prohibiting saloon-keepers from allowing minors to loiter in the place, and making them liable for harm to the family of the one to whom they sold liquor; and requiring that the effects of alcoholic drinks be taught in the schools; and fining minors for misrepresenting their age to obtain liquor, and intoxicated persons for being found so in public; and after years under laws making it the duty of county commissioners, prosecuting attorneys, mayors, police commissioners, and the judiciary to enforce these laws, another statute was tried. Under the Moore amendment to the Nicholson Law, to which the Supreme Court has given its approval, the citizens are now moving. Under this law, if a majority of the voters in any township or ward of a city shall file a remonstrance three days before any regular meeting of the commissioners against granting a license to sell intoxicating liquors to any individual applicant, or all applicants, then it will be unlawful for the commissioners to grant a permit for two years following. Power of attorney to sign a remonstrance may be delegated by a citizen to an agent or member of a committee who is on the watch for applicants for license.

This new law makes it optional with wards and townships whether they will have saloons or not. It is intended to adopt the measure also for counties. Working under this statute, the statistics for 1906 show that two-thirds of the townships of the State have now no saloons, and nearly three-fourths of the territory of Indiana is without a licensed saloon; and the Anti-Saloon League is pressing the campaign against the traffic everywhere. The Indiana brewers, alarmed by the broad sweep that this campaign has made, decided not to start any more saloons in the State. They also gave it out that they would discontinue the purchase of fixtures for their friends in the business, or advance funds for their support; and that the association would assist the authorities to enforce the present law, and help allay agitation by driving "dive-keepers" out of the business. Of this temperance movement, the Wine and Spirit Circular warns the liquor trade that "this league is a strongly centralized organization, officered by men of unusual ability, financed by capitalists, subscribed to by hundreds of thousands of men and women and children, advised by attorneys of great ability, and it is working with definite ideas to guide it. The retail liquor trade must mend its ways materially, or be prohibited, save from the business of tenderloin precincts of larger cities." It may be added that in August, 1908, Indiana added a statute known as the County Unit Law, which extends the present conditions under which license is granted, to whole counties, if the majority of voters so order by remonstrance.

Indiana has passed laws prohibiting the sale of cocaine and opium without a physician's prescription, and after one sale is made the prescription must be cancelled. It has also passed a prohibition on cigarettes. The fines authorized for violation of gambling laws, if imposed, might leave little to make the breaking of those sweeping statutes worth tempting the further infraction of the law. The enactments of pure-food laws are sufficient, if enforced, to protect the health of the State inhabitants. There is a regulation exacting sanitation of all food-producing establishments, and the assurance of the purity and wholesomeness of the products therein, and of the health of the operatives.

The laws in Indiana for the incorporation of cities have modernized the modes of city government, and the enactments for reform of county and township administration, which provide for supervision and legislation by Boards of Control, separating legislative and executive functions, are intended to regulate local abuses and insure business methods in county affairs. The new laws tending to equalization of taxation have been found worthy of being copied by other States. The decision of the Supreme Court of Indiana that, according to its laws, if a man is guilty of bribery of a voter whose support he desires to enlist, he is ineligible to hold the office, even if he is elected without including the purchased vote, shows the desire to maintain the purity of the ballot. This decision holds true of votes in convention also. Indiana was one of the first States to adopt the Australian ballot, and also introduced improvements which were copied by other communities. The State's fee and salary law, whereby officials are paid a fixed salary and the fees pass into the treasury, was a great moral advance, as also were the franchise license laws of 1891, regulating the granting of commercial privileges.

Besides the general codes for the benefit of wage-earners, common to many of the States, there are statutes in the interests of the laboring classes that show Indiana's regard for the welfare of her workers, and that their well-being is of the very greatest importance. A Labor Commission was created in 1899, one member of which must come from the employing class, and the other must represent the wage-earners. This Commission is to serve as a mediator, look after the interests of laborers, endeavor to conciliate in times of trouble, and arbitrate opposing interests. Factory inspection has been instituted to look after the bodily welfare of workmen, including the sanitation of buildings, protection of belts and machinery, fire-escapes in high buildings, safety appliances where needed, light and air, temporary floors in buildings which are in course of construction, and other measures of protection. Employers as well as employees are gratified with the results of these enactments. There are laws regulating the conditions of employment of women and children, including the prohibition of taking children under fourteen years of age, and under sixteen, except during school vacation, of children who cannot read and write. Ten hours is the longest day for labor by women, and night labor by them in manufactories between the hours of ten and six is prohibited. There is a statute to insure weekly payment of wages, and forbidding the assignment of future wages. A law fixes the limit of hours for a day's work, and provides for the noon hour. The large coal-mining business is on the eight-hour basis and the laws relating to labor unions are very liberal. Enactments have been passed forbidding the discharge of persons because they were members of labor unions. There are provisions for the protection of trainmen, miners, and engineers. There have been decisions from appellate and supreme courts, interpreting the laws affecting the liability of the employer for accidents, in a manner much more favorable to the employee than the interpretation of similar laws in sister States. Thoughtful citizens of Indiana look forward to state regulation of working men's insurance and laws providing pensions for old age. In the words of Charles R. Henderson, a native of Indiana, who has worked for years collecting international data for these measures, "We are laying a demand upon the legislatures of the country to make laws conform, not to conditions which have been outgrown, but to conditions as we face them to-day. I speak with the emphasis of conviction, with the hope that we are seeing the dawn of the result of a long study of a great subject, and of a successful striving for a righteous end."

As a result of the laws for the protection of laborers, and the conciliatory methods of adjustment by a commission, the conditions in Indiana have become

The State Capitol, Indianapolis.
From a photograph by the W. H. Bass Photo. Co.

more favorable to order. Annual contracts, and settlements of demands by arbitration, have reduced the number of strikes in the proportion of twenty to one. Especially is this the gratifying state of affairs in the case where the workers are skilled, and are members of a union.

Indiana's saving banks are organized on a plan to insure the safety of the people's savings. These banks were planned to be philanthropic institutions, and were not intended to make money for the incorporators, or for the directory. Their securities are on the basis of unimproved real estate values and farm property. Provisions for penny and dime savings have also been made by the State.

As mentioned in the chapter on Education, the State schools for the blind, deaf, the feeble-minded, and the soldiers' and sailors' orphans are regarded as part of the public school system. This is from the recognition of the fact that the infirmities of these children bar them from the regular schools established for all youth. These schools are also furnished with the appliances for industrial training.

It is conceded that the provision for the disbursement of charities, and the care of the flotsam and jetsam of humanity, is also a distinct gauge of the advancement made by a commonwealth. In Indiana there are higher planes to be attained, but by 1889 the State had advanced to the position of creating a Central Board of State Charities, to supervise the expenditure of the funds, and the whole system of public charities to which the State contributes. This board is intended to be purely advisory and represents the people in visitation, inspection, and reporting any recommendations considered desirable. It is composed of representative citizens serving without pay, and required by law to have the oversight of every department of charities and correction, from the great State prisons and insane hospitals to the small town lock-up, and the thousand and more township trustees, the county jails, poor asylums, and every children's orphan asylum. All these institutions are under the inspection of this strong board. It had long been recognized that the county is too small a govermental unit, with too restricted resources, to grapple successfully with all of the problems of relief. It was felt that a central supervisory body was the only wise and economical way in which to influence the administration of the affairs of the commonwealth. It is now this State Board's duty to see that every inmate of every public institution receives proper care; that the public funds are honestly expended, although it does not direct the expenditure; and that the institutions are properly conducted. No more important office can be bestowed upon a citizen of the State than that of an appointment on the Board of State Charities. At present, the care of 86,000 persons is under the board's supervision, and an oversight of the expenditure of over two million seven hundred thousand dollars. When a citizen recalls the haphazard methods of administering the charities and corrections under the former customs, and which are still practised in too many States, the wisdom of centralized control is most evident. Under the persistent recommendations of this board a steady improvement in the laws has been accomplished; and as a consequence, the conditions in the various institutions are so improved that it is extremely gratifying to the citizen who has a humane interest in the unfortunate. He can also feel assured that there is a continuous oversight and frequent inspection, that was not possible before. This board has secured laws which insure non-partisan boards of trustees; four trustees are appointed by the governor to administer the affairs of each State institution, not more than two of whom may be of the same political affiliation. Each board appoints its own superintendent, and the superintendent in turn appoints all officers and employees under him. No other qualification than fitness must be taken into consideration in making appointments; and the trustees are prohibited from interfering in the selection or discharge of employees. The appointment of separate trustees for each institution insures more direct personal responsibility and interest in the administration of that particular institution's affairs than if there was a general board for all of the State's wards. As the demands on the time of the trustees are less, they can be more faithful to the trust imposed in them by their acceptance of appointment. Non-interference on the part of any of the trustees in the selection of employees makes the superintendent entirely responsible for the work done by his assistants. Since the new régime of administering the State charities, under the watch-care of a strong advisory board, which has had the advantage of the valuable services as secretaries of such men of national fame as Ernest P. Bicknell, Alexander Johnson, and at present Amos W. Butler as field officer, the supervision has so greatly improved the business methods that the expenditures have been economized in many particulars. In the administration of townships' trustees' relief, an average saving of $300,000 a year has been accomplished.

In the State institutions, the annual expenditure would probably be $225,000 less than it was prior to 1895. At the same time the standards of the institutions have been raised in every particular. More humane treatment of the State's wards has been assured, and better instruction given than could have been imparted in the isolated county asylums. All of this improvement in administration has secured for the plan of central supervision the confidence of the people, the support of the press, and an influence with the legislative body for further betterment.

Among the wise laws, and amendments to laws, that the board has secured, a few may be mentioned, to show the position attained by the State, in comparison with other sections. The Board of Children's Guardians has been authorized for every county, and the terms *neglected* and *dependent* have been explicitly defined, so that there need be no doubt as to the rights of boards to act. It adds to uniformity of administration that, throughout the State, no child can be made a public dependent except by the judge of the Juvenile Court. Any citizen can, without personal expense, bring the case to the attention of the Juvenile Court. In cases where such children are brought before the Juvenile Court, the parents or those having the custody of the children, who wilfully neglect their duty to them, may be brought before the court and fined any sum not exceeding $500. But, in accordance with the new theories of dealing with the criminal classes, the court has the power to suspend the sentence, and release the person so found guilty, putting him or her on probation for two years, on condition that he or she shall appear before the court at such times as shall be designated, and show that he or she has provided and cared for the children. In such cases the children may be given to them, but if they, in any way, violate the parole they may be sentenced at any time. This gives the court the necessary hold on the parent or guardian, which is most effective in keeping them to their duties. Few parents will neglect their children, or contribute to their delinquency, if they are in danger of being sent to prison for a long term. At the end of two years, if there has been no violation of the court's order, the person is free from the sentence. The Legislature has also given the Board of Guardians a general power to take a child under their care where the associations of such a child are such as to contaminate and corrupt it. This gives the board the power to act when it may be unable to prove specific charges, although it is evident that the welfare of the child is at stake. Not only has Indiana provided for a special court for juvenile offenders, either by special judge in cities of 100,000 or more inhabitants, or in other counties, by the regular judge of the circuit court sitting, but it has increased his jurisdiction by empowering him to hear juvenile cases in vacation time. The powers of the court are almost concurrent with the jurisdiction of the criminal court, for the judge is given power to punish any person that the evidence shows is guilty of contributing to the delinquency of a child, if such contributing act be a misdemeanor. If it is shown to be a felony, the juvenile court is given the power to bind him over to the criminal court. An act has been passed making it a felony, and subjecting the offender to a term of two to fourteen years imprisonment, to contribute to the delinquency of girls under eighteen years, by enticing them into a wine-room, saloon, or other questionable place for immoral purposes. There has been State legislation authorizing county commissioners of adjoining counties to unite in the erection of asylums for the care of dependent children, who have heretofore been kept in the county poor asylums. Better still is the provision made for the placing of such children in homes, and the continuous watch-care over them afterward. Prolonged institutional life is recognized as a great wrong to a child, and a "childless home for every homeless child" is the object of this method of caring for dependent children, as soon as it is possible. All of the various State institutions especially designed for the care of defective children are equipped with modern appliances to insure their education, and industrial training; as in the State schools for the blind, the deaf, the feeble-minded, epileptics, the soldiers' orphans, and the boys and girls who are delinquents.

Desertion of wife and children has been made a felony. The granting of marriage licenses has been more strictly regulated by the law passed in 1905. This law makes the county clerks liable to a penalty should they issue a marriage license without the observance of its provisions. Under this statute, the first of its kind probably, no license to marry shall be issued where either of the contracting parties is an imbecile, epileptic, of unsound mind, or under guardianship as a person of unsound mind; nor to any male person who is, or has been within five years, an inmate of any county asylum, or home for indigent persons, unless it satisfactorily appears that the cause of such condition has been removed and that such male applicant is able to support a family and likely to so continue. Nor shall any license be issued when either of the contracting parties is afflicted with a transmissible disease, or at the time of making application is under the influence of intoxicating liquor or narcotic drug. Uniform blanks to be filled out are required for the whole State alike; and no license to marry shall be issued except upon written and verified application. This application, stating in full the previous history and condition of the applicants, becomes a matter of record, and open to public inspection.

Under the supervision of the State board, the poor asylums have been improved in administration, and their complete renovation urgently pressed upon the various counties that are remiss in this particular. Before the new régime, they were as great a stigma on the good name of the State as are the county jails. Legislation relating to the county jails and asylums must be the next step in advance in the history of Indiana's progress. Indiana has a provision for police matrons in the police stations of the cities of 10,000 population or over, and jail matrons in counties having 50,000 population or over. There is also a later law providing that condemned women, sentenced for ninety days, shall be sent to the State workhouse, where they are taught an industry, instead of lying in idleness in the county jail. These are all very gratifying advance measures. The State board also serves in an advisory capacity in the planning of new county jails, and poor asylums, as to their arrangement and sanitary provisions.

One of the most desired objects was obtained when the village of epileptics was authorized. With a number reaching four thousand in the present population, the wisdom of providing separate care for these afflicted ones, and a possibility of their having an opportunity to be self-supporting, was recognized by all workers for humanity. Twelve hundred and forty-five acres, near the town of Newcastle, was selected for the village; and the necessary buildings are to be erected as they are needed. This institution will, in time be partially self-supporting, as many of the inmates are capable people when not ill. Many of them will be able to help care for others who are stranded by this incurable affliction. The handicap of this disease will be less cruel when the conditions of living are accommodated to the inmate's misfortune.

The feeble-minded children are no longer to be kept in the county poor asylums, but have provisions made for them in a State school at Fort Wayne. This home is situated on a farm of three hundred and ten acres. More buildings are needed for the accommodation of other unfortunates that are suffering for the care given here; but the institution is managed on the most humane lines, and the children are taught all that they are capable of learning. It is recognized that accommodations are imperative in State asylums for both feeble-minded children and adults, as well as for the incurable insane.

By a law enacted in 1903, Indiana recognized the humanity of the State providing for its sick, and authorized the establishment of hospitals by county commissioners and their maintenance afterwards. They may do this in conjunction or without the aid of hospital associations. Indigent patients may be received into such hospitals from other counties, by a payment of the cost; and it is also provided that two or more counties may unite in building a hospital, for the use of those counties; making it possible, by either of these methods, for even the most backward communities to care for the sick and afflicted.

Aware of the awful waste of life from that dread disease tuberculosis, Indiana has made provisions for a State hospital for the treatment of patients suffering from this affliction. The State has authorized a commission to secure a site of five hundred acres for the important work. There care and treatment will be instituted by the trustees, without the delay of waiting for great buildings. A law has been passed directing the proper authorities to supply free antitoxin to citizens too poor to purchase it, at the expense of the Board of Health.

Indiana has four hospitals for the insane, in different districts of the State, and a fifth is under construction. There is also established a state soldiers' home, located at Lafayette, which is open not only to old soldiers and sailors, but also to their aged wives and widows. Here they may not have the hardship of separation added to poverty and old age. The orphans of soldiers and sailors are provided for in a home and school at Knightstown, on a farm of two hundred and forty-seven acres.

Since the Board of State Charities has suggested needed legislation, the whole system of out-door relief of the poor has been rearranged, and the duties of officers defined. Now, the township trustees are the overseers of the poor to give the temporary relief; and when permanent aid is found necessary, the recipient becomes a charge of the county and is transferred to the county poor asylum. This system of direct responsibility to the immediate constituency of the trustee, and the required reports, has effected an enormous saving to the taxpayers, amounting to hundreds of thousands of dollars; and also insures more careful investigation into the conditions of the family assisted.

The progress made in the State's laws for the prevention and punishment of crime has been most marked. First, the laws for the care of children are being modelled with the object of preventing crime and pauperism, if possible, before the evil is done; this is shown in the provisions for universal education enforced by truant officers, the establishment of the Juvenile Court, industrial reform schools, and the children's guardian laws, whereby it is provided that there should be a board of children's guardians in every county in the State.

In the laws for the punishment of criminals, Indiana has taken the position that it is correction, and not degradation nor vengeance, that the State wishes to accomplish by the punishment awarded. Says Alexander Johnson: "The fundamental principle of it all was adopted nearly a hundred years ago; for in the first constitution of the State is a magnificent declaration, never surpassed in a written constitution, on the subject. The eighteenth section of the bill of rights declares that 'the penal code should be founded on the principles of reformation and not of vindictive justice.'"[1] Although it was many years before this prophetic statement, of some advanced thinker, came to be fully incorporated in the statutes, still the truth has been gradually formulated in the later laws. In this spirit the four correctional institutions of the State are certainly administered. The Indiana Boys'

[1] Johnson, Alexander, in an address before the State Conference. *April Bulletin*, 1907.

School at Plainfield is an industrial school to which are admitted boys over eight and under sixteen years of age who are guilty of vicious conduct. Such boys are committed until they attain the age of twenty-one years; but through good conduct they may obtain release from the board of control by discharge, but are still under the watch-care of the institution. Should such a boy's presence in the school prove detrimental to its welfare, if committed for crime, he may be transferred to the Reformatory, with the consent of the governor, after he is sixteen years old. The State prison at Jeffersonville is the Indiana Reformatory and the State prison north, at Michigan City, is the real prison. "The Reformatory is governed," says Alexander Johnson, "by the best laws on the subject upon the statute books of any state of the Union."[1] All men between the ages of sixteen and thirty years who are found guilty of a felony, other than treason, or murder in the first degree, are committed to the custody of the board of managers of the Reformatory. Men guilty of treason, or of murder in the first or second degree, and all men convicted of any felony who are over thirty years of age, are sentenced to the State prison. To both of these institutions men are committed under the indeterminate sentence and parole law. There is an allowance for transportation, clothing, and necessary money, to all men who get out on parole. Another very advanced position was taken when the State added the law enabling circuit and criminal courts of Indiana to suspend a sentence which they had just imposed, and release upon probation persons convicted of crime and misdemeanors,

[1] Johnson, Alexander, in an address before the State Conference. *April Bulletin*, 1907.

in certain cases. While still keeping them under the surveillance and control of the prison authorities, the offender is subject to all of the laws applying to paroled prisoners; also subject to the court, which may revoke the parole at its discretion, and order imprisonment to begin. This vast change in penal law was undertaken to give guilty ones another opportunity to start right in life without the shadow of a prison record. There was also enacted a law ordering *life* imprisonment for all habitual criminals, upon a third conviction of crime in *any* State. This is to prevent degenerates from resuming their criminal careers upon release from every sentence, endangering the security of life and property. To check the important part played by heredity, a law was passed making it the duty of all State institutions intrusted with the care of confirmed criminals, idiots, rapists, and imbeciles, to have such surgery performed, by experts, on these specified incurable inmates, as would prevent procreation. Insane criminals are to be transferred from the State prisons to hospitals for the insane.

Indiana was the first State in the Union to establish a woman's prison. The State has also provided an institution called the Indiana Girls' School, which is located eight miles northwest of Indianapolis, and which is intended for the training of wayward girls. Its regulations are similar to the Plainfield school for boys, and it is constructed on the cottage plan. There are thirty girls in each cottage, which is a complete home in itself. Here they are taught life's tasks and given school lessons throughout their period of commitment. In maintaining this industrial correctional institution for girls, and a separate woman's prison, the State provides for the complete separation of

The Indiana Reform School for Boys.
From a photograph by Deweese, Plainfield, Indiana.

Her Civilization as Shown by Her Laws 513

the sexes, and also divides the adult female criminals from the younger delinquents. Industrial training, and the rudiments of an education, are provided in both of these institutions; and the indeterminate sentence and parole laws apply also to these inmates, the same as in the prisons for males. The State workhouse already spoken of has also been established for women who are sentenced for ninety days or less; they would otherwise have to serve out their sentence in the county jails, in idleness, and are here taught to be of some use.

Trade schools are conducted in the State Reformatory, intended to train men in useful trades, and to provide for the manufacture of products needed in the various State institutions. The State prison employs about half of its population on contract work, and the remainder are employed on the farm, or in the manufacture of binder twine, and on articles for the State. Under these arrangements, in all of the penal institutions, the inmates have the advantage of the saving grace of employment, at the same time lowering the cost to the State of their maintenance; combining conditions more favorable than any other State. Superintendent Whittaker has said that no State in the Union has as satisfactory laws upon the question of prison labor as has the State of Indiana. These were prepared, and passed, with the approval and co-operation of the labor leaders of the State, and of those citizens directly interested in the management of the penal institutions.

The *results* of carrying out the reform methods of punishment and the indeterminate sentence and parole system are of interest in making an estimate of the value of Indiana's humanitarian laws. Economy of funds, stricter oversight, more careful assignment to the institution best suited to the individual case, scientific treatment, home instead of institutional life for normal children, and less pauperizing of the derelict members of the communities, are some of the results of the modern methods in charities and corrections. In the ten years that the new penal laws have been in force, we find, says the superintendent at Jeffersonville, that boy prisoners from sixteen to thirty years of age are being educated and taught trades; that every influence is thrown around them to make them useful and respected citizens. It is not an uncommon experience for the management to be requested by the boy himself, that he be not paroled, but be held in the institution until he has finished his education and trade. These boys when paroled are given tailor-made suits, costing less than did the misfits that were given them ten years ago. Positions at good wages are found for them before they are allowed to go out. While on parole, friendly advice and encouragement are given when needed. Under these conditions, both in the State prison and reformatory, we find that sixty per cent. of the men and boys who leave the institutions become law-abiding and useful citizens. We find, further, that prisoners are now serving in the prison and reformatory, an average of two years and four months. Counting the year on parole, it amounts to an average of three years and four months that the State has control of the convicts; while under the old method of fixed sentences they were held but one year and nine months; which means that the management is not turning confirmed criminals loose upon society as rapidly as was done under the old law. An outline of the methods used with convicted prisoners, upon entrance, under the present laws, is useful in passing judgment on their desirability. After a boy is registered as an inmate, and his previous record and sentence have been duly recorded, a bath is administered and an entire suit of military clothes given him. He then undergoes a strict physical examination, and a school test. A complete history of himself and his family is taken. After instructions about the rules and regulations, and an invitation to the religious services, the boy goes to the general superintendent, who impresses him with the fact that each officer of the institution is there as his friend and adviser, and that they are there for the purpose of making a man of him; and if they do not help him, it will be his fault and not the fault of the management. They tell him that his sentence does not mean one year, nor fourteen years; but that he is sent to the institution exactly as a patient is sent to a hospital, with a case of typhoid fever; and that he will not be paroled, or discharged, until he is cured. He is informed that he is to be given an education to at least the seventh grade, and taught some trade, so that he will be an asset rather than a liability to the State when he is released. The boy is then placed in the school of letters, under a competent teacher, for two hours each day. Here he is given instructions on how to study, and how to prepare his lessons for the next day while in his cell in the evening, as he is provided with an electric light in his cell until time for retiring, at nine o'clock P.M. In addition to his school work, the boy is placed in one of the trade schools, usually the one that he prefers. The trade school, if it be printing, or any other, is under a competent instructor, who gives his time to teaching this boy, so that he may be a practical workman on leaving the institution. There is employment for every inmate. During the first year he learns to read and write, and to be able to earn at least seven dollars a week. Then the board of managers hear his story, and the reports of his good behavior in the institution. They may grant him a parole, if they think best. Employment is found for each one, before he goes out into the world; and a strict watch-care kept over him for the remainder of the sentence. Not, said Professor Freudenthal at the international penological conference, "by a police oversight, but a well-wishing friendly interest which is maintained by parole officers. These serve either for pay, or for the honor of it, or they represent a combined system of both kinds of parole officers as in the model state for parole, Indiana." The paroled one reports regularly to the superintendent his earnings and expenses. If he proves recreant to the trust placed in him, he is returned to the prison; but if, at the expiration of his time, his conduct is approved he is discharged free. Superintendent Whittaker reports on the life within the walls, and speaking from the experience he has had in the last ten years in the work says:

"I find there is nothing that will prevent crime more than education and instruction in some useful and practical occupation, and there is no better means of bringing about reformation with the class of our citizens such as we receive at the Reformatory than instruction from a competent educator in a school of letters, followed up with practical instruction in some useful trade. We also find that any method adopted in such institution that humiliates the inmate in the eyes of the other prisoners or of the officers brings no good results from the standpoint of reformation; hence we have discontinued the use of stripes for clothing, abolished the lock-step, and instead we give each inmate in the institution a suit of cadet blue clothing, cut in military style, and permit them to march in twos in military order. Seventy-five per cent. of the 1100 boys we have to-day come from broken homes and from environments that were bad when they were children, or where the parents were dead. Much has been said of our divorce laws. The best law, in my judgment, that could be enacted for those who secure a divorce would be, if they had children under sixteen years of age, for the court to take charge of such children and see that they are placed in proper homes and given a high school education, the parents having nothing to say in the rearing of the child after divorce has been granted." [1]

And what of these paroled men? Secretary Butler's reports show that more than half of them have remained faithful to the trust imposed in them. Of the 3755 prisoners paroled, since the law has been in force, he says that sixty per cent. have maintained themselves and been saved to society. Most of these men were not wage-earners before their incarceration, yet they have earned $949,773.63 while on parole, and eighty-six per cent. of their employers approved of the law as very beneficial. The paroled men, without exception, have a favorable opinion of it; and professional crooks, who do not expect to reform, all denounce the law. The secretary's deduction from all of his data is, that is it much better for the State as an organization that it be relieved of this expense; and for society that these men be returning to it professing reformation and willing to prove their

[1] Whittaker, William H., *Address at Fifteenth State Conference of Charities and Corrections.*

profession by becoming working, earning members of it, instead of coming out with the hopeless outlook of the discharged convict, under the old régime; since a much larger per cent. of those discharged under the old system return to lives of crime, and a far greater per cent. of those discharged on parole manage to keep out of prison. Under the new system, by far the larger number of those released after the parole test become law-abiding citizens, and but a small per cent. again find their way behind the prison walls. As stated by former State Auditor Hart, "to-day the reformatories are giving wayward boys and girls educational facilities, industrial training, and Christian counsel, so that, instead of being schools of crime, the worthy among the young offenders are coming back to society prepared for honorable responsibilities." For the older prisoners, the State Bar Association, in common with other citizens, had doubts of the wisdom of the reform statutes; but its committee reported at the last annual meeting that the law was "a distinct advance in the State's attitude toward the treatment of criminals. The great majority of men paroled sustain the confidence placed in them, and not only perform the conditions, but merit their discharges, and become honorable citizens."

In claiming an advanced position for legislation in Indiana, it is natural to ask what is left to be desired. Active citizens for the public good see many needs. Especially do they deplore and condemn the backward condition of county affairs in the buildings used for the jails and poor asylums, when it might be expected the citizens would demand better conditions in the local institutions, where the blame comes close to home. The tardiness of some of the counties in availing themselves of the empowering statutes, that are not mandatory, suggests the desirability of further State control. We hold no brief for Indiana where she is behind the civilization of the times. It is important that the counties should be more progressive.

Indiana has not taken her place in the advanced ranks of legislation on the subject of suffrage for women. Notwithstanding most of the instruction and the civilizing influences of life in the State have been furthered by the mothers in the commonwealth, the ballot has not been extended to them. Among other things to be desired, in both county and State institutions, is the doing away with the per capita method of providing maintenance and the retaining of convicted male prisoners to serve their sentence in idleness in the county jails, instead of in a State workhouse. In the above conditions, it is hoped there will be speedy improvement. The most fundamental need is the establishment of industrial training as part of compulsory education in all of the counties. If the combination of required education and industrial training has proved so effective in correctional institutions for convicts, it would seem that a like provision for enforced, universal training for all of the youth of the State, as a preventive measure, would be better economy of men and money than as a cure after the evil had come upon the community. If hand work must accompany head work to hold the average pupil within the civilizing influences of regular hours at school, and within moral environments, it would seem the part of wisdom to furnish such facilities for the youth still innocent of crime, rather than that he should have to commit a felony before he can obtain the training which will fit him for life work.

It will be seen from this cursory study of a few subjects of legislation in Indiana, that each year has marked some advancement; and that enough enlightened laws have been passed to insure a measure of support in the emergencies of existence, and humane treatment of the defectives and the delinquents, to serve as a guarantee of further progress. "Let us count ourselves, then, as not having attained, but as pressing forward," said Alexander Johnson in the State Conference of Charities. "Real and great progress has been made and the tendency is ever forward to sounder principles, to improved methods, to increased efficiency, to decreasing relative cost, to the saving of wasted money, to the saving of wasted humanity." It is also a significant indication of advance that the president of the State Conference felt justified in claiming that "to-day there is no State freer from partisan control, from scandal in the management of its public funds, than is our own, no state where the unfortunates are so humanely and scientifically cared for as in Indiana." [1] This improvement has resulted from the united efforts of an enlightened contingent of workers for the public good, acting upon the conviction that self-help and not pauperism must be inculcated. Insisting that education and criminality are opposite forces in civilization, and that prevention and reformation are the duties of the State in reference to wrong-doers, to carry out present laws and advance to higher planes it is evident that the thing most needed is personal interest

[1] Whittaker, W. H., *Bulletin of Charities and Corrections*, page 86. April, 1907.

in the public welfare, and *individual service* on the part of the best citizenship. "The patriotism of public duty enters very largely into the vitality of civic righteousness."

It will be seen that in her educational system, in the supervision of the health department, in administering charities and corrections, in the oversight of game and fisheries, in the appointment of city police commissioners, and in the methods of taxation, Indiana has steadily developed a closely centralized system of administration. It will be remarked that the State has taken the direction and control from the individual counties, and assumed the responsibility of enforcing uniform laws for the whole commonwealth. Formerly in other departments, as in the school system, "each community was a law unto itself. There was neither unity or uniformity. With closer organization order began to come out of chaos." This method has proved so efficient in accomplishing the wishes of the best citizens that it has attracted the attention of serious students from other States, as worthy of imitation. Indiana owes much to these general laws for all the counties. They have pushed forward civilization in the outlying districts a full quarter of a century. Professor Rawles gives us a most excellent valuation of the results of this centralization in his very illuminating thesis on the subject:

"Both theory and practice demonstrate that this gravitation towards centralization in administration is in harmony with our progress, our political ideas, our pecuniary interests, and our highest prosperity and happiness. This conclusion does not relegate the theory of local self-government to the limbo of obsolete doctrines. There will always remain a field within which the people of the respective communities will have free choice as to their policies. This conclusion does not, therefore, mean an abandonment of the ideals of the fathers. The evidence has been sufficient to demonstrate that this centralization has resulted in a more efficient administration, has secured a greater safety of funds, has protected more thoroughly the interests of the whole people, has ameliorated the condition of the unfortunate classes for whose care and education the State is responsible, has led to the reformatory in place of the vindictive principle, and has helped to elevate the social and moral tone by diffusing knowledge and culture through the agency of the common schools. An increase of population is of itself a sufficient cause for the extension of governmental functions and a more careful organization of the machinery of administration; for any form of government is devised and instituted to promote the welfare of the society within which it is established." [1]

Judged by the accomplishment of increased good to all of the people, there can be no doubt that State control in Indiana has resulted in a more scientific, humane, and economical administration of affairs.

Eminent statesmen try to impress upon the nation the importance of keeping the delicate balance of power between the States and the federal authority adjusted to prevent encroachments. Indiana has enacted such laws for the regulation of her local affairs and the establishment of a vigorous self-government that the State is often cited as an example of the direction in which the individual States should move to lessen the necessity of federal jurisdiction intervening.

[1] Rawles, W. A., *The Centralizing Tendency in the Administration of Indiana.* Columbia University, New York.

Her Civilization as Shown by Her Laws 523

In making a summary of the legislation in Indiana to determine her rank in civilization among the States, we quote the statement of one of her citizens of national fame—"We have led in many ways, we are behind the most progressive in but few."

BIBLIOGRAPHY

ANONYMOUS. *Annals of Pioneer Settlers on the White-Water.* Richmond, Indiana, 1875.
BALL, REV. T. H. *Northwestern Indiana.*
BANTA, D. D. *History of Johnson County.* Indianapolis, 1888.
BARTEL, FREDERICK J. "The Institutional Influence of the German Element of the Population of Richmond, Ind." *Wayne Co. Hist. Soc. Pub.* Richmond, Indianapolis, 1899.
BEARD, REED. *Battle of Tippecanoe.* Chicago, 1880.
BLATCHLEY, W. S. *Gleanings from Nature.* Indianapolis, 1899.
BLATCHLEY, W. S. *State Geological Reports.* Indianapolis.
BOLTON, NATHANIEL *History of Indianapolis.* Indianapolis.
BOONE, RICHARD G. *Education in Indiana.* Indianapolis.
BURR, S. J. *Life and Times of William Henry Harrison.* New York, 1840.
BENTON, ELBERT JAY. *The Wabash Trade Route.* Johns Hopkins Univ., 1904.
BUTLER, AMOS W. *Reports of Indiana Board of State Charities.*
BUTLER, AMOS W. *Bulletins of Indiana Board of State Charities.* State Department. Indianapolis.
COCKRUM, WILLIAM M. *A Pioneer History of Indiana.* Oakland City, Ind., 1907.
COLEMAN, CHRISTOPHER B. *Indiana Historical Magazine.* Indianapolis.
CONDIT, REV. D. B. *The History of Terre Haute.* New York, 1900.
CONKLIN, JULIA S. *Young People's History of Indiana.* Indiana, 1899.
COTTMAN, GEORGE S. *Indiana Historical Magazine.* Indianapolis.
COX, SANFORD C. *Recollections of the Early Settlements of the Wabash Valley.* La Fayette, Ind., 1860
DILLON, JOHN B. *History of Indiana.* Indianapolis, 1857.
DILLON, JOHN B. *Monographs on Indiana.* Indianapolis.
DINWIDDIE PAPERS. *Virginia Historical Society Publications.*
DUNN, JACOB P. *History of Indiana.* Boston, 1888.

DUNN, JACOB P.   *Monographs on the History of Indiana in Ind. Hist. Soc. Publications.* Indianapolis.

EGGLESTON, EDWARD.   *Tales and Articles about Indiana.*

EGGLESTON, GEORGE CARY.   *The First of the Hoosiers.*   Ferno, 1903.

ENGLISH, WILLIAM H.   *Conquest of the Northwest.*   Indianapolis, 1896.

FISKE, JOHN.   *Essays, Scenes and Characters in American History.*   New York, 1902.

FISKE, JOHN.   *Old Virginia and Her Neighbors.*   Boston, 1897.

FOULKE, WILLIAM DUDLEY.   *Life of Oliver P. Morton.*   Indianapolis, 1900.

HARDING, WILLIAM F.   "The State Bank of Indiana."   *Journal of Political Economy, U. C.*, 1895, Chicago.

HENDRICKS, MRS. THOMAS A.   *Popular History of Indiana.*   Indianapolis, 1891.

HENRY, WILLIAM E.   *Indiana Magazine of History.*   Indianapolis.

Historical Addresses, Sketches in State Newspapers, and Reminiscences of Pioneers.

HODGE, FREDERICK W.   *Handbook of the American Indian.*   Washington, D. C., 1907.

HOLLOWAY, WILLIAM R.   *History of Indianapolis.*   Indianapolis.

Indiana Historical Society Publications.

JONES, LLOYD.   *Life of David Owen.*   London, 1873.

JOUTEL, MONSIEUR.   *A Journal of the Last Voyage of La Salle.*   Reprint by the Caxton Club, Chicago, 1896.

LAW, JUDGE.   *The Colonial History of Vincennes.*   Vincennes, 1858.

LEMCKE, J. A.   *Reminiscences of an Indianian.*   Indianapolis, 1905.

LOCKWOOD, GEORGE B.   *The New Harmony Movement.*   New York, 1905.

MERRILL, CATHERINE.   *The Soldiers of Indiana in the War for the Union.*   Indianapolis, 1867.

MERRILL, CATHERINE.   *Essays.*   Indianapolis, 1902.

NICHOLAS, ANNA.   *Idyls of the Wabash.*   Indianapolis.

NICHOLSON, MEREDITH.   *Hoosiers.*   New York, 1900.

OGG, FREDERICK A.   *The Opening of the Mississippi.*

PARKMAN, FRANCIS.   *La Salle and the Great West.*   Boston.

PARKMAN, FRANCIS.   *The Jesuits in North America.*   Boston.

PARKER, BENJAMIN.   *Annals of Pioneer Settlers in Ind. Mag. Hist.*   1908.

PARKER, BENJAMIN, AND E. HINEY.   *Poets and Poetry of Indiana.*

PERSHING, M. M.   *Life of Gen. John Tipton.*   Tipton, Ind., 1906.

RAWLES, WILLIAM A.   *The Centralizing Tendency in the Administration of Indiana.*   Columbia University, N. Y.

RAWLES, WILLIAM A. *The Government of the People of the State of Indiana*, 1897.
ROOSEVELT, THEODORE. *Winning of the West.* New York.
SMITH, WILLIAM H. *History of Indiana.* Indianapolis, 1897.
SMITH, OLIVER H. *Early Trials.* Cincinnati, 1858.
State Superintendent of Public Instruction Reports.
STEIN, EVALEEN. *One Way to the Woods.* Boston, 1897.
STEIN, EVALEEN. *Among the Trees Again.* Indianapolis, 1902.
STICKNEY, IDA STEARNS. *Pioneer Indianapolis.* Indianapolis, 1907.
SULGROVE, BERRY. *History of Indianapolis.*
THOMPSON, MAURICE. *Stories of Indiana.* New York.
THORNTON, W. W. *The Government of the State of Indiana.*
WALLACE, LEW. *Autobiography.* New York, 1906.
WEBSTER, HOMER J. *Wm. Henry Harrison's Administrations of Ind. Territory.* No. 3, Vol. 4, Ind. Hist. Soc. Indianapolis, 1908.
WINSOR, JUSTIN. *Narrative and Critical History of America.*
WOOLEN, WILLIAM W. *Biographical and Historical Sketches.* Indianapolis, 1883.

INDEX

A

Adams, J. Otis, 407
Addams, Jane, 99
Ade, George, 356, 391
Agriculture in Indiana, 459, ch. xx.; French, 459; and early settlers, 461; fairs, 462; at Purdue University, 466; taught in schools, 469; women's part in, 472
Agriculture, Journals of, 468
Alexander, Miss, author of *Judith*, 388
Algonquin Indians, 10
Anderson, Melville B., 377
Anglo-Saxon love of the soil, 103
Art exhibition of great merit, 407
Artists of Indiana, 404
Audubon, John J., story of mill, 80
Automobiles, 237

B

Baker, Martha S., 405
Ball, Rev. T. H., 334, 382; on the culture in frontier homes, 96
Ball's paintings, 407
Bandits of the border, 192, 193
Banks, first, 160; in first constitution, 160; charter cancelled, 160; State bank of Indiana, 161; wildcat currency, 162; disastrous free banking laws, 163; Bank of the State of Indiana, 164; national banks begun, 164; present wise laws, 164; savings banks, 164
Banta, Judge D. D., 410, 413

Baptist Church first organized, 168
Barnes, Charles, 457
Bartel, Frederick, 382
Bee-hunters, 87
Ben Hur, 351
Benton, Elbert J., brochure on the Wabash and Erie Canal, 227, 228, 230
Beveridge, Albert J., 386
Bicknell, Ernest P., 503
Billings, Dr. John S., 456
Black Hawk War, 157
Blake, Mrs. Katherine, on pioneer life, 92; on Rappites, 245
Blatchley, Wm. S., 328, 333, 382, 474, 484
Bloomington, State University, 430
Blue grass carried to Kentucky, 125
Breeders of pure bred live stock, a source of wealth and improvement to the State, 476
British incite Indians to massacre, 45, 58
Bundy's pictures, 407
Burr, Aaron, his deluded followers in Indiana, 134

C

Cabins of pioneers, 64, 65
Campbell, Alexander, 173
Camp-meeting first held, 174
Canada, part of Indiana included in, 18; French ceded it to Great Britain, 23; the West wished it incorporated in the United States, 137
Cannibalism among the Miamis, 13

Index

Capitals of Indiana, first, 147; second, 148; present, 151
Carleton, Mrs., description of boarding-schools, 277
Carrington, General, 456
Catherwood, Mary H., 356
Chappelsmith, John, and wife, 259
Churches, early, 166
Civil War period, 293
Civilization measured by the laws, 493
Clark, General George Rogers, 46, 51, 57
Clay, John, quoted, 346 ff
Clay deposits in Indiana, 484
Clubs, 395; federation of, 397
Coburn, General John, tribute to Mr. Dillon, 379
Cockrum, Wm. M., 80, 81, 382
Coe, Dr., pioneer physician, 155
Coggeshall, Wm., Anthology, 350
Condit, Rev. Blackford, 203, 382
Conklin, Julia S., 382
Conner, J. D., Jr., Secretary of Registry Association, 476
Conner's paintings, 407
Constitutional Commission, in 1815, 140; in 1850, 435
Constitution, wise provisions of first, 140
Corn Club, 467, 469
Corydon, second capital, 137, 148
Coudert, Amelia Kusner, 405
Coulter, Dr. John, 457
Coulter, Dean Stanley, 457, 481
Counterfeiting, 189
Coureurs de bois, 8; pursuits, 8; character of, 9
Covington, thriving river town, 341
Cox, Jacob, 405
Cox, Sanford C., 382; story of Irish canal laborers, 196
Crimes of the border, 182
Culver Military School, 430
Cumberland Road, 214, 215

D

Dairy farming, 477
Dale, Miss, married Robert Owen, 249

D'Arusmont, Phiquepal, at New Harmony, 259
Davis, Jefferson, unfair in report, 290
De Frees, John, character of, 388
Democracy of the West, 449
Democratic party during the war, 300
Denby, Charles, 457
De Pauw University founded, 428
Dial, the, quoted, 449
Dillon, John B., 137, 379
Doctors of early times, 92, 93
Dooryards about farm-houses, 478
Dress in 1816, 146
Duncan, Robert, quoted, 119
Dunn, Jacob P., 59, 130, 380, 458
Duquesne, Marquis, regarding French colonization, 459

E

Eads, John B., 456
Earlham College founded, 426
Earthquake in 1811, 133
Economic waste, 489
Education in Indiana, 409; industrial, 441–443; compulsory, 442
Educational system, 446
Eggleston, Edward, 358, 367
Eggleston, George Cary, 457; quoted, 368, 454
Electric power from streams, 491
Ellsworth, Annie, sent first telegram, 286
Ellsworth, Edward E., at Centennial, 451
Ellsworth, Henry L., quoted, 460
English, Wm. H., 59, 382
Erie, Lake, crossed by La Salle, 4
Europeans, contact with Indians, 128
Explorers in Indiana, 4, 5

F

Factory Age lightens home labor, 99
Factory inspection, 499
Farmers, 475

Index

Farmers' Institutes, 446, 467
Federal and State authority, 522
Fellows sisters, writings, 384
Fertility of soil, 135
Finley, John, poem *Hoosier Nest*, 65
Fire companies in early times, 286
Fiske, John, 135
Flatboats, 199, 202
Fletcher, M., letter about the character of Indianapolis settlement, 156
Fletcher papers, extract from, 99
Ford, Simeon, 391
Forkner's paintings, 407
Forsythe's paintings, 407
Fort Wayne, 18
Foster, John W., 381, 457
Foulke, Wm. Dudley, 142, 305, 307, 380, 386
Franklin College, 426, 427
French dominion, 19, 20
Furnham, Lucy, 389

G

Game, wild, in Indiana, 63, 73
Gazette on live-stock improvement, 476
Genet, citizen, creates trouble in the West, 36
Gibault, Father, priest in Northwest Territory, 51
Gillilans' tales, 391
Girardin, Frank, paintings, 407
Glisson, Admiral, 456
Gold fever in '49, 290, 291
Goodwin, Rev. Thomas, 213, 382
Grange, 468
Griffiths, John L., 380, 394
Grist mills in early times, 70
Gruelle, Justin, painter, 407
Gruelle, R. B., painter, 407

H

Hamilton, Lieut.-Gov., instructed by Great Britain, 45; recaptures Vincennes, 52; loses it forever, 57
Hamilton's collection of Indiana writers, 352
Hannegan, Edward, 288, 341
Hanover College, 425

Harding, W. F., monograph on Indiana, 382
Harmonie Commune, 241
Harrison, Benjamin, 394, 455
Harrison, Wm. Henry, 125, 126, 130, 282
Hay, John, native of Indiana, 456
Hays, Prof., on high schools, 470
Hayworth, Paul, and O. G. S., 366
Helm, Captain, in charge of Post Vincennes, 51
Henderson, Albert, a memoir, 336
Henderson, Charles R., 381, 457, 500
Hendricks, Thomas A., 394, 455
Herndon, Commander, 456
Hibben, Helen, 406
Hines, Fletcher, Secretary of Registry Association, 476
Hiney, Enoch, collection of poems, 354
Hinsdale, Prof., on British colonization, 30; on American occupation of the West, 59
Hobbs, Barnabas, 411
Hoosier, origin of name, 366
Hoosier dialect, 358-362, 367
Hoosier Group of painters, 404
Hoosier writings, 390
Horse-thieves, 185
Hoshouer, Prof., as a teacher, 424
Hospitality of pioneers, 282
Howard, Judge Timothy E., History of St. Joseph County, 382
Howe, Judge, quoted, 190

I

Illinois, separated from Indiana Territory in 1808, 130
Indiana, first explored 1, 15; under French rule, 15; British, 26; territorial days, 106; fertility of soil, 135; State organized, 139; future rank of State depends on legislators, 165; in the forties and fifties, 271; slavery in, 293; provision for education, 409; character of population, 448; geographical position favorable, 478; natural resources varied, 479; character of laws, 493

Index

Indiana Farmer quoted, 477
Indiana prize corn, 469
Indiana Society of Chicago, 457
Indiana University founded, 431
Indianapolis, site of, selected, 151; capital moved to, 153; first sale of lots, 153; early settlements, 154-156; as a railway centre, 234; art school, 408
Indians, all Algonquins in Indiana, 10; barbarity, 10, 127; customs, 11-12; religion, 12; influence of friars, 16; intoxication, 16, 118, 119; send a "speaking bark," 60; conflict with white race, 106, 127-129; forms of warfare, 107; General Clark's dealings with, 108, 109; articles bartered with, 110; games, 119; treaties with, 120; names of, 120
Industrial schools, 501
Industrial training in the schools, 519
Internal improvement system, 214, 219-221; effect on State, 222, 225; abandoned by State, 231
Iron deposits, 489; iron oxide for paint, 489

J

Jeffersonville received General La Fayette, 153
Jenners, Anna, story of a pioneer, 102
Jennings, Jonathan, first Governor, 141
Johnson, Alexander, 503, 510, 511, 520
Johnson, Robert Underwood, native of Indiana, 457
Johnston, Gen. Jos. E., 456
Joliet and Marquette discovered the Mississippi, 3
Jones, Rev. Jenkin Lloyd, tribute to Thomas Lincoln, 104
Jones, Lloyd, *Life of Robert Owen*, 248
Joutel's Journal quoted regarding La Salle, 6
Judah, Mrs. John, stories by, 389

Julian, Geo. W., agitator for abolition of slavery, 300; author, 382

K

Kankakee River, La Salle's exploration of, 5; picturesqueness, 333
Kaskaskia, Fort, captured by Clark, 48
Kentucky volunteers, with Clark, 46; guard the frontier, 58; at the battle of Tippecanoe, 124; carry home blue grass, 125
Kindergarten Training School (State), 439
Knights of the Golden Circle, 307
Krout, Caroline, author, 389

L

La Fayette, General de, visits Indiana in 1825, 153, 208
La Fayette, city of, 204
Lakes in Indiana number one thousand, 333
Land Commissioners to adjust claims of settlers, 131
Land sharks in the early settlement outwitted, 133
Lane, Henry S., 274, 298
Lanier, Sidney, quoted, 357
La Salle, Robert Cavelier de, arrived in Canada, 3; learns Indian languages, 3; ambition to explore the West, 3; sells his estate to raise funds, 3; starts on his first voyage to find a passage to China and discovers the Great River, 3; makes another voyage west and down the Illinois to the Mississippi, 5; enemies in Canada, 6; goes to France to enlist the support of Louis, 6; Tonty's friendship for, 7
Laws for the new States, 141
Lawton, General, 456
Lawyers in early times, 146; riding the circuit, 147
Legislation in Indiana, regarding Australian ballot, 499; board of State Charities, 501,

Index

Legislation in Indiana (*Con.*) 502; bribery, 499; care of orphans, 504, 506; centralizing tendency of, 521, 522; child labor, 499; compulsory education, 442, 495; county administration, 502; county hospitals, 508; county poor asylums, 507, 518; criminals, 512; drugs, 498; elections, 499; epileptics' village, 507; factory inspection, 499; favorable to women, 494; family desertion, 506; feeble-minded, 508; fee and salary, 499; franchises, 499; incorporation of cities, 498; industrial reform schools, 511, 512; insane, 509; insane criminals, 512; juvenile court, 504, 505; labor regulations, 499; for libraries, 495; labor regulations for women and children, 499; marriage license, 506; out-door relief, 509; parole of prisoners, 514, 516, 517; police matrons, 507; prevention of crime, 510; pure food, 498; reformatory, 511-514; results of reformatory laws, 513; savings banks, 501; soldiers' home, 509; soldiers and sailors' orphans, 509; State workhouse, 513; suspended sentence, 511; temperance, 495-498; tuberculosis, 509; women's prison, 512

Legislators sent to Assembly hold State's destiny in hands, 165

Lemcke, Capt. J. A., his political canvass, 144; on steamboating, 201

Lesueur, Charles A., at New Harmony, 267

Levering, Mortimer, Secretary of Registry Association, 476

Liberty clubs, 400

Libraries, Maclure's, 261, 262; travelling, 397; Carnegie, 398

Library Commission, 397

Lincoln, Abraham, lived in Indiana, 260; Emancipation Proclamation, 304; signed agricultural college bill, 466

Lincoln, Thomas, pioneer, 105

Literary development in Indiana, 351-353

Live-stock Registry Association, influence of, 476

Log Convention, 144

Log rolling, 75

Logan, chief, speech, 116

Looms in every house, 99

Lotteries, common form of raising funds in the early days, 148

Louisiana, held dominion over Southern Indiana, 18; was ceded to France, 34; to Spain, 34; re-ceded to France, 34; Napoleon ceded it to U. S. in 1803, 41

Lowell, James Russell, on gayer spirit of earlier times, 281; on the first American, 337; people of wide reading, 395

Lutheran Concordia School, 430

M

McCulloch, Hugh, banker, Secretary of Treasury and author, 382; quoted, 163, 454

McCutcheon, Ben, 391

McCutcheon, George Barr, 387

McCutcheon, John, great cartoonist, 392

Maclure, William, geologist, 258; established schools at New Harmony, 259, 260; established libraries, 261, 262

Madison, 274; bank, 160

Mails in early days, 83

Major, Charles, novelist, 387

Maple sugar, groves in Indianapolis, 154; Indians fond of, 481

Marest, Father, wrote of the French posts, 409

Marl beds in northern Indiana, 485

Marquette and Joliet discover the Mississippi 132 years after De Soto, 3

Martin, Edward S., on the spirit of the West, 447

Maumee River and portage, 4, 18

Merom College, 430

Merrill, Catherine, quoted on the Civil War, 296; sketch of her work in Indiana, 375; paragraphs from her essays, 378
Merrill, Samuel, Treasurer of Indiana in 1824, 153
Methodist Church, early founded, 168; schools established, 428
Mexican War, 288
Miami Indians in Indiana, 10, 13
Milk sickness or "tires," 91
Miller, Elizabeth, writer, 388
Miller, Joaquin, the poet, born in Indiana, 456
Millerism in 1843, 175-177
Mills, Caleb, successful agitator for public schools, 433-436
Mills, old, 330
Mineral springs, 329
Mississippi River, discovered, 3; contention over its free navigation, 34, 35; commerce on, 40; contention settled in 1803, 135; battle of New Orleans in 1814, 136; element of dissension in the Civil War, 323.
Monetary craze in the fifties, 162
Moody, William Vaughn, writer, 384, 390
Moore's Hill College, 428
Morgan's raid during Civil War, 308-323
Morton, Oliver P., great War Governor, 296, 299
Morton, Oliver T., writer, 395
Mosler, Henry, artist, 407; native of Indiana, 456
Muir, John, tribute to Catherine Merrill, 377
Muster day, great event in pioneer times, 88

N

Natural gas, the first use in Indiana, 487; large area of, 487; added manufactures to State, 487; its waste, 489
Natural resources of Indiana, 479, 490
Negroes, slaves in Indiana, 22, 131, 139; Fifteenth Amendment passed, 165; free ones kidnapped, 295

Nesbit, Wilbur, writer, 391, facetious reference to Indiana's literary fame, 355
New Harmony, 240; location, 241; first in many movements, 255; principles in the Owen commune, 253; population attained, 254; variety of followers, 256; cause of failure, 264; after the passing of the commune, 266; the village at present, 266
New Orleans, founded, 34; the market place for the Mississippi and its tributaries, 40; ceded to U. S., 42
Newspapers in Indiana, 398; Elihu Stout establishes first one, 398; their influence and character, 398-401
Nicholas, Anna, author, 389; editor of Sunday *Journal*, 400
Nicholson, Meredith, writer, 385; quoted, 325, 358, 366, 372
Nordyke's paintings, 407
Normal Schools, State, 438; at Angola, 438; Danville, 438; Manchester, 430; Marion, 438; Rochester, 438; Terre Haute, 438; Valparaiso, 438; control of certificates by Board of Education, 438
North Manchester College, 430
Northwest Territory, of which Indiana was a part, 44; Clark's conquest of, 44; value of, 58, 59
Notre Dame University, 429

O

Oakland City College, 430
Ogg, Frederick, on favorable entrance of French into the continent, 15
Ohio River, discovered by La Salle, 4; open door to Southern Indiana, 60
Oil fields of Indiana, 483
Ordinance of 1787, 130, 140, 433
Ouabache (Wabash) River, first navigated by white explorers, 4

Index 535

Ouiatanon, first post in Indiana, 18; established in 1720, 18; location, 18; importance of, as trading station, 18; final disappearance of, in 1791, 24
Owen, David Dale, United States geologist, 267
Owen, Jane, married Robert Fauntleroy, 267
Owen, Robert Dale, State geologist, 268
Owen, Robert, sketch of, 248, 249; purchases New Harmony, 247; establishes a commune, 251; failure of community plan, 263; most valuable pioneer, 264
Owen, Robert Dale, work at New Harmony, 268; subsequent career, 269, 270; Indiana's chief citizen, 268; legislation secured by, 269; legislation for women, 269; Civil War record, 303
Ox teams in use, 213

P

Painters of Indiana, 402, 406
Parker, Benjamin, author, 351; early pioneers, 351; collection of poets, 354
Parkman, Francis, 4
Peat beds in northern Indiana, 490
Pennington, Dennis, letter regarding slavery, 139
Pershing, M.M., historical sketches, 382
Pestalozzian system of education introduced at New Harmony, 255
Petroleum in Indiana, 483
Pigeon Roost massacre, 126
Pioneering in the blood, 100, 107
Pioneers, 60; their amusements, 75-77, 79; agriculture, 460; bee-hunters, 87; buildings, 64; cobblers, 87; crude implements, 67, 68; culture, 96, 449; dances, 78; defence, 107, 108; dress, 69; field sports, 79; going to mill, 70; games, 79; help each other, 75; hopefulness, 97, 99; hospitality, 75,

83; industry, 96, 98; journey to the West, 61, 62; marriages, 86, 90; modes of travel, 71, 72, schools, 88; scarcity of letters, 83; sickness, 91; religious meetings, 86; women's part in pioneer life, 69, 97, 98, 105
Poetry by Hoosier writers, 353, 384, 385
Poets and Poetry of Indiana collected by Benjamin Parker and E. Hiney, 355
Poets, early, 352, 353
Political parties of Indiana, 494
Pontiac, Chief, warning, 106; war in 1764, 106
Poor whites from the South, origin, 359; character, 362; dialect, 362, 363
Portage at the head of the Wabash, 4, 18
Posey, Governor, message to the Territorial Legislature, 137
Posts established by the French in Indiana, 16, 17
Pottawattomie Indians, 118
Powers, Hiram, sculptor, born in Indiana, 456
Prairies in northern Indiana, 94; prairie fires, 95
Preachers of early times, 86, 87
Prentice, George D., publisher of early Hoosier poems, 353
Presbyterians, first church was organized in 1806, 168
Priests of the French settlement, 16
Prophet, the, received pension from the British, 121; at battle of Tippecanoe, 124
Purdue University, 445, 446, 466, 475

Q

Quakers in Indiana, 169; objection to slavery, 284; connection with the Underground Railway, 284; their schools, 426

R

Races, conflict of, 128, 129

536 Index

Railroads, first in the State, 221; later, 231; 233, centre at Indianapolis, 234
Ralston, Alexander, laid out the city of Indianapolis, 152
Rapp, Frederick, assisted in the commune at Harmony, 241, 244
Rapp, George, with his followers, founds settlement at New Harmony, 241; returns to Pennsylvania, 245; death, 246
Rawles, W. A., 382; on centralization of State administration, 521
Reading circle of State teachers, 438
Reeves, Arthur Middleton, 395
Reforestation urged, 481
Registry Associations, secretaries, 476
Regulators, 188
Republican party formed, 291, 299
Richards, William, marine painter, 407
Richmond, Dr. Corydon, 102
Richmond, Dr. John L., 102, 340, 426
Richmond, Rev. Nathaniel, writes of multiplicity of sects, 172; one of the founders of Franklin College, 426
Richmond's Art League, 406
Riley, James Whitcomb, 331, 355, 384; quoted, 70, 77, 236, 386; dialect, 367, 388; appreciated, 369, 370; reader of his own poems, 371; style, 372; degree of M.A., 372; humor, 390; characteristics, 391
Rivet, Father, held first school in the territory of Indiana, 409
Rose Polytechnic Institute, 429, 492

S

Saddle-bags, 202
Salt, scarcity of in pioneer times, 74; expedition to evaporate, 74; cost of, 184
Sample, Henry T., on the Wea, flatboating to New Orleans, 200
Sand of lake shore, valuable for building material, 485
School gardens, 444
Schools, early, 88, 411, 412; for blind, deaf and dumb, 439; books used in, 416; circulating teachers, 410; consolidated schools, 439; county seminaries, 422, 423; denominational, 425, 426, 428; industrial, 512; "loud" schools, 412; public, 432-436; at New Harmony, 259, 422
Scientific writers, 401
Shale deposits, vast and valuable, 484
Slavery in Indiana, 22; negro, 22, 130, 131; efforts in behalf of fugitives, 283, 284, 285
Slocum, Frances, story of her being kidnapped by the Indians, 110
Smith, Oliver H., riding the circuit, 147; writes of early preachers, 173; of horsethieves, 186, 187, 188; recalls pioneer gentlemen, 453
Smith, Roswell, founder of *Century Magazine*, 457
Smith, Wm. H., history of Indiana, 382
Snakes in early days, 79
Snow, Alpheus, writes of colonial possessions, 355
Social life before the war, 281
Sons of Liberty, 307
Southern settlers in the State, 228, 293, 363; many of them came because of disapproval of slavery, 131
Spanish money in Indiana, 32; dominion over the Mississippi, 33; goods confiscated, 34, 36; efforts to divert West to disloyalty, 37
Spinning in early times, 98
Squatters, a peculiar class, 101
Stage-coach days, 215, 216
Stark, Otto, artist, 407
State institutions of Indiana, 502; benevolent, 507, 509; reformatory, 511, 513

Index   537

Steamboats, first in Indiana waters, 203; offence to Indians, 204; importance to commerce, 204, 207; passengers on, 207; route of commerce, 207; Mark Twain's description of, 209; cause of decline, 232; decline of traffic, 233
Steel, manufacturing in northwestern Indiana, 489
Steele, T. C., artist, 407, 408
Stein, Evaleen, quoted, 331, 334, 335; stories, 355, 356
Stephenson, Henry T., 387
St. Mary's-of-the-Woods school, 428
Stone of Indiana unrivalled, 486; easily quarried, 486, many varieties, 486
Stout, Elihu, established first newspaper in the State, 399; his fine character, 399
Studevant, counterfeiter, 190
Stump speaking, 143
Sulgrove, Berry, journalist, 383
Sunday-schools, 178, 179, 180
Superintendent of Public Instruction, 437

T

Tarkington, N. Booth, writer, 271, 387
Tarkington, William, quoted, 205
Taverns of old times, 84; primitive accommodations in, 85; unique sign-boards, 85
Taylor, Dr., poem, *The Theng*, 362
Taylor, Zachary, elected President, 290
Teachers, early, 414, 416; high standard the aim, 437; reading circle, 438; debt of State to, 446
Teaming an occupation in early times, 156, 212
Tecumseh, Shawnee chief, 117, 122, 123; great leader, 121; opposed the advance of white race, 121; visits General Harrison to protest, 121; departs for the South, 122;

battle of Tippecanoe fought while he was gone, 124; died in the British service, 121
Terre Haute, the French boundary line between Louisiana and Canada, 18; early fire protection, typical, 286; school centre, 429
Text-books in pioneer times, 416
Thompson, Maurice, writer, 351, 352, 374; quoted, 357
Thompson, Col. Richard, *Recollections of Sixteen Presidents*, 382
Thompson, Will H., 375, 384
Thornton, W. W., writer, 382
Timber found in the State, 480
Tinder-box in every house, 72
Tippecanoe, battle of, in 1811, 121, 124, 125
Tippecanoe River, beauty, 326
Tipton, General John, passages from his journal, 149
Tomahawk right, 66
Tonty, Henri de, appreciation of La Salle's explorations, 7
Training for teachers, 438, 439
Travelling in the olden times, 208–215
Twain, Mark, description of steamboat traffic, 209
Tyler, ex-President, as a roadmaster, 473

U

Underground Railway, 284; extent of the movement, 284, 295; numbers of slaves helped to Canada, 284; work ceased, 286
Universities of Indiana, at Bloomington, 430; Purdue, at La Fayette, 445

V

Valparaiso College, 430, 438
Vevay scenery, 329
Viele, Hermann, writer, 390
Vigo, Col. Francis, acquaints Clark with condition at Vincennes, 53

Vincennes post established, 18; French life there, 19; Fort, 19; captured by American forces, 51; recaptured, 57; territorial capital, 147; university established, 148, 420; capital removed from, 148

W

Wabash College founded, 425
Wabash River, explored by La Salle, 3; highway of commerce, 204, 207
Wallace, Gov. David, quoted, 403
Wallace, General Lew, author, 373; quoted, 291, 424, 453
Wallace, Susan, author, 374
Water-power of the State undeveloped, 491
Waterways of Indiana, 237
Wea Plains, 225
Weaver, Col. Erasmus, 456
Western characteristics, 452
Whiskey used in early times, 74, 91, 92
Whitcomb, Gov. James, 460
White River declared navigable, 209
Whitewater Valley and other settlements of Friends, 131
Whittaker, Wm. H., quoted, 513, 516, 520

Wickersham's novel, 389
Wild fruits in the State, 73
Wild game found in Indiana, 63, 73
Wiley, Harvey W., 457
Wilkinson's treachery, 37
Willing, the, built for Col. Clark's expedition, 53
Willson, Forsythe, poet, 384
Wilstach, John A., translations, 386
Wilstach, Paul, author and playwright, 386
Wilstach, Walter, biography, 386
Winona Institute, 430; address quoted, 478
Winona Lake, 430
Winsor, Newton, quoted, 59
Winter, George, description of Frances Slocum, 110; painted Miami Indians, 402
Wishard, Dr., description of early practice of medicine, 154
Woman's suffrage, backward in the State, 519
Woods-Ulman, Alice, stories, 389; pictures, 406
Woolen, Wm. W., historical sketches, 382; natural history articles, 382
Wright, Frances, at New Harmony, 396; organized the first woman's club, 396